THE
MIND

BOOKS BY RICHARD M. RESTAK

Premeditated Man: Bioethics & the Control of Future Human Life
The Self Seekers
The Brain: The Last Frontier
The Brain
The Infant Mind
The Mind

THE
MIND

Richard M. Restak, M.D.

BANTAM BOOKS
TORONTO • NEW YORK • LONDON • SYDNEY • AUCKLAND

THE MIND

A Bantam Book / October 1988

Library of Congress Cataloging-in-Publication Data

Restak, Richard M., 1942–
    The mind.

    Bibliography: p.
    Includes index.
    1. Brain. 2. Neurophysiology. 3. Neuropsychology.
4. Neuropsychiatry.   I. Title.
QP356.R47 1988   152   88-19365
ISBN 0-553-05314-0

Published simultaneously in the United States and Canada

Bantam Books are published by Bantam Books, a division of Bantam Doubleday
Dell Publishing Group, Inc. Its trademark, consisting of the words "Bantam
Books" and the portrayal of a rooster, is Registered in U.S. Patent and Trademark
Office and in other countries. Marca Registrada. Bantam Books, 666 Fifth Avenue,
New York, New York 10103.

PRINTED IN THE UNITED STATES OF AMERICA

0   9   8   7   6   5   4   3   2   1

To my daughter, Jennifer,
who has made it all worthwhile

CREDITS

The author wishes to thank the many sources of illustration for their cooperation and assistance during the preparation of this book. They are listed below following the page number upon which their illustration appears.

2 (top); John Gajda/FPG; 2 (second from top): The Bettmann Archive; 2 (third from top): Comstock, Inc./Tom Grill; 2 (bottom); © Manfred Kage/Peter Arnold, Inc.; 4: The Bettmann Archive; 5: Kerry Herman; 7: Kerry Herman; 8: Kerry Herman; 10: Culver Pictures; 12 and xiv: Leonard Lessin; 14: UPI/Bettmann Newsphotos; 15: Culver Pictures; 16: Kerry Herman; 17 (top): The Bettmann Archive; 17 (bottom): UPI/Bettmann Newsphotos; 19: © Alex Grey; 21: The Burns Archive; 22: courtesy D. Mountcastle; 24: Kerry Herman; 25: courtesy Dr. Eric Courchesne; 28: WNET; 30: WNET; 32 (top), 34 and xiv: © Lennart Nilsson, *The Incredible Machine*, National Geographic Society, Washington, D.C.; 32 (third from top): Fotolab/FPG; 32 (bottom): Kuhn/Image Bank; 36-37: © Dr. Kathryn Tosney; 38: After W. Maxwell Cowan, *The Brain*, W.H. Freeman, 1979; 39 (left): © Francis LeRoy, Science Source/Photo Researchers, Inc.; 39 (right): CNRI, Science Source/Photo Researchers, Inc.; 40: Dr. Gary Aston-Jones, New York University Department of Biology; 42: © Matthew Neal McVay/Picture Group; 32 (second from top) and 43 (top): © Lennart Nilsson, *Behold Man*, Little, Brown & Co., Boston; 45: Leonard Lessin; 47: © Don Perdue; 50: © Gerard Murrell; 56: Vernon Burger; 59: © Gerard Murrell; 60: Jeffrey Dunn; 64 (top): © Manfred Kage/Peter Arnold, Inc.; 64 (second from top): AP/Wide World Photos; 64 (third from top): Comstock, Inc./Tom Grill; 64 (bottom): Comstock, Inc./Tom Grill; 67 (top left): Indianapolis Museum of Art, The Clowes Fund Collection; 67 (top right): Giraudon/Art Resource; Kassel: Staatliches Museum; 67 (bottom left): National Gallery of Scotland, on loan from the Duke of Sutherland Collection; 67 (bottom right): Giraudon/Art Resource; Florence: Uffizi; 72: © Manfred Kage/Peter Arnold, Inc.; 73: © Rescke/Peter Arnold, Inc.; 75: Kerry Herman; 78: Dr. William T. Greenough; 81 (top): © Dr. D. Dickson/Peter Arnold, Inc.; 81 (bottom): © Bob Sacha/Phototake; 86 and xiv: © Dr. Mony DeLeon/Brookhaven National Laboratory and New York University/Peter Arnold, Inc.; 91: WNET; 95 (top left): AP/Wide World Photos; 95 (top center): courtesy Sophia Smith Collection, Smith College; 95 (top right): UPI/The Bettmann Archive; 95 (middle left): AP/Wide World Photos; 95 (middle center): Culver Pictures; 95 (middle right): The Bettmann Archive; 95 (bottom left): UPI/Bettmann Newsphotos; 95 (bottom center): UPI/Bettmann Newsphotos; 96: Leonard Lessin; 99: © Dr. Mony DeLeon/New York University; 102: AP/Wide World Photos; 104 (top): Terry Qing/FPG; 104 (second from top): courtesy Monte S. Buchsbaum, M.D., University of California, Irvine, Department of Psychiatry; 104 (third from top): Paul Biddle and Tim Malyon/Science Photo Library; 104 (bottom): © Manfred Kage/Peter Arnold, Inc.; 106 (left): Comstock, Inc./Tom Grill; 106 (right): WNET; 109: © Alex Grey; 114 (top): UPI/Bettmann Newsphotos; 114 (bottom): The Metropolitan Museum of Art, Harris Brisbane Dick Fund, 1932 [32.35 (124)]; 116: © Dr. Edythe D. London, National Institute on Drug Abuse; 117: Floyd Gillis, A.F.C.G., Inc., based on data from Dr. Robert Livingston, University of California, San Diego; 118: Leonard Lessin; 119: UPI/Bettmann Newsphotos; 121: Larry Mulvehill; 122: Leonard Lessin; 124: Culver Pictures; 127: Dufor Photographers, Philadelphia, Pennsylvania; 130: Barry Boxall/BBC Enterprises; 137: courtesy Monte S. Buchsbaum, M.D., University of California, Irvine, Department of Psychiatry; 138 (top): Jeffrey Sylvester/FPG; 138 (second from top): Photo Researchers, Inc.; 138 (third from top): Dick Luria/FPG; 138 (bottom): Four by Five; 140: WNET; 141: Culver Pictures; 142 and xv: © Alex Grey; 144: Sebastian Lindberg; 146: Geoff Manasso; 149: © Alex Grey; 150: Photo Researchers, Inc.; 156: Jonathan Perry; 157: © Dean Cornwell; painting of "Osler at Old Blockley" reproduced with permission of Wyeth Ayerst Laboratories; 158: Movie Star News; 159: Bettmann Newsphotos; 164 (top): Comstock, Inc./Russ Kinne; 164 (second from top): © Drs. E.R. John and L.S. Prichep, Department of Psychiatry, New York University; 164 (third from top): Four by Five; 164 (bottom): © Manfred Kage/Peter Arnold, Inc.; 166: The Bettmann Archive; 167: The Bettmann Archive; 168: © Nimatallah/Art Resource; 173 and xv: The Bettmann Archive; 174: The Bettmann Archive; 174: courtesy Monte S. Buchsbaum, M.D., University of California, Irvine, Department of Psychiatry; 177: WNET; 188: WNET; 192: Dr. John Mazziotta, UCLA; 194: © Drs. E.R. John and L.S. Prichep, Department of Psychiatry, New York University Medical Center; 196 (top): Ed Lettau/FPG; 196 (second from top): FPG; 196 (third from top): © Manfred Kage/Peter Arnold, Inc.; 196 (bottom): The Image Bank; 200: Rick Malkames; 203 (left): UPI/Bettmann Newsphotos; 203 (right): The Bettmann Archive; 206: Dr. Patricia Kuhl; 211: © Erika Stone/Peter Arnold, Inc.; 214: © Alex Grey; 219 and xiii: © Drs. Michel Posner, M.E. Raichle, and Steven Peterson, Washington University, St. Louis; 222 (top): The Bettmann Archive; 222 (second from top): John Gajda/FPG; 222 (third from top): Robin Forbes/The Image Bank; 222: UPI/The Bettmann Archive; 223: Jerry Jacka; 227 and xv: Jonathan Perry; 228: Peter Bull; 234 (top): Peter Bull; 234 (bottom): WNET; 237: Thomas Hurwitz; 245 (top): The Bettmann Archive; 245 (bottom): The Bettmann Archive; 247: Jim Pilan; 259: © EEG Systems Laboratory; 260: J.J. Grandville, from 1838 French edition of *Gulliver's Travels*; Great Ocean Publishers, Arlington, Virginia; 261: © Eileen Cowin; 267: © Alex Grey; 268: © Dr. Patricia Goldman-Rakic; 269: courtesy Professor Francois Lhermitte; 272 (right): © Avraham Shifrin: *The First Guidebook of Prisons and Concentration Camps of the Soviet Union*; Bantam Books, New York, 1982; 274 (top): AP/Wide World Photos; 274 (second from top): © Manfred Kage/Peter Arnold, Inc.; 274 (third from top): Four by Five; 274 (bottom): Roger Allyn Lee/Four by Five; 281: courtesy Monte S. Buchsbaum, M.D., University of California, Irvine, Department of Psychiatry; 286: Leonard Lessin; 291 and xvi: Ian Calvert; 294: © Tripos Associates/Peter Arnold, Inc.; 302: courtesy Monte S. Buchsbaum, M.D., University of California, Irvine, Department of Psychiatry; 306: Sarah Leen; 309: AP/Wide World Photos; 311: AP/Wide World Photos; 313: Michael Paris

CONTENTS

ACKNOWLEDGMENTS

This book could not have been written without the help and cooperation of the many people involved in the creation of the television series, *The Mind,* produced by WNET/New York in association with BBC for distribution by PBS. Executive in Charge George Page, Executive Producer Jack Sameth, and Executive Editor Richard Hutton shared with me their intentions and objectives for the series at all stages of production. Bonnie L. Benjamin, Series Science Journalist, provided me with the necessary research papers, and her grace and courtesy never faltered even under the intense pressure of formidable deadlines. Douglas Lutz, Coordinating Producer, and Aavo Koiv, Production Supervisor, helped me maintain a sense of balance in the writing of the chapters, which coordinate with and expand upon the nine programs in the series.

I am most grateful to the producers of these programs for their counsel and willing assistance: John Heminway, producer of "Search for Mind" and "Aging"; Martin Freeth, producer of "Addiction" and "The Violent Mind"; Vivian Ducat, producer of "Pain and Healing" and co-producer of "Language"; DeWitt Sage, producer of "Depression"; Peter Bull, co-producer of "Language" and "Thinking"; and Richard Hutton, who, in addition to his responsibilities as Executive Editor, was the producer of "Development" and co-producer of "Thinking." These creative people offered their help at every stage, and were invaluable in reading and critiquing the manuscript.

My very deep appreciation and thanks go to Leonard Mayhew, Director of Program Development at WNET/Thirteen, whose guidance, wise counsel, encouragement, and support over the past three years have been of inestimable value.

Leonard Lessin, Picture Editor, sought out and found the remarkable images that accompany, complement, and enhance the book. His efforts were conscientiously and creatively seconded by intern Douglas Loynes. Alex Grey and Daniel Ross provided the drawings that elucidate the text.

Major funding for *The Mind* television series was provided by the James S. McDonnell Foundation. Control Data provided corporate funding for the series and educational programs. Additional support came from the National Science Foundation, agencies of the United States Public Health Service, the John D. and Catherine T. MacArthur Foundation, and Public Television Stations.

Several authorities were kind enough to read various chapters in the book, and I am especially grateful to Robert P. Friedland, M.D., Deputy Clinical Director of the National Institute on Aging, and Steven J. Philips, M.D., Professor of Anatomy, Temple University School of Medicine. It goes without saying that all responsibility for the accuracy of the content rests with me.

Finally, I thank my wife, Carolyn Restak, for her help and support, and my secretarial assistant, Constance M. Banford, for her word-processing wizardry. My most heartfelt gratitude of all goes to my editor, Ann Harris, for her dedication, determination, and commitment, which have advanced this project in so many ways. The encouragement and efforts of these three most important people have made this book possible.

RICHARD M. RESTAK, M.D.

PREFACE

The objective of *The Mind* is to provide the reader with a unique overview of the thinking of many varied authorities on the nature of mind. Obviously, no one book could deal with everything pertaining to the mind, a subject that has preoccupied human beings since the beginning of recorded history. Mind is an encompassing subject, so selectivity, emphasis, and "point of view" were needed from the start. I have tried whenever possible to include the thinking and contributions of many disciplines: the neurosciences, philosophy, psychology, linguistics, and history among them. There are innumerable questions about the origins, nature, and workings of mind. We know much more about mind today than we did even a century ago; yet we still have more questions than we have answers, and perhaps always will. But what we have learned is illuminating and often exciting, and the direction of further exploration promises increasing insight into this often mysterious aspect of the self.

This book, like the television series, concentrates on nine aspects of mind. There are others that might have been chosen in their stead, given the range and complexity of the overall subject; but taken together, these aspects offer a broad-ranging view of what we know, do not know, and think we may eventually know about the human mind.

Search Self-understanding is one of humankind's most ancient pursuits. Who am I? What is my relationship to the world around me? These questions marked the beginnings of philosophy. They also inaugurated the search for mind, for, at least in this one respect, we are unique among all creatures. Only *we* are curious about our origins, the meaning of our existence, and the nature of the inner world that we experience whenever we reflect, remember, daydream, or dream.

At various times in the past, the mind has been equated with the soul or the spirit. But such terms are religious or spiritual, rather than philosophical or scientific; and self-understanding is difficult enough without our presuming to be capable of understanding the nature of the divine. At other times, mind has been denied altogether, and behavior considered the only reality. Yet only a moment's reflection reveals a rich inner world that exists independently of any outward behavior. What is this mind that we experience so vividly, yet which eludes our best efforts when we try to describe it? Recently, specialists in a host of disciplines have set their sights on understanding the human mind. This chapter provides an overview of their ideas.

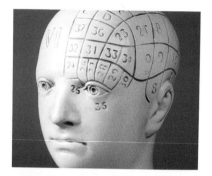

Development Within two weeks after conception, the process of brain formation is underway in the embryo. From the brain emerges the mind, present in primitive form even before birth, and developing throughout infancy and childhood in ways that are generally predictable, yet unique in each individual and always astonishing. Nothing is more vulnerable, however, than the brain of the fetus in the ensuing sixteen weeks after it first begins to form. Deviations from normal development can bring about profound alterations in mind. Alcohol and ionizing radiation can induce those alterations, leaving the baby that is born several months later deprived of the full and normal life he or she might otherwise have lived.

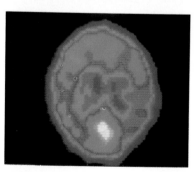

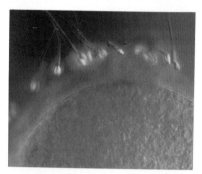

Aging Many of our ideas about aging are based on erroneous stereotypes. The mind is not preordained to suffer an eclipse in function as we age. Indeed, it can continue to operate at its best well into the eighth and ninth decades. Moreover, challenge and stimulation can exert a powerful influence on this optimal functioning. Neuroscientists now believe that throughout our lives, new information can actually be incorporated into the structure of the brain, through the creation of new synapses and the facilitation of existing nerve pathways.

Addiction Within the human brain are specific receptors on certain neurons to which addicting drugs bind. There are pleasure centers and nerve pathways that, once stimulated, exert a compelling influence on the individual to repeat this stimulation again and again. The mind can literally be enslaved by the pernicious and illegal substances that are readily available on the streets of cities of the United States and all over the world. Can scientists come up with chemical antidotes that will counteract the effects of these addicting agents? This is not only unlikely; a purely chemical approach to addiction ignores the larger aspects of the drug problem. Why are addicting drugs exerting so powerful an influence in our society? What does this tell us about ourselves?

Pain and Healing Not everyone reacts in the same way to an injury, an illness, or the death of a loved one. This is because the mind can influence our responses to stresses and unpleasant experiences. We now know that our mental attitude can alter physical processes within our body. Further, it can influence the effectiveness with which we fight off disease, the success with which we cope with stress, the way in which we respond to pain-producing illnesses such as cancer—and even, perhaps, how long we live.

Depression and Mood What is the difference between normal fluctuations in mood and clinical depression? Over the past two decades, neuroscientists have gathered convincing evidence that depression is biological as well as psychological. Early detection and treatment for specific forms of depression can now be expedited by the analysis of body tissues and fluids such as blood, urine, skin cells, or spinal fluid. Based on these analyses, appropriate drugs can be selected for the treatment of depression, and when joined to psychotherapy, promise better control of this most widespread of mental illnesses.

Thinking Thinking is as natural and inevitable as breathing, but when we try to pin down what it is that we actually *do* when we think, we run into difficulties. In part, this is because many aspects of our thinking are not accessible to our awareness. We cannot summon up *everything* that we believe, for example; yet the beliefs that we fail to articulate may be as or more important than what we speak about. This paradox has much to tell us about the nature of mind.

THINKING

Language All animals communicate, but only humans are capable of language. Indeed, it is safe to say that if there were not language, the mind would not have developed to its present stage. Language makes it possible for us to form representations of the world, and to communicate these representations to others. How much influence does our language have in determining how we perceive the world about us? Or our inner world? Does language create the mind, or does the process work the other way around, our language providing us with a critical aspect of mind: a highly personal representation of the world?

Violence Electrical discharges deep within the brain can produce violent outbursts that can result in murder. In such instances, is the violent person responsible for his actions? And what about the violence associated with some forms of mental illness, such as schizophrenia or uncontrolled mania? If a person afflicted with one of these disorders kills another person, should he be considered "not guilty by reason of insanity"? Do new discoveries about the brain and its role in rage and violence cast doubt on one of our most cherished beliefs about ourselves—our free will?

These are the broad topics that we will cover in this book. The beginning is the story of the search for mind itself.

THE
MIND

1.
SEARCH FOR MIND

In this book we are seeking no less than an understanding of who we are and why we are here. It is our mind that conceives these questions, searches for identity, and longs for answers. No one will ever know if the idea of mind first occurred to some caveman contemplating his image on the surface of a pond. But the earliest writing showing an awareness of something that resembles what philosophers later called the mind is a series of "dream books" composed on clay tablets by the Assyrians in the fifth or sixth millennium B.C. These deal with dreams about death, the loss of teeth or hair, even the shame of finding oneself naked in public—all matters implying belief in a personal identity.

A society's view of dreams may be a measure of its sophistication about the mind: A belief in the reality of dream content implies a failure to distinguish fantasy from reality, without which a concept of mind is impossible. The ancient Egyptians' preoccupation with a god of dreams, Serapis, probably coincided with a concern about the relation of the body to the mind or spirit. Their observation that life depended on breath, and that death coincided with the cessation of respiration, provided a basis for a belief that the spirit dwells within the body but does not depend on it for existence. It was the spirit that required the food, jewels, games, and other objects found in Egyptian tombs.

But long before the Assyrians composed their dream books or the Egyptians constructed their extraordinary tombs, early man created a remarkable picture of himself. It is about seventeen thousand years old, on the wall of the Lascaux cave in the French Dordogne. The picture is a simple

Cro-Magnon man's drawing of himself, on a wall of the Lascaux cave. Below the sticklike figure is a painting of a Paleolithic hunter killed by a bison.

stick figure topped by an eccentric image of a bird's head. In the same cave are paintings of animals so vivid and so imaginatively formed against the rounded contours of the rock walls that in the dim light they seem almost to be moving.

We will be taking many journeys in our search for mind. A journey back in time to the primitive figure on the wall of the Lascaux cave is an appropriate start to our search, for it is one of the earliest pictorial records we have of mind becoming aware of itself, the first clumsy groping toward a sense of "I."

It is also appropriate because, in a sense, what this figure reveals is a paradigm for the search itself. What do we mean by "mind"? As we shall see, it is a concept so complex, yet in a sense so amorphous, that over the ages it has resisted efforts to define it. It is *through* human thought, action, and behavior that philosophers and poets and scientists have sought to understand what mind is. It is *through* the Lascaux figure that we are able to form a sense of what mind was when thinking man first emerged. Our pictures of ourself, literal or figurative, are our access to understanding who we are and why we are here.

When Dr. Donald Johanson, a physical anthropologist, and Jonathan Kenworthy, an artist, look at the figure in the Lascaux cave, they are walking into the past and seeing the world of about seventeen thousand years ago through the eyes of the people who actually lived in it. The artist who created the paintings, says Kenworthy, has made this possible "in the most potent way imaginable. He's taking us through the world that he saw, through the creatures that he hunted, into the very innermost part of his mind."

The sticklike figure is simple, crude, flat—a startling contrast to the extraordinary richness of the animal paintings. "He's the first man we see in all these caves," says Kenworthy. "You look at all those wonderful images of animals, and here's man. And he's a pipe cleaner figure. Why? Why doesn't he draw himself? I think that at this stage of his thinking, his mind was in what he saw, not what he was. He was seeing himself through the things that he admired. It's the creatures that reveal his mind for us. He didn't have to look at himself. He was himself and that was the important thing in his world."

The Lascaux paintings portray the hunt, but this is not a hunting gallery. The Cro-Magnon artists who created them drew some creatures that were already extinct in the region, and others, such as the unicorn, that were fantasy figures. We know, therefore, that Lascaux is an effort by Cro-Magnon man to reveal the world as he *experienced* it, not as he literally saw it. "We are able to participate in that world," says Johanson, "because our minds are very similar to the minds of people in the Cro-Magnon period. This is a very different view of the world from the view of our earliest ancestors, who left behind only stone tools or other artifacts."

When Kenworthy goes on safari to Africa to study the movements of leopards, cheetahs, lions, and herds of wildebeest, he makes drawings of the creatures in front of him. "What the caveman was doing in Lascaux is exactly what I'm doing now," he says. "He went out and looked and saw and absorbed. And when he reproduced these emotional responses he'd had to what he had seen, he was not evoking images that were the same as the creatures he'd seen. He wasn't drawing those creatures. What he was drawing were his *feelings* about the creatures." When Kenworthy returns to his studio with his sketches, he begins an identical process. "When I come back here, the cheetah that I saw earlier becomes a reflection of how I feel. The composition recreates not the moment when I watched the cheetah but rather a sense of what was happening and how I felt about what was happening. Like Cro-Magnon, seventeen thousand years later I am drawing not just simply what I saw but what I felt about these creatures."

Artist Jonathan Kenworthy and anthropologist Donald Johanson stand before rock paintings in the Lascaux cave.

By looking at the cave paintings at Lascaux, we are able to enter into the mind of Cro-Magnon man. Indeed, through this art, Cro-Magnon man speaks to us in a language that is universal.

"If a caveman walked into my studio today and started talking to me, I would not understand a word he had to say," says Kenworthy. "He would be speaking cave language, whatever that is, and it would mean nothing to me. But if I look at his paintings, I have a complete area of feeling and view that I can share with him. This curious development of drawing the pictures of our minds is the most eloquent way of touching another person's mind that has ever evolved. It's a language without words, a language that links us through the whole history of mankind. If you like, it's a fellowship from one human mind to another."

At first glance, a definition of the mind seems obvious. After all, we speak of it daily. We talk of making up (or losing) one's mind, call some of our neighbors "mindless," and sometimes suggest that someone "does not know his own mind." But mostly we use the word as shorthand for memory, feeling, intelligence, reason, perception, judgment. Defining it is elusive. A telling reflection of the difficulty is the fact that there is no exact word for mind in some languages—even German, the medium of many philosophers and of the founders of psychology. When Immanuel Kant was trying to create an anatomy of the mind for his *Critique of Pure Reason* in 1781, he found that he could not even *invent* a precise word for the matrix within which, he claimed, are embedded sensibility, understanding, reason, and judgment. When they talk of the mind, Germans sometimes use the quaint term *Gemüt,* which refers to a person's nature. On other occasions they favor *Seele,* which corresponds to the Greek "psyche" and to "soul" in English. Then there is *Geist,* or "spirit."

Yet none of these is quite right. Many who seek to understand the mind do not believe in a soul. And what exactly is spirit?

Dictionary definitions are not very useful either. Culling from *Webster's Third New International Dictionary,* we read that mind is "the complex of man's faculties involved in perceiving, remembering, considering, evaluating, and deciding." This seems helpful until we realize that it is somewhat like the definitions of *inflation* and *entropy*—while we think we understand the meanings of these words, we finally have to admit that there is little there to grasp onto. A complementary definition, also from *Webster's,* says that mind is "an organized group of events in neural tissue occurring mediately in response to antecedent intrapsychic or extrapsychic events which it perceives, classifies, transforms, and coordinates prior to initiating action whose consequences are foreseeable to the extent of available information." In combination with the first, this rather cumbersome definition suggests that events within the brain, when suitably transformed and interpreted within other brain areas, result in the operation of mind.

The statement notes a fundamental link between mind and brain—our mind depends on our brain, and the human brain is the most complex organ in the universe—but the *operation* of mind is not a definition of mind itself. Since all this underscores the acknowledged difficulty of finding a satisfactory definition, it is more productive to search instead for the meaning of mind through those who have sought it before us, and who are seeking it still.

Scientists and thinkers in pursuit of mind have tried to identify those qualities that make it unique. One quality is the ability to be conscious of self, the ability to understand one's place on the planet and in time. Dr. Richard Leakey, an archeologist, believes that this capacity developed very slowly. "I would think that *Homo habilis* 1.8 or 1.9 million years ago was more conscious of self than is a chimpanzee. But, nonetheless, less conscious of self than perhaps we are today."

Leakey's comparison of the chimpanzee is telling because chimpanzees are our closest relative; the brain of a chimpanzee shares a striking structural similarity with our own. This animal also shares 99 percent of our genetic material, has many social structures and behaviors that resemble those of human beings, and is capable of comparatively sophisticated learning in some ways. Yet notable though these similarities are, there are fundamental limitations to the chimpanzee's mental capabilities. For this reason, studies of these animals make a valuable contribution to our understanding of the human mind.

Dr. Jane Goodall, who has been studying primate colonies since 1960, has taught us much about the behavior of the chimp. She believes that what accounts for the crucial difference between the minds of chimpanzees and humans is our development of a spoken language. "Language enables us to make meaningful plans not only for the immediate future, which even the chimp can do, but for next year or ten years ahead," says Goodall. "It enables us to pass on traditions and cultures to our children about types of behavior or objects which are not present. We can talk about them, we can explain them, and in this way we are completely and utterly different from the chimpanzees."

Dr. Desmond Morris, a zoologist, author, and artist, says, "Although chimps are much closer to us than some people would like to admit, we are somehow over a whole new threshold, even a whole new world. The human mind has

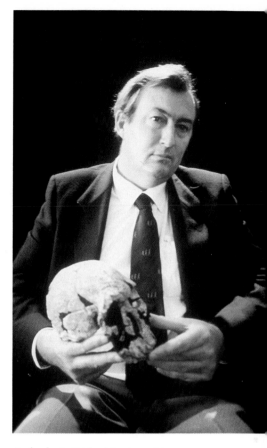

Archeologist Richard Leakey with a model of the skull of Homo habilis.

Primate researcher Jane Goodall in Gombe, Tanzania.

become just that little bit more complicated than the chimpanzee's mind. And that was enough to take us not ten degrees but a million degrees further. We can sit down and close our eyes and think for two hours, and when we open our eyes at the end of that time, apparently having done nothing, we are different people." Human beings are capable of introversion.

They are also capable of forming social relationships and getting along with their fellows, which experimental psychologist Nicholas Humphrey believes makes them different from all other animals. To do this, each must become his own personal psychologist, predicting and interpreting the behavior of other human beings as he encounters them. How? "By employing a mental model that makes use continually of the kind of information we get when we look in our own minds with the inner eye of consciousness. At such times, we see our own minds as being composed of desires, wills, emotions, sensations, and so on. It gives us a conceptual framework for understanding other human beings." Self-reflection is that inner eye of consciousness unique to the human species.

Self-awareness, symbolism, introversion, self-reflection, the formation of mental models—all are aspects of mind that searchers like Leakey, Goodall, Morris, Humphrey, and many others have pursued in their quest for the nature of mind. These searchers are part of a long history. The struggle to understand the meaning, purpose, and functioning of our mind is as old as civilization itself.

Our search for mind begins where philosophy, began—in ancient Greece. Greek philosophers were the first to understand that knowledge is not just the result of experience; it is something that can be studied in the same way a philosopher analyzes any object in nature.

Aristotle argued in the fourth century B.C. that the operation of the human mind was unlike anything else known. Our brain might physically resemble animal brains, but it was merely a hollow structure whose chief function was the regulation of body temperature. The mind existed independently of the body. This concept of *dualism* has influenced the idea of mind ever since.

Aristotle believed that the important organ of the body was the heart, not the brain. This emphasis differed from Plato's, who had placed the mind (then called "soul") in the brain, not the heart, because of his belief that the brain was round and thus conformed in its basic configuration to the perfect geometrical figure, the sphere. Galen, the second-century Greek physician, embraced Plato's brain-centered theory, but Aristotle's view never completely died out.

> Tell me where is fancy bred,
> Or in the heart or in the head?

In our own time, we seem to have settled on the brain, but not completely. A peculiar relic remains as a heritage, a blend of Aristotle's and Plato's ideas. Our emotions are relegated, at least metaphorically, to the heart. We suffer a "heartbreak" if our romances do not turn out as we wish. Our Valentine's Day cards show pictures of the heart, not the brain. "It is raining in my heart," not the brain, lamented the late rock and roll singer, Buddy Holly. For most of us, love—unrequited or otherwise—is consigned to the heart and not the brain.

But our thinking capacity, our intellectual resources, are brain-based. No doubt about it. "She is a real brain," we say in admiration of an outstanding student.

Galen, who believed that the soul—mind—resided in the brain, did more than speculate; he experimented with pigs, cutting the sensory and motor fibers to and from the brain. As it happened, he was wrong about the sites of these functions in the brain, reversing them, but he was correct about the concept. He was the first in the line of what would later be called the localizationists, who believe that parts of the brain are specialized to carry out specific functions.

René Descartes (1596–1650).

Galen saw sensory and motor activities as "lower" functions, but said very little about the "higher" functions of mind: judgment, memory, reasoning, and the exercise of will that makes possible motor activity such as moving the hand toward an object. Implicit in this division between the higher and lower functions was the belief, still encountered today, that such things as the "will" that initiates the movement of our limbs should not be considered on the same level as the lower functions. By implication, therefore, the functions of the mind are to be considered separate from the functions of the brain.

It was René Descartes, in the seventeenth century, who first made this mind–brain (or mind–body) dualism explicit.

In 1629, Descartes retired to an inn in Holland in order to explore the mystery of his own consciousness. His intention was to discover a principle that could not be doubted. Certainty mattered in a century following that in which Copernicus had dislodged the earth from the center of the universe and redefined it merely as an orbiter around the sun. Descartes saw the sun rise in the east and set in the west and knew his perception of this "reality" was questionable. He sat in his room and looked at the furniture. Even if it did not exist as it appeared, perhaps did not even exist at all, there was no possibility of doubting the consciousness that perceived it. The *fact* of consciousness—*cogito, ergo sum;* I think, therefore I am—had priority over the objects of the external world.

Further, the brain, which Descartes compared to a machine, was part of the body and must also be separate from the mind. He was fascinated by the hydraulically operated automata, life-sized statues, in the Royal Gardens of Saint-Germain in Paris. In *Traite de l'homme,* published in 1664, he described a visitor walking in the Gardens who stepped on particular tiles arranged to operate valves so that water flowed from a reservoir through pipes and activated these statues. The brain, he supposed, was organized on principles similar to the automata. Sense organs responded to stimuli in the environment, just as the statues responded to pressure on the tiles. The brain, too, had pipes and valves and a reservoir of fluid in the *ventricles,* and the reasoning mind could influence the opening and closing of these valves. To Descartes, the reasoning mind was like a master engineer in the Royal Gardens, stationed near the main reservoir, who kept his eye on how things were progressing, and occasionally intervened to open or close a valve on his own.

Descartes placed the site of the mind in the brain, writing in *The Passions of the Soul,* "Let us then conceive here that the soul [mind] has its principal seat in the little gland which exists in the middle of the brain, from whence it radiates forth through all the remainder of the body by means of the animal spirits, nerves, and even the blood, which, participating in the impressions of the spirits, can carry them by the arteries into all the members."

Strictly speaking, however, Descartes was not a localizer, despite his apparent localization of the mind to this "little gland," the pineal; he saw the pineal as an infinitely small area of contact akin to a mathematical point, rather than a site in the physical sense. One could no more locate the position of the mind within the brain than one could pick up a mathematical point and pass it around for inspection. Further, he was localizing not so much a relation between a structure (the brain) and a function (the mind) as a philosophical relationship between the preeminent mind ("I think") and the body ("therefore I am"). In this equation mind was far and away more important than the body, including the brain, and could conceivably exist without it.

Many of our contemporary ideas about mind and brain can be traced back to Descartes. Though it has long been recognized that mind does not exist somehow apart from brain, the tendency to separate them persists in many ways. If we have a migraine headache or suffer an epileptic seizure, we seek out a neurologist. But if we feel sad, weep a lot, lose our appetite, and have trouble sleeping, we're encouraged to visit a psychiatrist. The neurologist is the expert on the brain; the psychiatrist holds forth on matters pertaining to the mind. This gap is narrowing at last; neurologists recognize that emotional and behavioral disorders cannot be accounted for wholly by brain and nervous system dysfunction, and psychiatrists are now becoming proficient in the neurosciences and no longer believe that mental illness or even problems in living can be understood without reference to the brain. But ingrained patterns die hard, and relics of Cartesian dualism have not yet vanished.

Opposed to dualism (mind as separate from matter—brain) is the view that neither mind nor brain is the primary reality. The extreme of this position was taken by Bishop George Berkeley, the Irish-born eighteenth-century idealist philosopher. He maintained that the material world does not really exist; it simply consists of images in the mind, with God as the source of all perception. Said Berkeley: "To be is to be perceived."

Berkeley's idealism is hard to confirm or deny since it does not lend itself to investigation; it must be taken on faith. But a moment's thought must convince anyone but the most intransigent idealist that material objects indeed exist independently of our experience of them. Samuel Johnson took just this tack in his riposte to Berkeley; in James Boswell's words, "Striking his foot with a mighty force against a large stone till he rebounded from it, 'I

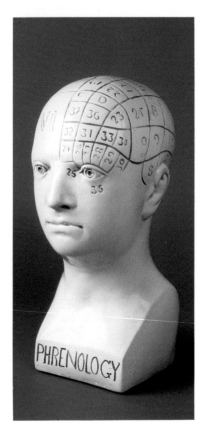

The faculties of the brain, as charted by anatomist and phrenologist Franz Joseph Gall.

refute it *thus!*'" All that Johnson knew of the stone, of course, was his experience of it—precisely Berkeley's point. But how in fact does one prove that a thing exists apart from one's perception of it?

La Peyronie, an eighteenth-century French surgeon, described the changes in human behavior that accompanied specific brain injuries. His observations were largely confined to "lower" functions—paralysis, loss of sensation, blindness—and to this extent he remained a thoroughgoing Cartesian. Nonetheless, he and surgeons like him were bringing about a revolution in thinking about the mind. In 1741, when surgeon to the king, he delivered a paper in Paris that reported on a patient with a severe wound to the head extending to the depths of the *corpus callosum* (the bridging mass of fibers connecting the two *cerebral hemispheres*). La Peyronie injected a squirt of water into the wound. The patient lapsed into unconsciousness. When the water was removed, the patient became alert once again. La Peyronie thought, ludicrously, that he had discovered the site where the soul "exerts its function." What *was* important was that he and others no longer held that mind existed somehow apart from brain. Rather, the two were interrelated in ways yet to be discovered.

In 1819, *Anatomie et Physiologie du Systeme Nerveux,* by Franz Joseph Gall, was published, and influenced the direction of brain research for the next fifty years. Gall, an anatomist, believed that the brain was the seat of all mental functions. He divided these functions into twenty-seven separate faculties, and was convinced that each was associated with a discrete area of the brain. He came to this conclusion on the basis of a childhood observation that he pursued into adulthood:

"At age nine I noticed that those who continued to learn most easily by heart had prominent eyes. . . . Although I had no preliminary knowledge, I was seized with the idea that eyes thus formed were the mark of an excellent memory. It was only later on . . . that I said to myself: if memory shows itself by a physical characteristic, why not other faculties; and this gave me the first incentive for all my researches, and was the occasion for all my discoveries."

Gall looked harder at the human face and head than anyone before him. He studied his patients, as well as portraits and busts of famous people. He examined and preserved skulls; he made hundreds of head casts. In hospitals, schools, prisons, and orphanages he examined and recorded the configuration of skulls. He was particularly interested in individuals with exceptional abilities or talents—the savant and the retardate, the criminal and the saint, the scholar and the artist, the musician and the statesman. Indeed, when Gall looked at a skull, he was convinced that he was also looking at a brain. Today we recognize this as absurd. Whatever "bumps" exist on a person's skull, one can be certain they are not the result of enlargements of the underlying brain. Lord Macaulay captured the nonsensical character of phrenology, the pseudoscience of "bumps," in a diary note for January 16, 1851:

"We talked much together until another party got into the carriage: a canting fellow and a canting woman. Their cant was not religious but phrenological. It was all we could do to avoid laughing out loud. The lady pronounced that the Exhibition of 1851 would enlarge her ideality and exercise her locality."

But phrenology did perform a useful and critical service; it advanced the cause of localization.

In 1861, Paul Broca, a French surgeon and neuroanatomist, described his patient, Tan, who as a result of a stroke in the left hemisphere had lost his ability to speak. Soon, many other reports appeared of patients who exhibited various functional losses as a result of discrete lesions in the brain. Indeed, for a time, early neuroscientists believed that for every brain lesion a specific deficit must exist, and vice versa.

New insights into the mind–brain relationship came with the study of reflexes by the Russian physiologist, Ivan Pavlov, in the early twentieth century. Pavlov observed that if you put food in front of a dog's mouth, it will begin to salivate. But the same salivation can be brought about in other ways; the sight of the man who customarily fed the dog, or any other action associated with feeding, is in itself sufficient to initiate salivation. Pavlov referred to these *conditioned responses* as "psycho secretions," and they provided the basis for a lifetime of investigation.

Consider for a moment salivation not in a dog but in yourself. Salivation is not ordinarily under conscious control. You do not say, "Now I'll start the salivary reflex"; you think about eating, or the first bit of food touches your tongue, and the response occurs automatically, a simple reflex arc. But most reflexes do not conform to simple stimulus/response patterns. If you're suddenly bitten on the leg by a mosquito while walking and swat at it, you must make numerous postural adjustments. Without conscious awareness your weight must be redistributed from one leg to another, your balance must be realigned, and so on. According to the English neurophysiologist Sir Charles Sherrington, these adjustments are the essence of what a reflex is all about.

In one of Sherrington's experiments, a dog was hooked up to a harness and a bell was sounded, followed by a brief electrical shock to one of its paws. The dog raised the paw in order to avoid the shock. After several repetitions, it had become conditioned to raise its paw at the sound of the bell alone. But the response was far more complicated than the simple reflex described by Pavlov. A dog cannot lift one foot without realigning its whole body in order not to topple over. Many muscles must be brought into opposition with each other, so as to maintain a stable base from which the necessary postural readjustments can be made. This is *integrative* reflex activity. Nerve signals pursue a path involving a number of reflex arcs that work together, creating an integrated response involving the whole organism.

These two theories concerning reflexes, Pavlov's and Sherrington's, have exerted differing influences on researchers engaged in the search for mind. Sherrington's work was appropriated by physiologists, while Pavlov's simple reflex arc was enthusiastically taken up by psychologists. In the 1920s, J. B. Watson based his theory of behaviorism on Pavlov's conditioning, describing behavior in terms of physiological responses to stimuli. His best known (and rather perfidious) "experiment" involved an eleven-year-old child, Albert, who was conditioned to fear a white furry rat. Whenever Albert tried to touch the rat, Watson struck a loud gong. The noise so frightened the child that he not only began to fear the rat but generalized his conditioned fear to other white furry objects, including Santa Claus's beard.

B. F. Skinner later expanded the theories of Pavlov and Watson by elaborating a new form of conditioning, *operant conditioning,* in which the animal learns to "operate on" the environment. A pigeon, for instance, learns to peck at an illuminated button or key to get the reward of a food pellet, or to avoid pecking at a key if the end result is an electric shock, a punishment. Complex behaviors can be conditioned on the basis of this system of rewards and punishment.

In effect, behaviorists decided that the mind was irrelevant and demanded that psychology restrict itself to what can be observed. A generation of psychologists explored the workings of stimulus and response, "Skinner boxes" and maze-running rats, and ignored decision making, changes of "heart," resolutions, religious conversions, and other operations of mind that occur in the absence of any observable behavior.

The path from Gall to Broca to Pavlov to Sherrington to the behaviorists constituted a search for mind that focused on the brain and behaviors explicitly linked to it. A concurrent search took a different and equally influential direction.

Though Charles Darwin is popularly remembered for *On the Origin of Species,* it was another of his works, *The Descent of Man* (1871), that provoked the greatest storm. Darwin's theory rejected Aristotle's basic distinction be-

Behavorial psychologist B. F. Skinner, who greatly influenced psychological theory and practice from the 1930s through the 1950s.

tween the human mind and the mental life of other species. He proposed that all minds adapted to their environments over time. His theory of evolution said that the human mind has its roots in a past shared with other animals, evolving as part of a continuum.

Darwin's thought powerfully affected our view of ourselves and our world, and at the beginning of the twentieth century it had a powerful effect on the thinking of Sigmund Freud, the creator of psychoanalysis and probably the most influential psychologist in history. Trained in anatomy and physiology as well as medicine, Freud practiced as a neurologist before he turned to the development of the theories that revolutionized thinking about the mind.

Freud's investigation of the mind began with the uncloaking of repressed sexual, aggressive, and hostile drives that had evolved from our animal orgins. Unlike the rest of the animal kingdom, human beings must function within a society, a civilization, so these instinctual tendencies have to be brought under control and socialized. There is an eternal war, therefore, between what might be called the Darwinian side of our nature and the civilized side. Chiefly because of Freud, we recognize today that there is a dynamic process by which unconscious processes of mind—hidden instincts, desires, memories, reactions—provide the energy for higher processes of thinking, learning, and creating. The mind has learned to harness the power but repress the content of much of the unconscious.

Freud's theory of the unconscious has exerted a powerful effect on therapeutic approaches to problems and disorders of mind, as is widely recognized. Now neuroscience is demonstrating that what is happening in the unconscious literally registers in the brain, a further confirmation of the intricate relationship between mind and brain. In experiments done by Dr. Howard Shevrin, of the University of Michigan Medical Center, a word like *fear* is flashed on a screen for a thousandth of a second, too fast for conscious perception. We call a stimulus such as this, which can be visual or auditory, *subliminal.* Electrodes on the subject's head, which register electrical activity at the surface of the brain, convey a very brief response to the subliminal flashing of *fear,* and then, a quarter of a second later, a sharp burst of activity. However, when the word is flashed supraliminally, that is, at a rate slow enough for conscious perception, it takes twice as long for the brain to react.

Shevrin concludes from this difference in reaction time that all messages to the brain are selectively transmitted first to the unconscious in a filtering process. It is this process that causes the delay. "When the words are presented supraliminally, so that the subject can actually see them," says Shevrin, "there is some kind of inhibition or delay of the

Sigmund Freud (1856–1939).

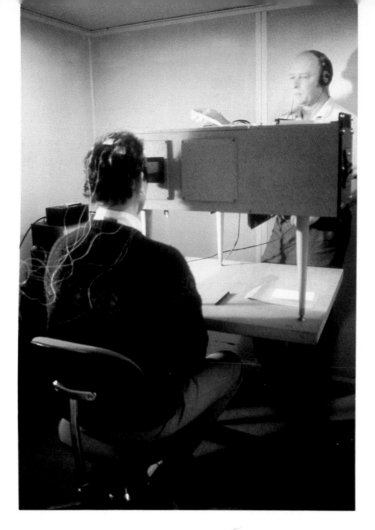

When Dr. Howard Shevrin flashes an emotionally loaded word like "fear" at subliminal speed, the subject does not realize he has seen it. His brain, however, responds measurably to the stimulus.

brain's responses to those words. This is of great interest from the psychoanalytic standpoint because it suggests a link to Freud's idea of repression. There is reason for the person to repress those unconscious words and their related ideas and feelings, because to become conscious of them would be very distressing."

From these experiments, an image of our mind emerges. We all take in more than enters our conscious awareness, first in the unconscious and then only selectively into consciousness. This process takes time. "What we're trying to demonstrate," says Shevrin, "is that what is meaningful to the mind has an existence in the brain. It isn't simply a matter of electrical or biochemical activity. That which is going on is part of the meaningful transactions in human life."

Mind is present at birth in an elemental form; indeed, as we shall see in Chapter 2, in the fetus before birth. Thereafter mind emerges gradually, in a developmental sequence that was elucidated by the Swiss psychologist, Jean Piaget. Through ingeniously designed experiments based on observations of his own and many other children, Piaget charted the stages that infants and children go through as mind matures and learning is accomplished. He began his investigations in the 1920s, when designing IQ tests to be administered to schoolchildren. He saw that children consistently gave the same sorts of incorrect answers to certain questions. The systematic character of these "errors" suggested certain universalities of childhood thinking at different stages of development, and from this recognition came Piaget's formulations of these age-related stages. In one famous series of experiments, very young children demonstrated a gradually evolving ability to find hidden objects, and finally to appreciate that objects remain the same when hidden and when revealed. This appreciation cannot be hurried. It is a function of experience and maturation, and will not show itself until the child's mind is ready. Crucial attributes of mind such as space, time, causality, number, and hierarchical structures, which are essential to the functioning of our internal world, appear only in their own time.

Piaget concluded that the mind evolves by active *construction*. We do not passively perceive and process information from the world around us. We transform it, and this transformation evolves in developmental stages according to certain preestablished guidelines.

Studies on the human brain within the last three decades confirm the existence of these and other guidelines and make it clear that our minds are not simply "blank slates" on which is sketched an unfolding representation of the world.

Only moments after birth, an infant will turn toward the sound of a human voice. Such a performance is the result of inherited patterns: neural networks connecting visual and auditory pathways so that what is heard is automatically associated with the expectation of something to be seen. Even a blind newborn will turn its eyes toward the source of a sound, although for that infant there will be nothing to be seen. Shortly thereafter, based on experience, this reflex turning will cease.

Within the animal kingdom, newborns come into the world predisposed to what the ethologist Konrad Lorenz refers to as the "following response." Newly hatched birds of many species will follow the first moving object they encounter after hatching. It need only move and emit a clucking sound. Anything will do. It can be a human being or even a piece of metal pipe with a stripe. In a famous experiment, it was Lorenz himself. This "imprinting" serves a purpose under ordinary conditions: an identification with the mother bird. But within the context of Lorenz's experiment, the innate disposition to accept as "mother" anything that grossly simulates the mother bird results in a situation that is sadly comic. One of Lorenz's favorite pictures shows him strolling through high grass trailed by several grown

Jean Piaget (1896–1980).

Ethologist Konrad Lorenz. Geese who had been "imprinted" with his image moments after hatching cluster around him.

THE AREAS OF THE BRAIN

The brain and the spinal cord comprise the central nervous system and are enclosed within the bony structures of the skull and spinal column. In general, regions of the brain are specialized for different functions. Starting from below and working upward, we encounter:

1. The **spinal cord.** This long, tapering structure runs the length of the spinal column and lies within the curved enclosure formed by the spinal vertebrae. The spinal cord receives information conveyed from the nerves of the skin, joints, muscles, and ligaments, and conveys motor commands for movement. If the spinal cord is cut (transected) as a result of an accident or other injury, sensation and voluntary movement are lost in those parts of the body below the point of damage.

2. The **brainstem.** There are three parts to the brainstem. The *medulla,* a vital inch of tissue at the place where the spinal cord enters the brainstem, controls such tasks as breathing, talking, singing, swallowing, vomiting, and the maintenance of blood pressure and even (partially) heart rate. The *pons* ("bridge"), just above the medulla, is a broad band of fibers that neurally links the cerebral cortex and the cerebellum. Continuous with the pons is the third structure, the *midbrain,* the smallest division of the brainstem, which permits elementary forms of seeing and hearing. The *cerebellum,* lying behind the pons, is chiefly concerned with modulating the range and force of movements; lacking a cerebellum, you would not be able to move an object without dropping it.

3. Centimeters above the brainstem is the **diencephalon,** which includes the *thalamus* and *hypothalamus.* The thalamus processes all the senses except smell. Immediately below it is the hypothalamus, which is the regulatory center for vital activities, many of which lie outside conscious awareness: endocrine levels, water balance, sexual rhythms, food intake, and the autonomic nervous system. It is also the command center for many complex mood and motivational states, including anger, placidity, fatigue, and hunger.

4. The **limbic system,** also called the emotional or primitive or old brain, is a network of nerve centers above the hypothalamus. It has connections to both the cortical centers in the temporal lobes (concerned with thought and higher cognitive functions) and the hypothalamus, and is involved with the same emotions and motivational states: rage, fright, aggression, hunger, and sexual arousal. This dual relationship allows emotions to reach conscious awareness, and cognitive fantasies and observations to affect us emotionally.

5. The two **cerebral hemispheres** are involved with our highest conceptual and motor functions. They consist of the overlying *cerebral cortex;* the *basal ganglia,* which together with the cerebellum coordinate all body movement; and three large nuclear groups, the *caudate nucleus,* the *putamen,* and the *pallidium.* The two hemispheres resemble each other, almost as if we had two brains. Each hemisphere is divided into separate but ultimately artificial territories: the frontal, parietal, occipital, and temporal lobes, which have specialized roles to play. Nonetheless, the more that neuroscientists learn about the brain, the more it becomes clear that the boundaries separating one brain area from another are much less distinct than had been previously thought.

The *frontal lobe* is concerned with movement and the formation of complex motor "programs." The most forward portion, the prefrontal fibers, exert an inhibitory control over our actions, bringing them into line with social expectations. Injuries to this area may cause offensive, socially unacceptable behaviors. Injuries—as in stroke—to the motor cortex, the areas that control movement on the opposite side of the body, can cause paralysis.

The *parietal lobe* contains the primary sensory cortex, the "feeling" part of the brain, which receives impulses from all the body's sensory receptors. Each area of the body is represented in the parietal lobes in proportion to its functional significance; thus, the hand has greater representation than, say, the small of the back.

The *temporal lobe* is important for hearing, memory, and a person's sense of self and time. This is also where déjà vu experiences originate. Because it has connections to the limbic system, the temporal lobe also plays an important part in emotional experience.

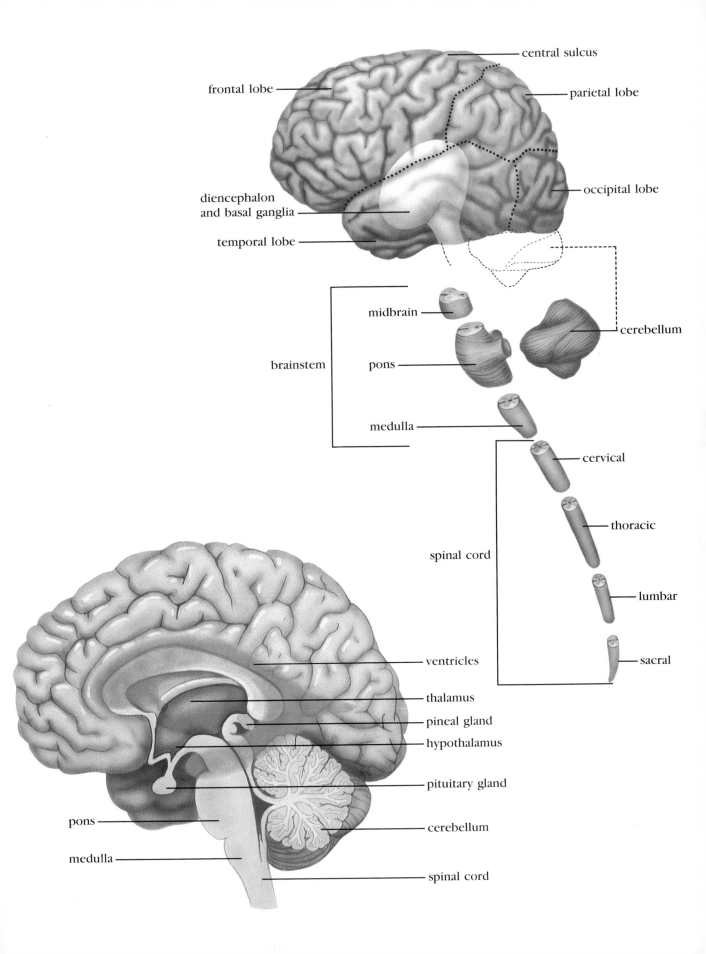

central sulcus

frontal lobe

parietal lobe

occipital lobe

diencephalon
and basal ganglia

temporal lobe

midbrain

brainstem

pons

cerebellum

medulla

cervical

thoracic

spinal cord

lumbar

sacral

ventricles

thalamus

pineal gland

hypothalamus

pituitary gland

pons

cerebellum

medulla

spinal cord

The *occipital lobe* is the visual center of the brain, carrying out the extraordinarily complex transformations of the information conveyed from the retina of the eye. A stroke or other injury to this area can cause severe visual impairment or blindness.

The "two brains": Though the two hemispheres look very much alike, they process information in different ways. The right hemisphere operates holistically. Thus, forming a mental picture of one's living room is best done by the right hemisphere. The left hemisphere, in contrast, excels in breaking things down into their component parts; mentally counting the number of chairs in that living room is best done by the left hemisphere, which draws upon the right hemisphere's vision of the entire living room and then mentally subdivides it according to the individual chairs it contains. Since language involves the stringing together of separate units—words—in order to form a phrase or sentence, the left hemisphere is specialized for language in 96 to 99 percent of right-handed and 70 percent of left-handed people.

Because of its holistic processing, the right hemisphere is better at visual–spatial tasks, such as forming mental maps, rotating geometrical figures in one's head, or recognizing the face of a friend. But the left hemisphere comes into play when the mental map must be converted into verbal instructions—"Take the first right turn, then make a sharp left"—or when one analyzes distinguishable aspects of a friend's face—"Is Janet wearing a different hairstyle today?" But it is important to remember that at all times the brain *functions as a whole,* both hemispheres communicating with each other as well as with other parts of the brain deep below the cerebral cortex.

geese that had been imprinted with his presence moments after hatching.

The response that is functioning at birth confers an adaptive advantage on the organism; the gosling, recognizing the mother and attaching itself to her, is helped to survive. The process confers an adaptive advantage on the species as well. Both individual and species adaptation are extremely important in terms of our search for mind.

Darwin's theory of evolution suggests an explanation for this. While an individual brain may be heavily dependent upon experience for its maturation, the development of the brain over countless generations depends upon whichever assemblage of genes happens to prevail and thereby determine the structure and function of the individual brain. That genetic ensemble is the end of a process of natural selection that operated on our distant ancestors. Those ancestors with brains that incorporated the attributes of time and space (detecting movement in the high grass and darting off at just the right instant) survived. Those whose brains lacked these attributes died in the grasp of their predators. Over time, "knowledge" about the world was incorporated into the genetic ensemble that determines the structure and function of the human brain. Thus, the human brain has both an individual and a phylogenetic (species) history, and the brain's organization and its expression as mind represent phylogenetic adaptations evolved for coping with the "real world." Our knowledge of the "real world" is therefore heavily dependent upon the organization of our brain.

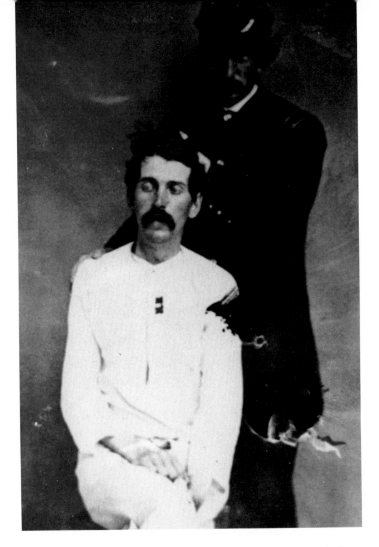

A Civil War doctor inspecting a gunshot wound in a soldier's head. Wartime head injuries have been a fertile source of new knowledge about the workings of the brain.

It is ironic but true that much that has been learned about the brain and the mind has come as the result of wars and preparation for wars. From the study of head injuries incurred during the Civil War and especially the First World War, neurologists learned which areas of the brain are concerned with vision and what happens when selective parts of the visual pathways are injured by shrapnel. Based on the care and treatment of soldiers suffering from brain injuries in World War I, neurologists, notably Kurt Goldstein and Henry Head, came to the conclusion that, in Head's words, "No function is localized strictly to any part of the cortex." This does not mean that there are not areas in the brain particular to specific functions; it means, rather, that other areas—sometimes many of them—may also be involved in these functions. The great neurologist Hughlings Jackson illuminated this when he said, "To locate the damage which destroys speech and to locate speech are two different things."

A telling argument for holism rather than localization came from the work of the psychologist Karl Lashley. In *Brain Mechanisms and Intelligence,* published in 1929, Lashley analyzed the effect of removing parts of the brains of rats

Dr. Vernon Mountcastle's experiments have greatly expanded our understanding of functional areas in the brain.

that had been trained to run mazes. He found that the formation and retention of the rat's ability to make its way successfully through a maze varies with the *extent* of the brain injury but not its specific location. In general, the defect in performance as a result of a lesion was directly proportional to how much brain had been removed.

Beginning in the 1960s, neuroscientists began achieving new insights into the brain, based on three discoveries about brain organization. First, major brain structures, most notably the *cerebral cortex,* were found to be composed of multiply replicated, more or less similar modules, each containing hundreds of thousands of neurons. This discovery was based on the finding by Dr. Vernon Mountcastle, a neurophysiologist at the Johns Hopkins University School of Medicine, that cortical cells are organized in vertical columns, extending from the surface down through the six layers of cortex.

Second, the connections between cells within the cerebral cortex were found to be far more numerous and specific than previously believed. Third, the total set of processing modules within the cortex is divided into subsets. Each of these modular subsets is linked to similar subsets in other brain structures and areas. According to Mountcastle, "These connective subsets are distributed systems, each composed of modular elements in several or many brain regions, connected in both parallel and serial arrays. They form the neuronal pathways for distributed and parallel processing within the brain."

Contemporary conceptions of the brain are based on distributed rather than localized networks. A distributed system has no "center" from which all action emanates. There is no master neuron or "ghost" resident within the neuronal machinery. Indeed, in a distributed system, "motor" and "sensory" areas are only terms of convenience.

"There is nothing intrinsically 'motor' about *motor cortex* or 'sensory' about *sensory cortex.* It is their extrinsic connections—the inputs they receive and the connections they make to other brain areas—that make them distinctly motor or sensory," Mountcastle says.

If we could understand the operation of a single area of the cortex, or a single vertical column, Mountcastle believes, this would have important implications for understanding other areas of the brain, as well as enhancing our understanding of the brain itself.

A large number of cortical areas have now been identified, corresponding to each of the major sensory systems. There is not an "auditory center," but four auditory areas; not a solitary "visual center," but no less than twelve visual areas. Further, all of these sensory areas, in Mountcastle's words, "impose their own abstractions and syntheses upon the representations that reach them; they also function as distribution centers."

As we have noted, consciousness—awareness of the self—is a uniquely human quality. The French critic, M. Auguste Bailly, writing about James Joyce, saw a symphony as an analogy of the relationship of consciousness to the mind.

"The life of the mind is a symphony. It is a mistake, or, at best, an arbitrary method, to dissect the chords and set out their components on a single line, on one plane only. Such a method gives an entirely false idea of the complexity of our mental makeup, for it is the way the light falls upon each element, with a greater or a lesser clarity, that indicates the relative importance for ourselves, our lives and acts, of each of the several thought-streams. . . . We do not think on one plane but on many planes at once. It is wrong to suppose that we follow only one train of thought at a time; there are several trains of thought, one above another. We are generally more aware, more completely conscious, of thoughts that take form on the higher plane; but we are also aware, more or less obscurely, of a stream of thoughts on the lower levels. We attend or own to one series of reflections or images; but we are all the time aware of many series which are unrolling themselves on obscurer planes of consciousness."

To Descartes, the simple thought, "I think, therefore I am," exerted such compelling force on his attention that he was convinced all competing elements within his own mind were no more than distractions, mental gnats to be slapped away so that he could concentrate on the mental landscape he considered the essence of his consciousness.

Descartes willed away the full complexity, even chaos, that makes up our consciousness during every moment of our waking life. (And our dreams as well, where in most instances many different themes and subthemes, sometimes tenuously related to one another, are taking place in our dreamscape at the same time.)

But Descartes was undoubtedly correct on one point. Consciousness at all times and under all conditions is experienced as a unity. Even the obsessive, who balances dozens of reasons why he should attend the board meeting with a dozen other reasons why he should not, experiences himself as a unity, *one person,* if a rather tortured unity. The schizophrenic who hears voices, or the PCP user bedeviled by hallucinations of bloody faces with gaping eyes, experiences himself as the *singular* victim of these frightening experiences.

We take this unified, *integrated* consciousness for granted. But some people from birth onward encounter a world without this integration, without meaning.

"Ed" is a twenty-four-year-old man who can remember

Autistic bicyclist "Ed,"
ready for his weekly journey.

(Opposite) *Recent studies indicate that the brains of most autistic persons have defects. One of the defective areas in some patients is the cerebellum, a region not normally linked to higher brain function. The lower MRI (magnetic resonance imaging) scan shows a normal, fully functional brain. The upper, of an autistic person, shows a much diminished cerebellum.*

and vividly describe every bicycle that he has ever owned. Every Saturday morning, he rides his current bike to towns, and to stores in these towns, that he selects, one at a time, from a Chamber of Commerce map. He has formulated a strategy that permits him to visit these towns and stores only in alphabetical order. He allows himself one visit each week. Having ridden a few hours to the next town on his list and to a shop there beginning with "A" he may find himself close to the next shop on his list, which begins with "B." But he will not even glance at it. He will return next Saturday to see that. And what does Ed do at each of these stops? He merely looks at his destination for a while, checks it off his maps, and sets off on the long ride home.

In many ways, Ed functions at a normal level. He is not retarded; he is *autistic*. What is missing is the capacity to find normal meaning and purpose in the places and people of his environment. To give order to his life, he makes lists. They offer him the framework he cannot otherwise construct. As a result of his autism, Ed represents a mind unable to self-reflect, a mind that is therefore ill-equipped to ascribe meaning and relationships and motives to others. "He seems to go through life week after week trying to hold on to a sameness," says Ed's father. "He never asks for anything. If we did not encourage him, he would not initiate any social behavior at all. He would sit in his room, look at his maps, and listen to his radio. There are three things that have never entered his behavior. He does not request, share, or demonstrate."

To neuroscientist Eric Courchesne, of the University of California, San Diego, who has known Ed for many years, the deficiency in autism is a failure in the ability to synthesize. "In their social interactions and in every other interaction, autistic people are recording as faithfully as they can what they see and what they hear and what they feel. They collect pieces of unconnected information, and then, rather than synthesizing all the facts into something new which is their own unique creation, they simply take these pieces; and when a certain button is pushed in their nervous system, they respond with the appropriate piece of information or the appropriate rule. But it is the same rule, the same piece of information, that they had in the first place. It has not been changed. It has not been combined with anything. It has not been synthesized and turned into a unique symbol or a unique idea representing that person's experience of his or her own world."

Because of his autism, a disorder now recognized to involve damage to the brain, Ed lacks an important component of mind. Despite adequate intelligence, the ability to

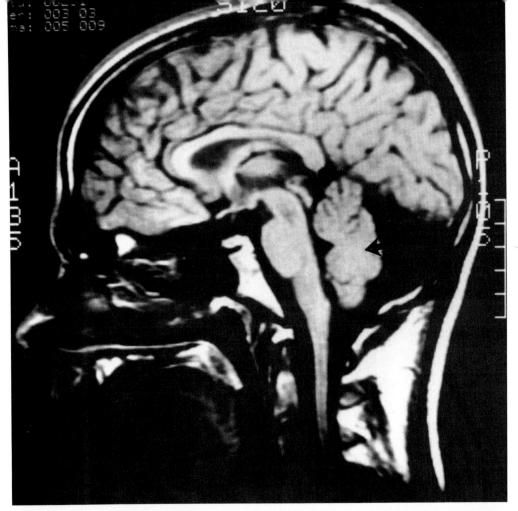

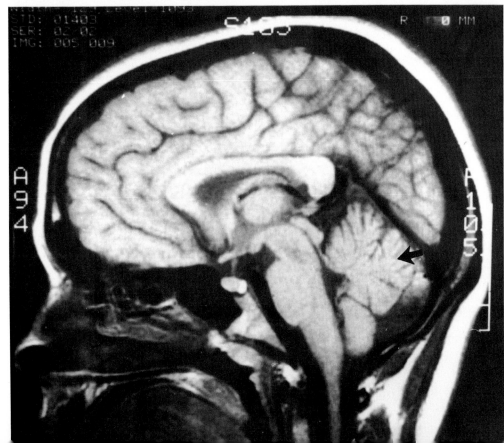

learn, curiosity, and an intense interest in subjects such as his bicycles, he cannot transform the information that he learns into symbols and ideas from which he can build and construct his own mind. "For normal people, life is like a novel, a personal story with a beginning and a sequence of events involving people acting for certain reasons," says Courchesne. "But in autism there is no story. Rather, there is a set of facts and rules and lists, like a crossword puzzle. Sometimes these things overlap, and sometimes they do not. There is no essential communication between these facts. They simply are. They do not build up to any personal story."

But for most of us, integration and synthesis do not *seem* to present a problem. We can give reasonably coherent explanations for our behavior; we experience ourselves as in control of our destiny; we are conscious of ourselves as a unity. To philosopher John Searle, "Consciousness is essential to the mind. Any theory of the mind that does not make consciousness a central part of the investigation has missed the point." But traditionally, scientists have been reluctant to study consciousness. This reluctance is based on the belief that consciousness is not "scientific"; instead, it has something to do with mysticism or religion.

"There is nothing more mysterious or mystic about the mind than there is about digestion," says Dr. Searle. "What the brain does for the mind is what the stomach does for digestion. We have got to start treating mental life and consciousness as just an ordinary part of the physical world like anything else. I think of the mind not as a separate kind of thing or arena, but rather as the sequence of thoughts, feeling, experience, and so-called mental phenomena that go on in it. 'Mind' is the name of a process, not a thing. We've got to demystify it. We have this tradition that makes it seem spooky, but there's nothing spooky about it. It's part of our biological life. The thing is, it's what matters most about our biological life. We can give up our thumbs, or in a pinch, our eyes. But if we give up our consciousness, that's it. We're dead."

The "biological life" of which mind is a part is very specific. The brain, that three-pound mass of tissue encased within our skulls, is the physical embodiment of mind. Further, identifiable alterations of mind result from damage in specific parts of the brain. Studies of the results of such damage play a major part in the search for and understanding of mind.

Studies of patients who have undergone "split brain" operations are particularly illuminating in this respect. Normally the right and left hemispheres of the brain are tethered together by means of the corpus callosum, a thick band of nerve fibers that makes cross-communication between the hemispheres possible. (It is this area in which La Peyronie's patient was injured.) In certain epileptic seizures, electrical discharges originating in one hemisphere pass across the corpus callosum to the opposite hemisphere, causing the entire brain to be involved in the seizure. When these seizures become life-threatening and no other form of treatment is effective, the corpus callosum is surgically severed, depriving the electrical discharges of their passage. Thereafter, the seizures can often be controlled by drugs and the patient can lead a comparatively normal life; but as with any drastic surgical procedure, split brain operations exact a price—the transmission of information between the two hemispheres is halted. This can produce some bizarre (and intriguing) situations that reveal significant processes of mind.

In one experiment, Dr. Michael Gazzaniga, a neuroscientist at Dartmouth College, flashes the word *walk* for an instant on a screen in front of "Joe," an epileptic patient who has undergone a split brain operation. The signal is delivered only to his left visual field. Since the left visual field projects only to the right hemisphere of the brain, Joe's left hemisphere, which in most people is responsible for language, is not aware that the word *walk* was transmitted. Yet several seconds later, he gets up from his chair. When asked where he is going, he answers, "I'm going to get a Coke."

What Gazzaniga has done is to put information into the patient's disconnected, mute right hemisphere and produce a behavior that is going on outside his conscious awareness. Joe responds nonverbally to the direction "Walk," but when asked what he is doing, feels it is necessary to articulate a plausible reason.

From experiments like this, according to Gazzaniga, we have reason to believe that there are all kinds of complex processes going on in the brain that we are not aware of. A case like Joe's, says Gazzaniga, "allows you a window into the unconscious, and shows how powerful unconscious processes are in influencing our conscious self, our personal self. What Joe and patients like him—and there are many—teach us is that the mind is made up of constellations of semi-independent agents or processes that can carry on a vast number of activities outside our awareness."

Instead of a unitary self residing within the brain, Gazzaniga suggests that the "normal brain is organized into modules and that most of these modules are capable of actions, moods, and responses." One of these modules, which Gazzaniga refers to as the "interpreter," organizes the various behaviors produced over time by the brain's separate modules. This provides the individual with the subjective sense of unity, a sense that he or she is of "one

mind" instead of "a confederation of mental systems." In the absence of such an interpreter, behavior becomes fragmented and the personality splits into subselves that work at cross purposes.

In another experiment, Gazzaniga flashes the word *car* to Joe's right hemisphere. "With your left hand, draw a picture of the word I flashed," Gazzaniga requests.

Since the left hand is under strict control of the right hemisphere, Gazzaniga is asking for a performance based on the perception of that hemisphere alone. But since Joe's language-processing left hemisphere has not seen anything, he can only protest, "I can't. I didn't see it."

"Go ahead and let that left hand try," Gazzaniga urges. Joe stops talking and his left hand picks up a pencil and draws an accurate picture of a car. Most fascinating of all, however, is his verbal response to this performance. "I don't know why I drew that," he says.

In this experiment, thought—the correct reading of the word and the rendering of that word into a drawing—occurs without reference to language and, in fact, contrary to the patient's own statement. He says one thing about himself while his performance proves the opposite.

Such a performance raises disquieting questions. Does the intact brain—yours as you're reading this book and, presumably, mine as I'm writing it—also operate according to this double bookkeeping system? We do not know; and obviously, no control experiments can test this because no one performs a commissurotomy (surgical cutting of a band of nerve fibers) on a normal person. If this should be true, and split brain studies have more universal application, self-understanding, a goal that can be traced back at least to Socrates ("Know thyself"), would seem to elude accurate verbal rendition. Our left hemisphere interpreter selects one explanation among many for our behavior, no single one of which can be confidently identified as the "real" one.

"The data suggest that our mental lives amount to a reconstruction of the independent activities of the many brain systems we all possess," according to Gazzaniga. "There's some final stage, or system, which I happen to think is in the left hemisphere, that pulls all of this information together in a theory. It has to generate a theory to explain all these independent elements. And that theory becomes our particular theory of ourself and of the world."

Writing in the *Principles of Psychology* about a century ago, William James suggested that the key to consciousness is self-reference. "The universal conscious fact is not 'feelings exist' and 'thoughts exist,' but 'I think' and 'I feel.' " In other words, for experience, thoughts, and behavior to become conscious, a link must be made between mental representations of these thoughts and feelings and some mental representation of the self as experiencer.

These linkages exist in memory. An extraordinary example of what happens if the linkages are broken is the case of Clive. Clive is a victim of viral encephalitis, an inflammation of the brain, which in his case attacked his right and left *temporal lobes* and a good portion of the left *frontal lobe*. Within the temporal lobe, on both sides, is the *hippocampus*, a structure absolutely critical for meaning. Clive's hippocampus on both sides has been destroyed. Formerly a distinguished medieval and Renaissance musicologist, an organist of virtuosity, and a choral master of renown, Clive now spends his time sitting in a twelve-by-twelve hospital room playing endless games of solitaire and making entries in a notebook.

The entries are always the same. "Now I am completely awake, for the first time in years." And each time Clive returns to his notebook and sees what he has written before, he disclaims it. "I do not know who wrote that. It was not me," he says. If the similarities in the notations and handwriting are pointed out to him, he gets angry. Here is his wife Deborah's description: "Clive's world now consists of a moment, with no past to anchor it and no future to look ahead to. It's a blinkered moment. He sees what is right in front of him, but as soon as that information hits the brain it fades. Nothing makes an impression, nothing registers. Everything goes in perfectly well, because he has all his faculties. His intellect is virtually intact, and he

Clive joyously greets his wife as if he had not seen her in years.

perceives his world as you or I do. But as soon as he perceives it and looks away, it's gone for him. So it's a moment-to-moment consciousness, as it were, a time vacuum. And everything before that moment is completely void. And he feels as if he is awakening afresh the whole time. He always thinks he has been awake for about two minutes."

One of the most poignant moments in the filming of the television series *The Mind* occurred when Deborah entered Clive's room, and he got up from his chair to greet her with a burst of laughter and happiness that shone all over his face. He greeted her as if he had not seen her in years. Yet only moments before she had been with him. He had forgotten. To have once been so brilliant, to have accomplished so much, and then to have come to *this*. "You're not dealing here with somebody who is demented, who is oblivious, who is gaga," Deborah said later. "You're dealing with a perfectly lucid, highly intelligent man who has been robbed of the knowledge of his own life. And he feels deeply humiliated to be put in that position; very, very frustrated. He can't grasp what's wrong with him because even as you are telling him something, he is forgetting the previous sentence. So he can never take in or understand what is wrong with him."

Dr. Alan Parkin, of the University of Sussex, describes the tragic situation in which Clive finds himself. "He is extremely different from any normal human being. He has to a large extent lost part of his mind, because part of what we call the mind is our ability to perceive ourselves in a continuum of time. Sitting here, I know how I got here and I know what I am going to do when I leave here. Clive does not have that kind of experience. He is just living in the present. So in a sense he feels like a man adrift."

Notice that Clive's consciousness hasn't disappeared. He knows who he is, and he can recognize his wife Deborah. But his consciousness is reduced to moments. On either side of this brief continuum of time lies a fearful abyss. But to Deborah, who knows and loves Clive, the horrifying brain damage has, mercifully, left an important part of him intact.

Deborah: "His being, his center, his soul is absolutely functioning as it ever did. The fact that he is so despairing, so much in anguish, so angry, so much in love with me—those are all real, human passions. And he is showing them almost to the exclusion of everything else. All he shows us is raw human passion, straight from the heart of the mind."

Unlike Clive, cursed by being able to live only in the now, we can excape through our minds from the limits of the present. Thanks to mind, we can project ourselves into the future and reexplore the past. We have memory. We can empathize and identify with the feelings and actions of others. We can create works of imagination and art. Mind gives us meaning and direction and the possibility of progress over time. Mind orchestrates the realization of the brain and binds consciousness and unconsciousness together. Mind is the astounding interplay of one hundred billion neurons. And more.

As we search for mind in the pages of this book, we shall be treading an age-old path. Today, it is one that is being illuminated by often astonishing new insights derived from the neurosciences and psychology. As this chapter suggests, the nature and definition of mind have fascinated and perplexed thinkers throughout history. We have touched on some of its aspects here, in pursuit of the elusive totality: mind itself. New explorations and new knowledge are the focus of the chapters that follow. The logical beginning for the search is the point in our development that the mind first appears.

2.
DEVELOPMENT

Birth is not the place to start. The shift from the dark aquatic world of the womb to the world of air and light in which we spend the rest of our lives is certainly a profound environmental disruption, but it is not a beginning so much as a transition. The true beginning and most critical *event* in our lives is clearly the moment of our conception. The Chinese recognize this by calculating age from that moment; a baby is considered one year old at birth. Therefore, our search for the development of the brain and the emergence of mind must begin with the sperm and egg of our parents. These structures contain the *genes* that constitute the blueprint for our development.

The maternal contribution to who we are dates back to when our mother was herself a fetus. The ovarian structures containing the genetic material for our mother's eggs were formed at that time. Later, at her puberty, the primary follicles, all present in her ovaries at the time of her birth, matured under the influence of hormones secreted by her pituitary gland. Still later, at the midpoint of each menstrual cycle, 1 (or occasionally 2) follicles out of roughly 300,000 ruptured and released a mature egg, ready for fertilization, into the fallopian tube.

In sharp contrast, the sperm cell carrying our father's half of our genetic heritage was formed only two or three months prior to insemination. Approximately one hundred million sperm are released during a single ejaculation. Each sperm exhibits marked differences in shape, motility, and the capacity to fertilize eggs. Out of the myriad released, only one sperm eventually fertilized our mother's egg.

From this single fertilized egg comes the staggering number and diversity of cells that comprise the human being. A portion of these cells will form a network called

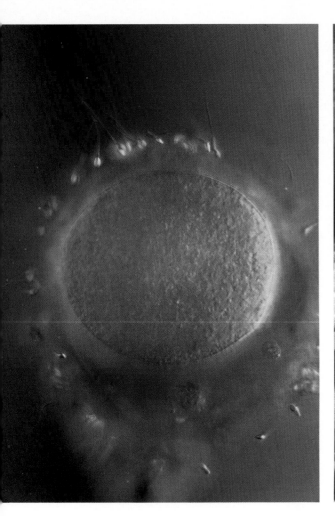
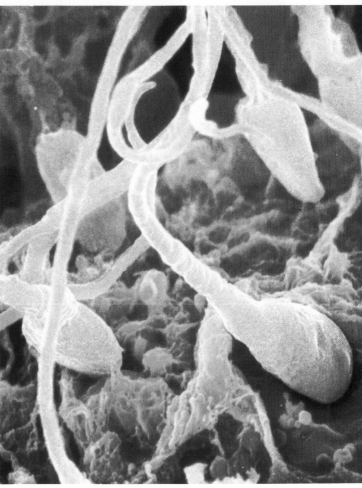

(Above, left) *Sperm are seen swarming about the ovum (egg) prior to fertilization.*

(Right) *One sperm successfully penetrates the ovum. The membrane of the ovum then seals itself off, preventing other sperm from entering.*

the brain. The connections between brain cells must be similar enough from person to person so that we perceive objects in the same way, understand the same symbols and language, and recognize what others mean when they use a term or present an abstract idea. Yet those same connections must be flexible enough to give each of us a different sense of self, to leave each of us in possession of an utterly unique mind. This is the story of how the human brain develops and the mind emerges from that single cell.

Within hours of fertilization, the egg begins to divide. Gradually that first cell becomes a ball of hundreds of cells. They seem identical, but hidden within each is a chemical blueprint that controls what it will become. Some will form muscles and bone. Others will become the heart, the liver, or the brain.

This process begins with a startling metamorphosis of the embryo. At about day 14, the tiny ball of multiplying cells begins to fold in on itself. A portion of the outer layer on the surface of the embryo migrates inward and advances underneath another portion of the outer layer. Pushing

GENES, BEHAVIOR, AND ENVIRONMENT IN UTERO

The influence of the environment begins very early. The sperm in the female genital tract encounter a variety of conditions. A woman's hormonal status may affect the consistency and thickness of the mucus in her uterus and cervix. Her central nervous system may affect the strength of uterine contractions. Each of these factors may influence the speed of sperm transport. So it is difficult to avoid the conclusion that sperm are single-celled organisms capable not only of movement but of reaction to their environment. This has all the appearance of *behavior* at the cellular level.

There are many other environmental influences that can help determine the genetic makeup of an embryo. A variety of hormones, neurotransmitters, peptides, even the mother's behavior and mood, have all been shown to influence fertilization. Thus, even at the cellular level "selection" and "choice" are taking place, whereby certain sperm with certain characteristics will be favored over others.

The genetic composition of the sperm themselves may also influence this selection process. Although many presumably acceptable sperm are available to the egg, only one actually fertilizes it. Why this sperm and not another? Problems like this, formerly considered unresolvable, or credited simply to "chance" or "fate," are now potentially answerable because of what scientists are learning about selection, choice, and discrimination at the cellular level.

It is true that the words *choice, selection,* and *discrimination,* used to describe the events surrounding conception, are normally reserved for describing the behavior of human beings. But their use to describe the behavior of single-celled organisms may seem less anthropomorphic if we consider that behavior is the central element of *all* organized systems. We are not speaking metaphorically, therefore, when we use the same terms for a chemical reaction, the movement of a blood cell, and the action of a child picking up a doll. At each of these levels, small differences in genetic composition and environment can have an effect on the final "product."

Besides affecting the selection of sperm, genes exert influences on each other as well. In one environment, certain genes may be "turned on" to influence development along a certain line. Alter the environment and another aspect of that vast genetic potential will be activated. (Probably no more than 10 percent of the genes in the mammalian cell are activated in an individual's lifetime.) Thus the development of our mind—how we think, the behavior we display, the emotions we experience—is affected in important ways by the formative influence of the environment.

The formation of neural networks within the brain, the orchestration of the body's hormonal system, the interplay between the newborn infant and his parents—each of these involves an increasingly complex interplay of genes, behavior, and environment. As we move from single-celled organisms such as sperm swimming upstream toward the uterus to the intricate behaviors of someone reading this book, the interplay of forces becomes increasingly difficult to sort out. But it is certain that genes, behavior, and environment influence organisms ranging from the sperm and the ovum to the whole person functioning in a complex world.

---

one's finger through the skin of an orange and advancing it in the act of unpeeling the orange approximates this process. The end result is the formation of three cell layers. The underlying advancing layer, corresponding to the finger in our orange analogy, is the *mesoderm.* Below it is the *endoderm,* and above it the *ectoderm.* It is from the ectoderm that the brain develops.

At first, the future brain is no more than a thin layer of cells, known as the *neural plate,* on the surface of the

(Above) *The central nervous system begins with the formation of a thin layer of cells on the surface of the embryo known as the* neural plate.

(Opposite, top) *The neural plate then folds in upon itself to form the* neural groove.

(Bottom) *The groove closes into the hollow* neural tube.

embryo. But from that inauspicious beginning will develop the most marvelous organ in the known universe. It will emerge gradually and synchronously according to a rhythm that is repeated in every brain in every person born on this planet. No more than perhaps 125,000 cells are present in the beginning. But eventually they will multiply into some one hundred billion neurons that are the basis of all functions of the brain.

To form the brain, the neural plate first folds in on itself forming the *neural groove*. This groove then closes into a hollow structure, the *neural tube*. From one end of the tube will come the spinal cord. From the central canal will come the ventricular system of the brain. And from the other end of the tube three swellings will emerge. These are the precursors of the three major regions of the brain—the *forebrain* (the cerebral cortex and basal ganglia), the *midbrain,* and the *hindbrain* (medulla, pons, and cerebellum). By the eighth week, the main divisions of the fetal brain are in place. At this point, it resembles the adult brain sufficiently for a trained observer to identify each structure and appreciate its resemblance to its adult counterpart.

The transformation of apparently identical cells into the different parts of the brain is called *differentiation*. This involves a three-stage process, though each stage and the

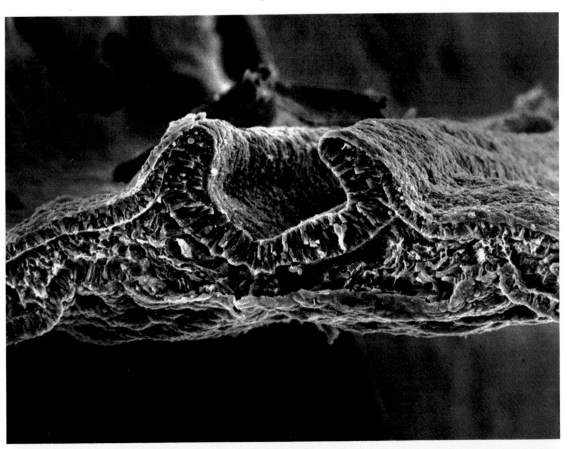

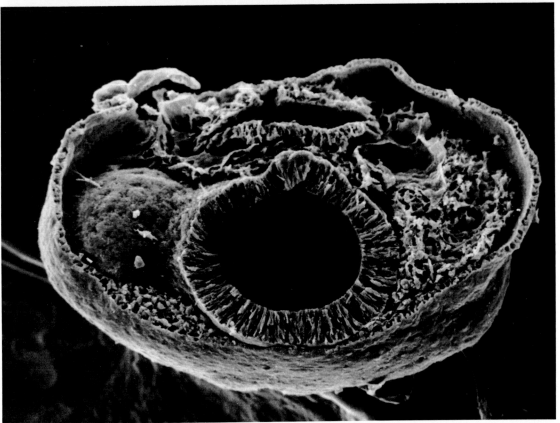

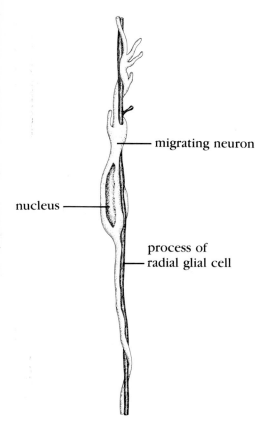

migrating neuron

nucleus

process of
radial glial cell

*Neuron migrating along a radial
glial cell.*

various controlling factors involved are not completely understood. In the first stage, the nerve cells proliferate and specialize. Then the *neurons* migrate to their final positions within the brain. Finally, they mature and establish specific interconnections with other neurons.

The first stage, nerve cell *proliferation,* begins after closure of the neural tube at about the end of the third week. This proliferation involves both neurons and the supporting *glial cells,* which nourish the neurons and guide them to their final destinations. These glial cells form the greatest proportion of cells within the human brain; there are between ten and fifty times more glial cells than neurons. Together neurons and glial cells orchestrate a pattern of development that will emerge in the first small stirrings of the human mind.

Starting with a single layer of nerve cells lining the cavities, or ventricular walls, of the neural tube, the number of cell layers rapidly builds up. The nuclei of each of the actively dividing young neurons, which are known as *stem cells,* move in an oscillatory pattern from the inner layer outward, and then back again. With each movement away from the ventricular wall, the nucleus within each neuron begins doubling its DNA content—the genetic information in the gene. Once the DNA has doubled, the cell oscillates back to the ventricular wall. Then it divides. Where there was only one, now there are two neurons. Each of the daughter cells then repeats the pattern.

This crossing and recrossing of nuclei from the ventricular wall to the outer layer occurs with the rhythmicity and delicacy of dancers working their way across a ballroom floor. The movements are foreordained, as in a formal dance, and yet, thanks to the dancers themselves, nuclei express a certain whimsicality. No one knows exactly when a neuron precursor will lose its ability to replicate, but when it does, that neuron migrates to its permanent position within the brain.

Neuronal migration presents a particular challenge to our understanding. How do millions of neurons "decide"

*Stages of nerve cell development in the
evolving fetal brain.*

PROLIFERATION	0 - 12 WEEKS
MIGRATION	13 - 25 WEEKS
DIFFERENTIATION	
CONTINUED DIFFERENTIATION	26 - 39 WEEKS

about a location within the brain? From studies of the cerebellum, neuroscientists have learned that special radial glial cells, which appear in an early stage of embryonic development, send out long "processes" that extend from the ventricular wall to the outer margins of the neural tube. These radial fibers form a trellislike frame upon which the migrating neurons travel on their way to their final destination. As they do so, the cell layers thicken and the brain becomes larger. The brain's growth and final form depend on this brain cell multiplication, a process that continues at a rapid rate throughout the nine months before birth.

Each of the neurons that comprise the brain is an independent unit consisting of a cell body containing the *nucleus,* a long fiber called the *axon,* and a varying number of branching fibers called *dendrites* that reach out toward other neurons. Information is conveyed through electrical signals sent along the axon of one neuron to the dendrite of a second one. At the *synapse,* or tiny cleft between neurons, the electrical signal is converted into a chemical code. This releases a chemical substance, called a *neurotransmitter,* which slips across the synaptic cleft to specialized receptors on the second neuron. Neurons form specific and precise functional connections with certain neurons but not with others.

The brain's complex functions are related to the number of neurons and their interconnections. No function is carried out by a single neuron. Instead, behavior is the result of the activity of many, many nerve cells linked together in neuronal networks. At birth, a newborn brain

(Below, left) *The neuron. The terminals of one axon are seen communicating across the synapse with the dendrites of another neuron.*

(Right) *Photomicrograph of the synapse between two neurons in the cerebral cortex. At the synaptic cleft (the deep red area in the center), the neurotransmitter is released from the axon of the neuron and diffuses across the minute gap to the receptor site on the target neuron.*

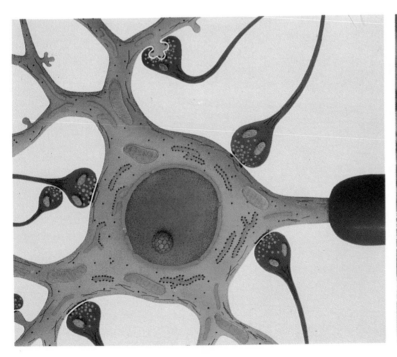

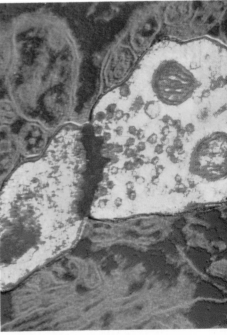

NEUROTRANSMITTERS

In the wet landscape of the human brain, neurons communicate with each other by means of neurotransmitters. These are chemical messenger molecules released in minute amounts from the *presynaptic membrane* on the axon of the sending neuron, and diffused across the synaptic cleft to a receptor site on the *postsynaptic membrane* of the dendrite of the target neuron.

Neurotransmitters are stored in tiny packets, or synaptic vesicles, on the presynaptic membrane of the axon. They are released in response to an electrical signal in the neuron, called an action potential, which travels along the length of the axon to the terminal site. A neuron may be linked to one target neuron or to many. If it forms a network with other neurons, its axon will have branches, each storing a neurotransmitter that will connect with a specific target cell.

A neurotransmitter exerts either an excitatory effect on the target neuron, causing it to fire, or an inhibitory effect, preventing it from firing. It acts by altering the permeability of the receptor cell membrane, thereby affecting the voltage within the cell. This action is not an on/off process like a light switch, however; rather, it is graded, as in a dimmer control, and requires a certain strength to have an effect.

At present, the number of chemicals in the brain thought to function as neurotransmitters exceeds forty. Chemically, neurotransmitters are of three main types. The most prevalent ones are simple amino acids, which act directly and rapidly on the target neuron; among these, GABA (gamma-amino butyric acid), an inhibitor, is the most completely understood. Monoamines, which include acetylcholine, dopamine, serotonin, and norepinephrine, are associated with more diffuse pathways in the brain, and perform modulatory functions (see Chapter 6). Neuropeptides, chains of different amino acids in specific sequences, are found in the lowest concentration, but are extremely potent. They include the brain's natural opiates, the endorphins, described in Chapter 4.

If each of the forty or more neurotransmitters discovered thus far functions like a letter in the alphabet, then the number of "words" that results from their various combinations approaches infinity. This would seem to be more than sufficient to provide the basis for the incredibly complex chemical interplay that takes place in the brain—and for the consequences of that interplay in body and mind.

Photomicrograph of the neurotransmitter norepinephrine in the locus ceruleus of the brain.

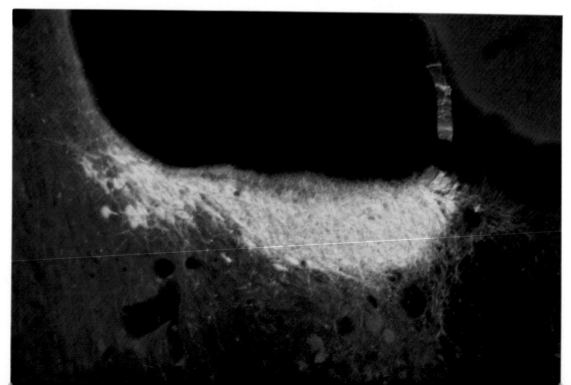

has more neurons with which to form networks than it will ever have again. Within months, our genetic programming calls for more than half of those neurons to die.

All the steps described thus far, with the exception of synapse formation and dendritic branching, occur only once, very early in development. The determination and differentiation of neurons from other cells, the proliferation of nerve cells, migration, axonal growth, the cell death of excessive neurons, neuronal recognition that enables neurons to reach their final destination—each of these phases is choreographed in space and time by various controlling factors that are not completely understood.

But already what may be the most critical period of the brain's development has passed. The formation and migration of neurons is the time when the developing brain is most vulnerable to environmental insult. Recently, scientists have turned their attention to what those insults are, and what effects they may have on the emerging mind.

In 1899 a Liverpool physician, William Sullivan, carried out a controlled study of babies born to women in prison. He compared the children of heavy-drinking mothers with those of their nondrinking counterparts and discovered that the rate of infant mortality and stillbirth was two and a half times higher among the children of drinking mothers. He also found that several women who had borne children with severe birth defects in the past gave birth to normal healthy babies while they were in prison and had no access to alcohol.

Although Sullivan's study was the first scientific investigation into the effects of alcohol on fetal and infant development, warnings to mothers-to-be about alcohol can be traced back to biblical times. In Judges 13:7, an angel tells the wife of Manoah, "Behold, thou shalt conceive and bear a son; and now drink no wine or strong drink." Perhaps the warning was heeded, for a healthy child named Samson was born.

After Sullivan's study, no further research on the effects of alcohol on infants was reported for three quarters of a century. Then, in 1973, the distinctive pattern of abnormal development resulting from alcohol intake during pregnancy was described for the first time by Dr. Sterling K. Clarren and his colleagues at the Pediatric Department of the University of Washington School of Medicine in Seattle. Clarren called this pattern "fetal alcohol syndrome." Serious alcohol abuse in the mother can lead to growth and mental retardation, limb and heart malformations, and a distinctive facial abnormality. In instances of milder alcohol abuse, the damage may involve disorders of attention, be-

In Dr. Sterling K. Clarren's experiment, the baby macaque on the left responds to a new object with normal curiosity, touching and examining it. But the macaque on the right, suffering from fetal alcohol syndrome, is listless and unresponsive.

havioral disabilities, hyperactivity, temper tantrums, impulsiveness, short memory span, and perceptual disorders that interfere with learning.

Scientists now know that alcohol wreaks its damage on the fetus by crossing the placenta and entering the fetal circulation. Because the fetus lacks an enzyme, known as alcohol dehydrogenase, which is responsible for metabolizing alcohol, the level of alcohol builds up in the fetus, particularly in the brain, and causes havoc.

Brains affected by fetal alcohol syndrome are frequently small, shrunken, and malformed. The microscopic differences between normal and alcohol-damaged brains are extraordinary. "The brain density is really reduced," says Clarren, "and that normal convolutional pattern of the brain is lost." These microscopic abnormalities result in part from faulty cell migration in the cerebellum and cerebral cortex. "It's as if the cells of the brain, when they were migrating to their final homes, didn't know when to stop."

In an attempt to pinpoint when the damage occurs, Clarren ran a study of baby macaque monkeys. By giving different doses of alcohol to pregnant monkeys, he made a chilling discovery. Moderate levels of alcohol consumed during the first half of the first trimester of pregnancy caused greater damage than higher levels of alcohol con-

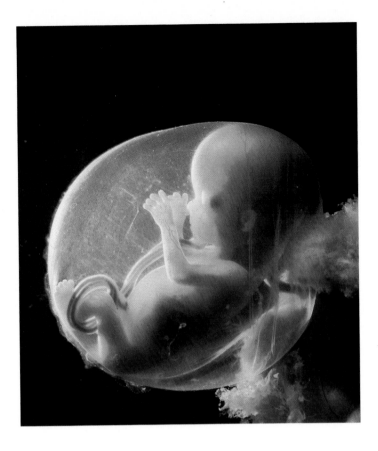

sumed later in the pregnancy. These results are particularly significant if they prove to apply equally to humans, for many women do not realize they are pregnant during those early weeks.

Clarren concluded that the severity and extent of defects depend not only on the amount of alcohol imbibed—in general, women who drink more produce children with more severe defects—but also the period of gestation when the heavy drinking occurred. His findings suggest one or more windows of vulnerability. The cerebellum, for instance, is most vulnerable to damage at about forty-five days of gestation; the cerebral cortex at about eighty-five days. But curiously, alcohol seems not to be harmful in every instance. Some women in the study drank at alcoholic levels and still produced apparently normal children.

Just which children will be born with fetal alcohol syndrome cannot be predicted. One thing, however, is clear. Alcohol use, particularly heavy drinking early in the pregnancy, increases the likelihood that the infant will suffer from the syndrome. And if subtle behavioral difficulties can result from even small amounts of alcohol taken at critical periods during the pregnancy, it is important to alert women to the risks. Many communities have already passed ordinances requiring that signs be posted in drinking establish-

The fetus at three months, more than three inches long and weighing almost one ounce, is astonishing and vulnerable.

WARNING

DRINKING ALCOHOLIC BEVERAGES DURING PREGNANCY CAN CAUSE BIRTH DEFECTS

 NEW YORK CITY DEPARTMENT OF HEALTH
THE CITY COUNCIL Local Law 63

ments warning pregnant women of the potentially harmful effects of alcohol on their unborn children.

Such efforts can be effective. In 1979, Dr. Marita Aronson surveyed babies with fetal alcohol syndrome in Götenborg, Sweden, noting that "our favorite drug, alcohol, can devastate the developing brain." Aronson's findings of impaired brain functions triggered a successful public information campaign in Götenborg. "Before we began, we saw one fetal alcohol syndrome baby in every six hundred births. But the campaign has caused mothers-to-be to stop drinking and thereby change their fetus's environment. We're now down to one case of the syndrome a year for every twenty-five hundred births and dropping."

Fetal alcohol syndrome demonstrates that brain development, when it goes awry, has social, ethical, and even political implications. It is proof that any interference with the process of normal brain development—in this instance the orderly migration of neurons—has devastating repercussions on the mind of the newborn child.

Seven months before she was born, Nurumi Toda's mother stood half a mile from where the atomic bomb was dropped on Hiroshima. Nurumi suffers from severe retardation.

Dr. William Schull, a geneticist at the Radiation Effects Research Foundation in Hiroshima, has been studying people like Nurumi for the past forty years. "I first came to Hiroshima in 1949," explains Schull, "to study the consequences of exposure to ionizing radiation. And I found that among children who had been exposed in utero, a small number were severely retarded."

Schull followed up on sixteen hundred women from Hiroshima and Nagasaki who had been pregnant when the atomic bombs were dropped on their cities in 1945. Within this group, thirty went on to bear children with severe mental retardation. Eighty percent of these retarded children, Schull discovered, had been exposed to the bomb and its radiation between eight and sixteen weeks following conception. This, of course, is the period during which the neurons are completing their cell division and are migrating along the glial fibers to their final destination. In fact, it is during about the tenth week that the largest number of neurons begin migrating.

"The evidence is overwhelming," says Schull, "that any time within the period from eight to fifteen weeks, ionizing radiation has a profound and significant effect on brain development. There are important analogies between the effects of ionizing radiation and chemicals that we know will do similar things to the brain. Fetal alcohol syndrome, for example, produces a degree of retardation that is very similar to what we see in radiation exposure. We know that in both conditions the primary fault is mismanaged cell migration."

But while alcohol causes the neurons to continue past their destinations, radiation seems to stop the neurons short of their targets by disrupting the glial cells. "Imagine yourself boarding a train destined to go to a specific location and expecting to be in that train for eight hours. But suppose six of these hours were spent in the railway station because of a snowstorm. After traveling for two hours you obviously would not have reached your destination. Otherwise, everything would be as expected: the train and everything about it would be functioning normally. The same thing happens when neuronal migration is interfered with by radiation or other factors. The neurons simply don't arrive at their predetermined destination. And since we know that brain function depends upon brain cell position, cells have to be in the right place to do the right thing. They don't perform the proper function if they are not in the proper site."

On April 26, 1986, the nuclear reactor at Chernobyl in the Soviet Union suffered a disastrous meltdown. Scientists trying to estimate the rate of mental retardation among fetuses exposed to Chernobyl's radiation based their figures on the outcome of the events at Hiroshima and Nagasaki forty years earlier. They project that mental retardation resulting from Chernobyl will be five times that which normally occurs in the general population.

For centuries people have speculated about the intrauterine environment. References to the umbilical cord, the "waters" (amniotic fluid) within the womb, and the mystery of how one person, a fetus, can be contained within the body of another, the mother, are encountered in the myths and folklore of every age. During the Middle Ages great emphasis was placed on the mother's emotional state. A mother was required to ponder only "elevated thoughts" lest her infant develop along malevolent lines. Fright, sudden shock, despondency, and other unsettling emotions were held to exert an influence on the timing of the birth process, the infant's personality, and in some extreme instances even to cause the death of the fetus.

With the advent of new discoveries in the biological sciences, many of these early concerns about the influence of the mother on her developing fetus are being taken seriously. Alcohol, malnutrition, and tobacco are now known to cause fetal malformation, prematurity, and gross or subtle learning disabilities. So the mother's experiences—what she drinks, eats, and breathes—can have a profound influence on the development of the infant mind. But what about the claim that a mother's thoughts and feelings—her emotional state—can influence her fetus?

The after-effects of Chernobyl.

In the 1960s and 1970s scientists began carrying out experiments on rats that would be unthinkable to contemplate in humans. Pregnant rats were given electric shocks, housed together in crowded and noisy cages, or subjected to restraint or the glare of bright lights. Depending on the timing, intensity, and duration of the distress to the mother, these disruptive influences affected all kinds of behavior in the rats' offspring. For example, rats born to mothers who had been subjected to overcrowding during their pregnancy tended to avoid exploring new territory. And male rats born to mothers exposed to bright lights or restraints during the last third of the pregnancy failed to exhibit normal sexual behavior around female rats.

The evidence indicates that maternal hormones, altered by the stresses induced by the scientists, acted directly on the brain of the developing fetus, as well as on the fetal endocrine system, so as to modify the neuronal networks that were then forming. Similar reactions are believed to operate in humans.

There are several ways in which the mother can modify neuronal networks within her fetus. One path, of course, is the placenta, the organ that directly unites the fetus to the maternal uterus. The mother is also able to influence her fetus through the same senses that enable us to palpate our environment, for to a limited extent the fetus too is able to hear, see, taste, smell, and feel in the intrauterine world.

As early as the first trimester of the pregnancy, the fetus possesses functioning receptors for balance and motion detection. Each time the mother moves, the fetal brain is stimulated to an extent that will not be equaled until months after birth when the baby begins taking his or her first steps. If the fetus is deprived of some of this movement within the womb because of a premature delivery, that baby will lag behind full-term infants in sensory–motor and visual responsiveness.

Midway through gestation the fetus also begins to hear. Brain scientists infer this on the basis of fetal movements observed in response to sudden noises. Hearing in the womb is also inferred by the fact that newborns can be calmed by low frequency sounds produced at the rhythm of the mother's heart rate. It is believed that the fetus's exposure to the sound of the mother's heart rate in the uterus exerts a comforting effect. After birth, in most cultures, mothers hold their infants against the left side of their chest where the sound of their beating heart is loudest.

Vision within the uterus, however, is severely limited. Opening one's eyes underwater in a lake late in the afternoon is probably very similar to fetal vision in the uterus. At best, all that can be seen are variations in diffuse light coming through the mother's abdominal wall. But it's likely

PREMATURE BABIES

The premature baby has a host of problems to overcome. Among them are the instabilities in temperature regulation caused by diminished body fat, faulty respirations due to immature lung tissue, and feeding difficulties caused by the infant's underdeveloped gastrointestinal tract and weak sucking reflex.

Years ago the French physiologist Claude Bernard described *homeostasis,* the body's ability to maintain its own internal processes within certain narrowly defined ranges. If blood pressure or pulse or respiration or body temperature varies from normal, mechanisms are brought into play to bring these functions back within normal ranges. In the case of body temperature, normal is 98.6°F, for instance. But in premature infants, these correcting mechanisms aren't working as efficiently as in babies born at term.

There can be dire consequences for the premature brain in the wake of disturbances in blood pressure or breathing. During spells of *apnea,* or stopped respiration, the premature infant's intracranial pressure goes up, blood pressure rises, and carbon dioxide levels in the blood skyrocket. Together these events bring about an abrupt change in the baby's intracranial blood flow. This additional stress, combined with the fragility of the capillaries within the brain, often leads to a blood vessel rupture. Intracranial bleeding is, in fact, one of the principal causes of severe disability and mortality in the premature infant.

Until just a few years ago, very few premature babies survived. Today, thanks to technology developed principally during the past two decades, they stand a good chance of survival. As we learn more and more about the intra-uterine world of the fetus, we can move closer to recreating important aspects of it for babies unlucky enough to be born before they and the world are ready for each other.

When the environment of neonatal intensive care units is carefully controlled, it is often possible for the brains of premature infants to grow normally. Joy Williamson was born at twenty-eight weeks' gestational age, thirteen weeks prematurely. In such a unit, and under the care of Dr. Cecilia McCarton, Joy has been helped to survive, grow, and eventually thrive, and at one year of age the delight on the faces of her parents is testimony to the fact that technology, sophisticated medical care, and love have achieved something like a miracle.

Dr. Cecilia McCarton holds premature baby Joy Williamson.

One year later, Joy and her happy parents beam at her very first birthday cake.

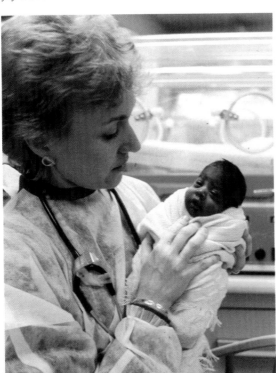

that *something* is seen, since retinal structures appear to be functional by about five months of gestation. The eyelids themselves open at seven months, and late in the last trimester, the fetus may be capable of a murky view of its own hands and feet.

Taste is also operative in a fetus. Infants tend to swallow more amniotic fluid when saccharin is injected into it. And moments after birth an infant will prefer a sugar solution to one containing quinine. This taste preference begins in the womb, is expressed in earliest infancy, and for most of us, endures throughout our lives.

Much of our knowledge about the extraordinary extent of fetal development has come from studying premature babies. This work has helped us understand the remarkable adaptive powers of the newborn child. "If you watch babies after they are born," notes Dr. Cecilia McCarton, of the Albert Einstein College of Medicine in New York, "they are exquisitely awake and tuned into their environment. They are responsive to their mothers. They turn toward sounds. And they fixate on their mother's face. Obviously babies have to have the equipment well in hand before birth."

Scientists have known for years that all is not quiet or quiescent within the womb. Intrauterine recordings reveal the sounds of the mother's heartbeat along with muffled speech and sounds from the environment. But important questions remained unanswered. After birth will the newborn recognize the sounds heard in the womb, perhaps even prefer them over other sounds? Although this was an intriguing possibility, there was no way of knowing the answer until scientists developed a way of measuring newborn preferences. The breakthrough came with the use of a non-nutritive nipple, which monitors the rate and amplitude of an infant's sucking.

It was then demonstrated, for example, that a newborn provided with a non-nutritive nipple that is attached to a tape recorder shows a change of sucking rhythm when recordings of the mother's voice are switched to recordings of another woman's voice. Newborn babies tend to suck in the pattern that elicits a recording of the mother's voice, according to Dr. Anthony J. DeCasper, a psychologist at the University of North Carolina at Greensboro. Infants only a few days of age will do this. How is this possible unless they learned to recognize the mother's voice within the womb? "It looks as though auditory preferences after birth are influenced by what is heard prenatally," says DeCasper.

But just how much can the fetus learn? Can it progress beyond the mere recognition of the mother's voice? To find out, DeCasper elicited the aid of sixteen pregnant women who were asked to read *The Cat in the Hat* to their fetuses twice a day for the last six and a half weeks of pregnancy. By the time the babies were born, the story had been read to them for approximately five hours.

Shortly after birth, the babies were hooked up to the nipple. This time they had the opportunity to listen to *The Cat in the Hat*—the story they had been exposed to during their last six and a half weeks in utero—or *The King, the Mice and the Cheese,* which is also rhymed but has a very different meter. The babies sucked in the rhythm that let them hear *The Cat in the Hat.* So it seems to DeCasper that prenatal auditory experience is sufficient to influence post-natal auditory preferences. Fetuses, in other words, are capable of auditory *perceptual* learning in the uterus months before they actually need it or could be expected to make use of it.

In an attempt to establish the limits of fetal learning, DeCasper next turned his attention to testing the fetus's learning ability while it was still in the womb. He wondered just how much the fetus is influenced by the sounds that reach it in the uterus. Researchers were aware that fetuses as young as twenty-four weeks react to loud, brief sounds by movement or by the speeding up of their heart rate. But no one had measured the response to less intense rhythmic stimuli such as speech.

To explore this idea, DeCasper asked thirty-three volunteer women between the thirty-fifth and thirty-eighth weeks of pregnancy to help him discover the effects of repeated but nonstartling sound stimuli. When pairs of speech syllables were presented every three seconds, for two minutes, through a loudspeaker placed on the mother's abdomen, the fetal heart rate decelerated. Deceleration is an indication of attentiveness. As the stimuli continued, however, the heart rate accelerated. When the stimuli were changed, there was deceleration again. "Responsiveness [of fetuses] to changes in stimulation," DeCasper concluded, "demonstrates that they are competent to perceive some acoustical characteristics of speech."

The next stage was to ascertain whether the fetus could actually recognize a story while still in the womb. And could it recognize a story if it were read by a woman other than the mother? To answer these questions, researchers collaborating with DeCasper recruited thirteen healthy pregnant women in the thirty-fourth week of pregnancy to read a short children's story aloud. Eight read *La Poulette* and five read *Le Petit Crapaud.* (This time the studies were carried out in Paris and the language spoken was French. This provided a nice check on the possibility, however remote, that the previous findings were valid only for spoken English.) Each woman, according to her assignment,

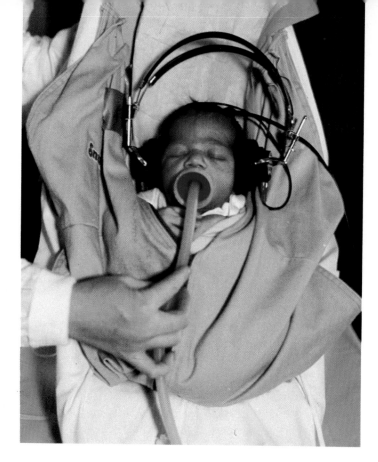

In Dr. William Fifer's experiment, a newborn increases the vigor of his sucking on a non-nutritive nipple when he hears the sound of his mother's voice through the earphones.

read her story aloud three times in succession each day for the next four weeks.

During the thirty-eighth week of the pregnancy the mothers reported to the laboratory. Fetal heart rates were monitored during the playing of recordings of the story previously recited by the mother and a control story that had never been recited. At the time of the testing the women had recited their stories an average of ninety-three times during the thirty-one days preceding their trip to the laboratory.

During the testing the recordings played for the fetus were renditions of *La Poulette* and *Le Petit Crapaud* read by female graduate students, not by the mothers. The result? Fetal heart rate consistently decreased with the familiar story and increased with the control story—even though they were read by a stranger.

Dr. William Fifer, of the New York State Psychiatric Institute, has used the non-nutritive nipple and a pair of earphones to test the preferences of newborns. Infants express a preference for certain voices heard through the earphones by the vigor and rhythm of their sucking. The test procedure is simple but elegant, the results clear-cut. Fifer learned that babies prefer a woman's voice over a man's, their mother's voice to the voice of other women, their mother's voice filtered so as to sound as if coming through the walls of the uterus rather than their mother's normal voice, and their mother's real voice over the filtered voice of other women. But by three weeks of age, an infant's preference for the quality of the mother's voice is reversed. The infant prefers her real voice to the filtered one.

Fifer's research, together with DeCasper's, provides a window on the marvelously complex behavior of which a day-old baby is capable. This is possible only because the fetal brain has been actively engaged in learning. Far from being a passive and uninvolved passenger, the third-trimester fetus is working optimally within the environment in which it finds itself. Clearly the infant brain isn't a primitive brain or a second-class version of the adult brain. It is a brain exquisitely and beautifully adapted to the womb and to the inevitability of birth.

Newborn babies are biologically programmed to seek new information. "The baby's world is a world full of things that are changing very rapidly," says Dr. Eric Courchesne, some of whose work was described in Chapter 1. "What it has to do is reach out with its sensory system and with its nervous system and grab on to those pieces and try to hold on to them so that it can build a continuous picture of what is happening."

To explore this process, Courchesne has been investigating how the baby's brain manages to distinguish what is familiar from what is new. In one experiment, a single image, a human face, is flashed, again and again, until the baby gets used to it. Then, quickly and without warning, the face changes. A set of electrodes on the infant's head picks up the brainwaves that are evoked when the infant notices the change of face. Even three-month-old infants can perceive this change. In fact, a change in image evokes a much stronger response in the infant's brain than it does in the adult's.

"It's a big response in children," Courchesne explains, "because they have a lot to learn, and they had better get it right because it may be important for them later on."

It is known that the number of synapses multiplies markedly during the first year, and Courchesne suspects that this response to novel stimuli is related to the increase in synapses. "The response gets larger and larger across the first year of life," he notes, "just as the number of synapses grows."

If you turn out the lights and leave a newborn in the darkness, the baby will reach out, look around, and search for stimulation. Dr. Jerome Kagan of Harvard University compares this presence of mind to a well-fed seagull flying around on a summer afternoon. "It has no reason to fly around," explains Kagan, "but that's the way seagulls are built. Human beings, too, are built to seek new information, to learn from it, to consolidate that knowledge, and move on."

As the young brain develops, it begins to lose its flexibility. To discover how long this flexibility lasts, Dr. Hendrik Van der Loos has been studying the whiskers of mice at the University of Lausanne in Switzerland.

A mouse, he explains, explores the world by means of its sixty-six whiskers. Obviously, these whiskers are very important to the mouse because a large portion of its brain is devoted to processing information relayed by them. In fact, every whisker has an area in the brain devoted exclusively to that whisker. This area is called a barrel.

Van der Loos has discovered that snipping off a whisker in a mouse that is no more than five days old will cause the barrel for that whisker to disappear and the adjacent barrels to incorporate its neurons. In other words, the removal of one whisker changes the structure of the mouse's brain. But if this experiment is repeated in a mouse that is six days old, the barrel devoted to the missing whisker remains, even though its function has been taken over by the adjacent barrels. "The map that is in the brain—the visible map, the barrel ensemble—will remain in place," says Van der Loos. "So that means the brain is now *committed.*"

Van der Loos's mice offer a possible explanation for what happens in humans. It is known, for instance, that if an infant or small child develops a brain tumor in one hemisphere and that hemisphere must be removed, very often the child's other hemisphere will take up the slack. Years later, only the most sophisticated of tests can reveal that the remaining hemisphere is actually doing the work of two. This flexibility, or *plasticity,* as it is known, is one of the hallmarks of the infant's brain. But if the same operation is carried out on a twelve- or thirteen-year-old, a wide variety of disabilities, including impairments of speech, touch, vision, or movement, may result.

This loss of the brain's plasticity has benefits as well as drawbacks. Think of it this way. If you wish to build a house, the best and most efficient way of going about it is to hire specialists—plumbers, electricians, carpenters, and so on—who restrict their efforts to what they know best. The brain also functions at its best by parceling out specific "assignments" to specific areas. In time, the infant brain, a generalist, is transformed into the adult brain, a specialist. Though the price usually paid for such commitment is the adult brain's inability to reorganize itself following cell injury or cell death, more is gained than lost by this new arrangement. For through commitment, what the brain loses in flexibility it gains in efficiency and stability.

Genetic programming developing in tandem with envi-

METAPHOR FOR THE DEVELOPING BRAIN

How does one conceive of the events going on within the developing brain? Since there is nothing remotely similar to this process in the known universe, we reach for metaphors in order to make sense of the process. Metaphors can be helpful as long as we remain mindful that the "map is not the territory." All metaphors are only partially correct.

One useful metaphor suggested by Dr. Eric Courchesne is that the brain is like an island born of the sea. At first the island is barren. Then slowly, almost imperceptibly, isolated patches of life appear. They follow their own patterns of development while at the same time always remaining open to the influences of local events. Programmed, fairly predictable, and unalterable events occur alongside events that take their cues from environmental variation.

No two islands look exactly alike: beaches, forests, inland waters all vary according to the conditions that prevailed during the formation of the island. Some islands are rich and lush, teeming with trees and birds and fish. Others are rocky and inhospitable with few living creatures visible for our inspection. But they are still recognizable as islands. Each is the end result of unique patterns of development influenced at all times by local events. At a certain point in this process the isolated patches of life, flora and fauna, begin to influence each other, interact. An independent, unique island is then formed.

"To create an island like this requires more than programming, more than simply seeds. It requires an accumulation over time of millions of events, each of which affects the island both locally and globally," says Courchesne.

"If by some miracle we could miniaturize ourselves and enter the brain, we would find connections that would remind us of a forest of incredible beauty. We would find neurons of different sizes and shapes and with different positions one to the other. And these neurons would be making connections which are critical for proper brain function. This is very similar to how a forest forms: plant life of different sizes and shapes finding their own positions within the system. Each is adapted to a particular function within the ecosystem. On your imaginary journey within the brain you may find neurons that remind you of plants. You will find branches and trunks and stems. You'll find neurons that climb like vines.

"Both the forest and the brain are alive. Both systems have come about through processes that are very similar to each other. This is why you'll find things within the brain that remind you of forests and vice versa. Biology repeats itself when it finds something good. It does it again. That's what's so beautiful about biology. The rules that one finds in one part of the natural world can be used in other parts.

"Both a forest and the brain are parts of the natural world and, therefore, brain development is governed by principles which are very much analogous to those principles which govern the formation and development of other natural phenomena in the world around us, such as an island ecosystem."

Like an island, the brain, too, develops according to specific principles. Further, mishaps at specific times—"critical periods"—can produce permanent alterations in brain function. This translates into impairments of mind that may extend over a lifetime.

---

ronmental influences; plasticity; flexibility; potentiality—and only then commitment. This is the sequence followed by the brain as it develops.

Scientists near Vancouver, British Columbia, are hoping to discover the exact moment when commitment for human language takes place in the brain. In infants, the flexibility to learn *any* language is present from birth, but there is a certain critical moment when they lose that potential. Dr. Janet Werker, of the Department of Psychology at the University of British Columbia, has been testing babies for their ability to distinguish a set of consonants in an obscure Indian dialect—the Thompson, or Inslachetin, language. "This language," Werker explains, "has a set of consonants that are not used in English and that English speakers cannot distinguish between."

These consonant sounds are recorded and played back to young infants. When a sound changes, a toy appears behind the baby. "We teach the baby to turn her head when the sound changes," says Werker. "When the baby has learned this, we can tell if she can distinguish the sound change because she turns her head in anticipation of seeing the toy appear."

Werker has found that eight-month-old infants have no trouble anticipating the appearance of the toy, turning their heads as soon as they hear the change in sound. But for a baby one year old or older, the sound change no longer registers. "There's a reorganization in speech perception across the first year of life," Werker explains. "The young infant is born ready to learn any language. Experience then narrows that universal set of abilities, that universal discriminatory ability, to the particular language that the baby is learning."

The acquisition of language sheds new light on an old controversy: Is genetic predisposition or the environment more important in human development? Over the centuries, the notion prevailed that the human infant learns to speak by parroting; that the infant, in other words, acquires language largely from environmental cues. Then, in the 1950s, this theory fell out of favor through the work of the linguist Noam Chomsky. Language acquisition is not a learned activity, Chomsky claimed, but a biological process as natural as breathing. Any normal child raised in a reasonably normal environment and exposed to human speech will eventually learn to speak. Language, he believed, is innate.

Unfortunately, the work on fetal and newborn language recognition isn't likely to resolve this controversy. While it is true that from day one the newborn demonstrates certain language preferences, it's also evident that these preferences are based on experiences. (The mother's voice heard from inside the womb, said one researcher, is "like the sound of a person's voice heard through the walls of a motel room.") Or, as Anthony DeCasper suggests, if an infant's sensitivity to speech is influenced by prenatal auditory experience, then language acquisition may be more of a learning process than Chomsky and other innatists would suggest— a process that may be dependent to some degree on what is heard in the womb. But since it would be impossible—not to mention unethical—to design an experiment in which a fetus never heard the sound of human speech, the best we can do is look for existing instances in which this happened.

Legend has it that, centuries ago, an Assyrian king was intent on learning which language a child would grow up to speak if that child was deprived of the opportunity of hearing any language. A peasant couple was selected and their child isolated from the sounds of human speech. The child was fed and clothed and generally taken care of adequately enough. But everyone who handled and cared for the child was ordered, under the threat of grievous punishment, not to speak in front of the youngster. The child, according to legend, grew up speaking no language at all.

Beyond legend, however, there are actual cases in which children never learned to speak. Probably the most celebrated case was the "Wild Boy of Aveyron," a child, purportedly raised by wolves, who never learned to speak despite intensive efforts to teach him. Even more poignant is the experience of "Genie," a thirteen-year-old girl who was kept confined by her psychopathic father, isolated from human speech, and abused. In the decade or so since she was rescued, Genie has not learned to talk. An innatist would argue that all bets are off because neither the Wild Boy of Aveyron nor Genie was raised in a normal environment. But perhaps there is an innate biological predisposition for language that involves critical periods during which environmental stimulation is absolutely necessary. If that stimulation is missing, commitment within the brain cannot take place, thereby interfering with the normal unfolding process of language acquisition.

Tiny infants spend most of their time sleeping and, particularly in the earliest weeks, exhibit many behaviors that are reflex in character, so as recently as a decade ago many scientists believed that babies were born with very few inherent behavioral traits. They thought that almost everything was learned from the environment. The opposing position—that even tiny infants are predisposed toward certain perceptions, behaviors, and competencies—was barely granted a hearing. Now all that is changing.

Researchers have been using four- and five-month-old infants in an experiment that involves showing them a pair of movies with soundtracks. One film depicts two yellow wooden blocks striking each other in an unpredictable fashion. The second film shows two yellow, water-soaked sponges being squeezed individually or against each other, also in an unpredictable rhythm. When the sound track that corresponds to one of the two films is then played on its own, infants direct their gaze toward the film that it accompanied. Somehow they detect a similarity between what was just heard and what was seen.

In slightly older infants the inferences are even more striking. Eleven-month-old infants are presented with a continuous or discontinuous sound and then see a pair of visual stimuli that consists of a continuous line set alongside a discontinuous line. These older infants look longer at the discontinuous line if the tone heard was discontinuous, but look longer at the continuous line if the exposure was to the continuous tone. In essence, infants at eleven months can extract the quality of discontinuity from two different sensory inputs.

This activity, called intermodal (or cross-modal) transfer, demonstrates that the infant can take information conveyed by one sense, such as sound, and assimilate it into another sensory sphere, usually vision. Intermodal transfer challenges our traditional ideas about the mental life of children. Infants seem to be less a "buzzing, blooming mass of confusion," as William James once claimed, than "cognitively analytic in their approach to experience," as psychologist Jerome Kagan believes.

They even seem friendly to abstract representations. Dr. Leslie Cohen, of the Children's Research Laboratory at the University of Texas at Austin, has been studying the development of a baby's mind by testing infants for their ability to form abstract concepts. He does this through a technique called habituation. "What this really means," explains Cohen, "is that if you show the baby the same thing over and over again, the baby's going to get bored. He's not going to be interested, and he's not going to look very long at it. The reason the baby is bored is that he's experienced it before. But that, in turn, means that the baby has remembered something about it. We can exploit the baby's boredom to discover what it is babies perceive, and how perception changes with age."

Habituation, in Dr. Leslie Cohen's experiment, as demonstrated by a baby's response to different angles.

In Cohen's experiments, he shows a baby an angle and habituates him to it. Then he shows the baby other angles. One is identical to the first. The second is the same angle, but rotated so that its sides point in different directions. The third angle is unequal to the first two, but it is oriented so that its sides point in the same direction as the first angle.

Cohen found that babies six weeks old respond quite differently to the angles than babies three months old. The younger infants lose interest when they see only angles whose sides point the same way. Older infants, however, lose interest when the angles themselves are equal. The younger infants seem to be processing the angles in terms of the lines that form them—in effect, reacting to the component parts—and the older ones seem to be able to put those component parts together to form a more abstract whole, the concept of "angleness." This capacity to grasp an abstract concept seems to develop in the infant mind in a span of only six weeks.

"Infants form categories at a very early age," says Cohen. "In fact, imagine what it would be like if an infant could not form some simple concepts and categories. Each time the infant saw a person from a different point of view, that person would seem to be totally different. The world would be chaotic and the infant would be unable to learn from experience."

Jerome Kagan suggests that such internal transformations of information may not be limited just to sight, sound, and touch. Certain hitherto inexplicable language performances by young children depend on internal transformations, too. "One of the puzzles in early speech," says Kagan, "is the appearance of expressions that are not part of the child's past experience. When a three-year-old calls a thin slice of lemon a 'moon,' she is telling us she detected the similarity in form between a piece of lemon lying on a saucer and the picture of a new moon in a coloring book. When she calls a dark cloud 'mad,' she is informing us that she detected the affective dimension of unpleasantness shared by a storm and an angry face."

Researchers looking for new insights into the formation of mind have taken a variety of approaches in their studies of infant speech perception. In one approach, the baby's heart rate is monitored while he or she listens to a repeatedly presented word or speech syllable. (As we have seen, a slower rate is an indication of infant attention.) After a number of repetitions of the same stimulus, the heart rate no longer slows down. Then the speech syllable or word is changed. The heart rate once again decelerates. This effectively demonstrates that the infant can discriminate a new speech sound from an old one.

A second approach for assessing speech and language capacities capitalizes on babies' desire to control their environment. Babies are not passive creatures who don't care one way or the other about what's going on around them. They seek novelty and change. This has been demonstrated in experiments using the non-nutritive nipple. When infants are fitted with earphones and the nipple, they soon discover that sucking produces speech sounds delivered through the earphones. The infants therefore increase their sucking when the sounds are heard. This increase is followed several minutes later by a slowing of the sucking rate. At this point a new word or syllable is introduced and the sucking increases once again. The infants recognize a new speech sound and respond accordingly. Interest, the recognition of novelty, and the desire to control the environment are all present in the infant long before the time that we have usually associated with the first stirrings of mind.

The mind does not appear suddenly like a butterfly from a chrysalis, but emerges—from the fertilized egg to the migration of neurons, from birth to the interaction of the brain with the environment—slowly, gradually, and inevitably. The infant's mind is not a "blank slate," for it comes fully equipped with certain perceptual and behavioral biases. It is not an "empty bucket"—the term favored by the philosopher Karl Popper—for it possesses a rich innate structure that matures biologically according to an orderly sequence of brain development. At the same time, it constructs increasingly elaborate rules and structures with which to organize experience and adapt constructively to reality. Infants seem to grow and develop in accordance with some universal milestones of development.

This modern notion of milestones began with Swiss psychologist Jean Piaget and his experiments with his own children. Piaget made three pivotally important suggestions about the development of mind. First, the mind changes over time. Second, the mind changes in ways that depend on the environment. That is, our thinking about everything from the nature of the world to morals depends to an incalculable extent on the features of the physical world in which we happen to be immersed. And third, the mind changes not only in regard to the specific content of our thoughts, but in our mode of thinking as well.

The thinking of a bright sixteen-year-old girl is different from that of a bright two-year-old not only in obvious matters of content—music and fashion as opposed to toys and the sandbox—but in form as well. The sixteen-year-old is able to foresee the consequences of her actions, express herself in complex sentences, mentally rotate a geometric figure, and employ quasi-logical arguments to buttress her opinions. These formal and structural features that differentiate the sixteen-year-old and the two-year-old are not present at birth but develop according to the interaction of the genes, the environment, and the brain. Jerome Kagan, who has studied infant development for the past two decades, has formulated his own set of "miraculous universal milestones of development." "The young child is prepared to react to the world in very special ways that are unique to our species," he explains. "The one-day-old infant can hear, smell, taste. He is attracted to certain things: a checkerboard rather than a plain pattern, dark lines on a white background. Intermittent sounds are preferred over continuous ones. Even certain colors, such as red, are preferred. At an emotional level the infant is prepared biologically to attach himself to the people who care for him. He will respond to a vocal pattern that matches the human voice rather than a high-pitched violin or a low-pitched bassoon. He smiles, babbles, cries to certain stimuli."

At two to three months of age the first major change occurs. The baby doesn't cry as much and starts to babble more. Most importantly, he smiles at the people around him. It's as if the two-month-old recognizes an unfamiliar face as similar to the face of his mother or father and assimilates it. "We call that the smile of assimilation," says Kagan. This indicates that some form of early memory must be working. How could the infant recognize similarities unless he was capable of shaping some form of recognition memory? It's probable that this emerging memory capacity corresponds to enhanced development within the frontal lobes, which grow rapidly in the period between three and eight months and participate in a major way in memory.

Then at eight months, memory changes. The infant is now capable not only of recognition but retrieval. If I tick off a list of people who were at a cocktail party last evening and you select from that list the ones you had met—that's recognition memory. But if I ask you simply to tell me who was there, the task is more difficult. You have to be capable of retrieving the information from your memory bank— retrieval memory.

Diversity as demonstrated in a group of babies.

THE MYSTERY OF EXCEPTIONAL CHILDREN

Christopher is a seven-year-old with mechanical and chess-playing abilities far beyond his age. He is a challenge to any theory that insists that the development of mind occurs in an inevitable pattern.

"Development is not something which occurs universally in all people in the same way," insists Dr. David Feldman, of Tufts University. "Sometimes things don't march along in sync. A case like Christopher's, where logical reasoning so outdistances everything else, makes you at least entertain the idea that mind is actually made up more of a confederacy than it is some kind of overall integrated capability. With Christopher one sees at least a couple of areas of capability that stand out very sharply from the rest of his development. And when one sees such a distinctive capability, it raises the question of whether the mind is one thing or several things or many things."

The teachers at Christopher's school make the assumption that it is the child's special qualities that dictate what will be done. "There is no formula," says Feldman. "There is no single way to do it. The gift of teaching and the gift of parenting have to be rediscovered with each child."

In order to do this, Christopher's teachers are helping him integrate his special abilities in some areas with his more conventional development in others. If they are successful, and so far things are going well, Christopher will be able to employ his special talents in ways that won't alienate or distance him from his peers.

While the mind appears to develop according to fairly predictable sequences such as described by Jerome Kagan, there are exceptions, like Christopher, who serve to remind us that the mind will always evade our paltry attempts at definition, no matter how cunningly these are crafted.

Christopher, at seven, numbers inventiveness among his many gifts. Here he holds the model of an energy-efficient roof he has designed.

We know that eight-month-olds are capable of retrieval memory, a major milestone in their development, thanks to the delightful experiments of Piaget on what he termed "object permanence." If the eight-month-old sees a rattle being hidden under a blanket, he can briefly remember where it was hidden and lift up the blanket. But if too much time passes, ten seconds or more, he won't be able to do this. Retrieval memory is only weakly developed. Not until fourteen or fifteen months can the infant respond correctly in the face of a delay of a minute or more.

"This ability to retrieve the past exacts a price," says Kagan. "That price is a vulnerability to fear or anxiety. One of the main milestones of development in all human beings occurs at eight or nine months of age: fear of strangers and fear of separation."

It seems reasonable to suppose that memory must be involved in "separation anxiety." The infant cannot "miss" the mother unless he can recall her presence thirty seconds earlier and compare this with her absence at the moment. When the infant is aware that something is amiss, his awareness leads to anxiety, crying, and all-around fussiness.

"It's analogous to being on a jet plane about to take off and you notice that the motor sounds funny," says Kagan. "You can retrieve from your memory how jet engines normally sound and match that with how this particular engine is sounding now. If they aren't the same sounds, you get anxious. That's how the baby feels at eight or nine months of age when the mother leaves the room."

Along with this enhanced anxiety comes an increase in the infant's ability to manipulate symbols. Ten- or twelve-month-olds in play will treat pieces of cloth as blankets and shards of wood as cookies. Toys are recruited into service as the components of a playhouse. At about the same time—in the twelve- to fourteen-month period—the infant begins to speak. Children can comprehend some words before the first year is over, but this is when they actually start to employ language: single words at first, and then in the second year partial sentences of three, four, or five words. There is a big burst in vocabulary by the end of that year. Language is the second major milestone in human development.

The third major milestone—one that distinguishes us from all other species—is the growth of a sense of self, self-consciousness, self-awareness. "Between eighteen and twenty-four months," says Kagan, "children, for the first time . . . become aware that they have intentions, that they have feelings, that they can act. . . . A child has to have interactions with people. But all the interactions in the world won't lead to the sense of self until you're in the middle of the second year because the brain is not yet mature."

This sense of self can be experimentally verified. Children of nine or ten months of age with a spot of rouge brushed on their nose won't touch their nose when staring at themselves in a mirror. But by eighteen or twenty months, children reach up and touch their nose. They recognize themselves in the mirror, their curiosity piqued by the spot of red that they've never seen before. *I, me, mine,*—these words begin appearing at the same time. Or the eighteen-month-old may begin to order others about: "Give *me* that toy."

Kagan believes that there is a set timetable for the emergence of self and the other milestones in the development of mind. He cites the work of Laura Petito at McGill University in Montreal, who has demonstrated that deaf children learning to communicate by sign language will make the sign for "I" at about the same time as hearing children will begin to touch the rouge brushed on the tip of their nose. "That," says Kagan, "is a marvelous discovery."

The other milestone of the second year, according to Kagan, is a moral sense. This first appears as a primitive understanding that there is an integrity to objects. Children at this stage are bothered by a broken doll, a broken car, paint that's peeling from a table. They show concern, and say "broken," "dirty," "bad." Or they'll take the doll or car to their mother, implying that something is wrong. These children begin to use and understand words like *good* and *bad*. Culture increasingly influences the direction of this moral sense. A child growing up in India is likely to have a somewhat different sense of right and wrong than a child growing up in Chicago.

"A moral sense is one of the most profound of accomplishments," Kagan emphasizes. "We should view it just as we view singing and speaking and walking. It is a maturational milestone that will be acquired by every child as long as they live in a world of human beings."

With this moral sense, the emotions so characteristic of the "terrible twos" begin to appear. The incomprehensible aggression of this period of life is probably the result of the child's attempt to establish what is right and what is wrong. Indeed thought, or cognition, seems to precede emotion.

Nineteenth-century theorists wanted to make emotions primary and saw thought as a necessary coping device to deal with conflict. Freud made the emotions the basis for cognitive development. He said that the id came first, and the ego, which represented thought and logic, followed as a result of the resolution of conflict.

But modern developmental theory suggests that cognitive processes must appear before emotions. A child can't react with "stranger anxiety" until he or she is capable of remembering human faces and recognizing that this face isn't familiar. So, contrary to Freud, emotion cannot be the stimulus for the development of mind. Instead, our cognitive abilities seem to emerge as an accompaniment to brain maturation.

From the second to the sixth year, a child's vocabulary expands dramatically and his or her knowledge grows astoundingly. One can begin to see what the child's actual potential may be. It is the time to begin building the basis of formal education. The child's "social self" emerges.

By the seventh year of life, another major milestone appears. The child becomes capable of "logical thinking." He or she can accept responsibility and recognize the need to tell the truth. This is the age, according to English law, when a child can be considered responsible for a crime. It's the period in the Catholic Church when children first go to confession.

At this age, thanks to the accelerated maturation of the human brain, the child begins to perform in some areas almost up to adult standards. "If you go to Indian villages in Africa or Latin America," Kagan notes, "parents tend to assign to the child of about age seven a responsibility like taking care of the cow or taking care of a younger sibling. In our own culture a child starts school at about that time."

Children of this age appear responsible to adults because by this time they have also gained the ability to see where they fit into the huge and amorphous world around them. Living things are distinguished from nonliving things. Objects and people are understood as belonging to separate categories. The pet cat is an "animal" and at the same time a "living thing," a "companion," and a "friend." The child learns that there is a hierarchy into which categories fit. For all logical thinking, Kagan points out, you have to have this understanding.

"One of the consequences of this new ability to relate concepts," says Kagan, "is that now the child whose sense of self has been growing continuously since the second birthday is able to relate the concept of self, which is abstract, to the concept of events in the outside world. Once you can do that, then you can begin to think about abstract events that might happen to you. Four-year-olds are afraid of simple things: darkness, ghosts, and big dogs. But the abstract fears occur after age six. Now children will tell their mothers they're afraid of things like being kidnapped or nuclear war."

The mind has emerged.

3.
AGING

It is hard to think of another period of human life for which we have coined as many euphemisms as old age. If we are to believe this vocabulary of wishful thinking, "senior citizens" can spend their "golden years," "the sunset of their lives," in "retirement communities" and "leisure villages" in which they can "age gracefully" amid the rich green of sweeping golf courses, the companionability of nostalgic rocking chairs on front porches, and strolls hand in hand down Memory Lane with the glow of the afternoon sun behind them.

These bromides, however, are only half the story. Every sugar-sweet cliché has its savage counterpart. Behind their backs, the elderly are often "crocks," "old bags," "geezers," and "hens" who are empty vessels, past their prime, in their dotage, washed up, done and gone.

Two powerful emotions underlie this contradictory vocabulary: fear and denial. Fear of physical illness, indignity, dependence, and most terrible of all, of "losing one's mind," that which above all defines us as human. Denial of the inevitability of death. "Tell us the secret of your longevity," interviewers always ask the very old, as if there were a formula, if only we knew it, that would assure us too of reaching ninety or one hundred.

What *is* the reality of growing old? It is certainly not the golden age of the clichés, but examples abound of people who have remained mentally vigorous, indeed have made some of their richest contributions in their later years. We think of George Bernard Shaw, Pablo Casals, Georgia O'Keeffe, Marianne Moore. Konrad Adenauer became chancellor of West Germany at seventy-three; Clara Barton was seventy-seven when she served in Cuba during the Spanish American War; Benjamin Franklin at eighty-one helped to frame the Constitution of the United States; Henri Matisse and Pablo

Picasso were still painting well into their eighties; Claude Monet's large "Water Lilies" were begun when the painter was seventy-six; Sophocles is said to have written *Oedipus at Colonus* in his very old age. The distinguished musicologist Nicolas Slonimsky, in his nineties, is the world's authority on nineteenth- and twentieth-century music, and shares his enormous knowledge with a delighted radio audience every Saturday afternoon. Golda Meir became prime minister of Israel at seventy. "It's no crime to be seventy," she observed with characteristic wryness, "but it is no joke either."

But for every Nicolas Slonimsky and Golda Meir, and for every more obscure but equally lively and productive old person we know, there are old people who have great difficulty in remembering, understanding, finding the right words; whose minds, as well as bodies, seem to deteriorate with age. Clearly, there are vast differences separating one aged mind from another, so that one person in his eighties is a mentally vigorous Supreme Court Justice, another confined to a state hospital with organic brain disease. Science calls these differences *variability*. Dr. Marilyn Albert, Professor of Psychiatry and Neurology at Harvard Medical School, notes that in no other group except infants do we find individuals so different from one another as among the elderly. "If you take very healthy individuals across the age range," says Albert, "the variability among the young is very narrow, whereas the variability among older individuals is much greater. So you have seventy-year-olds who are performing at the level of thirty-year-olds and seventy-year-olds who are performing much more poorly." As we explore the changes that occur in the brain and the mind with aging, we will be seeking the reasons why this is so.

We shall also be talking a good deal about loss or diminishment: of cells and functions and capacities and skills. Aging of the body and the mind entails this; it is a fact of life. Two things need to be remembered in what may seem at times like a litany of losses. One is that neuroscientists do not always know how significant these changes may be. The other is that the *effects* of these changes are by no means always dire. As we shall see, the mind is remarkably flexible and adaptable, often able to exploit the strengths of experience and wisdom to compensate for lessened abilities.

What do we mean by "old"?

The number of years a person has lived, for one. In order to reach a ripe or even not-so-ripe old age, he or she must approach as closely as possible the "maximum achievable life-span." *Homo sapiens* achieved a maximum *potential* life-span of just over 100 years millennia ago, and this figure remains the same today. (The longest life that can be documented is 114, and very few people actually live to 100.)

1629.

1634.

1657.

1664.

But the maximum *achievable* life-span has changed greatly in recent times. For tens of thousands of years, life expectancy was only about 30 years, and it rose only 10 years between prehistoric times and the classical Greek and Roman periods. Indeed, it was still a mere 40 years for a child born in this country in 1860. Then, as throughout recorded history, wars, accidents, and infectious diseases were the major killers.

By the beginning of the twentieth century this figure had risen to 48.2 years in Western nations, thanks largely to improved public hygiene; by 1964 to 70.2 years; and by 1978 to 74 years. The chief factor in the great jump in the latter half of this century has been the development of vaccines and drugs such as antibiotics that prevent and treat once-lethal infections. It is only in the last twenty-five years, however, that these gains in life expectancy have really affected the longevity of people over sixty-five. The improvement has come about because of a significant decrease in heart attacks and strokes. In addition, the "old old"—people over eighty-five—are surviving longer because of more effective treatment and control of influenza.

We are individuals, of course, and not statistical averages, and for each of us the significant factors in longevity are two: how close we are to the age at which our parents and grandparents died, and the presence or absence of disease factors. But age matters. The older we are, the more likely we are to be afflicted with one or more diseases.

Thus, chronological age cannot be dodged in defining what "old" means, even if Uncle John, who is sixty-five, has difficulty thinking of himself as old, particularly on Sundays when he sees his mother, age eighty-six. She, in turn, may well consider herself as not so old, certainly not when compared with her friend, Thelma, whom she visits in the nursing home and who just yesterday turned ninety-two.

"It's not how old you are but how young you feel." "Attitude is more important than chronological age." We reassure ourselves with these truisms. Doctors do, too. "The patient acts and looks considerably younger than her chronological age," the intern in his mid-twenties is likely to write on the history sheet of the sixty-six-year-old patient he is examining. But while these assumptions are comforting—and attitude certainly does play a part in a sense of well-being—there is little evidence to support the view that "looking younger" or "feeling younger" has much to do with how long the mortician can be held at bay.

Our young intern gauging his patient's health and longevity would be better advised, therefore, to ignore the presence or absence of such conventional marks of aging as graying hair and wrinkled skin, and to think less single-mindedly of weight, height, grip strength; or hearing or personality; or blood pressure, lung capacity, blood sugar, cholesterol levels, or a host of blood chemistries. None of these is as important in predicting aging changes or death as simple chronological age. Our doctor will do better to seek answers to some questions: At what age did her parents die? Of what? Does she smoke? Does she have any current or chronic medical problems? Did anyone in her family ever have Alzheimer's disease? But most important: focus on her age.

"Death increases exponentially during aging": a simple rule first laid out in 1825 by a statistician interested in life annuities, Benjamin P. Gompertz, in a paper presented before the Royal Society of Medicine. Gompertz was the first to observe and codify what now seems so obvious: death is more common among older people than among younger ones, the death rate doubling about every eight years after the age of forty.

But death is only half of it. Before there's death there's aging, and that's the part that hurts. "Old" means changes in mind and body. Psychologists and physicians have measured and recorded changes that every septuagenarian and octogenarian can testify to from personal experience. Things aren't learned as easily as before; it can take disconcertingly longer to dredge up a name to match a face; reaction time increases; muscular strength declines (harder to pick up that bag in the supermarket).

What do these changes signify? Are they interconnected? What is the nature of the aging mind, and how does it differ from the younger one?

Contrary to popular opinion, the older person, at least up to the mid-seventies, doesn't show much change in intellectual performance. Older people still know what they knew decades ago, and if you're willing to wait a bit, will get the information to you. Psychological tests show that vocabulary, general knowledge, and comprehension, which reach a peak at about twenty to thirty, for the most part are maintained pretty much intact until at least the mid-seventies—though in the presence of brain disease of any sort, of course, all bets are off.

It is the clock that is the old man or the old woman's enemy. Ask him or her to name the presidents back to Roosevelt and if you don't ration the time, the performance will be credible enough. But pull out a clock or a watch and measure how long it takes the person to recite Reagan . . . Carter . . . Ford . . . Nixon . . . Johnson. The performance slows markedly with time, a steady decline that occurs over a person's lifetime. That's one of the reasons why few older people appear on quiz shows. "I know the answer," says the contestant. "Just wait a second or two and I'll tell it to you." Although part of the slowing may be attributed to alterations in motor speed or perceptual ability, there is now unequivocal evidence that the speed of central processing is dampened with age.

We are, of course, talking *averages* here. Some seventy-year-olds perform better than twenty-year-olds on tests of mental speed, just as some seventy-year-olds can run marathons while some twenty-year-olds are put off by a brisk walk to the office if it's more than a mile away. The same can be said for reaction times. A former boxer forty years into retirement can still deliver a punch fast enough to dispatch most muggers. But we must remember that such performances are the exceptions, the things we love to read about over our morning coffee. It's the exceptions that cheer us up, make up for the reality we must face: that we, too, are getting older.

With aging, slowing occurs in such tasks as running and finger tapping, copying words, adding up figures. Endurance, strength, and coordination are affected equally: with age it takes longer to do a task than before; it takes more out of the doer; it isn't done as smoothly. Even for people in good health, the changes in physical function are real. As writer Malcolm Cowley said on reaching his eightieth birthday: "Age is not different from earlier life as long as you're sitting down."

What happens when one must stand up? What about walking? Posture tends to be stiffer, forward bent, and inflexible. There's reason enough for such changes, including arthritis; the loss of height secondary to thinning, wedging, and even collapse of the discs in the spine; compression and narrowing of the vertebral bodies secondary to calcium depletion. And these are only changes that don't involve the brain. With aging, the motor cortex in the frontal lobes can lose a high percentage of its neurons. Many of these cells send long axons descending along the spinal cord to spinal motor cells that communicate with peripheral nerves and muscles. With the loss of these Betz cells (named after their nineteenth-century discoverer, the Russian anatomist V. A. Betz), motor coordination can be affected. Flexor and extensor muscles can no longer be kept in balance.

Ask a twenty- or thirty-year-old to stand on one foot with his eyes closed and that prosaic task doesn't present much of a challenge. Ask an eighty-year-old to do the same thing, even an eighty-year-old who still jogs and does calisthenics, and he will be unsteady, likely to fall unless he uses the other leg to steady himself. Dr. Robert Katzman and Dr. Robert Terry, now at the University of California, San Diego, School of Medicine, tested and confirmed in the laboratory at Albert Einstein College of Medicine in New York what Malcolm Cowley discovered by observing his own performance: a man is old when he "can't stand on one leg and has trouble pulling on his pants."

With aging, the elderly person's muscles must come into a clumsy and uneasy balance with one another. That's why there is frequently weakness, pain, muscle contraction, tremor. Along the *peripheral nerves*—the outpost where sensory signals are first detected—many of the axons are lost. No message or a garbled message is conveyed back to headquarters. The largest fibers are affected first, and since the largest fibers carry messages with the utmost dispatch, the aging individual first loses his or her ability to respond quickly. That's why old people fall, embarrassed and angry at their impaired responsiveness, hoping that this time they haven't broken a hip. Finally, the muscles themselves thin out, and fail to contract as adequately as they once did years before on the tennis court. For the muscles, however, the news isn't unrelievably gloomy. That thinning can be reversed through exercise. Not so the combined changes in brain, spinal cord, and large peripheral nerves that link up with muscle. Along this highway the damage is additive, leading to Cowley's vexed experience: "Everything takes longer to do . . . it becomes an achievement to do thoughtfully, step-by-step, what was once done instinctively."

At birth the human brain contains perhaps as many as one hundred billion nerve cells (some believe the figure to be fifteen billion). From then on there is a continuous process of attrition. Brain weight decreases gradually but surely—about 10 percent over a normal life-span—because of neuron death. But not every part of the brain loses neurons at the same rate. In most *brain stem* regions—areas located below the cerebral cortex that are responsible for automatic unlearned activity— there is little or no cell loss with advancing age. The cerebral cortex, including the motor cortex and the frontal lobes (the thinking part of the brain), loses neurons at a maximum rate of fifty thousand a day, according to Dr. Stanley Rapoport of the National Institute on Aging. Multiply that by the number of days a seventy-year-old has lived and you get the kinds of numbers that interest a statistician. Furthermore, even in a specific area, certain types of cells disappear more frequently than others. Overall, the pattern of neuronal loss is a patchy one: significant in parts of the frontal and *temporal regions,* little or none slightly farther back in the postcentral region and, further downward, in the inferior temporal regions.

More common than actual cell death—and perhaps more important—are the losses with aging of connections between neurons. Fewer synapses are seen along the dendrites, an indirect measure of the number of nerve cell connections.

Moreover, as we age, the dendritic branching of many

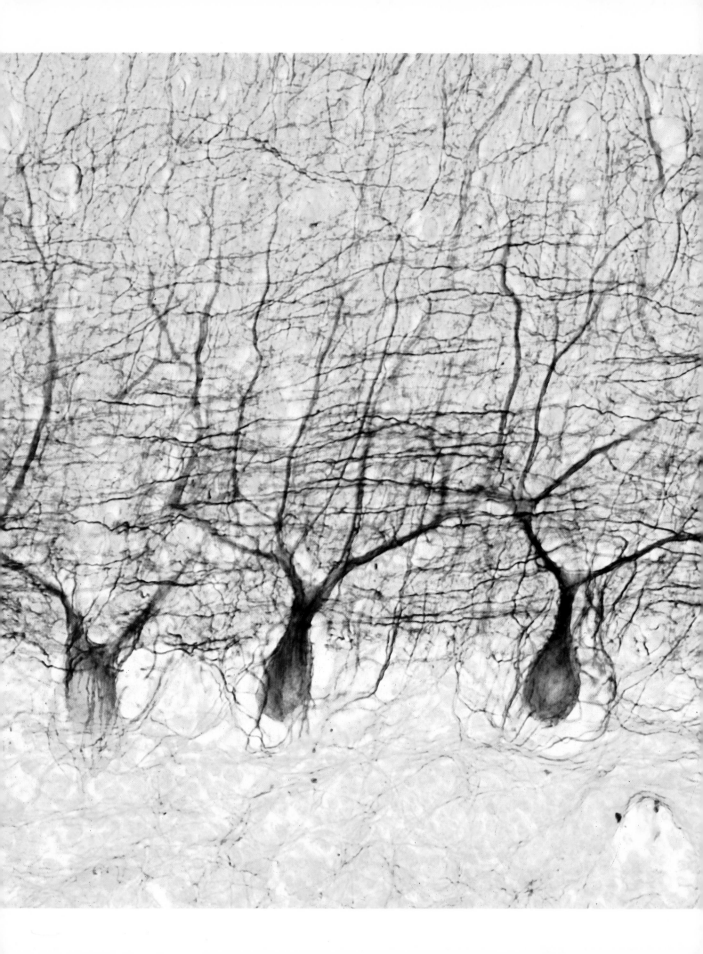

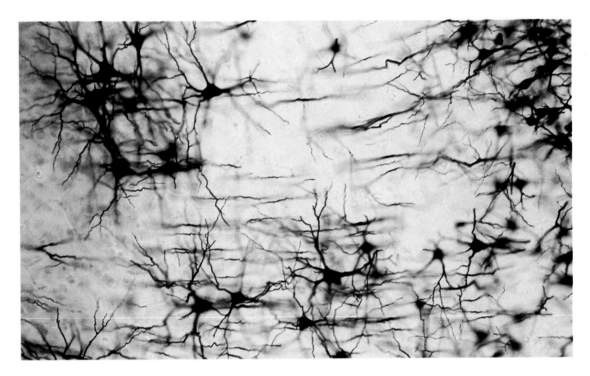

of the surviving nerve cells is no longer quite so elaborate. When photographed after special staining, the branches appear thinned out, like trees that have lost their farthest twigs. Many of those that remain are drastically reduced in size. The quantity of neurotransmitters decreases as well. Some neurons appear swollen. Indeed, a skilled neuropathologist scanning this scene under the microscope can make an educated guess about the age of the patient at the moment of death.

All this means fewer messages to be sent, fewer neurotransmitters to convey these messages, fewer receptor branches on the terminal neurons to receive them. Neuroscientists at scientific meetings debate among themselves the reasons for these changes. According to one explanation, abnormal protein metabolism within the nerve cell may lead to an accumulation of bits of debris within the cell. Since the distant dendrites of the neuron are dependent on material transported from the center of the cell, sufficient quantities of such debris could conceivably prevent the flow of substances that normally enable the dendrite to perform its function of communicating with its fellows, and cause it to die off.

While this scenario seems reasonable, it's not the whole story. Another intriguing possibility is suggested by comparisons between aging neurons and neurons that for one reason or another have been isolated and deprived of their normal cross talk with neighboring neurons. Neurons remain inherently "social" throughout the lifetime of the brain. Each, if it is functioning normally, strives to "reach

(Above) *With aging, in contrast to the picture opposite, dendritic branching decreases, reducing the connections between neurons.*

(Opposite) *Photomicrograph of neurons in the cerebellum showing the cell body, axon, and numerous dendrites.*

out and touch someone." If this process is interfered with, as it often is in the aging brain, neuronal degeneration and death may occur.

Further, this process of death and destruction may involve many, many neurons scattered throughout the brain but linked by synaptic connections, a process known as "cascading." There is speculation that the aging brain may be particularly susceptible to cascading effects: widespread degeneration occurring as a consequence of minor damage such as that caused, for example, by high blood pressure.

Research carried out by Stanley Rapoport points to the effects of this damage on the brains of otherwise healthy elderly men. Rapoport and his colleague, Dr. Barry Horowitz, showed that in the aging brain the frontal regions and the *parietal lobe,* a receiver of sensory information and a regulator of coordinated body movements, are out of synchrony with each other.

Rapoport and Horowitz believe that this may be caused by the reduction in number and complexity of dendritic interconnections. The result is a loss of integrative function. The aged individual is less capable of integrating his or her sensory inputs: vision with hearing, movement with sensation, memory to bind everything together into a meaningful whole. Thus, older people have great difficulty recognizing by touch alone a figure embedded in a complex geometric pattern. Decreases in memory span and the ability to process information rapidly are also thought to be a consequence of losses in integrative skills.

The disturbed frontal–parietal relationship and its effect on integrative skills is an example of a brain–behavior correlation. Other regions of the brain that may be involved in decreased brain–behavior correlations because of cell loss include the locus ceruleus, an area associated with sleep and wakefulness cycles, emotion, and memory, which shows a 40 percent loss of cells with aging, and the hippocampal cortex, a "memory center" that shows a decline in certain nerve cell types after age sixty.

Because of the somber observations of neuronal loss and functional deterioration, as well as tests on elderly people, neuroscientists used to believe that brain blood flow and oxygen consumption (which are linked to glucose utilization) —two indirect measurements of how much energy the brain is expending—must also decrease with aging. With fewer cells, less glucose and oxygen should be needed to stoke the Machine.

But this assumption proved invalid. It turned out that many of the old people who had cooperated in the testing of brain blood flow and oxygen use suffered from a smorgasbord of illnesses that have an effect on brain function:

hypertension, arteriosclerosis ("hardening of the arteries"), diabetes, and psychosis. It was important to look at the *healthy* old. How would they measure up to their younger counterparts?

To find out, healthy twenty-year-old men were compared to healthy seventy-year-old men. To everyone's surprise, except perhaps the healthy seventy-year-olds, blood flow and oxygen consumption differed hardly at all in the two groups. Overall, the functional capacity of the brains of normal healthy men does not change over a fifty-year period. Further, the amount of glucose utilized in specific brain regions of the elderly men sitting quietly in the laboratory didn't differ significantly from that of the twenty-year-olds also sitting quietly.

To the careful thinker, the above observations are puzzling. If there are fewer cells, fewer branches on the remaining cells, and fewer neurotransmitters, what can be going on that would result in *no change* in blood flow and oxygen and glucose utilization? In other words, shouldn't fewer cells generate less energy and thereby need less blood to deliver a reduced amount of oxygen?

While thinking about that question, recall that the psychological testing of the elderly reveals no change and, in some instances, even improvements in what we call *crystallized intelligence:* vocabulary, general information, and comprehension. The "wisdom" of the aged is an everyday recognition of the fact that the observations and experiences accumulated over a lifetime can count for a great deal—one of the reasons our Supreme Court justices on the average are in their sixties and seventies and not their thirties and forties. Only *fluid intelligence*—memory span and the ability to process information rapidly—decreases significantly with age.

Given this, how does one account for these islands of preserved function (retained crystallized intelligence, no alteration of glucose use, blood flow, or oxygen consumption) within a setting of massive brain cell loss: 18,250,000 cells per year?

Whenever observations and what seem to be reasonable conclusions from these observations produce a paradox, scientists try to discover an underlying principle. In this instance, not one but two principles have emerged: *redundancy* and *plasticity.*

If the brain can suffer the loss of fifty thousand cells per day, then it's likely that many more cells are initially present than are required. This is certainly true for fetuses and infants; as we have noted in Chapter 2, we never have as many brain cells as we do while in the womb. This suggests that the brain, to borrow an analogy from the world of art, is sculpted: form is produced by the discarding or elimina-

Supreme Court Justice William Brennan at 82. As with many of his colleagues, age and experience have not altered judgment.

tion of materials (neurons) rather than an accumulation of materials (additional neurons).

Think of it this way: if only 50 percent of a group of neurons is truly required to carry out a specific task, then half the cells in that group could die and still leave a sufficient number to function, though perhaps with slightly less efficiency or with an increased tendency toward error or "breakdown." We have far more neurons than we need. That is *redundancy*.

Furthermore, undamaged brain cells in the elderly can grow more dendrites, thus enhancing communication throughout the brain. That's *plasticity,* also noted in Chapter 2. More is done with less because those fewer neurons are more active, search out new connections, intertwine and interdigitate in an arabesque creation more complex and dazzling than the most celestial of Persian carpets. This activity requires energy—the reason that blood flow, oxygen consumption, and glucose utilization remain unaltered in healthy older people.

In the elderly, growth and development square off against degeneration and death, the brain doing the best that it can under the circumstances and, judging from the overall result, often doing more than might be expected.

Dr. William T. Greenough, Professor of Psychology and Chairman of the Program in Neuroscience and Behavioral Biology at the University of Illinois at Champaign-Urbana, suggests that the structure (and therefore the function) of an individual's brain at any point reflects the dynamic interplay between the growth and the degeneration of neuronal processes. As the person ages, the relative weight of the degeneration aspect increases. But Greenough's experiments also show that if you increase the complexity and interest of an organism's environment, the complexity of that organism's brain will increase correspondingly. It happens in rats.

Neuroscientists have long suspected that the strength of the connections between neurons in the adult brain is susceptible to modification by ongoing neuronal activity. For example, if an adult rat is trained to run a complicated maze and its companion isn't, the two rats will exhibit differences in the number of connections between their brain cells. The maze-running rat is the proud owner of a brain with a greater number of synapses. More experience, more synapses.

In a chocolate chip cookie experiment, Greenough trained rats to reach for this treat with a specific paw. One gluttonous rat obliged by stabbing 219 cookie pieces in twenty minutes. Microscopic examination of its brain revealed that the brain hemisphere that controlled the trained paw exhibited a dramatic increase in dendritic branches compared to the same area in the brains of its untrained companions.

AGED MACAQUES

At Johns Hopkins University, Dr. Donald Price has assembled a colony of some of the oldest macaques in existence. "We have animals here that are in their thirties, and we have to multiply their ages three times to get the human equivalent. So some of our animals would be the equivalent of ninety to a hundred years of age."

The animals are tested every day for the purpose of discovering the biologic basis for the abnormalities in performance that occur in aged animals. Not every animal shows the same falloff in performance. "As they grow older," Price says, "there are some animals that are quite impaired while others are much more preserved. And that finding has its parallel in humans."

Price and his associates have designed experiments that test specific regions of the brain by selecting tasks that are specific for those regions. Thus, the *prefrontal cortex* is the objective in the delayed response test, in which the macaque observes in which of two wells a food pellet is hidden. Then a screen is brought down between the animal and the wells. When it is lifted soon afterward, the animal is rewarded only if it remembers the correct well. If an aged animal does poorly on the test, Price predicts that an autopsy of its brain after it dies will uncover abnormalities of brain structure and chemistry in the prefrontal area.

In another test, the monkey is required to remember one rule: A peanut reward will always be located under a novel object, not a familiar one. Young macaques have no difficulty learning this rule; when the screen is raised, they reach toward the newly introduced object, such as a bottle, knock it over, and retrieve the peanut. But monkeys of an age equivalent to a human's ninety don't do very well. Price believes these aged monkeys suffer from damage to the frontal lobes and possibly the amygdala and the hippocampus deep in the temporal lobe.

At no time is anything harmful done to the animals; verifications of the researchers' assumptions will be undertaken only after the macaques die. Price and his associates are maintaining the colony under the highest standards of animal care. "We are only looking at what nature does to the animal as it ages," Price says. "In that sense, this is a unique opportunity to examine age-associated behavioral abnormalities and the biological abnormalities in structure and chemistry that underlie the behavioral deficits."

More learning, more synapses.

In another pair of experiments, Greenough provided middle-aged or elderly rats with toys—"the rat equivalent of a Disneyland," as he put it. The result of this complex environment? Heavier brains and larger nerve cells in some brain areas than are found in animals reared in barren laboratory cages. More stimulation, more synapses.

According to Greenough, the increase in brain weight is the result of the increase in synapses. Further, dendritic branching is increased in animals reared with play objects. Most exciting of all, this plasticity isn't confined to young rats. Adult brains, elderly as well as younger, can be modified as well.

"We can offset and even reverse late brain aging in rats by providing changes in experience on a regular basis," says Greenough. "It's known that old rats lose synapses and old

Dr. William T. Greenough's "Disneyland" for rats. This enriched environment stimulated the formation of new synapses in the rats' brains.

people do, too. Are they lost because they're forming fewer connections? There's a good possibility that experience can govern the number of synapses that are born and the number of synapses that survive."

Greenough's results fly in the face of traditional wisdom. "Historically, neuroscientists assumed that as the brain developed, it formed connections which stayed in place indefinitely until the aging process took over. Generally speaking, people didn't think of the adult brain as being susceptible to changes in its actual structure." But in reality, he notes, connections continue to form throughout most, if not all, of the life of the brain.

"Basically what's happening is that new information is being incorporated into the structure of the brain, into the pattern of connections. Both the young animal and the old animal can form new synapses. The young animal forms more, the old animal a few less. But the brain retains an important part of the younger brain's character in its ability to form new synapses."

Obviously, the question still to be answered is whether the increase in synaptic connections has any *practical* significance. Greenough is convinced that it does. "If you look at the animals, they seem more alert and may be happier. It's as if they're really enjoying life for the first time instead of this boring routine that they'd become accustomed to earlier in their lives, when they spent their time in a cage with nothing to do."

Of course, one must be cautious about extrapolating from rats to humans. But many of the things that have been learned about the human brain have come from judicious comparisons between animals and humans. "I think that the rats are trying to tell us something," says Greenough. "What they're saying, basically, is that mental exercise is a very good thing for the health of the brain. It's similar to the effect of physical exercise on the rest of the body. The Disneyland for rats is really an attempt to mimic a mentally stimulating world for a human being."

Dr. Peter Davies, of the Department of Pathology at the Albert Einstein College of Medicine in New York, is convinced that there is a correlation between retained intellectual capacity and the state of the elderly person's brain. "I've been struck that some of the brains from normal elderly people over ninety are really indistinguishable from the brains of twenty-five-year-olds. Absolutely nothing wrong at all. A perfect brain," says Davies. "I do not believe there is good evidence for an effect of age alone on the brain." What this suggests is that the changes in the brain that accompany normal healthy aging may not be as significant in the functioning of the mind as the data on neuron loss and other degenerative processes might seem to indicate. It is an important area for further research.

As noted, what has been described above refers to the normal healthy brain as it ages. But not every brain is so lucky. Plasticity and redundancy may not work. Brain function may be impaired by disease. Translation: the old man or the old woman can't recall what happened a month ago, yesterday, or, if the impairment is severe enough, even what happened only a few minutes ago. He or she may be disoriented, clumsy, rambling in speech; may fail to recognize neighbors, friends, eventually even relatives; may wander in and out of rooms or in and out of conversations. The standard term for this condition is "senile dementia." It is defined by Robert Terry and Robert Katzman as "progressive mental deterioration, loss of memory and cognitive function, with resultant inability to carry out activities of daily living, that occurs in some elderly individuals."

Cognition, as defined by Dr. Marian Perlmutter, a gerontologist at the University of Michigan, includes not only memory but intelligence, reasoning, and decision making, "the representational thinking and problem-solving skills that expand human abilities, enabling us to conceptualize, experience, and communicate with each other." As life expectancy increases, the possibility of a person's exhibiting some form of cognitive disturbance or dementia increases as well. Ten percent of people over the age of sixty-five and 20 percent of those over eighty have significant dementia. But despite the increased frequency with age, dementia isn't simply an extreme form of aging. It is a complex of symptoms that often indicates the presence of disease, and it affects approximately three million people. By the year 2010, one out of every six persons in the United States will be sixty-five or older, and these numbers will continue to grow. Because of these demographics, it is estimated that dementia will be epidemic by then, afflicting six to seven million people at a cost of close to $40 billion a year. The magnitude of the problem makes it clear that either we find cures for the conditions and diseases that cause dementia, or we will see our nation turned into a huge extended care facility in which the healthy old administer to their aged contemporaries who haven't been so fortunate.

Efforts to identify and study dementia can be traced back to the turn of the twentieth century, when Alois Alzheimer, a psychiatrist at the University of Breslau in Germany, identified the disease that bears his name: Alzheimer's disease, a degenerative, progressive, irreversible illness that gradually erodes all mental functions and is characterized by accelerated neuron loss and other specific changes in the brain that leave it shrunken into a caricature of the normal brain.

About 55–60 percent of all cases of dementia are caused by Alzheimer's disease. Of the other types of dementia, about 20 percent develop as a consequence of disrupted blood flow to the brain (stroke) and subsequent cell death. From 5–15 percent of persons with dementia have a mixture of Alzheimer's and vascular disease. The remaining 10–20 percent of dementia cases have a variety of causes. Some of these dementias are reversible or curable when the underlying cause—such as depression, thyroid disease, vitamin deficiencies, and the side effects of one or multiple medications—is treated. Others are not.

These statistics mean, put in the plainest possible terms, that many of the persons suffering from dementia who are brought to the neurologist for diagnosis have little chance of improving. And in the late stages of this terrible disease, it is the family, not the patient, who will need counseling.

Memory loss is usually the first symptom of Alzheimer's disease. It is progressive, and numerous cognitive dysfunctions, disorientation, depression, mood swings, personality changes, and gradual physical decline also develop, until ultimately its victims become incapable of caring for themselves. The majority of cases—called senile dementia of the Alzheimer's Type, or SDAT—begin in the late sixties and the seventies; presenile dementia, a form whose onset is

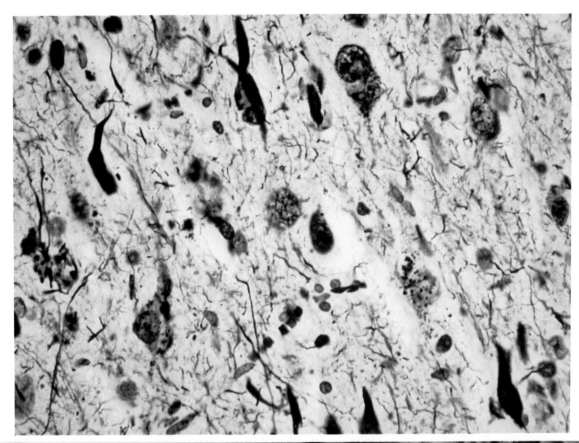

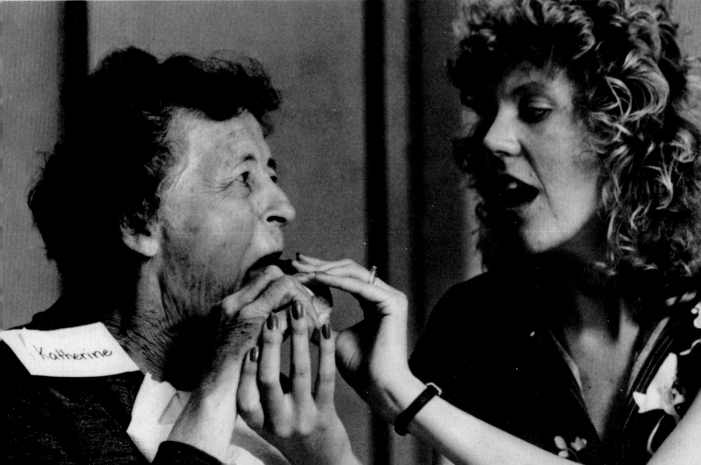

earlier, in the fifties or sixties, runs a more rapid downhill course. Because there are no laboratory tests that can confirm the presence of the disease, Alzheimer's is diagnosed on the basis of a combination of symptoms, the exclusion of other possible causes for these symptoms, and the patient's progression to incapacity. An absolute diagnosis can be made only on autopsy. The brain is atrophied and many neurons are filled with black fibers called *fibrillary tangles*. *Senile plaques,* degenerated networks of axon terminals, are found in the hippocampus, the temporal lobe, and, if the disease has been present long enough, the frontal and parietal lobes as well.

The cause or causes of Alzheimer's disease are still unknown. Most instances of the illness affect a single individual and leave other family members unscathed; one identical twin can have the disease and the other be free of it. But there does seem to be a genetic factor in Alzheimer's and this factor is more difficult to determine than in other diseases because the expression of the gene is often delayed until very old age. The incidence of Alzheimer's increases greatly among eighty- to ninety-year-olds. (A significant number of people ninety years of age or older have some changes in their brains that are also found in Alzheimer's disease.) Since gene expression leading to the disease doesn't occur in these people until the ninth decade, however, most genetically predisposed individuals escape the disease by dying before then. As life expectancy increases, this situation can be expected to change and familial patterns of inheritance to become more apparent.

But key questions still remain unanswered. Are all forms of Alzheimer's disease inherited or only some of them? What factors determine when or under what conditions the gene or genes responsible for the illness "turn on"? This last question is particularly important, since most cases of Alzheimer's disease strike when people are in their seventies. If scientists could learn to retard the expression of the gene by five or ten or more years, the incidence of the disease could be cut in half.

The next step for genetic researchers involves learning as much as possible about the location of the defective gene responsible for Alzheimer's. But as with any severely disabling or fatal heritable disease, genetic research on Alzheimer's disease is both promising and fearsome. While it's true that great benefit can come from knowing the chemistry and genetics of the disease, until it is possible to retard its onset such knowledge is a mixed blessing to the person who is told ahead of time that he or she is destined to develop this dreadful illness at some time in the future.

Peter Davies notes that "Genetic therapies for Alzheimer's are still some distance away. In fact, it's not really clear that would be the appropriate way to go. To correct a gene defect that may never be expressed in the lifetime of the patient would seem silly, a waste of time. Patients with this genetic defect can live sixty and seventy years of perfectly normal life. It would seem much more fruitful for researchers to find out what triggers the expression of that genetic defect."

To do this Davies is currently running a brain bank for the Alzheimer's Disease Association. By studying the brains of Alzheimer's patients, he hopes to understand further how this tragic illness destroys the biologic underpinnings of the mind, the human brain. Much has already been learned.

In addition to genetic studies, neuroscientists are concentrating on the possibility that Alzheimer's may be the result of the havoc produced by a "slow virus." Slow viruses can invade the body twenty years or more before the telltale signs of a disease appear. Although such viruses have not yet been implicated in Alzheimer's disease, they have been found in the brains of individuals suffering from other forms of dementia. Neurologist Carleton Gajdusek, of the National Institutes of Health, won a Nobel Prize for his discovery that a slow virus was the cause of one such illness, the fatal disease kuru, found in New Guinea, which in its terminal stages reduces the sufferer to a helpless dement.

Linked to the virus theory is the possibility that Alzheimer's disease may result from an immune system that has somehow gone awry. It is known that older people, as a result of a weakened immune system, are less able to fight off viral and other infections. Might this be the reason that slow viruses that have established a beachhead within the brain become activated years later in elderly individuals? Although appealing in its simplicity, this theory has remained simply that, a theory.

Neurotransmitter synthesis is another major focus of research because it is known that Alzheimer's patients have 60 to 90 percent less of the enzymes that synthesize acetylcholine, a neurotransmitter that plays an important role in memory. On autopsy, the brains of these patients show a loss of up to 90 percent of the cells of the *nucleus basalis of Meynert,* a tiny area in the forebrain that sends nerve terminals into wide and diverse areas of the cerebral cortex. These are acetylcholine-releasing cells, so the consequence is a deficiency of the neurotransmitter.

Based on these findings and others, neurologists Dr. Donald Price and his colleagues at Johns Hopkins, Drs. Joseph T. Coyle and Mahlon R. DeLong, have suggested as a possible scenario that as the neurons in the nucleus basalis of Meynert begin to fail, their cortical projections swell and form plaques. As a result, the malfunctioning neurons can

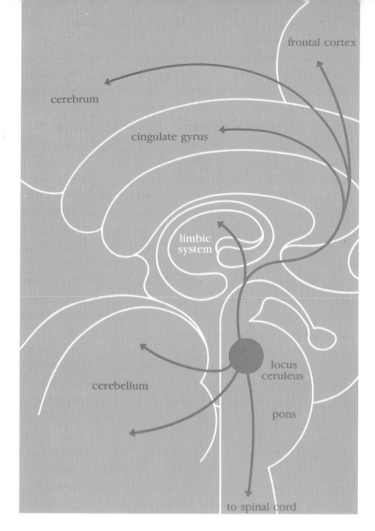

The locus ceruleus area in the brain, associated with sleep, wakefulness, emotion, and memory, shows a marked loss of nerve cells in the elderly.

no longer make sufficient acetylcholine to allow the end terminals in the cortex to function normally.

The discovery of acetylcholine deficiency in Alzheimer's disease made some early enthusiasts propose that all that was necessary was to provide the brain with the missing substance. For a short period in the early 1960s, therefore, soybean extract, choline, and other precursors of acetylcholine were recommended as possible palliatives for the disease. Alas, the conundrum of Alzheimer's did not yield to this simplistic approach. Other chemical substances, too, are contributors to the conversation among neurotransmitters that provides the chemical underpinnings for the human mind.

"There's increasing evidence that other transmitter systems are involved, although not so severely or so consistently as the cholinergic [acetylcholine-producing] system," says Price. "The cholinergic system may be the tip of the iceberg."

To appreciate the difficulties faced by neuroscientists, imagine yourself listening to a symphony in which one or two of the instruments are being played in a time frame that is out of synchrony with the other instruments. Before very long, even an unsophisticated listener could recognize distortions and errors in the symphony. Eventually the underlying themes and subthemes would almost be unrecognizable. Would one be able to correct the situation by pinpointing the original instruments and adjusting time signatures? Perhaps, but only if one was sufficiently familiar with the musical composition being played. In the case of the brain, the difficulty arises from the fact that the underlying "composition" is unknown. As a result, neuroscientists shift the emphasis from one instrument (i.e., neurotransmitter) to another. But even when a particular neurotransmitter seems most important, as with acetylcholine, the exact contributions of the others remain as a confounding variable.

One neuroscientist who has done a lot of thinking about what happens in the Alzheimer's-afflicted brain is Professor Alan Davison, of the National Hospital, Queen Square, London. Davison believes that many of the behavioral changes associated with both normal and unhealthy aging are brought about by alterations in the number of nerve cells in specific brain areas. He has targeted the hippocampus as another site in which there is a loss of acetylcholine-producing cells that may affect memory.

He has been studying another region as well. "We know that a specific group of cells, the locus ceruleus, extends from the brainstem upwards to the outermost frontiers of the cerebral cortex. This area is responsible for controlling mood. With increasing age we may lose as much as 50 percent of our nerve cells in this particular region. And so an explanation of the changes in behavior may be that there's a deficiency in the amount of chemical transmitter—noradrenaline—in this area which affects behavior.

"For example, in the older person there's often a flattening of mood. The older person is impassive. His reactions are slow in comparison to the younger person. Older people are perhaps less bright, less vigilant and attentive. Sleep patterns are altered. We can account for these changes, I believe, based on the loss of cells from the locus ceruleus. As a consequence of this cell loss there is less noradrenaline available elsewhere in the brain," says Davison.

In summary, damage to two comparatively small brain areas—the locus ceruleus and the hippocampus—results in profound disturbances in memory and behavior. This can come about, Davison believes, only because these small areas are important in sustaining cells in other brain areas. "In the normal aging brain perhaps it's the loss of nerve cells in different parts of the cortex or in the brainstem which influences the death of nerve cells in other selective regions." If this is true, a method of treatment suggests itself.

"If in normal aging we lose nerve cells in certain se-

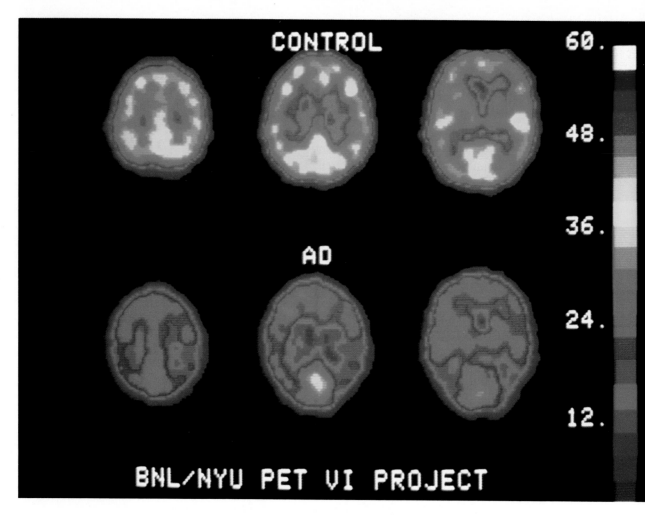

CONTROL 60.

48.

36.

AD 24.

12.

BNL/NYU PET VI PROJECT

PET scan showing glucose utilization in a normal brain (top) *and the brain of an Alzheimer's disease patient of the same age. As the scale at the right indicates, glucose utilization—indicating energy expenditure by the brain—is greatly diminished in the Alzheimer's patient.*

lected areas, the hippocampus and the locus ceruleus, for example, it's really exciting to think that it may be possible to intervene, either to prevent nerve cell loss and thereby prevent damage from occurring or maybe to restore the missing neurotransmitter activity."

Another potential treatment might involve finding ways to increase the branching of existing nerve cells. This would make greater amounts of neurotransmitter available and thereby enhance nerve cell communication. With greater branching there would also be more surface area upon which other nerve cells could establish synaptic connections.

Davison: "I see a great future in the restoration of normal behavior and intellectual functioning in our elderly population. Many scientists have taken up the challenge of investigating the changes that occur in the normal aging brain as well as in the diseased brain. I think in the next decade or so we are going to see new treatments, new approaches to the whole problem. The future, I think, should be bright and promising."

There is another encouraging area of research that involves attempting to save dying nerve cells. This research has recently become practical with the demonstration of the existence of neurotrophic (nerve-nourishing) factors within the brain that in and of themselves help keep brain cells alive. The most important of these neurotrophic factors is nerve growth factor (NGF). In the brain, NGF is manufactured by glial cells adjacent to neurons, and travels along dendrites until it reaches nerve terminals which, in a sense, it "fertilizes" or recharges. This is a process necessary for the survival of neurons. Any interruption of the transport mechanism can lead to the death of the cell.

In order to clarify this relationship between NGF and cell survival, Dr. Fred Gage, of the Department of Neurosciences, University of California, San Diego, purposely damaged acetylcholine-producing cells in the basal forebrain of rats. When this is done, the cells are observed to die off. But if NGF is infused early enough after the damage is inflicted, these cholinergic nerve cells survive. This observation may prove particularly relevant to Alzheimer's disease, since in this illness cholinergic neurons are especially affected. "With further experiments," says Gage, "one can think of a time when NGF could be introduced to early-diagnosed Alzheimer's patients in the hope that you could protect those cholinergic cells from death. The hope is that by protecting these cells from dying and getting them functional again, you can arrest some of the symptoms of the disease and perhaps prolong efficient and successful life for these patients."

Promising though this research direction is, however, several considerations currently limit the application of neurotrophic factors in the treatment of Alzheimer's disease. For one thing, unlike Parkinson's disease, there is not a localized population of damaged cells in Alzheimer's that is responsible for all of the deficits. Secondly, trophic factors cannot pass through the blood–brain barrier. That means that instead of a pill or an intravenous injection, they must be introduced directly into the brain through a cannula lowered into a ventricle or other area of the brain that is damaged. This is a neurosurgical procedure that by its nature entails risks. Finally, no one can be certain at this point that the saved neurons will be functional. Will the cells that are rescued by the intervention of NGF or other trophic substances be capable of establishing functional contacts? "This is the next step in demonstrating the potential clinical application of these approaches," says Gage. "We must show that, in fact, the surviving cells have function in a freely moving animal."

Trophic factor administration is aimed at restoring function to dying nerve cells. Implantation of neural tissue involves a replacement of cells that have already died. Each approach complements the other.

BRAIN GRAFTS

The concept of brain grafts is one of the most fanciful, provocative, and intriguing approaches to degenerative brain diseases—fanciful because it smacks of science fiction, provocative because it appeals to our sense of possibility (it was not so long ago, after all, that a transplanted heart sounded like a plot out of Edgar Allan Poe), and intriguing because in a world full of technical miracles, why should this be out of the question?

The brain is certainly not a Mercedes 300SEL, in which one can open up the hood, troubleshoot what's malfunctioning, and slip in a replacement part that lets it zoom back up the highway. What works for an automobile doesn't hold for brains. Except in rare instances such as Parkinson's disease, a specific "part" of the brain cannot be implicated as the offending agent in brain disorders.

But before dismissing out of hand the possibility of replacing brain parts, consider the following:

- Vision can be restored in surgically blinded frogs by transplanting whole eyeballs. These grafts reestablish new connections with the visual center of the frog, the *tectum*.
- Fetal neurons that secrete specific neurotransmitters can reestablish damaged connections in the brain of a rat. This is how it works: A specific part of the rat's brain

is surgically destroyed. As a result, cells in that region are no longer capable of forming connecting links with other cells, or of transmitting impulses through their neurotransmitter. Cells that secrete this same neurotransmitter are taken from rat fetuses and implanted at or near the site of the surgical damage. Formerly lesion-impaired rats soon begin to act like normal, untampered-with rats.

And indeed, in humans, brain grafting has been tried and has been claimed to work, at least briefly. The disease in question was not Alzheimer's, which is marked by diffuse changes in brain tissue, but by Parkinson's disease, in which, as we have noted, the problem is localized.

The victim of Parkinson's is almost a caricature of old age. The hands tremble, the posture is stooped, the voice is feeble, all movements occur as if through molasses. The disease is caused by a loss of nerve cells in an area of the brainstem called the *substantia nigra,* which results in a deficiency of the neurotransmitter dopamine. Patients are treated with the drug L-dopa, which is converted to dopamine in the brain.

But there is a new and potentially more effective alternative to L-dopa. More than half a dozen laboratories within the United States have been working with animals for the past

The implantation in the brain of both neurons and glial cells is now an established field of investigation, says Gage. "The concept here is to understand something about the cells that have died and attempt to replace them with other cells, and then get these cells to grow back to the right location and to function. At one time this kind of thing was considered science fiction. It's now becoming a reality."

Research into all aspects of Alzheimer's disease and the other dementias of aging has accelerated in recent years, and we have reason to be encouraged by how much more we have learned. "It's incredible to see the progress in this area over the last three or four years," Peter Davies notes. "Our understanding of Alzheimer's disease has gone from minimal to almost having the cause in our grasp. It's a most exciting time to be involved in this research."

several years in an effort to transplant dopamine-secreting cells from one brain to another. In some instances tissue from the substantia nigra of animal fetuses has been used in the transplants, which is chemically the simplest approach since the transplanted tissue matches the tissue in the damaged site of the animal's brain. If and when this approach is used in humans, however, the ethical issue of how fetal substantia nigra is to be obtained will have to be confronted.

Other research groups have elected to use tissue from the medulla of the adrenal glands. Minced adrenal medullary tissue is injected with fine needles so that it lies on top of the *caudate nucleus,* a part of the dopamine system in the brain. This has been tried in humans with limited success. In March 1982, two Parkinson's patients in the Karolinska Hospital in Stockholm were injected with tissue taken from their adrenal glands and deposited in and around the caudate nucleus. "The first patient showed transient and relatively minor signs of improvement during the first couple of weeks after surgery," the researchers reported, "after which his clinical status has remained essentially unchanged." In the second patient, and two others operated on subsequently, there was some benefit, but this "slowly vanished during the first two to three months postoperatively."

By far the most controversial results were reported in April 1987. A group of neuroscientists led by Dr. Ignacio Madrazo Navarro at the La Roza Medical Center in Mexico City removed the right adrenal gland from a thirty-five-year-old man suffering from Parkinson's disease and transplanted the medullary tissue into his brain. They performed the same procedure on another patient, age thirty-nine. The researchers reported that within three months in one case, and ten months in the second, the patients became less rigid in their movements, their tremors decreased, and for the first time in several years, they were able to eat on their own, dress themselves, and even play football.

At this writing, neuroscientists throughout the world are curious but very wary about the results that Madrazo and his team have reported. Among the unanswered questions is why the procedure appears to have worked in Mexico City when other teams in other locations, using the same technique, have failed. Also unknown is the factor of the Mexican patients' ages; they were significantly younger than most Parkinson's sufferers (the disease usually has its onset between the ages of fifty and sixty-five). Results in approximately eighty patients who underwent the procedure in U.S. medical centers in the year following the report of La Roza operations have been discouraging.

Most researchers in the field view the prospects for brain grafts as limited for some time to come. Nothing at this point makes them seem a likely approach in treating the dementias of aging.

Unhappily, though, there has been no real progress so far in treating the irreversible forms of these illnesses. Many approaches have been tried: reduction in stress, decreased use of alcohol, tobacco, and caffeine, nutritional supplementation, antiviral drugs, medications aimed at altering the body's immune responses—but none have met with success. Alzheimer's remains a scourge and an anguish whose burden falls as heavily on the families who must watch their loved one deteriorate as on the victims themselves.

Prevalent and terrible though the dementias of aging are, the great majority of older people do not suffer from these diseases. Nonetheless, we all recognize that there are vast differences in cognitive and emotional function among them. These differences are found even though in normal aging, all of us undergo the same kinds of changes in the brain that have been described earlier in this chapter. In the absence of disease, what other factors may cause some minds to flag while others flourish with age?

Neuroscientists have long suspected that stress plays a major role in the aging process. But formidable difficulties lie in the way of incorporating this hunch into a workable theory. All of us are exposed to stress; no one is free from it. Yet not everyone ages at the same rate or with equal grace. If stress is important, why does it seem to affect only some of us adversely?

To investigate this intriguing question, Dr. Robert Sapolsky, of the Department of Biological Sciences, Stanford University, concentrates on the stress-related hormones, the *glucocorticoids*.

"Glucocorticoid secretion by the adrenal glands during stress is absolutely critical for everything your body has to do to get out of a stressful emergency. But just as critically important, it's becoming clear that too much glucocorticoid in response to too much stress can get you sick," Sapolsky says.

Imagine a gazelle running across the savanna in an attempt to escape from a predator. The animal's glucocorticoids raise its blood pressure and give it that extra bounce to the ounce that may make the difference between escape and sudden death. But those same glucocorticoids can also produce a chronically elevated blood pressure in a constantly harassed executive. In this instance the end result isn't helpful but pernicious.

Further, Sapolsky has discovered that chronic exposure to glucocorticoids kills brain cells. "In the aging person, the death rate of neurons in the hippocampus increases. Under conditions of stress, exposure to high levels of glucocorticoids can accelerate the rate at which these neurons die during aging."

Sapolsky found that if neurons from a rat's hippocampus are put in a laboratory dish and exposed to glucocorticoids, the cells no longer store energy at an efficient rate. "And when you have a neuron that's run out of energy, it's very vulnerable to anything that comes along at that point that challenges it. And the net effect during aging is a lot more neuron damage."

But stress in a gazelle or a rat and stress in a human obviously differ. For most of us, stress comes from societal pressures rather than running for our lives to escape a predator. Given these differences, some critics have claimed that demonstrating glucocorticoid-induced damage and death in rat neurons is irrelevant to understanding the relationship between stress and aging in humans.

To resolve this reasonable objection, Sapolsky turned

his attention to creatures much closer to human beings, a population of baboons living freely at the National Park in the Serengeti in East Africa.

"If you're a baboon, living in the Serengeti is about as great a place as you could hope to wind up in. The food is terrific, they don't have a lot of problems with predators, the infant mortality rate is low. They have, in effect, an affluent society that gives them the free time to generate social stress for themselves. Much like ourselves, their lives revolve around social stress."

Over the past eight years Sapolsky and a Kenyan assistant, Richard Kones, have been studying these baboons, concentrating on the structure of their society, the stresses this structure induces, and how they respond to stress.

Once a year Sapolsky and Kones capture each of the animals and run a series of chemical tests on them. "We do the same sorts of tests that you might do on any patient in a hospital: standard clinical tests as to how the adrenals are functioning, what the level of cholesterol is, and so forth. Essentially, we're asking the question, Does your social rank, or the quality of your life, or the number of stresses that you're exposed to, have something to do—at least in this baboon society—with how well your body works? Ultimately we're trying to discover if these things have anything to do with successful or unsuccessful aging."

The chemical findings are then correlated with the kinds of questions that are important in understanding any socially generated stress. "What is the quality of their lives? What stresses do they have? What grudges are they in the middle of? What coalitions are they in the middle of? What unrequited affairs are they having? However you want to put it in human terms."

Sapolsky has found that "consistently there are tremendous differences in the physiology of these animals, depending on their social rank. In bodily system after bodily system, it's the highest ranking animals that have the more efficient stress responses."

The tests have shown that the animals that rank *lower* on the social scale are under chronic stress and that this stress leads to the overproduction of glucocorticoid hormones. This affects their blood pressure, cholesterol levels, and the effectiveness of their immune systems in fighting disease. Thus far, Sapolsky has not demonstrated a direct effect of glucocorticoids on the primate brain, but he suspects this effect exists, and in human brains as well.

"Suppose it does turn out that stress by way of glucocorticoids can damage neurons in the human brain. What can we do about it? There are at least two things. First, scientists like myself can try to figure out how you can repair a damaged neuron. But even more important are the

Richard Kones with one of the baboons in the Serengeti.

TWIN STUDIES AND AGING

Investigations into the process of aging that seek to differentiate between genetic and environmental influences have always been difficult. Studies of twins would seem to be an ideal mode, but identical twins, who by definition have the same genes, usually share the same environment. Then an extraordinary opportunity presented itself. A collaborative project was undertaken by the University of Colorado and the Karolinska Institute in Stockholm to identify the genetic and environmental influences in people's response to medication. Professor Jerald McClearn, now of Pennsylvania State University and then at Colorado, and an associate noticed that among the subjects in the study were more than seven hundred pairs of identical twins who had been reared apart. "This discovery," McClearn says, "was like stumbling on a bonanza because it offered an opportunity to identify the separate contributions of genetics and the environment on the aging process." The study was further enriched by the inclusion of twins who had been reared together.

McClearn and his collaborators see "environment" as extremely inclusive, ranging from factors we can never know, such as subtle gradients in the distribution of chemicals in the cytoplasm of the egg and the sites of implantation of each twin egg, to those that are more easily identified: the rearing styles of the parents, the food eaten, childhood experiences, playmates, the home, the school, religion.

The bulk of this study still lies ahead, but its promise is great. There are already some fascinating findings. For one, the notion that genetic influences operate only early in our lives isn't turning out to be true. Genetic influences with respect to temperament, personality, and health variables are found in the elderly individual, and are equal in magnitude to those found in younger people.

As McClearn notes, "In recent years, exciting advances in molecular genetics have made it clear that genes can turn on or off throughout our lives, so that we're genetically different beings when we're older than when we're younger. Further, the genes that are involved when we are younger may not be the same ones that are active later in our lives. We're talking about a kind of two-part harmony composed of genetic and environmental determinants that goes on all our lives."

Dr. Nancy Pedersen, McClearn's colleague at the Karolinska Institute, says, "Research can give us a better understanding of all the variations in aging that are seen in different people. Since we're studying twins reared apart and twins reared together, we'll have the opportunity to separate the environmental from the genetic factors."

McClearn and Pedersen expected from the beginning that both genes and the environment would exert an influence on aging. On the genetic side, the hope is that ultimately "we'll be in a position to identify genes and enzymes and other proteins that are produced by the genes. This may make possible rational interventions that can minimize or reduce some of the consequences of aging."

Such interventions might involve medication in some instances, and in others a more challenging environment. Still further in the future, specific genetic or hormonal treatments may help to retard certain aspects of aging. Although aging will always be inevitable, we may in the future be able to control some of its more tragic aspects through modification of genes or the environment. McClearn says, "We expect to find that some of the processes of aging are under greater genetic control than others. We do not expect to find any that are fully under genetic control. That means that every individual has the prospect of increasing his or her possibilities of aging better."

things that can be done to avoid ending up with a damaged neuron in the first place."

What are the factors in psychological stress that Sapolsky found most important? Loss of control, loss of the ability to predict events—these are crucial in inducing and sustaining prolonged stress and, Sapolsky believes, an unhealthy aging process in the brain and other body systems. But there's a hopeful aspect to this, too. "We have a tremendous power to affect whether or not these disease states come about in the first place. How we live our lives, how we perceive the events that happen to us, are very important. If you can't control events—and how many of us can control all the stressful events that occur in our lives?—then it's very important to work on changing your perception of the events."

Sapolsky's research leads not to a fatalistic acceptance or resignation but to the kind of good advice that wise men and women have suggested for centuries:

"It's ironic that after all of this laboratory work, all the biochemistry coupled with all the work with something as unlikely as a troop of baboons, that the take-home message is something that our grandmothers told us. We should be happy, we should relax, we should take things in stride. Maybe that's basically the final lesson."

His findings also suggest that reactions to stress may be one factor in the wide variability found among the elderly. Those who utilize the coping experience of a long life to adapt positively to tension and change are likelier to maintain their vigor than those who let the stress of these factors overwhelm them.

There are other factors less obviously unfavorable than stress that also play a part in healthy or accelerated aging of the mind. One way to identify them is to concentrate on differences in mental function between the old and the young, and on the implications these differences may have for healthy aging.

Imagine a child and an older person standing on the sidewalk just as the first float appears at the Macy's Thanksgiving Day Parade. Which of the two would you expect to be most enthusiastic and thrilled at the sights and sounds? Which of the two might behave as if nothing all that wonderful were going on? Although there are, of course, exceptions, the child is more likely than the older person to become animated, talk excitedly, jump on and off the curb to get a preview of what's coming a block or two away.

Dr. Robert Kastenbaum, former Director of the Adult Development and Aging Program at Arizona State University, suggests that "aging" may involve the ascendancy of the attitude that "I've seen most of this before; there's not much I now have to notice or respond to." Kastenbaum

(Opposite) *For all these men and women, old age was vigorous and productive.* From the left, in each row:
Konrad Adenauer (1876–1967).
George Bernard Shaw (1856–1950).
Robert Frost (1874–1963).
Pablo Picasso (1881–1973).
Clara Barton (1821–1912).
Henri Matisse (1869–1954).
Golda Meir (1898–1978).
George Burns (1896–   ).
Louise Nevelson (1900–1988).

suggests that aging begins "when normal events and situations are treated as though they are repetitions of the familiar." *Habituation* is the technical term for this process. "We tend to think of a person as 'old' when this person has relatively little exchange with the environment," says Kastenbaum.

"Environment" involves not just objects and events (the Thanksgiving Day Parade) but work and activities aimed at maintaining, perhaps even expanding, occupational skills. Older people who remain active in some aspect of their work find a continuing sense of purpose, and are motivated to depend upon themselves and their own resources. The environment should also include vigorous involvement with family and friends; an active rather than a passive life-style (walking or exercise routines, a weekly bridge game rather than mindless hours staring at television), and flexible attitudes. These are key factors in maintaining mental sharpness. Put another way, "Use it or lose it." That's the bottom line of a twenty-eight-year study of four thousand people on Puget Sound in the state of Washington carried out by Professor K. Warner Schaie, of Pennsylvania State University.

Schaie found social involvement played a major part in maintaining mental vigor. Elderly people who live with their families or maintain an active social life outperformed their contemporaries who lived alone. The greatest decline was among widowed housewives who had never had a career of their own and led restrictive, often reclusive lives. "After a while the pressure isn't on you any more to engage in mental exercises. It's very much like physical skills: once you stop using them, they get rusty."

Schaie believes that mental exercises, like physical exercises, can help older people sustain and in some instances even improve their mental capabilities. Through the use of specially designed exercises, Schaie and psychologist Sherry Willis, also of Pennsylvania State University, brought about improvement in about half of their volunteer subjects in such areas as spatial orientation and numerical and verbal skills. Memory, too, can be improved if an older person uses a mnemonic system—a device to aid recall.

It is true that certain other mental performances improve only slightly, if at all, with training. We have noted that reaction time, for instance, declines steadily as a person moves through middle age. But raw speed of response is in itself rarely that important in most ordinary activities. Besides, alternative strategies are often available. In one study, for instance, older typists, although exhibiting slower reactions, typed just as fast as younger ones. They did it by scanning farther ahead, a neat demonstration of the power of experience over speed.

In addition, the tests and laboratory settings and stop-

Cognitive testing of an elderly man. Appropriately chosen tests can be useful in differentiating normal changes from those caused by organic brain disease such as Alzheimer's.

watches that so fascinate the psychologist and his Ph.D.-seeking graduate students are often of little interest to the elderly person, who may perform poorly on formal testing because of simple boredom. It can seem idiotic to be asked to place a white disc in the red hole if you are a septuagenarian who has seen ten presidents come and go and lived a full and complex life.

Gerontologist Marian Perlmutter notes that "the relevance of laboratory learning and memory performance to everyday learning and memory situations remains unclear." Under everyday conditions, learning and memory depend on one's previous experience. New knowledge is acquired and retained with the help of old knowledge. One learns the alphabet, then acquires the knack of reading, and only later tackles Plato. But too often, laboratory tests measure performances such as basic learning and memory processes that are not correlated with what is already known. "To the degree that performance depends upon basic learning and memory processes, younger adults will be favored over older adults; to the degree that performance depends upon acquired knowledge, older adults will be favored over younger adults," Perlmutter has found.

She and others believe that traditional measures of intelligence ignore important components in the assessment of how intelligent an aged person may actually be. "How appropriate is it to measure the 'scholastic aptitude' of a seventy-year-old?" Perlmutter and psychologists such as Dr. Robert Sternberg, at Yale University, believe that laboratory and clinic-based tests underestimate how effectively—"intelligently," in a functional sense—the older person performs in the real world.

"Indeed, to the extent that intelligence comprises somewhat different skills for different people, there's no one wholly appropriate test for it," according to Sternberg. "If we had more comprehensive tests of intelligence, I suspect that older people would score at least as well and probably better than younger people," says Perlmutter.

"Many of the tests used to assess the cognitive abilities of the elderly are biased in favor of younger people," says Dr. Leonard Poon, a psychologist at Harvard. "One test involves remembering pairs of nonsense words. . . . Older people just don't care about nonsense words. What looks like a diminished ability in the elderly may partly be lack of interest."

It may also be due to depression. Within any group of elderly people initially diagnosed as suffering from dementia, up to one third may actually be depressed. Outwardly the initial manifestations of the two conditions are strikingly similar. Poor memory, a slowed reaction time, difficulty in communication, sleep and appetite irregularities, characterize both depressed and demented people. But depression is often reversible. Older people may have good reason to be depressed; loneliness, frailty, the fear of illness and dependency, the side effects of medications they are taking—these and other factors can all contribute to depression, and if recognized, usually be remedied.

Psychologists who limit testing of the elderly to laboratory situations alone can almost be guaranteed to overlook an older person's primary asset: the wisdom that accompanies normal aging. Indeed, rather than a liability, the older person's poor performance on laboratory tests may be just one aspect of this "wisdom of the aged."

Dr. Paul Baltes, of the Max Planck Institute in Berlin, has a different perspective on assessing the abilities of the elderly. He measures their wisdom in a series of carefully structured interviews.

"Wisdom for me is a state of knowledge about the human condition, about how it comes about, which factors shape it, how one deals with difficult problems, and how one organizes one's life in such a manner that when we are old, we judge it to be meaningful," says Baltes.

Baltes tests wisdom by having his subjects consider how

STROKE

Aging and dementia are both accompanied by the loss of nerve cells. Both evolve over a period of years. Not so the nerve cell devastation that occurs with strokes. Within minutes after a stroke, a fit fifty- or sixty-year-old can be robbed forever of the ability to speak or walk. Four hundred thousand Americans are victims of stroke every year. Approximately two million people in this country are impaired by the consequences of stroke. The incidence of stroke has declined in recent years because of improvements in the treatment of high blood pressure (hypertension), which, together with hardening of the arteries (arteriosclerosis), is the chief cause of stroke, but it remains the leading cause of adult disability and the nation's third biggest killer after heart disease and cancer.

Stroke, or *cerebrovascular accident (CVA),* the term preferred by most physicians, is an interruption or marked reduction of blood flow to the brain. A stroke can be caused by the blockage of a blood vessel by a clot (an occlusive stroke) or by the rupture of a weakened blood vessel (a hemorrhagic stroke). If the blockage is temporary and largely reversible, it is called *ischemia.* Ischemia severe enough to produce tissue damage is called an *infarction.*

The brain is very susceptible to disturbances in its blood supply. Fainting is the most harmless and reversible example of what happens when there is a temporary decrease in the flow of blood to the brain. With stroke, the decrease may be permanent; nerve cells in the area formerly supplied by the affected blood vessel die off, and the functions served by those damaged areas cease or are severely impaired. The degree of impairment depends on the site and extent of the damage. There can be total recovery, or effects that range from minor handicaps to widespread paralysis. A significant number of strokes are fatal.

Neurologists diagnose the area of brain damage by skilled interpretation of the symptoms (the patient's complaints, provided he or she can still speak) and signs (the physician's observations that, for example, the patient can no longer move his or her right arm). Because many strokes occur without warning, and because even control of known risk factors (hypertension, diabetes, smoking) is not an assurance a stroke will not occur, neuroscientists are concentrating on (a) ways of determining how much damage has been done and whether treatment will be beneficial, and (b) how the pattern of blocked blood supply/ischemia/infarction/nerve cell death can be reversed or prevented.

The brain requires a certain amount of oxygen per gram of tissue per minute or irreversible damage occurs. By measuring oxygen metabolism in brain areas affected by stroke

they might go about solving a specific life problem such as the following: "Michael, a mechanic aged twenty-eight years with two preschool-aged children, just learned that the factory in which he's working will close in three months. There is no possibility for further employment in this area. His wife has recently returned to her well-paid nursing career. Michael is considering the following options: He can plan to move to another city to seek employment, or he can plan to take full responsibility for child care and household tasks. What should Michael do and consider in making these plans?"

In order to solve a problem such as this, the older person must be able to put himself into the situation, explore the possibilities, foresee the consequences, and sug-

and comparing these findings with such measurements in healthy brain areas, it is possible to make an educated guess as to whether a damaged area can recover once blood flow is restored. PET scans (short for positron emission tomography) are used to make such determinations, but these procedures are expensive and infrequently done, generally only in major medical centers and research facilities. "But if PET becomes crucial for making clinical decisions in stroke, additional instruments will be built. Nothing else can supply the same sort of physiologic information," says Dr. William J. Powers, Associate Professor of Neurology and Radiology at Washington University in St. Louis.

Another approach in the treatment of stroke, pioneered by Professor Brian Meldrum, of the Institute of Psychiatry in London, involves the administration of compounds that counteract the effects of injurious chemicals that are released by a stroke. Neurons that are temporarily deprived of their blood supply release excitatory amino acid transmitters in large quantities, and when the blood supply is restored, these substances induce bursts of activity in the cells. These bursts of activity cause calcium to accumulate in the cells and kill them. Meldrum and his colleagues are working to develop compounds that will stop this process by neutralizing the excitatory amino acids, thereby quieting the neurons and inhibiting the accumulation of excessive calcium. Their research suggests that if the amino acid antagonists can be given early after a stroke, damage can be minimized and the patient granted a reasonable chance for restoration to a normal life.

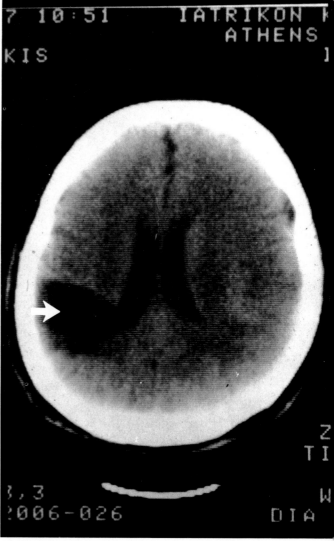

CAT scan showing a stroke (infarction) in the parietal lobe of the brain.

gest a resolution. Here's the response of a man who rates high on the wisdom scale:

"First of all, Michael should consider what his life is all about. What are his aims? And how is his life related to his job on the one hand, and to his family on the other? If he has in mind starting a career and he hopes to bring his family later to the place he's moving to, that's one choice. The other choice would be to stick to his family, to take over the role of the houseman, and so give his wife a chance. However, I wonder if his intention to do this would hold if he really had to do houseman's work week after week. Further, in case he did move, would his marriage hold up? I would also ask you for data about the wife, the kids, the social environment in which he is living now. What is his wife's thinking? How will the children react if he goes off to another city?"

Not everyone tested by Baltes performs with this much circumspection. But most older people, in contrast to many people decades younger, demonstrate at least some degree of wisdom.

Among the criteria for assessing wisdom are an appreciation of context and the ability to take a long overview rather than a narrow "here and now" approach. The wise older person also asks what might happen in the future. Perhaps he or she, in relying on experience, perspective, and a sense of proportion, is enjoying what Schaie calls the privilege of "selectively ignoring a good many things."

The question of whether or not aging is necessarily accompanied by mental decline involves far more than an academic quibble. If mental agility can be maintained into the seventh or eighth decade, then mandatory retirement at a certain age is unjust and unfair.

Contrary to popular belief, older workers can be just as productive as their younger counterparts. Drs. David A. Waldman and Bruce J. Avolio, psychologists at the State University of New York at Binghamton, analyzed forty-three years of research on the relationship between age and job performance. "The older worker who may appear to be dull as compared with a younger, more enthusiastic worker may have become so due to years of accumulated boredom. Offering older workers renewed stimulation at key points in their careers may help to maintain high levels of productivity," Waldman and Avolio assert.

Further, if experience and enriched environments result in less neuron loss and the growth of new synapses in the brain in experiments with aging animals (as noted in Greenough's research, pages 76–79), is it not reasonable to assume that enriched and fulfilling environments *might* have the same effect on humans? Obviously that question can't be answered experimentally. We cannot pair human beings into groups, one of which is allowed friends and provided with stimulation, and the other doomed to isolation and inactivity, so that at a later point we can cut into their brains, count cells, and quantify neurotransmitters. Brain–behavior correlations in humans can only be *inferred*.

But such inferences are possible, based on measures of how older people respond to different living conditions. Dr. Ellen Langer, at Harvard University, attempted to assess what happens when older people are given responsibility and choice. Ninety-one patients in a retirement home, all of them up and about and ranging in age from sixty-five to ninety, were funneled into one of two groups.

One group of patients was told in essence, "It's your life and you make of it whatever you want." Members were urged to try to change things they didn't like and pretty much make up their own minds on various matters. ("We're showing a movie two nights next week. You decide which night you would like to go or if you want to go at all.") On another floor, the second group was told things like, "We feel it's *our* responsibility to make this a home that you can be proud of and will make you happy. If you have any problems or suggestions let us know what they are." In mentioning the movie, they were told, "We're showing a movie next week. We'll let you know later which night you're scheduled to see it."

Langer discovered that, simple though this may sound, the group urged to assume responsibility for themselves became more alert and more active, were happier and healthier, participated in more activities, even lived longer. In general, Langer found that people did better in a reasonably demanding environment that encouraged them to make good use of their cognitive abilities. Another study, this one in a nursing home, found that even meeting for an hour or so a week to do nothing more than to reminisce about themselves and their families increased health and happiness, and even improved memory in about 40 percent of the participants.

Outside nursing homes the facts are the same: enriched environments motivate, postpone impairments, enhance health, give pleasure. And if that doesn't move you, maybe this will: The State of California Health Service estimates that the state saves $3 million a year in reduced nursing home costs thanks to thirty-four adult day health programs in that state. The elderly don't want our charity, our pity, our money. When the aging brain is stimulated, a measure of self-respect, peace, even joy, can be restored. Everybody gains, not only the old. The future for all of us, it turns out, need not be as bleak as we have feared. "Careful input into the nervous system is an antidote of sorts for senility," says neurologist Charles Wells.

Isolation, boredom, lack of intellectual challenge—these are the path to mental deterioration. Good friends, keen interests, mental vigor, continued curiosity, refusal to become "habituated" to the wonders both of the world outside and the world within one's own mind—that's the prescription, assuming reasonably good health, for continued productivity and creativity. This requires flexibility and adaptability. One's life changes as one grows old. Children disperse; the decades of work and structured routines wind down or come to an end; deaths—of spouse, relatives, friends—become more common. There may need to be a

move to a new home shaped to these changed circumstances, and the need as well to find useful activities and fresh purpose. The way in which the older person meets these changes determines the quality of his or her life. If new choices and fresh demands are seen as challenges, not defeats, the possibility for growth and opportunity continues in old age.

But certainly aging has a social dimension as well. Loneliness, fear, isolation, sensory declines like hearing loss, and financial problems all contribute to conditions such as poor nutrition, apathy, the ignoring of reversible medical problems, and the depression that is so prevalent among the elderly. Sound mental health and function can be hard to sustain when friends and spouse have died and one is balancing a meager pension or Social Security payments against unremitting bills and an uncertain future. Fear of losing one's independence is the surest road to deterioration, mental and physical.

As a corollary, the ability to sustain that independence is the best impetus there is to "using it instead of losing it." Since every one of us is growing older and may some day experience what it's like to be seventy or eighty, self-interest as well as neighborly concern should motivate us to care and care deeply about the condition of the elderly among us. Neuroscience can point the way toward what must be done to improve the physical lot of the aging brain and mind. But only social action, individual and collective, can enrich the lives of the elderly. Only then will our later years become a period all of us can accept, even enjoy, rather than a time we must fear.

Hulda Crooks, age 91, beams at the summit of Mount Fuji. She is the oldest woman to have climbed to the top, thereby besting the previous record holder, who was 90.

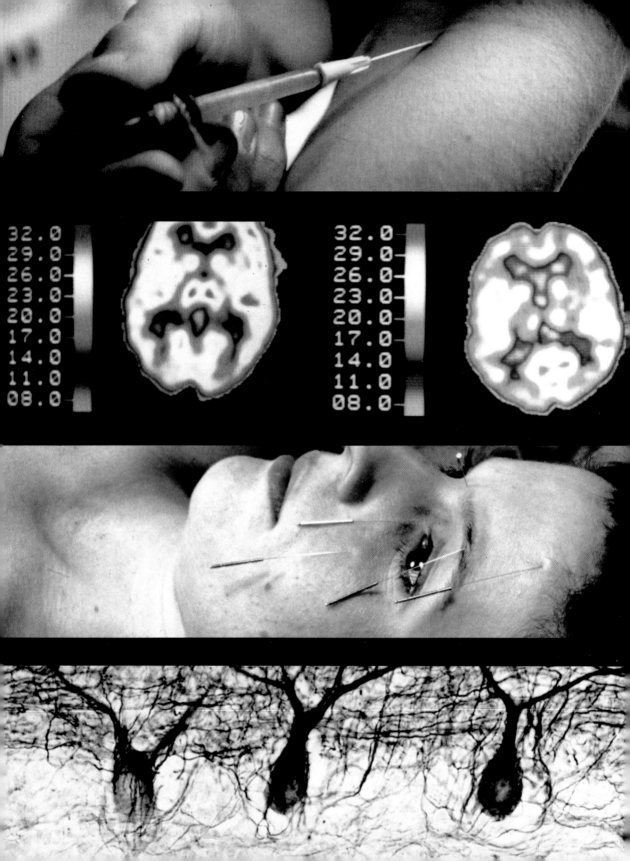

4.
ADDICTION

Throughout history human beings have been conducting an uncontrolled experiment on the mind. They have used, and often abused, substances capable of acting on the brain to produce pleasure so overwhelming that the mind is wholly concentrated on attaining this pleasure. It becomes the motivating force in their lives—more important than food, companionship, sex, safety, even life itself.

This drug taking is found worldwide. It exists in every culture. The drugs may be alcohol, which can be distilled from a wide variety of substances; cocaine, whose source is the coca leaf; marijuana, hashish, and related substances derived from cannabis, a hemp plant; and the opiates, from the poppy, which have morphine-like properties, and include opium, morphine, and heroin. Today, in addition to these naturally occurring substances, there are a wide variety of synthetic drugs—among them prescription sedatives, barbiturates, amphetamines, and mood-altering medications such as tranquilizers—whose potential for abuse is also often exploited.

When we talk about the potential for abuse, we mean that a substance has the capacity to induce dependence in those who use it, whatever their need may be: the intense pleasure these substances arouse, or the blocking out of a reality the user finds frightening, disturbing, or in some other way unendurable. Some authorities make a distinction between psychological and physical dependence. Psychological dependence is a form of obsessive behavior whose objective is the attainment of pleasure or the avoidance of unpleasantness. Compulsive practices like overeating, gambling, and promiscuity are forms of psychological dependence. So is the repeated taking of pills that enable the user to evade distressful events or realities. We hear often that we are a drug-dependent society, relying on these substances to help us sleep, pep us up, control our appetite, calm our nerves, ease our headaches, soothe our stomachs, enable us to relax, rather than addressing the ways in which we live our lives that generate insomnia, lassitude, tension, and stress. The staggering figures of pill consumption confirm that there is justice to this charge. Curbing psychological dependence is complex because it can be extremely difficult to alter ingrained behaviors.

Physical dependence, which technically is termed addiction, occurs when the brain itself becomes biochemically changed because of the continuing consumption of a drug. Tolerance develops, causing the user to need increasing amounts of the drug for it to have its customary effect. Because of these biochemical changes in brain function, an abrupt stopping of the drug causes acute physical and mental symptoms, the withdrawal syndrome.

But whether or not there are changes in the brain, dependence so persistent and consuming that individuals organize their lives so as to sustain the behavior can properly be called addiction. Dr. Richard Miller, the director of a drug treatment program near Sacramento, California, says, "Of all the drugs and the compulsive behaviors that I have seen in the past twenty-five years, be it cocaine, heroin, alcohol, nicotine, gambling, sexual addiction, food addiction, all have one common thread. That is the covering up, or the masking, or the unwillingness on the part of the human being to confront and be with his or her human feelings."

Addictions: alcohol and heroin.

Addiction to drugs is the most visible and shattering of all forms because it threatens the fabric of society itself. All too often, the risks—whether the anguish of the withdrawal syndrome or a drug's harmful or even potentially fatal consequences—do not matter to the addict. The drive to secure the drug is overwhelming. Abuse of addicting drugs has become epidemic in recent years, at appalling cost not only to the individuals whose lives (and the lives of those close to them) have been shattered by drugs, but to the civility and very structure of the social order.

How can the need for a drug become so urgent that the user forsakes health, companionship, even life itself? A partial answer to this question is emerging from research on the brain, and the discovery, unknown until the 1950s, of the relationship between pleasure and pain and the brain.

There were two important findings during these years. The first came out of the work of Dr. Robert C. Heath, a neurologist and psychiatrist at Tulane University School of Medicine in New Orleans, who thought it might be possible to help deeply disturbed mental patients—most of them schizophrenics—by electrically "altering circuits" within their brains. Heath implanted electrodes within the brains of several patients in order to test a theory that schizophrenics suffer from an impairment in hedonic experience—a technical term for the sensation of pleasure.

In pursuing this, Heath was influenced by observations he had made in experiments on cats. He had discovered that if a portion of the brain known as the *septal area* was destroyed, the animal often became inactive and lay immobile in whatever position the experimenter placed it. In humans, this tendency is known as "waxy flexibility," and it is seen principally in schizophrenics. Other experiments involving septal destruction had resulted in a decrease in the cat's response to stress, and this too had its parallel in schizophrenics, in whom biochemical evidence showed a diminished stress response.

Implicit in Heath's experiments was the assumption that the septal region was responsible for emotional expression. In schizophrenics, for some unknown reason, this region was under active suppression by the cortex. This was thought to be the cause of their characteristic withdrawal from reality and sleeplike state of reverie. Therefore, the treatment seemed obvious: electrically stimulate the septal area and produce an excitation that might activate the cortex and prove beneficial to the patient.

Pleasure did not enter into Heath's conjectures at this point; he was directing his efforts toward overcoming the patient's passivity and restoring and improving emotional experience. But over the course of the next several years, patients with implanted electrodes reported that the brain stimulation aroused pleasurable sensations. This finding re-directed Heath's focus; he concentrated thereafter on learning as much as possible about the brain's role in pleasure. His 1964 book on the subject of brain stimulation was called *The Role of Pleasure in Behavior*.

As Heath gathered additional experience with septal stimulation, his initial enthusiasm for the technique began to wane. It was true that some of the patients showed an improvement in mood that, on occasion, lasted several days after stimulation ceased, but others didn't improve much at all. In addition, attitudes toward experiments such as these changed. Both laypeople and scientists grew uneasy about patients with electrodes implanted in their brains; they aroused visions of a society in which behavior is manipulated by electrical stimulation rather than evoked through discussion and reason. Mounting criticism of the technique, fears of behavior control, and the growing dominance of talk-oriented therapies in the treatment of mental illness all led to the abandonment of the septal stimulation experiments.

But the research was not a failure by any means. Robert Heath had made a major discovery about the human brain: stimulation in certain areas can lead to changes in mental alertness and, even more important, to arousal of the sense of pleasure that can persist beyond the application of the electrical stimulus. The brain, in other words, had pleasure "circuits" or "centers."

But pleasure is only one half of an emotional equation. The other half is pain. Discovery of these pleasure circuits raised an important question: Are there also areas in the brain associated with pain and the feelings that accompany it?

In the early 1950s, Dr. Jose Delgado of Yale University noticed that after cats were stimulated in subcortical brain areas, they would go out of their way—indeed, scratch and claw—to avoid further stimulation. They also turned fearful at the prospect of being placed back in the same chamber where the stimulation had taken place. Their behavior suggested that they were undergoing an extremely unpleasant emotional experience.

It also suggested that the commonly held belief that animals are capable of responding only to direct stimuli might be wrong; the cats were reacting intensely to the *prospect* of returning to the chamber. It seemed as if the cats had "learned" from their experience and fought not to repeat it.

This finding indicated that it might be useful to investigate the brain mechanisms involved in this learning, and it was this goal that brought about the second important discovery.

At McGill University and the Montreal Neurological

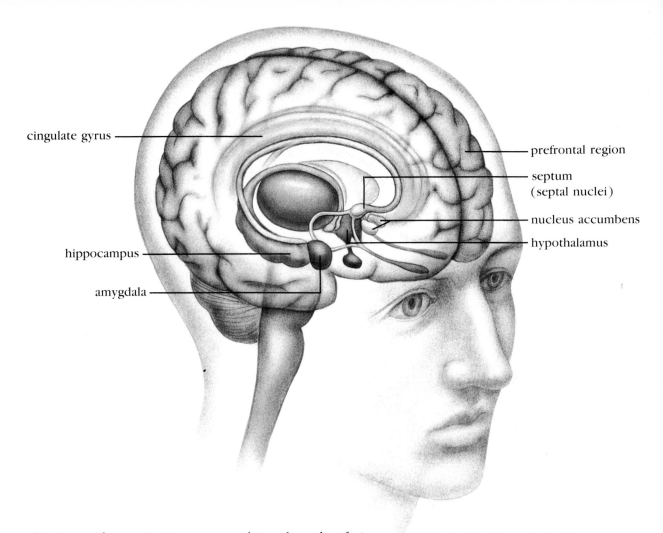

cingulate gyrus

prefrontal region

septum
(septal nuclei)

nucleus accumbens

hypothalamus

hippocampus

amygdala

Addiction is primarily associated with the limbic system of the brain.

Institute, where scientists were studying the role of the brain in learning, Dr. James Olds wondered whether electrical stimulation of the reticular formation, a diffuse and convoluted network extending from the brain stem up to the cerebral cortex, might enhance learning. With the help of a graduate student, Peter Milner, Olds threaded an electrode into what they thought was the reticular formation of a rat. But as luck would have it—chiefly because of faulty surgical technique—the electrode wound up not in the reticular formation but a considerable distance away, in the hypothalamus. (It is believed now that the electrode was accidentally bent during its insertion.) When the current was applied, the rat, instead of shying away from the stimulus as expected, sought it over and over again. Rather than reacting in a manner appropriate to an "adverse stimulus," the animal, in Olds's words, "seemed indubitably to be coming back for more."

The experiment was repeated with other rats and with a change in design. The rat itself was given the opportunity to determine the frequency of this rewarding stimulation. It was placed in a small box with a large lever. Each time the animal pressed on the lever, a brief electrical pulse was applied to its brain. Soon it began pressing the bar repeatedly. In some instances the self-stimulation reached one hundred bar pressings per minute—a frenetic rate that the rat maintained for hours. The strength of this reward was remarkable. It differed from rewarding stimulation for food and water in that there was no satiation. The rats would keep pressing to exhaustion. Olds had discovered that animals could be powerfully motivated to stimulate their own brains for what appeared to be an intensely pleasurable reward.

Additional investigation revealed that the self-stimulation response was not limited to rats. Goldfish, rabbits, cats, guinea pigs, monkeys, dolphins, dogs—and humans, too, —will self-stimulate for a pleasurable reward. Brain researcher Elliot Valenstein, of the University of Michigan, recalls that "animals that had not received any brain stimulation for several days have been known to jump from the experimenter's hands into the test chamber, where they would immediately make the responses that had previously been rewarded by brain stimulation."

When brain stimulation experiments were extended to human subjects, a new dimension was added. A dog and a human volunteer may both shy away from an adverse stimulus or actively seek to repeat a rewarding one, but only the human can convey the subjective sensation. When human participants described their reactions, it became clear that stimulation influenced their moods. In some areas of the brain, it generated elation and feelings of immense well-being similar to the description of drug experiences addicts give. At other sites, it produced variations on the theme of pain that perhaps are unique to humans: feelings of anxiety, foreboding, isolation, and abandonment. Could it be that mood, and a sense of well-being, are the result of a balance between the pain and pleasure centers within the brain?

The discovery of these centers confirmed what hedonic theories of human behavior (people seek what is pleasurable and avoid what is painful) have held over the centuries. "Nature cries aloud for nothing else but that pain may be kept far sundered from the body, and that, withdrawn from care and fear, he may enjoy in mind the sense of pleasure," wrote the poet Lucretius. Closer to our own time, Sigmund Freud held that "Our entire psychical activity is bent upon procuring pleasure and avoiding pain." But Freud never maintained that *immediate* gratification of the pleasure instinct was inevitable. "The ego learns that it must inevitably go without immediate satisfaction, postpone gratification, learn to endure a degree of pain, and all together renounce certain sources of pleasure. Thus trained, the ego becomes 'reasonable,' is no longer controlled by the pleasure principle but follows the reality principle."

This is indeed what most of us do much or most of the time, though this does not alter the underlying reality that in doing so, we are motivated by the desire for pleasure and the avoidance of pain. Even when we endure "pain" in the present (finishing a thankless task, coping with an unpleasant situation, tackling a difficult problem), we do so with the hope of achieving a heightened pleasure at a later point (feeling free of the burden, having time to do something enjoyable).

But there are indeed those who do not postpone gratification, who give in to the peremptory demand for pleasure now, whatever the consequences. For a long time such pleasure-driven behavior was looked at from a strictly moral point of view. Then, thanks to the research of Heath, Delgado, Olds, Milner, and others, the stage was set to consider this behavior as the result not of "moral weakness" but rather of alterations or an imbalance in potent neural systems within the brain.

This was a crucial underpinning in the efforts to understand the epidemic of drug abuse that began in the early 1970s. Moral judgments persisted, of course, especially in the early years of surging drug use, and addicts were labeled as ethically or psychologically deviant. But scientists pursued a different course, although, as often happens in the absence of a solid body of basic research, conflicting theories abounded. For a while, many thought that addicts were using cocaine or heroin to relieve depression—in essence, to restore themselves to their normal mood. But if this was true, abuse problems should be encountered with every therapeutic drug aimed at relieving depression. This was the period in which psychotropic (mood-altering) drugs were widely used in the treatment of mental and emotional disorders. However, with some exceptions, abuse problems did not arise with these drugs. There seemed to be something specific about addicting and habituating drugs that distinguished them from other mood-altering agents.

Dr. Conan Kornetsky, now at the Laboratory of Behavioral Pharmacology, Boston University School of Medicine, recalls the time. "It was utterly frustrating. We had very few treatments to offer. We hadn't any idea why some people got addicted and others didn't. And our conventional psychotherapy wasn't working."

Part of the problem, Kornetsky remembers, was that there was no way to tell whether addicts were using a drug for the high it gave them or for its ability to block out something they wanted to avoid. The drugs that cause addiction do not allow for a distinction between the positive and negative reinforcement properties of the drug. In terms of the Olds and Milner experiments, was the animal pressing the lever because there was a positive reinforcing effect ("pleasure" that results from this behavior) or because it wished to avoid or escape from a negative withdrawal effect ("pain")?

To clarify this, Kornetsky stimulated a pleasure or "reward" area of an animal's brain and recorded the reaction. Then he administered morphine. The recording showed that the animal had now become *more* sensitive to stimulation of this reward area; the threshold—the point at which a sensation, or any other stimulus, is perceived—had been reduced. It was clear that morphine (and other opiates) heightened the pleasurable response in the brain.

The next objective was to learn whether, in humans, the opiates' activation of the reward area of the brain was related to their euphoria-producing and reinforcing effects, including the craving that follows drug use and the drive to get more, whatever the cost.

In pursuing this research, Kornetsky and his associates decided not to restrict their research to opiates. They believed other frequently used drugs, such as cocaine, were also important to investigate, though cocaine had traditionally not been thought of as addictive. Kornetsky was, of course, not the first scientist to be curious about cocaine. Sigmund Freud was convinced that cocaine could be used to cure heroin addiction. He tried it and discovered that people would indeed exchange cocaine for heroin. Unfortunately, however, this neither freed them from their addiction to heroin nor prevented their becoming addicted to cocaine. But since cocaine wasn't considered a dangerous drug at the time, Freud declared a victory of sorts. It wasn't until later that the ravages of cocaine became obvious and Freud had to acknowledge that he had entered into a devil's bargain.

Kornetsky heard what cocaine users were saying about the drug's ability to heighten pleasure in food, in sex, in a wide variety of activities. This suggested to him that there was a relationship between the drug's effect on the pleasure centers of the brain and its potential for abuse. Research confirmed this.

"Every study in the 1970s showed that cocaine, along with opiate drugs, amphetamines, and stimulants, increased the sensitivity of animals to brain stimulation. In our own laboratory, we found that *every* drug that increases the sensitivity of the animal to brain stimulation has abuse potential. This suggests a common neural behavioral basis for the rewarding or pleasurable effects of drugs. Even those drugs that are chemically different—cocaine is certainly chemically different from morphine—affect the same system in the brain."

One of the impediments to recognizing cocaine as an

abuse problem for so long stemmed from the incorrect but persistent assumption that, unlike heroin, there was no withdrawal syndrome if the user stopped. At most, people thought, it "only" caused psychological dependency. Those who have tried to end their dependency on cocaine know otherwise. "Everything is about getting high," says former cocaine user Jim Sloan, "and any means necessary to get there becomes rational. If it means stealing something from somebody close to you, then you'll do that. If it means lying to your family, borrowing money from people you know you can't pay back, writing checks you know you can't cover, you do all of those things. It's hard to understand how you continuously spend money and do things that are totally against everything you have ever believed in and get nothing out of it.... Each time you use the drug again you just sit there and look at yourself like, 'Here I go again, and why?' "

Kornetsky's findings force a rethinking of our traditional ideas of why people abuse drugs. The most common "explanation"—that drugs are adaptive and thus help people overcome various personality deficiencies—fails to account for the wide diversity of those who at one time or another have abused drugs. Prior to the restrictions imposed by the Harrison Narcotics Act in 1914, eating opium and laudanum (liquid opium) were widely available in the United States. Users were principally women and older people (Eugene O'Neill's lifelong hatred of doctors stemmed from his mother's addiction to laudanum given to her by her physician). In the nineteenth century, opium use was more common among the prosperous than the poor—just the opposite of heroin use today. Here's how one observer put the matter in 1881:

"Opium eating, unlike the use of alcoholic stimulants, is an aristocratic vice and prevails more extensively among the wealthy and educated classes than among those of inferior social positions; but no class is exempt from its blighting influence. The merchant, lawyer and physician are to be found among the host who sacrifice the choicest treasures of life at the shrine of Opium. The slaves of Alcohol may be clothed in rags, but vassals of the monarch who sits enthroned on the poppy are generally found dressed in purple and fine linen."

Kornetsky thinks it unlikely that a substance could be adaptive for such a wide variety of people. "The question that one must ask is, What is the common denominator of opiate use among the Oriental opium smokers, the females of an earlier era, wealthy opium eaters, and the young heroin users of today?" He believes that abuse is based on "the hedonic nature of humans.... Simple euphoria is

probably sufficiently reinforcing to maintain drug-seeking behavior. . . . We should really be looking at why these drugs are reinforcing, why they are rewarding. . . . Until we understand that euphoric effect, we won't understand how these drugs affect people."

As a neuroscientist, Kornetsky's focus is on learning about the biology of reinforcement, rather than the psychological aspects of addiction, and discovering the circuitry that leads to rewarding effects from a drug. "We would have no behavior unless somehow what we do is reinforcing. It can be biologically reinforcing or psychologically reinforcing. But we do what we do because we get pleasure out of doing it. If we didn't, we probably wouldn't do it too well or we would stop doing it."

A rat pressing a lever in order to receive brain stimulation under the effects of cocaine may provide important parallels, Kornetsky believes, with a human user. "Animals will work very, very hard to get this brain stimulation. They will choose brain stimulation over eating. They will work to get this stimulation even in the presence of pain. [It] seems to be an overriding force. We are really tapping into a very primitive reward area of the brain, and we must remember that a man or a woman has the same reward areas in the brain as does a rat. The rat brain and the human brain have a great deal of similarity. The things that drive the behavior in the rat are the same things that drive the behavior in humans. Both rats and people respond to reinforcers in the same areas of the brain."

Today, using new techniques like positron emission tomography (PET scans), researchers can at last actually visualize the sites where drugs of abuse act on the human brain and thus pinpoint the ways in which different drugs do indeed make us into more primitive animals. Morphine shuts down the higher cortex and leaves the older, emotional brain in charge. Cocaine gives a boost to the whole brain but especially stimulates the primitive centers of emotions. This confirms findings in the early 1980s by Dr. Roy A. Wise, of the Center for Studies in Behavioral Neurobiology at Concordia University in Montreal, who applied cocaine to animal brains and identified the region in the brain strongly linked to the craving for cocaine as the *nucleus accumbens*.

The nucleus accumbens is located in the same septal area where Heath experimented, and is also the reward site for amphetamines. The reward site for heroin is the *ventral tegmental area*. These two sites are bridged by a bundle of nerve fibers whose cells produce the neurotransmitter dopamine. Wise and his colleagues have discovered that when they use chemicals that block the dopamine receptor cells,

(Opposite, top) *An opium den in New York's Chinatown, 1926.*

(Bottom) *William Hogarth's etching,* Gin Lane—*a view of alcohol in the eighteenth century.*

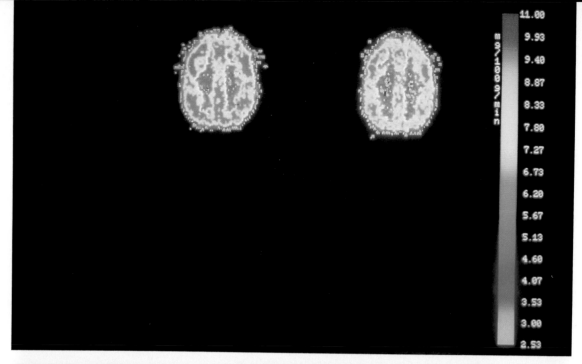

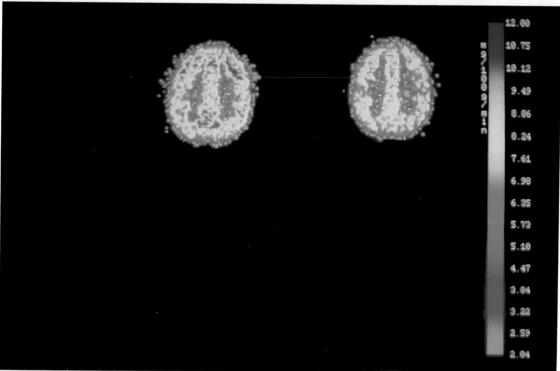

PET scans (top) *showing the rate of glucose utilization in the cerebral cortex of a human volunteer when given a placebo injection* (left), *and cocaine* (right). *Cocaine produced a feeling of euphoria and simultaneously reduced glucose utilization. The reduction is seen as a shift from red to yellow.*

Below are PET scans under similar conditions, except that the abuse substance is morphine.

the rewarding effects of cocaine, amphetamines, heroin, and morphine vanish.

Neurobiologist Hans C. Fibiger, who has worked with brain researcher Anthony G. Phillips, both of the University of British Columbia, on the involvement of the nucleus accumbens in a variety of rewards, describes the mechanism at work here. "When you take cocaine, it causes the neurotransmitter dopamine to remain longer in the synaptic cleft. [Cocaine] does this by blocking the re-uptake mechanisms

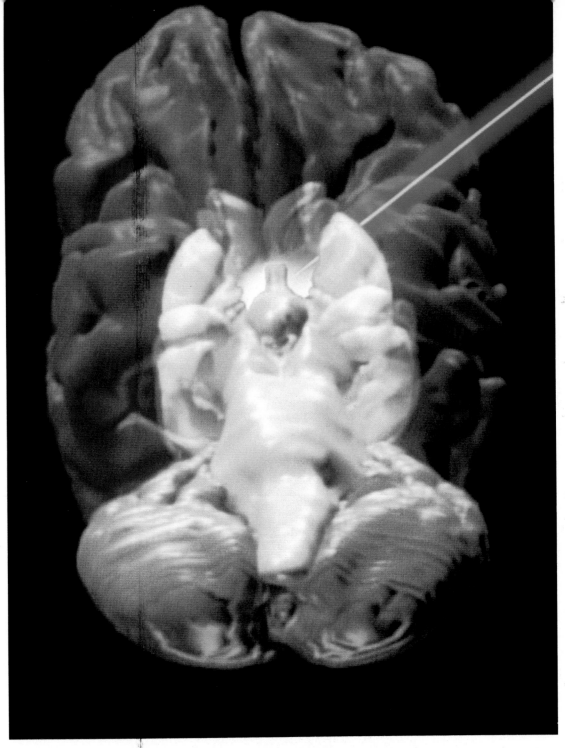

The nucleus accumbens, the "pleasure center" in the septal area of the brain, is shown "flashing" at the end of a stimulating probe.

whereby a neuron releases dopamine's action at the synapse. Now here's the interesting point: If we selectively destroy the dopamine-containing neurons in the nucleus accumbens in the septal area—roughly the area where Heath did his original work—the animal loses interest in self-administering cocaine. The drug is no longer reinforcing. The same thing happens with amphetamines." Dopamine appears to be crucial to the pleasurable effects of these drugs.

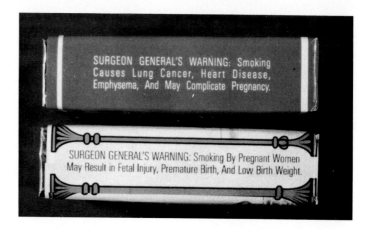

Despite the documented health risks of cigarettes, smokers often have great difficulty quitting because nicotine is addictive.

Interestingly, research on another self-administered substance, nicotine (the major rewarding agent in tobacco), suggests that it too activates dopamine systems. It therefore seems possible that nicotine shares a common mechanism of action with opiates, cocaine, and stimulants.

In a study released in July 1986 by the Center for Health Communication of the Harvard School of Public Health, tobacco was judged to create physical dependence, result in a withdrawal reaction and frequent relapse upon discontinuation, and lead to major alterations of mood and behavior. The report noted that tobacco shares other characteristics of addictive drugs as well; overuse is frequently associated with overuse of other agents such as coffee, alcohol, tranquilizers, marijuana, and aspirin. This is similar to the multiple drug use of opiate addicts.

"Nicotine has a profile of behavioral and physiologic effects typical of other drugs of abuse and, like the heroin derived from opium, meets rigorous experimental criteria as a drug with considerable potential to cause dependence," the report concludes.

But establishing the addictive or abuse potential of a substance, or knowing its mechanism of action in the brain, is not enough to tell us why some people become addicted and others do not. Not every smoker is addicted to tobacco. Not everyone who drinks alcohol is an alcoholic. Not even everyone who uses opiates is a "drug addict." We also need to know why it is that some people can "take it or leave it" while others can only take it and take it and keep taking it.

The same kinds of moral labelings that were used when drug use began to be epidemic in the early 1970s tend to be offered as explanations of these problems; some people are "weak" and others are "strong." But value judgments like this, dubious at best, ignore psychological complexities and tell us nothing from a scientific point of view. Neither does a related banality about addiction that says, "Once an addict, always an addict." In this last respect, however, scientists now know otherwise. They stopped believing this might be valid on the basis of a large scale study carried out in 1974 by Dr. Lee Robins, of Washington University in St. Louis.

Almost half the enlisted men who fought in the army in Vietnam tried one or more narcotic drugs. According to Robins's survey of men returning to the United States during the month of September 1971, one third had experimented with heroin, one third with opium. Most who had tried one of these narcotics had also tried the other. What *was* surprising was the behavior of these men upon their return to the United States. Most of those who used narcotics heavily in Vietnam stopped when they came home. Further, eight to twelve months later they had not resumed drug use.

"To our great delight and to the government's great surprise, we found that most of these men had little trouble with drugs after they got back. It turned out that among men who had been addicted in Vietnam, only about seven percent were re-addicted after they got back. This is an absolutely unheard of low rate as compared to the experience in the United States, where about two-thirds of addicts have usually relapsed within six months after treatment."

Equally surprising, there was no firm way of predicting which of the soldiers would become addicted. There were, however, certain general indicators: "High school dropouts,

Soldiers sharing vials of heroin in Quang tri province, South Vietnam, 1971.

delinquents, kids who had done a lot of fighting and been in a lot of trouble, were more likely to use drugs when they got back to the United States." Psychological factors were also found to be important; for instance, men with depression and anxiety symptoms were more likely to become re-addicted. But this doesn't nullify Robins's startling conclusion: "Contrary to conventional belief, the occasional use of narcotics without becoming addicted appears to be possible even for men who have previously been dependent on narcotics."

Robins's Vietnam study was viewed with skepticism at first, and it was predicted that as time went on the soldiers who had used drugs in Vietnam would eventually go back to them. "Once an addict, always an addict." These predictions have not been borne out.

"The really interesting question for me in 1974, and today as well," says Robins, "is, what makes the difference between someone who can walk away from drugs and those who become addicts?"

The question is crucial because the truth is that the overwhelming majority of people who use opiates eventually develop addiction. Nothing that has been said so far, including Robins's study, contradicts this tragic fact. If we could understand why it is that on some occasions drug dependency develops and on other occasions it doesn't, we might have reason to hope that some day we will be able to prevent addiction in those susceptible to it.

One obvious route to follow is genetics, the possibility that there is an inborn factor in those who become addicted that has made them vulnerable to drug dependence. With one exception, research has not yet produced hard evidence to support this theory. The exception is alcohol. Genetics does play a major role in alcohol abuse. (Also, interestingly, in tolerance to alcohol. For instance, nearly half of all Oriental people get a severe "flushing reaction" whenever they drink alcohol. Since this reaction is often acutely unpleasant, it should come as no surprise that the "flushers" tend to drink very little or not at all.) This finding helps to account, at least in many instances, for the difference between those of us who can drink socially all of our lives without becoming dependent on alcohol and those who become alcoholics.

Genetic studies reveal that the sons of alcoholic fathers, even those who have been separated from their fathers at birth, are at high risk for developing alcoholism themselves. Studies of boys who have been adopted reveal that it is the biological rather than the adoptive parent who is predictive of later drinking problems. Additional evidence for a genetic predisposition comes from twin studies. Alcohol abuse in identical twins is almost double that for fraternal twins.

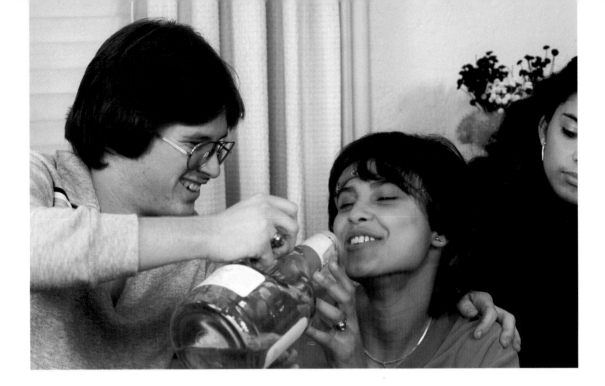

Teenagers drinking.

In fact, patterns of alcohol consumption are highly concordant among identical twins: if one twin drinks heavily, the other is likely to overindulge as well.

But establishing a genetic predisposition to alcoholism is only a beginning. What is needed is some way of identifying those with this predisposition so they can be alerted to their vulnerability. Neuroscientists have now found a way of doing this through a genetic marker.

The scientists have studied the brains of alcoholics using CAT (or CT) scans, the computer-assisted x-ray technique that makes it possible to "unpeel" the brain and view its structures layer by layer. The alcoholic's brain, as revealed by the CAT scan, is abnormal; there is a loss of cortical tissue, particularly in the frontal areas. CAT scans, however, are better able to reveal damage in some brain areas than in others that may be equally affected. In addition, they provide only a static picture of the brain—its *structure*. They cannot provide any information about *function*.

To assess function, scientists utilize another computerized technique, the evoked potential, which measures the brain's reaction to stimuli and produces a record of its functioning in response to these stimuli. Through electrodes placed on the scalp, signals register the progress of a stimulus, such as a flashing light, as it is processed at succeeding levels from the eye to the brain: at the retina, the optic nerve, the brain stem, the visual cortex. The nerve impulse at each of these levels is processed through a computer and recorded as a wave form, which is compared to a wave form standard for the patient's age and sex.

Evoked potentials (EPs) are particularly useful in exploring problems like the effects of alcohol on the brain because they are able to elicit subtle, dynamic, moment-to-moment changes in brain function. When a person is intoxicated, the evoked potential changes in a specific way. The amplitude (height) of the wave decreases and the conduction velocities of signals along the brain stem are prolonged. Chronic alcohol overindulgence results in a similar pattern (though often less pronounced) after tolerance develops. Withdrawal also has its characteristic evoked potential "signature."

As neuroscientists have gained additional experience with the evoked potential technique, its usefulness and applications have increased. There is now substantial evidence that EP wave forms are genetically determined. Identical twins show waves that are as similar to each other as those obtained from a single individual tested on two separate occasions. This remarkable similarity suggested to Dr. Henri Begleiter, of the Department of Psychiatry, State University of New York Downstate Medical Center, that EPs might provide a biological marker that would allow potential alcoholics to be identified *before* they become addicted to alcohol.

Research on alcoholism has discovered two basic types of alcoholics. In type 1 alcoholics, one parent—either the mother or the father—is alcoholic, alcohol-related difficulties begin after age twenty-five, and there is no history of antisocial or criminal behavior. In type 2 alcoholics, the father and not the mother is alcoholic, problems begin in the teen years and, typically, are accompanied by antisocial experiences such as fighting, arrests, and criminality.

"In type 2 alcoholics, the environment plays only a minor role," says Begleiter. "Genetics plays a stronger role. But you must remember that it's not a *disease* that's inherited, but instead a propensity or predisposition."

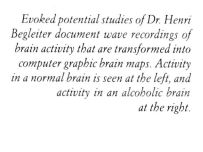

Evoked potential studies of Dr. Henri Begleiter document wave recordings of brain activity that are transformed into computer graphic brain maps. Activity in a normal brain is seen at the left, and activity in an alcoholic brain at the right.

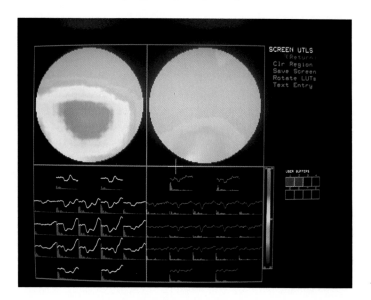

The evoked potential of type 2 alcoholics shows a deficit—a reduction in amplitude—in the third positive component of the wave, the so-called P3 component. Begleiter wondered whether it was possible that the children of these alcoholics, known to be at risk for alcoholism themselves, might show the same pattern.

First, he investigated evoked potential activity in the sons of both type 1 and type 2 alcoholics. He found that he could identify through their evoked potential wave forms 89 percent of the individuals whose fathers were type 2 alcoholics.

Then he and his associates measured evoked potentials in two groups of boys between the ages of six and eighteen, one group the sons of alcoholics and the other age- and education-matched sons of nonalcoholics. When he compared the results, he found that the P3 components in the sons of the alcoholics were lower in amplitude than in the control group. "These studies suggest that individuals with a family history of alcoholism tend to manifest different wave forms than do those without a family history of alcoholism," says Begleiter. In short, he appears to have found his genetic marker in those wave forms, though like any conscientious scientist, he remains cautious about his findings and would like to see further confirmation.

When it comes to addiction for agents other than alcohol, we have no evidence of genetic markers at all. In spite of much talk about the "addictive personality," or the very tenuous observations about those Vietnam veterans who became re-addicted, scientists have not discovered anything that predicts who can use drugs safely and who cannot.

In fact, neuroscientific research is demonstrating that drug "safety" involves more than simply the chemical effects of a drug on a receptor. All too frequently, drug overdose victims die after self-administration of a heroin dose that they had tolerated the day before. The body's response to an accustomed dose changes abruptly. How? Why?

In 1975, Dr. Shepard Siegel, of the Department of Psychology at MacMaster University in Hamilton, Ontario, made a discovery that bears on human addiction, overdose, and death. Siegel was working with rats that he had addicted to morphine. He then moved the rats to a different room and gave them their usual dose of morphine. Though the dosage had not changed, many of them became hypersensitive again; indeed, a number died of what in humans would be labeled unmistakable evidence of overdose. The experiments were repeated with different environmental changes. There were similar results. It was clear that in some mysterious way, the final effect of an addicting drug depended upon the conditions—the environment—in which the drug was taken. Change that environment, and the animal's usual response to the drug changes as well. It was as if the animal had become conditioned to responding to a drug under specific circumstances, and reacted differently when those circumstances were altered.

Is it possible, Siegel reflected, that addiction might be explained by the establishment of a conditioned response (CR)? If so, could a change in tolerance, drug overdose, and death result from a modification of this conditioned response? To find out why people become addicted and why, without any escalation in dose, this addiction sometimes kills, Siegel pored over Pavlov's original research (see Chapter 1).

All living organisms, Pavlov had pointed out, respond not only to stimuli, but also in anticipation of the stimuli. In his conditioning procedure, a bell was sounded (the conditioned stimulus) just prior to giving the dog food (the unconditioned stimulus). After several repetitions of this link between bell and food (conditioned and unconditioned stimuli), the animal started to salivate not only in response to the food but also in anticipation of the food that was announced by the bell. The dog, in Pavlov's terms, was said to display a conditioned response.

Pavlov had also demonstrated conditioning whenever a drug was given to an animal. He paired a tone with the

Ivan Pavlov with his class of students at the Military Medical Academy, and the famous dog of his experiments on conditioned reflexes.

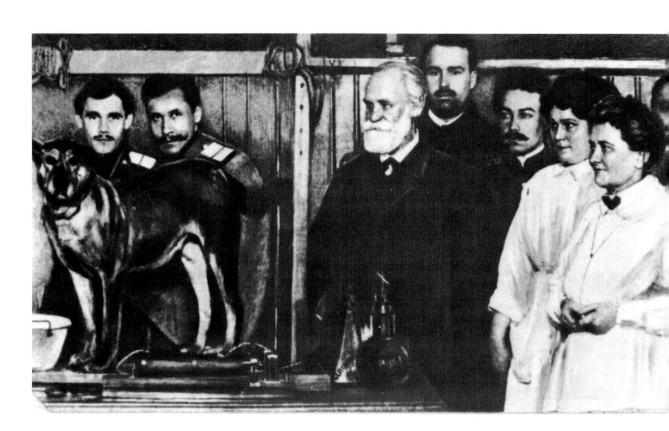

injection of apomorphine. The drug induced restlessness, salivation, and frequent vomiting. Following several tone–apomorphine pairings, the tone alone "sufficed to produce all the active symptoms of the drug, only to a lesser degree." After a while even the tone could be dispensed with. Merely opening the box containing the hypodermic syringes was enough to serve as the conditioning stimulus.

Then additional research experience with drugs and the conditioning response turned up a surprise: the conditioned response didn't *always* replicate the drug effect. A dog given repeated doses of epinephrine, a medication that normally causes an increase in heart rate, developed a *decrease* in rate after it was conditioned to the drug. It was almost as if the body were attempting to compensate for the anticipated effect of the drug on the heart. If the drug given was morphine, a pain-killer, rather than epinephrine, the conditioned response resulted in a *decrease* in morphine-related tolerance to pain. As long as the environmental conditions remained stable, the conditioned response increasingly weakened the effect of the drug, so that it would take a larger dose to achieve the same effect. "The progressively diminished response to a drug over the course of repeated administration defines tolerance," according to Siegel. "It's likely that Pavlovian conditioning contributes to tolerance to any drug."

But this effect ceases if the animal is subjected to unfamiliar environmental cues; without the familiar cues, there is no conditioned response—and no tolerance.

Translation: the same dose of a drug to which an individual is accustomed, when given in a different environment, can lead to death.

Additional research on addiction in animals explains why drug addicts sometimes undergo withdrawal reactions months after their last "fix." Drug-associated "cues" are at work.

In one experiment, monkeys were repeatedly injected with morphine while tape-recorded music played in the background. Soon the music alone could elicit withdrawal distress. Then the animals were weaned from the drug and maintained drug-free for several months. When the tape-recorded music was again played, it evoked restlessness, yawning, urinating, and runny noses, and the animals immediately sought a drug injection.

Dr. Charles P. O'Brien, of the Department of Psychiatry at the University of Pennsylvania School of Medicine, injected rats with morphine under specific environmental conditions, such as a particular cage or a familiar smell. The drug was then withheld and the animals went through withdrawal under these same conditions. After they were detoxified, the researchers put them back into the familiar environment, they went through withdrawal again, and in some instances this conditioned response led to death.

Anyone who has worked with drug addicts knows that drug-associated cues can elicit withdrawal symptoms. Drug paraphernalia, the presence of other users, even a visit to the neighborhood where the addict used to make his drug buys—any of these can lead to withdrawal and renewed drug taking. This is one of the reasons why the best outcomes occur when the treated addict is encouraged to move to another neighborhood or even another city. There he or she will not be repeatedly confronted with the drug-associated cues that elicit a conditioned response: withdrawal symptoms followed by the resumption of drug taking. The veterans addicted to opiates while in Vietnam returned to a different environment than the one in which they had become addicted. This may be one reason why comparatively few of them remained addicted.

If a person can be conditioned to take drugs, the question arises as to why he or she can't be cured by deconditioning. Dr. O'Brien has developed a treatment program for addicts based on deconditioning, after observing discharged patients who were fine until they returned to drug-associated neighborhoods and went into withdrawal and relapsed. The program he designed with his associates, Drs. Anna Rose Childress, A. Thomas McLellan, and Ronald Ehrman, measures physiological as well as psychological arousal.

Jim Sloan, the addict who described the hold cocaine had over his life earlier in this chapter, was filmed as he underwent the deconditioning procedure. When he began, his skin temperature was about 8°F below normal—a strong indication of physiological arousal—and he felt an intense craving for the drug. For twenty sessions, over a period of five months, he listened to audiotapes of cocaine talk, viewed videotapes of "cook-up" procedures, and handled drug paraphernalia over and over again. "You'll get into the actual ritual of getting high without getting high," Jim explains. "Or you'll cook up cocaine, you'll put it in the pipe as if you're going to smoke it, and then they'll take it from you. You go through this ritual three times in a row. And then you'll watch a tape and then you'll do it again. And after doing that over a period of time, you get desensitized to the point where you can handle these things without the craving because you know you're not going to complete the act."

This was confirmed by Jim's physiologic measurements, Childress reported. "He got to the point where his arousal was in the one- to two-degree range of change in body temperature that is normal for neutral stimuli."

The treatment procedure emphasizes a stimulus hierar-

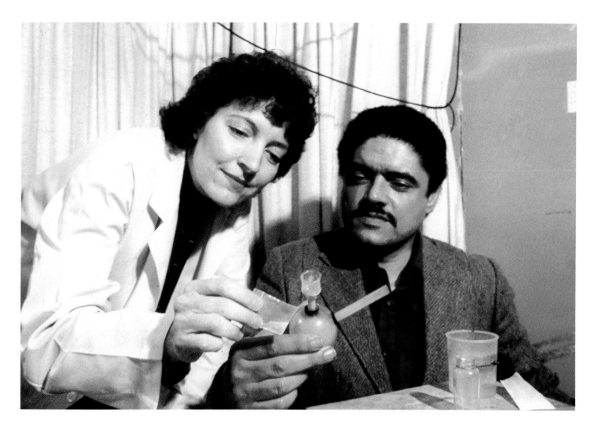

chy: the least arousing stimuli at first (listening to audio-tapes of heroin or cocaine use), then escalating to videotapes, and finally to actually handling drugs and drug-related para-phernalia. This stimulus hierarchy is designed to help addicts gradually tolerate exposure to the most evocative and influential cues. If the deconditioning method is successful, they won't relapse when re-exposed to the cues and situations that had conditioned them to crave drugs.

Three important findings have emerged from the efforts of O'Brien and his associates. First, drug-related cues are specific to each individual. What is arousing to one addict may have little effect on another. For deconditioning to be effective, the process must identify and focus on the particular situations—sights, sounds, smells, associations—that generate craving in the individual concerned.

Second, the O'Brien team discovered that physiologic responses, such as skin temperature and heart rate, don't always correlate with an addict's subjective report. Often, marked physiologic responses were present at times when the addict wasn't aware of experiencing craving or with-drawal. At other times, the addict reported craving without measurable evidence of physiologic changes. The team now feels that to treat addiction successfully, deconditioning may be necessary for each of these physiologic components if they are to be suppressed.

Cocaine addict Jim Sloan undergoes deconditioning under the direction of Dr. Anna Rose Childress.

The third and by far the most intriguing finding has been the major part that emotions and thought patterns play in the expression of conditioned responses.

"Many cues are mood related," Dr. Childress notes. "For example, a patient may have used heroin initially because he was anxious and depressed and found that it relieved these moods. After many, many repetitions of this process the mood state becomes a good predictor for the drug. At that point, anxiety or depression may arouse cocaine craving. Thus, the patient suffers from two disorders: an underlying mood problem and a craving for the drug set off by or at least associated with the mood disorder."

The reward circuits that are active in substance disorders are also active in other addictive behaviors, Childress believes. She anticipates that the repeated exposure techniques employed with cocaine and heroin abuse may be applicable to such behaviors as compulsive gambling. "We expect that the arousal that a compulsive gambler experiences is similar to drug-related arousal. It should be, because it's the same reward system. Whether a person is anticipating food or sex or drugs or gambling, he's anticipating a reward or reinforcement."

Behavior that is pleasurable tends to be repeated. When taken to an extreme, repetition leads to compulsions. In evolutionary terms this reward system is important to survival. "We're sort of prewired so that things that are important to keep us alive—food, water, and eventually sexual behavior—are very pleasurable," Childress notes. "We go for these things, they meet our needs, and they provide us with pleasure. In the case of drugs they have an unfair heartline to these reward systems, absent the usual governors and inhibitors. It's as though the person says, 'My goodness, this is probably the most important reward I've ever encountered. I'd better delay everything, defer everything else, and follow this.'"

Because addiction is a process that involves far more than conditioning, and addictive drugs not only modify behavior but the brain itself, neuroscientists have long known that these substances act on the cellular level. Beginning in the 1950s, they suspected that opiates must act on specific receptors—sites to which they would bind—on the membranes of certain neurons. For one thing, these drugs are incredibly powerful. One opiate, etorphine, relieves pain in doses only one five-thousandth of the effective dose of morphine. A dart saturated with etorphine can stop a charging elephant in its tracks. An effect this overwhelming couldn't possibly result from the action of the drug over the surfaces of a great many neurons. There simply aren't enough molecules of etorphine to go around. It seemed likely that etorphine locks onto the sites on the surfaces of those neurons specifically structured to accept it.

Secondly, the brain can recognize subtle differences in the chemical structure of different drugs in the opiate family. Opiates usually exist in either of two forms that are identical in chemical structure but which are mirror images of each other. Nonetheless, the brain can distinguish between these two forms and respond to only one of them.

Finally, the existence of substances that inhibit the action of opiate drugs—antagonists—argued for a specific binding site. In emergency rooms throughout the nation, suspected heroin abusers are injected with a tiny dose of naloxone, an opiate antagonist with a chemical structure similar to morphine. Within seconds after injection, naloxone brings on a withdrawal reaction. Naloxone has the opposite effect of morphine; rather than relieving pain or inducing euphoria, it prevents or abolishes the effects of opiate drugs. Furthermore, these are the only substances on which it acts; it has no effect on other drugs of abuse such as barbiturates, amphetamines, or cocaine.

These observations, taken together, suggested that opiates react with specific opiate receptors on certain neurons in the brain. The key question facing neuroscientists was where in the brain these binding sites might be.

At Johns Hopkins University School of Medicine in Baltimore in 1972, Dr. Candace Pert and Dr. Solomon H. Snyder were able to bind a radioactively tagged opiate drug to brain cells, proving that opiate receptors existed. Next, they discovered that opiates in low doses bind with specific receptors. Further, the tendency for a drug to bind to the receptor paralleled the drug's effectiveness as a pain-reliever in humans and in animals. The opiates with strong analgesic (pain-killing) and addictive properties bound firmly to the binding sites; weaker opiates did not.

The findings were not only a gratifying confirmation of something that had long been suspected; they also showed that the locations of these receptor sites corresponded with the known effects of particular drugs. For instance, opiates are most successful in relieving deep, chronic, burning pain. This pain is mediated by the medial portion of the thalamic area, which is rich in receptors. The limbic system is another brain area with a large number of receptors. The amygdala, part of the limbic system and a particularly important region for emotional expression, contains the highest concentration of opiate receptors in the brain. This correlates very well indeed with the euphoric effects of opiates: "the rush," the warm, joyous feeling after taking an opiate that is often compared to an orgasm.

But the discovery of opiate receptors was only half the battle. Most people in the world live out their lives without

Dr. Hans Kosterlitz, who, with Dr. John Hughes in their Aberdeen laboratory, identified the brain's own opiates, which they called enkephalins.

ever coming into contact with an opiate drug. How peculiar, therefore, that the human brain should contain opiate receptors. Why would the brain contain receptors for distillations of the poppy? A possible explanation—not immediately obvious—is that these receptors are present because the brain contains its own pain-relieving compounds. The receptors are the targets for these endogenous (internal) compounds.

This intriguing prospect provided the impetus for one of the most exciting and competitive efforts in the history of science: three different teams working at breakneck speed to be the first to isolate and identify the brain's own natural opiates.

In Aberdeen, Scotland, Dr. Hans Kosterlitz, a highly experienced pharmacologist, had been experimenting on the effects of opiate compounds on muscle tissue. He chose muscle tissue because opiates inhibit electrically provoked contractions of certain smooth muscles (the ileum, or small intestine, of the guinea pig, for instance) in direct proportion to their ability to relieve pain. Kosterlitz was certain that such a reaction could be possible only if this muscle system possessed opiate receptors similar to those that occur in the brain. To test this hypothesis, he and a young associate, Dr. John Hughes, put extracts of pig brain together with the muscle tissue and administered morphine. Contraction of the muscle was inhibited. When they then added an opiate antagonist, this reaction was blocked: the muscle contraction proceeded as it had prior to morphine administration. Using this simple but elegant procedure, Kosterlitz and Hughes identified an opiatelike material in the brain cells and then isolated it and analyzed its chemical structure.

"John Hughes extracted large quantities of pig brain which he collected at an unearthly early hour at the local slaughterhouse," Kosterlitz recalls. "Within a few weeks he obtained a crude extract in which our bioassay systems indicated the presence of opiate compounds beyond any doubt."

In the December 18, 1975, issue of the prestigious British science journal, *Nature*, Kosterlitz and Hughes and their collaborators published the structure of the morphine-like material they had isolated from the brain. It was a peptide consisting of two chemicals of only five amino acids each. Dubbed *enkephalins* (from the Greek word meaning "in the head"), the two molecules differed in possessing either leucine or methionine as their terminal amino acid.

At about the same time as the enkephalin story was unfolding, another researcher, Dr. Avram Goldstein, of Stanford University, discovered that the pituitary, the master gland suspended from the underside of the brain just above the roof of the mouth, also possessed opiatelike substances. Further, one component of the pituitary, beta-lipotropin, discovered ten years earlier by Dr. C. H. Li, of the University of California at San Francisco, and shelved for want of any particular application, contained within its ninety-one amino acids the same short chemical sequence as the natural opiate, methionine-enkephalin, that Kosterlitz and Hughes had isolated and analyzed in Scotland.

This suggested to three research teams, headed by Roger Guillemin at the Salk Institute in La Jolla, Dr. Derrick Smyth at the National Institute for Medical Research in London, and C. H. Li in San Francisco, that lipotropin is broken down in the pituitary to *beta-endorphin* (from the words *endogenous morphine,* "the morphine within"). It is beta-endorphin that accounts for the opiatelike activity of the pituitary.

With the discovery of the brain's own opiates, now renamed endorphins, the stage was set for efforts to synthesize these substances and for the first truly scientific investigation of the nature of pain relief, addiction, and drug-induced euphoria. The first step was to actually visualize the enkephalin molecules within the brain. Dr. Thomas Hokfelt, at the Karolinska Institute in Stockholm, and Drs. Rabi Simantov, Michael Kuhar, and Solomon Snyder at Johns Hopkins accomplished this feat through a special technique that lets the enkephalin-containing regions light up as bright fluorescent areas on a colored photomicrograph.

The scientists saw that enkephalins, like neurotransmitters, were highly concentrated on the membranes of nerve endings. This suggested that they functioned as neurotransmitters. In general, those neurons that possessed high concentrations of enkephalin also possessed the highest number of opiate receptors, and as Pert and Snyder had discovered in 1972, were found in large numbers in the medial thalamus and amygdala.

Outside the brain, enkephalins and opiate receptors were also found within a dense vertical band of fibers in the first two layers of the spinal cord. Known as the *substantia gelatinosa,* this area is the first way station to which pain information is relayed on its path from the sensory receptors up to the brain.

Armed with this information about the enkephalins and opiate receptors, neuroscientists in the mid-1970s were then able to sketch a convincing picture of how pain is experienced and relieved.

Imagine yourself sitting in a restaurant and touching an extremely hot plate that your waiter has neglected to warn you about. Nerve endings at the tip of your fingers are stimulated, and fire off impulses that proceed up your arm into the spinal cord. Nerve endings in the substantia gelatinosa of the spinal cord release an excitatory neurotransmitter that provokes other neurons in the cord to fire, a cascade of events that results ultimately in your perception of pain. Then enkephalin-containing neurons nearby impede this sequence by releasing enkephalins that inhibit the discharge of additional excitatory neurotransmitters. This is why the pain impulse first has a burning, intense quality, and is followed moments later by a dull, aching sense of discomfort.

Neuroscientists have formulated a convincing model of how enkephalin neurons act to relieve pain; and because opiates produce "good" feelings and, at the same time, occupy enkephalin sites, it seems reasonable to assume that enkephalin normally plays some part in regulating mood. But the models for euphoria and mood alteration are less satisfactory than the pain model. At this point, the most important achievement resulting from the discovery of the brain's own opiates remains the demonstration that the brain contains specialized receptors for drugs like heroin.

Over the ensuing decade, more and more receptors for natural brain chemicals—neurotransmitters—have been discovered. Certain exogenous (externally administered) substances also bind to the same receptors.

For example, where the acetylcholine molecule binds, nicotine adheres.

Where serotonin binds, LSD adheres.

Where noradrenaline binds, mescaline adheres.

All of these substances—nicotine, LSD, mescaline—subvert the brain's natural chemical controls in ways that no one—neither the drug users nor neuroscientists—ever anticipated.

When the brain is flooded with an unusually large quantity of a drug, the nerve cells respond by cutting down the number of receptors. That's why drug abusers need more and more of the drug to get the same effect. Then, when the drug is taken away, the brain's *natural* chemicals have fewer receptors to lock onto. Both opiates and the benzodiazepines (Valium and other drugs of similar chemical structure) act as sedatives. When the receptors that normally accommodate these drugs fail to do their job because of drug-induced inhibition in their numbers, the result is an increase in anxiety and "nervous excitement." That's withdrawal. Its intensity varies from drug to drug. Opiates such as morphine and heroin produce an intense withdrawal reaction; with the benzodiazepines, withdrawal, although easily detectable, is usually—but not always—less severe.

This is how Lisa Harrison, after sixteen years of taking benzodiazepine tranquilizers, describes her physical and emotional withdrawal: "I would experience electric shocks going all over my body, and my skin felt as though I had been scalded with hot water. I felt as though my body was actually falling apart, that my arms and legs would come off, that my chest would just fall open. I felt as though my brain was clogged up with the debris and the dead stuff from tranquilizers and sleeping tablets. So when I stopped taking them, it was as though my thought processes were rivers, and there were thousands and thousands of these rivers and some were still blocked. The water couldn't get through. Some were flooding and some were crossing over. There were so many thought processes forming a sort of river, and it was crazy. I couldn't cope with it. I felt demented, absolutely insane. It's as though my whole body was screaming—my body and my brain. I can't describe it any more than that; it was the worst thing I'd ever experienced."

To cope with heroin addiction, since the early 1950s, many thousands of addicts have been treated with a synthetic opiate, methadone, which occupies the same receptors as heroin. At first, scientists thought that methadone would prove a "cure" for heroin addiction. They anticipated that it could be employed for a short period as a substitute for heroin and then stopped, and the patient would be drug-free. They were wrong. Methadone proved to be equally addictive. But because it is less deleterious than heroin, at this point and in the absence of something better, it continues to be utilized as an interim—and legal—approach to opiate addiction. It is a telling reflection on the desperation scientists and therapists feel as they struggle to find solutions to the massive problem of addiction that a substitute dependency seems a reasonably acceptable means of handling the situation.

Neuroscientists suspect that if an addict can be forced to stay drug-free for an extended time, receptors eventually return to more or less normal levels. At least this is what happens in individual nerve cells grown in culture.

But receptors are only one aspect of a nerve cell. What longer term changes might an addict's nerve cells have undergone?

In London, researcher John Littleton has been looking at how nerve cells are affected by alcohol and the benzodiazepines, as well as addicting drugs. He has found that alcohol and the benzodiazepines decrease—inhibit—the excitability of the cells. Drugs such as morphine and barbiturates do the same. Later, when the substance is removed, the cells not only regain their excitability but become *hyper*excitable.

Littleton believes this may explain why addicts go into withdrawal. The nerve cell excitability induced by these substances is brought about at the cellular level by inhibiting the normal entry of calcium into the cells through special calcium channels on the cell membrane. The number of these channels increases under drug abuse. "Of course, while alcohol or the drug is there, this increased number of calcium channels doesn't make any difference to cell excitability because a lot of them are being inhibited," says Littleton. "But when we take the alcohol or drug away, the increase in the number of calcium channels is responsible for the increase in cell excitability that leads to the withdrawal syndrome."

One possible way of combating these withdrawal symptoms is by using drugs called calcium channel blockers. "But we're talking a new kind of calcium channel," Littleton says. "If we could block that channel without affecting the normal calcium channels on the cell membrane, we might have a cure for the withdrawal syndrome."

As we have noted, it is likely that enkephalin has a role in our moods. We know that the amygdala, which contains large numbers of enkephalin receptors, is important in emotional experience, including the emotional aspects of memory. Scientists have therefore speculated that the normal release of enkephalin in the brain acts as the body's own "tonic" against loss and disappointment. Some suggest that a deficiency of enkephalins in certain brain regions coincides with emotional pain and depression.

Explanations like this cannot be dismissed out of hand, but to assume a cause and effect relationship here oversimplifies very intricate processes. A good deal of caution is called for lest a devotion to tidy explanations does us in. The "runner's high" frequently reported by joggers, orgasm, and anorexia are only three of a number of behavioral states that have been "explained" in terms of an excess or deficiency of enkephalins. But such behavioral states are much more complicated than pain. So are attitude, mood, and "states of mind." It is unlikely that a single chemical or family of chemicals could fully account for such complex behavioral states as happiness or the feeling that one's life is "in sync." Nor is it likely that an insecure or emotionally distressed human being is ever going to be able to change his or her feelings by the process of injecting or snorting or swallowing an enkephalin-like drug.

The fact is that in the past fifty years, we have come a long way in learning how drugs affect the brain, in understanding the *mechanisms* of addiction. But we know comparatively little about *why* people choose to use drugs, or what the individual differences may be that allow or induce some people to become addicted and others not.

The epidemic grows and the drugs themselves proliferate. In desperation, doctors, therapists, and rehabilitation specialists are trying anything that may prove helpful: antidepressants, tranquilizers, group therapies, support groups, even acupuncture. A pilot study on acupuncture in treating alcoholism showed that of those who received acupuncture in the correct way—at the standard acupuncture points—nearly half managed at least for a short period to stay away from alcohol. The deconditioning program of Charles O'Brien and his associates was described earlier in this chapter. Another treatment program is that of Coke-Enders. Dr. Richard Miller, the director of the program, reminds us of the power denial exerts among addicts.

"Addiction to drugs is one of the very few illnesses that human beings encounter in which they can actually be suffering and still be denying that they have the problem. If I'm bleeding, and I look down and see blood all over my clothing, I'm going to go for help. But when we're bleeding from the spirit, we can't see the blood and we can easily deny. We lie to ourselves. That's why many of the people that I work with have been using drugs for ten and twenty and thirty years."

Miller believes that families play a significant part in this denial and in generating patterns that help induce addiction. "The addicted family is really nothing more or less than a symptom of the entire society," he says. "In the same way, when I have an infection in my hand that keeps recurring, I can keep treating the hand. But if I don't eventually look at my entire system, and say, 'What is there about my own system that's creating the infection?' eventually the infection will recur over and over."

Miller uses group therapy in treating cocaine addicts, who can "experience in the group the intimacy of true sharing, of letting their guards down, and still being accepted. That sense of being accepted by others when revealing the things that they are sure they are going to be rejected for gives them a spiritual connection that is unmatched by any drug that they can take."

Miller's Coke-Enders, Alcoholics Anonymous, and similar groups focusing on other addictive behaviors like gambling and overeating, enable addicts to face themselves, register their emotions (including guilt and shame), and in time to acknowledge their behaviors without denial. The group itself provides massive support, both by its presence and because its members know, as no one can who has not endured similar experiences and feelings, exactly what the addicted individual has been going through.

Originally, these groups were often regarded as aberrant kinds of treatment, useful chiefly to those who had a need for spiritual commitment and reinforcement. This attitude has now changed because the groups appear to work as no other forms of therapy have. Their effectiveness is forcing thoughtful people to scrutinize them in a more open-minded and analytical way. Though there seems no doubt that the members are intensely dependent on these groups in order to sustain their abstention from drugs or alcohol or addictive behaviors like overeating or compulsive gambling, dependency does not account for the groups' success in arresting these addictions. Clearly, there are processes here, not fully understood, which work on the mind and enable one-time addicts to lead reasonably functional, productive, and satisfying lives.

But these groups do not provide a cure, and cures are a long way off. Almost certainly there will never be any therapy that will work for every addict. Human beings are individuals, and their lives—and minds—are unique. The prospect of an enkephalin-like drug to cure addiction also seems unlikely, in part because these substances, like all peptides, cannot pass through the blood–brain barrier; in part because, thus far, every such substance pharmaceutical laboratories have synthesized in their pursuit of such a drug has proved to be powerfully addictive; and in part because addiction is almost certainly too complex to be susceptible to medication alone.

What's worse, the immediate future is far from encouraging as far as restraining the tide of destructive substances is concerned. Technology, like the Sorcerer's Apprentice, will no doubt continue to make possible new and perhaps even more potent chemicals. Each time we think we have encountered the "most" addictive drug, something worse emerges. Crack, the most recent, lethal, addictive, and readily available form of cocaine, has taken over the streets of the entire country. Until a few years ago, PCP was a drug known only to veterinarians, who used it as a horse tranquilizer. Now it can be cooked up in any well-equipped kitchen. It is the most treacherous drug known, and has led to bizarre and violent outbursts that have left many people dead or severely maimed.

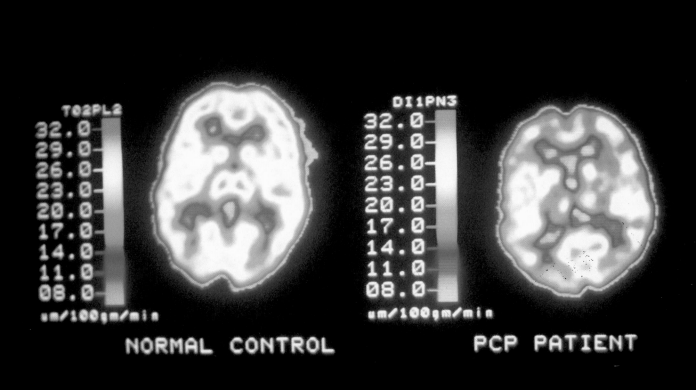

NORMAL CONTROL

PCP PATIENT

The addicted brain is a changed brain. The molecules and networks of our brain have been designed to make us creatures of habit, and drugs have a hotline to these networks.

The addicted mind is a changed mind. When we alter our minds by experimenting with the astonishingly complex and delicately balanced brain bequeathed to us by evolution, we do so at our peril.

This vast, uncontrolled experiment on the streets of the world grows vaster every day. In a way, drugs provide only a heightened, more intense version of what large numbers of people who do not use them consider desirable: the maximum pleasure and satisfaction in the shortest period of time with the expenditure of the least amount of effort. The mechanisms of drug use are the province of science. The problems of drug use are societal. As long as our culture is set up to gratify and dignify such goals, the demand will continue, the worldwide commerce will prosper, and the prospects of curtailing the epidemic seem dim.

PET scan of the brain of a normal person (left) *and a PCP patient* (right).

5.
PAIN AND
HEALING

Pain is an experience common to virtually every person in the world. Yet curiously, no one can ever be certain whether or not another person is experiencing pain. It is a private anguish. You may infer from my behavior or my words that I'm in pain, but you can never experience my pain directly. Only I know for certain that I am in pain. To learn about my pain you must ask, Where does it hurt?

It turns out that when you get right down to it, there is only one answer to that question, regardless of the actual site of the injury. When Bertrand Russell was asked by his dentist, "Where does it hurt?" the late English mathematician and philosopher came up with a startling reply: "In my mind, of course." Russell was correct. Pain is not a stimulus, it is a perception, and as such it can be influenced by a variety of psychological factors. For this reason, pain or the lack of it can provide us with a unique view into the human mind.

For all living things, avoiding harm is crucial to a strategy of survival, and pain is a part of that strategy. Pain is information. It warns us, protects us, and teaches us about what is harmful in the world around us. Our need for pain can no more clearly be illustrated than by someone with a congenital indifference to pain. Seven-year-old Sarah is one such person with this extraordinary deficit. She hurts herself repeatedly and doesn't realize it. A wound on Sarah's knee is protected from further harm by a cast on her leg. Her arm is bandaged to heal a bruise on her elbow. It took some time before her parents realized that Sarah was oblivious to her injuries because she felt no pain.

Pain is of great importance to our well-being. Sarah, age seven, is prone to injury because she was born lacking the crucial capacity to feel pain.

"When she was a few months old and starting to crawl around," her father explains, "we did notice that she didn't seem to cry and that she took some pretty good-sized bumps. We kind of chalked it off as a high pain threshold. As time went on, we realized she was also a bit difficult to discipline, or to train with the normal slap on the hand. She was awfully persistent. It wasn't until . . . I suspect she was something over a year old . . . that her teeth began to loosen and eventually come out. Through a series of dentists we finally came to the conclusion that she was biting them out. It was some time later that she had a significant burn on the foot, and in treating that burn we realized that she had virtually no pain, that she could lie there with a limp leg while that burn was dressed."

Little Sarah has something wrong with the nerve fibers that normally transmit the signals that the brain interprets as pain. The system that is dedicated to pain is simply not sending its messages. Her misfortune not only helps us understand how much we can learn from pain, but how much we need to learn about it.

Pain and the relief from pain is probably the clearest and most dramatic example of how the mind may come to influence our health. Can our minds actually be used to modulate our pain, to return us to health, and to make our body whole again? Certainly, if all the talk, folklore, and popular notions about the power of mind over the body are correct, then this mental power of ours is the most ne-

"GREAT SCIENTIFIC DISCOVERY!"

"MARVELOUS"··"QUICK CURE"

"STEP UP, LADIES & GENTS"

glected of all human assets. Or is all this talk about the powers of the mind just a ploy used by quacks, charlatans, and snake oil salesmen to gull the unsuspecting and the desperate? To find out, researchers have been applying the methods of the laboratory to separate the fact from the fantasy, the mind from the body, for the past three centuries. It was Descartes who first suggested that pain followed specific pathways from the skin to the brain, and present-day research bears him out. To understand just how pain is communicated to the brain, let's look at what happens when a person stubs a toe on a bedpost. The pain message begins with the release of chemicals (substance P, prosta-glandins, bradykinin) that can normally be found in or near the nerve endings. Together these chemicals sensitize the nerve endings and help transmit the pain message from the toe upward toward the brain. (These chemicals also contribute to the swelling, redness, and overall "angry response" of the tissues at the end of the toe. This response in turn lures the white blood cells that will stave off the efforts of bacteria looking to take advantage of the momentary disruption in tissue physiology.)

The pain signal from the stubbed toe is converted into a series of electrochemical nerve impulses that travel along the fibers of the peripheral nervous system to the central nervous system and up the dorsal horns of the spinal cord, a site in which many fibers from pain receptors form synapses with other ascending fibers. In a person six feet tall, the travel time of such a signal would be about two seconds.

The pain signal, which then becomes a veritable cascade and employs a host of chemical messages, is relayed to the thalamus, where distinctions are made between touch, hot and cold, and pain. From there the message is routed to the

The quick-talking traveling purveyors of remedies for whatever ailed their eager audiences are part of America's folklore. The term placebo was not yet in use, but though the "medicines" contained nothing therapeutic, belief in them was often enough to restore the users to health.

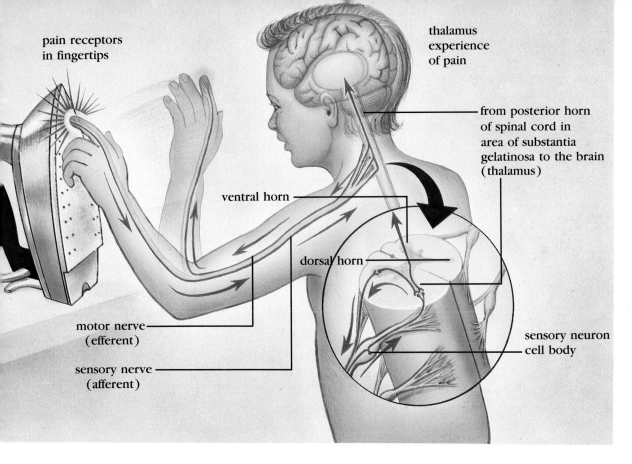

pain receptors
in fingertips

thalamus
experience
of pain

from posterior horn
of spinal cord in
area of substantia
gelatinosa to the brain
(thalamus)

ventral horn

dorsal horn

motor nerve
(efferent)

sensory nerve
(afferent)

sensory neuron
cell body

*The neural pathway, as pain is
experienced by touching a hot iron.
Afferent nerves convey messages to the
central nervous system; efferent
nerves convey signals from the central
nervous system.*

cerebral cortex, where the intensity and specific location of the pain is identified.

It's also in the cortex that the pain is symbolically interpreted, that it becomes a confection of the mind. The "ouch" that escapes us almost against our will may be accompanied by the annoyed recognition that the pain in our toe is the result of our clumsiness. Symbolic elaboration can make the pain acceptable, even welcome in the case of martyrs and patriots.

The attempt to heal begins immediately. The person with the stubbed toe does what everyone else would do in such a situation: leans down to massage it. Shortly afterward, the pain seems to vanish.

The reason this treatment so often succeeds is best explained by a sophisticated theory of pain first formulated in 1965 by Drs. Patrick Wall and Ronald Melzack. They found that the nervous system can process only a limited amount of sensory information of any kind—whether it's pain, or touch, or anything else—at any given moment. Wall and Melzack found that when too much "information" comes through the nervous system, certain cells in the spinal column impede the signal. The researchers envision the process as the closing of a gate, hence their term, "the gate theory of pain." Rubbing the stubbed toe sends a series of signals into the spinal cord, which, if all goes according to theory, slams the gate in the face of competing pain signals.

That the gates of pain should close in the presence of extreme stimulation also helps explain certain puzzling psychological aspects of acute pain. It helps us understand why, for instance, the same injury can produce different degrees of pain in a person depending on the circumstances. When the British army landed at Anzio in Italy in 1943, hundreds of soldiers were severely wounded. But according to the surgeon in command, three quarters of them refused morphine. So surprised was the surgeon that he later questioned a group of civilians with similar, though far less severe, wounds and found that 80 percent requested the analgesic. The surgeon concluded that pain is not a state of the body, but a state of mind.

Several years ago Fred Lay's right foot was crushed in an industrial accident. Eventually, the foot was amputated. Yet today Fred Lay feels pain as if his foot were still there. He describes the raw feelings in the phantom limb: "The pain from the foot is there continually. My toes are actually clawed over and the top of the toes are actually burning. They really are red. And it feels like smoke is coming out of them."

Nature has made the worst possible bargain with Fred Lay. He doesn't have his foot, but somehow, mysteriously, he still has pain from the missing foot. One wonders, quite naturally, how can this be? Perhaps the pain has a peripheral origin. False signals may be originating in what remains of the limb, because, after all, there are cut nerves in that limb. Compounding the problem is the fact that the cells in the spinal cord may somehow recognize that they are cut off, and thereby increase their excitability and generate false signals.

When pain such as this takes over, it ceases to be informative and begins to seriously interfere with daily life. This is the most troublesome type of pain to physicians—chronic, unremitting pain. It is the kind of pain that occurs in cancer, advanced arthritis, and phantom limbs. Many doctors, including myself, have a great deal of difficulty helping patients with chronic pain, since in most cases, the two mainstays of the physician's armamentarium, drugs and surgery, are ineffective.

Why they fail is no mystery, for pain is not simply a matter of "what hurts where?" It involves issues such as self-esteem, independence, the sympathetic attention of others—factors that pain specialists refer to as "secondary gain." Certainly there is no drug or surgical operation in the world that will relieve your pain if the secondary gain benefits are too enticing.

BEYOND PAIN

Not all pain is bad. Indeed, for some people, like Lesley Collier, principal dancer with the Royal Ballet in London, pain is an old friend with whom she has learned to live. "Perhaps more painful than anything are bruised toenails," she says. "The pain goes all the way up my leg. And it's something one tends to want to pull away from. But if you can make yourself go into the pain—this sounds masochistic, I know—but if you can make yourself go into the pain, it will improve."

During rehearsal Collier must force herself through the barrier that pain erects. At such times she is encouraged by the thought that on the night of her performance, the pain won't be so bad. That's because when she is on stage Collier can separate herself from the pain by totally immersing herself in her character role. "At such times," she explains, "your mind is totally occupied. It's too busy to think of being in pain."

Lesley Collier on point.

"Pain is not simply a sensory experience," says Dr. Wilbert E. Fordyce of the Multidisciplinary Pain Center at the University of Washington Medical School in Seattle. "Pain is a very complex matter. It involves the intensity of the injury, how well the injury is transmitted to the brain, and what the person's expectations are about the injury. As human beings, we have a very important characteristic when it comes to pain. Because we have language, we have the capacity to anticipate the future. When we're injured, our brain will attach meaning to what happened and that meaning will be greatly influenced by what we anticipate, what we think is going to happen in the future. As a consequence, whenever a pain stimulus occurs, the intensity of the reaction produced will inevitably be influenced by what it means to the person."

Years of treating thousands of pain patients has led Fordyce to conclude that people who have something better to do often don't hurt as much or suffer as much as those who don't. Call it Fordyce's rule, if you will, but Fordyce is only half joking. He's found that job and personal unhappiness are the best predictors of which patients will develop back pain. "I haven't got time for the pain"—a current jingle for an over-the-counter pain-killer—captures the key concept. A person who is active and personally fulfilled is less likely to enter into a chronic pain cycle.

It seems that for certain individuals the rewards resulting from pain and illness outnumber the rewards of everyday life. To disconnect the pain from the reward system, a number of new, behaviorally oriented, multidisciplinary pain clinics are focusing on the patient's mind. Using hypnosis, psychotherapy, biofeedback, and behavioral modification techniques, the patients are taught to take responsibility for their own care, increase their activity, reduce drug intake, and avoid manipulating their spouses or friends in order to gain sympathy and attention.

Nonetheless, it would be wrong to think of chronic pain as fantasy. "People who come to a program like this clearly are suffering," says Fordyce. "People will ask, 'Is the pain real?' That's a nonsense question. Of course the pain is real. The proper question is, 'Why is the person suffering?' "

One patient at the Seattle Pain Center, whose X rays fail to reveal any reason for pain, insists: "Hardly a minute goes by that I don't feel some sort of pain somewhere. I have constant pain all the time. My back hurts. My leg hurts." Like many of the patients seen at the clinic, she is an anxious person and easily upset. In Fordyce's opinion, she's likely to confound suffering, anxiety, depression, and fear with pain. The pain becomes chronic, explains Fordyce, when people overprotect themselves. "They rest too much, guard too much," he says. "We call that disuse. A second reason why pain becomes chronic is because once the per-

Fran Brooks undergoing therapy at the Seattle Pain Center to relieve chronic pain. As her physician at the Center notes, the absence of an organic cause does not mean her pain is not "real."

son begins to express the suffering, people around them overprotect them."

This experience of pain is uniquely human, very much a product of a person's mind. "There is no animal model for this kind of problem," observes Dr. John Loeser, the psychologist in charge of the Seattle Pain Center. "Can you imagine what would happen to a deer that said: 'Well, I just can't go out and forage for a living. And I'm going to lie down here and let the world take care of me.' If he didn't starve to death, the wolves would eat him overnight. It's only in an industrialized society such as ours where human beings can survive saying: 'I am unable to work and I am unable to take care of myself.' "

To establish the reality of the mind's influence on health, scientists needed to find a link between the brain and the immune system. This first step took place at the turn of the century when anatomists discovered that important components of the immune system—the thymus, bone marrow, and lymph nodes—were richly endowed with nerve fibers. A closer examination later revealed that the ends of these nerve fibers were closely enough intertwined with the immune system's lymphocytes to suggest a direct means of communication between the brain and the immune system.

But the most convincing evidence came just a few years ago with an elegant series of experiments carried out at the University of Rochester by Drs. Robert Ader and Nicholas Cohen. The researchers had fed rats a saccharin solution and then injected them with a drug (cyclophosphamide) that made them sick. Not surprisingly, the rats stopped

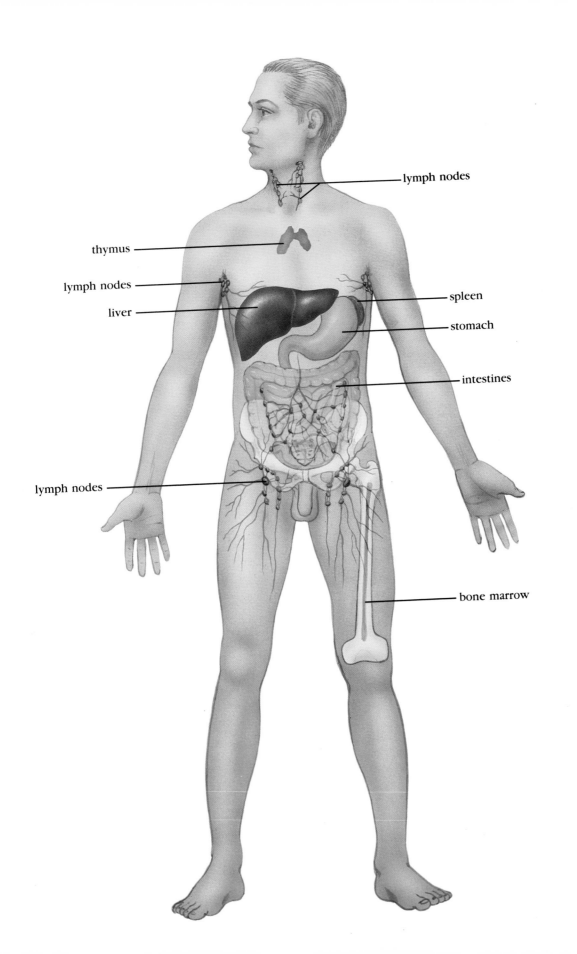

lymph nodes

thymus

lymph nodes

liver

spleen

stomach

intestines

lymph nodes

bone marrow

THE IMMUNE SYSTEM

"No man is an island," wrote the poet John Donne in reference to our social nature. But biologically speaking, we are very much like islands. For one thing, we are enclosed in a layer of skin that protects us from the organisms and toxins in our environment. Infections, sometimes death dealing, are the end result of violations in our insular integrity. Through a scratch on the skin, a virus or a bacterium can gain entry and produce an abscess, a sore throat, a blood infection—the end result depending on the organism and how well equipped our body is to fight off the invader.

The need for defenses against bacterial, viral, and chemical invaders must have arisen early in the development of life. Primitive defenses exist even in one-celled creatures like the amoeba. And insects attacked by bacteria can produce substances that inactivate the intruder. Still higher up the evolutionary scale, specialized cells appear capable of ingesting assailants. Such mobile scavenger cells also exist in humans in more developed forms. They occur in combination with a number of other defensive components of the immune system, which together can remember, recognize, and eliminate harmful invaders.

Our immune system is a sophisticated ensemble of mobile and stationary cells, killer cells, antibodies, and chemical substances whose goal is the destruction and removal from the body of everything that does not belong there. In terms of complexity and sheer number of components, the immune system is a fitting counterpart to the brain. Extracted and concentrated, our immune system weighs about two pounds; the adult human brain, on the other hand, weighs three pounds.

The immune system consists of about a trillion white blood cells called lymphocytes and about a hundred million trillion molecules, or antibodies, produced and secreted by the lymphocytes. In contrast to the brain, whose neurons endure over our lifetime, the immune system continually renews itself. During the few seconds it takes to read this sentence, your body has produced ten million new lymphocytes and a million billion new antibody molecules. The mind boggles at such profligacy. Even more astounding, these antibody molecules are not identical. Millions of different molecules are required in order to function as the body's main line of defense against disease.

Despite significant differences in structure and function, the brain and the immune system display some intriguing similarities. Both have the capacity for memory. In the immune system, a foreign invader, an antigen, stimulates lymphocytes to produce a specific antibody directed against the invader. Years later, the reintroduction of that antigen will trigger the production of the same neutralizing antibodies. This memory is as specific as the brain's storage and recall of a familiar face.

Lymphocytes.

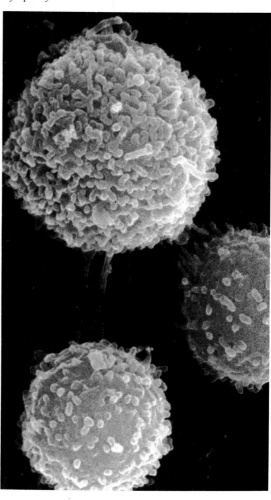

hormones in order to communicate with just about every other system in the body, according to Dr. J. Edwin Blalock, an immunologist at the University of Alabama in Birmingham. During an infectious illness, for example, endorphins produced by immune cells serve as a pain reliever or mood elevator. Thyroid-stimulating hormones might exert a stimulating effect on the heart rate, breathing, or general metabolism. And sex hormones might decrease potency, sexual interest, or fertility.

Blalock suggests that the immune system may even provide us with a kind of sixth sense for bacterial and viral invasions. If the classical sensory systems can only transmit taste, smell, sound, and touch, how then does the brain know when it is invaded? Perhaps, says Blalock, "the immune system serves as a sensory organ for stimuli not recognized by the classical sensory systems." Once the brain recognizes a chemical message forwarded from the immune system, it can orchestrate appropriate hormonal reactions and physiological changes to protect the body.

But neuroscientists are not yet certain of the precise mechanisms involved in brain and immune system regulation. An immune cell's activity might also be directly regulated via activations of specific receptors on the cell membrane. Immune cells possess receptors not only for hormones and peptides, but for several of the neurotransmitters, including two of the earliest and most thoroughly studied of the brain's messenger chemicals, norepinephrine and acetylcholine. These neuroactive agents can enhance or diminish immune cell activities, depending on the immune cell type targeted and the specific neurotransmitter employed.

All these recent discoveries are leading us to a new and dynamic view of how the mind can influence our health. What the brain, the immune system, and the endocrine system have in common is cell-to-cell communication. Whether this involves neurons in the brain, lymphocytes in the immune system, or insulin-secreting cells in the pancreas is not important. In fact, the distinctions between neurotransmitter and hormone begin to fade when the same chemicals are found to influence the brain, the immune system, and the endocrine systems. This allows us to view the brain as a gland controlled by hormones that it and the other glands in the immune and endocrine systems produce.

"Many kinds of illnesses, especially those related to stress, will be more easily treated by understanding the hormonal signals that move back and forth between the body and the brain," notes Dr. Richard Bergland, author of *The Fabric of Mind*. "Central to this concept that the mind is modulated by hormones is the recognition that the stuff of thought is not caged in the brain, but is scattered all over the body; regulatory hormones are ubiquitous."

So mind, it turns out, is not a matter of brain alone, but of coordination of brain, immune system, and endocrine systems.

Bereavement puts people—men in particular—at risk for illness and death. Dr. Marvin Stein and his colleagues at the Mount Sinai School of Medicine in New York have looked at what happens to the immune system of husbands who grieve after the death of their wives from advanced breast cancer. They found that the ability of their lymphocytes to respond to an invader such as a bacterium or a virus decreased dramatically within a month or two of the death of their wives.

Bereavement is regularly accompanied by depression, and indeed may be considered a particularly intense form of depression. Stein and his investigators next looked at the lymphocyte responses of patients hospitalized for severe depression. They, too, showed *immunosuppression*. The circumstances under which the stress occurs and the attitude of the person undergoing the stress were found to be particularly important. Furthermore, different kinds of stress can leave people vulnerable to a variety of diseases associated with the immune system. Many conditions are known to alter the response to stress. They include time of day, duration and frequency of the stress, even the kind of stress applied (e.g., noise versus electric shock). But not everyone is vulnerable to stress.

Studies have shown that the more life stress a person experiences, the greater the likelihood of developing a physical disorder like heart disease, infection, allergies, even cancer. A large study conducted over several decades by Dr. George Valliant of Harvard University found that poor mental health was associated with poor physical health, even when such variables as alcohol, tobacco abuse, and obesity were statistically controlled. "Stress," Valliant concluded, "does not kill as much as ingenious adaptation to stress—call it good mental health or mature coping mechanisms—facilitates our survival."

One of the most important factors in the response to stress—indeed in defining whether or not a particular situation is even stressful at all—is whether anything can be done about the stress. Rats that are given repeated, unavoidable electrical shocks become passive. This "learned helplessness" increases their susceptibility to disease, according to Drs. Martin E. T. Seligman and Steven Maier, who were at the University of Pennsylvania when this research was carried out in the mid-1960s. When they injected the rats with tumor-causing cells and then gave them shocks from which they could not escape, a high percentage of the rats developed cancer. But rats that could escape the shocks by moving to another part of the cage tended to reject the tumor cells. Also cancer-free were other rats, which were injected with the cells but not given any shocks.

Humans also show wide variations in the effects of stress. Research by Dr. Steven Locke, of Harvard University, shows that the immune system's natural killer cell activity against cancerous tumors diminishes in people who cope poorly with life-change stresses. Such people easily become depressed. Their depression eventually leads to the kind of situation wryly described by Woody Allen in one of his movies: "I don't get depressed; I grow a tumor instead."

People who cope well with stress, on the other hand, show no decline in natural killer cell activity even when they experience what appears to be the same stress. I say "appears to be" because, in truth, no two people ever experience the same stress. Stress, under all circumstances, must be viewed in the context of how each person interprets what's happening to him or her. "The care of tuberculosis depends more on what the patient has in his head than what he has in his chest," wrote Sir William Osler, the "Father of Modern Medicine."

How one responds to stress largely depends on the amount of control one has over the stress. Steven Maier has studied the effects of control in rats by introducing a new rat into an established colony. Almost immediately, the rats started investigating each other and sooner or later an established male would attack the intruder.

"Some rats will give up very quickly," explains Maier, "and adopt the defeat posture. Other rats will not, and will continue to fight. But sooner or later, given that this is another rat's territory, that rat, too, will give up. If you reintroduce the defeated animal the next day, it will almost immediately adopt the defeat posture."

The intruder is seldom injured in the fight. But by giving up, he has lost control of the situation. And it's that simple psychological shift—from control to a loss of control—that leads to clear physical changes that affect the rat's health. "The total outcome of the situation," says Maier, "is determined by the way the intruder perceives the situation. It's specifically under the situation where there is no control that you see deleterious consequences of stress. You see ulcer formation. You see a large steroid release. You see changes in metabolism. And consequently, down the line you also see immune changes that are undoubtedly a function of [this change in control.]"

It's not actual control that is important to the maintenance of health under conditions of uncertainty and stress, but the mere *belief* that one is in control. Remember what the dentist says when he's performing a painful extraction: "If it hurts too much, just lift your finger and I'll stop."

Most of us experience a good deal of relief from being told this.

"But in fact, most people will almost never raise their finger," notes Maier. "The dentist, in turn, probably wouldn't be able to stop that fast anyway, certainly not if he or she was in the middle of some delicate procedure. Yet thinking that you have control or might have control is sufficient to blunt many of the negative effects of stress."

If the mind does indeed exert a powerful, perhaps overwhelming influence on bodily health and integrity, one conclusion is inevitable: If my attitudes and interpretations can have such a powerful effect on my physical health, then it seems reasonable to conclude that to a very real extent I'm *responsible* for my health and well-being. This is certainly a revolutionary and, I would submit, disturbing reevaluation of the relation of mind to body. It may also have practical consequences of the gravest sort.

Is there a link between stress and cancer? The notion is an ancient one. In the second century A.D., Galen, the Greek physician and writer, claimed that "melancholic" women were more prone to developing breast cancer. But no one examined this question scientifically until 1954. Researchers then looked at the longevity of cancer patients who had reacted to their illness with a great deal of depression. As a group they did poorly, succumbing to their disease earlier than was expected. Over the past two decades researchers have pursued the effects of cancer patients' attitudes toward their illness on how long they live.

Of course, many factors other than mental attitude could be responsible for differences in survival rates. Age is one. So is the clinical stage of the cancer, in other words, whether it's localized or widespread. The tumor grade also plays an important role, for the more primitive or less differentiated the cancer cell, the poorer the prognosis.

So there is naturally much doubt on the subject. "It is very controversial in the medical profession," says Dr. Steven Greer, of the Royal Marsden Hospital in London, "to accept even the possibility that mental processes could affect cancer. I think this is partly because as doctors we're all taught, and have it drummed into us in medical school, that there is a rigid division between the mind and the body. Of course, that's nonsense."

It's nonsense also to Greer's patient, Rachel Beales. For Beales there isn't any doubt that her attitude is making a difference in her survival. Cancer has been her enemy for a long time. Her breast was removed six years ago. A lung collapsed three years ago under the weight of a tumor, and she was told she had only about one year to live. Recently the disease has reappeared twice, but she hasn't given up.

She is teaching and active in sports, but most important of all for her continued survival, she believes, is her attitude. "I'm sure I would not be here now if I hadn't developed this absolutely total and utter determination that I personally am going to beat this thing, and I was going to win."

Rachel Beales is part of Greer's latest study, designed to discover whether an attitude changed through therapy can prolong a cancer patient's life. In a group of sixty-nine women with early breast cancer, he's found that attitude is very highly correlated with survival. The women with an active "fighting spirit" had the best outcome and were twice as likely to be alive and well ten years later when compared to women who showed helpless or hopeless attitudes.

No one claims that attitude is everything, however. "I think you're crazy if you don't also use conventional drug treatments," says Beales. "They've worked in my case. But you've also got a body and a mind and a spirit. You've got to utilize all of these."

Cancer, of course, may not be a fair test of the influence of mental attitude on health. By the time a patient comes down with an advanced cancer, the odds may be so stacked against survival that even the powers of the mind may be ineffectual in prolonging life.

For the past seven years, Gail Scheiber has been using self-hypnosis to control the pain from her arthritis. "You're not aware of any pain when you're in a hypnotic state," she explains, "because your mind, your attention span, is somewhere else. You're ignoring it, you've tuned out. When you come out of a hypnotic state your subconscious has accepted your fed-in thoughts, your phrasing, so it naturally carries out the orders that you've given it. It's a matter of tuning in and tuning out to your pain."

HEALING WORDS

"A suitable explanation or a comforting word to the patient may have something like a healing effect which may even influence the glandular secretions. The doctor's words, to be sure, are 'only' vibrations in the air, yet they constitute a particular set of vibrations corresponding to a particular psychic state in the doctor. The words are effective only insofar as they convey a meaning or have significance. It is their meaning which is effective. But 'meaning' is something mental or spiritual. Call it a fiction if you like. Nonetheless, it enables us to influence the course of the disease in a far more effective way than with chemical preparations. We can even influence the biochemical processes of the body by it. Whether the fiction rises in me spontaneously or reaches me from without by way of human speech, it can make me ill or cure me."

—Carl Jung

Dr. David Spiegel uses hypnosis to help his patient Patsy Frazier manage her leg pain better.

That pain can be managed through hypnosis is not surprising. "Pain is a product of two factors," explains Dr. David Spiegel, of Stanford University. "One is the physical signal itself, the irritation, the damage in the body. The second factor is the message, or the meaning of the pain. Hypnosis can be very useful here. It alters the way people interpret the pain signal that is sent up to the brain. If a person knows that he's got cancer or arthritis, and the pain is simply a nuisance, he can learn to use hypnosis to basically put the pain outside that circle of attention by focusing on other images or metaphors."

Hypnosis allows us to disassociate ourselves from the sensations we feel. It happens like this: At all times, certain sensations and thoughts are filtered out of our awareness. As you sit reading this sentence, for instance, you are not aware of the position of your legs until I call your attention to this fact. In doing so, your focus of awareness shifts momentarily to an area of your body that seconds before was outside your consciousness. Hypnosis reassigns priorities in the same way, by shifting our perceptions.

This hypnotic state is reflected in a definite change in the pattern of brain waves, indicating that this reassigning of priorities originates in the cortex of the brain. "What

distinguishes humans from other animals is the size of this enormous neocortex that has evolved," says Spiegel. "Many animals can perceive things more accurately than we can. But we have an amazing ability to reorganize signals and decide to choose some and not others."

One afternoon about a decade ago a woman of forty-five came to my office with a very unusual complaint. She was angry, depressed, and disillusioned because she had discovered that her doctor of over a decade had been exposed as an impostor. But she had improved over the period she was under his care and she was curious what my response would be to her question: If he wasn't a doctor and didn't know anything about medicine, how was it that she did so well under his care? Inquiry revealed that her "doctor" always spent a good deal of time with her, inquired about her family, encouraged her to think well instead of ill of her appearance, intelligence, and personality. In a word, he made her feel good about herself.

Was this sufficient reason for my patient to have maintained her blood pressure and weight under good control? There's no way anyone could answer such a question with certainty. There are too many variables, too many loose ends, too many equally plausible reasons for why she had done so well. But I do remember how impressed I was with my patient's intensity when discussing how helpful her former "doctor" had been to her.

While I have personal reservations about making too much of what may only be an incidental accompaniment of good medical care, I have noticed that many of the most successful doctors I've encountered over the years have regularly aroused positive emotions in their patients. The ability to arouse these positive emotions has, of course, nothing to do with the breadth and depth of the practitioner's medical training.

But we should not underestimate the benefits of positive feelings. Only a few years ago, Norman Cousins, the former editor in chief of *Saturday Review,* published an article on the beneficial effects of laughter on his own serious illness. Among other things, Cousins had watched Marx Brothers films in his hospital room and gave a good deal of credit for his recovery to the amusement and laughter they aroused in

Norman Cousins credits laughter, like that generated by the Marx Brothers' A Night at the Opera, for much of his recovery from serious illness.

him. But until he had explained himself further, I was skeptical.

"One of the common characteristics of serious illness is panic," said Cousins. "Medical science has been able to identify the negative effects of such emotions. It's well known, for example, that panic will constrict the blood vessels, even as it increases sharply the presence of catecholamines in the bloodstream. The catecholamines, in turn, can destabilize heart rhythm and can even rupture muscle fibers of the heart. It is essential to control the panic. Many physicians make a special effort to encourage their patients' will to live and, indeed, the full range of the positive emotions. For the best way to deal with the panic is to replace it. It is in this context that laughter—and the positive emotions in general—perform a useful function. By changing the mood of the patient the physician is able to set an auspicious stage for treatment. It is useful, I believe, to reach beyond laughter to all of the positive emotions—hope, faith, love, will to live, purpose, and confidence."

Some three hundred years earlier the same point had been made by Thomas Sydenham, one of the foremost physicians of the time. "The arrival of a good clown," he said, "exercises a more beneficial influence upon the health of a town than of twenty asses laden with drugs."

One would of course like to believe that all this is true. But do things actually work this way? At this point, the fairest answer is that we can't be certain. The data is intriguing and suggestive, but firm correlations have not yet been made. One of the difficulties here, it seems to me, stems from the deeply ingrained schism in our ideas about mind and body.

As I write these words, I experience aspects of mind—what effects these words will have on you the reader, for instance—influencing a bodily activity, the movement of my pen across the paper. But as a neurologist, I know that each word I write is inextricably bound up with a sequence of nerve potentials and movements in the muscles of fine control in my hand. I know that these are not two separate processes, but a single unitary activity: *I* am writing these sentences.

But try as I might, I can't escape feeling that somehow I exist apart from the body that is forming these words. It's as if I use the hand in order to set down what my mind is thinking. The analogy here is to a machine, and, indeed, Descartes described the body as a marvelous clockwork that must be set off against the mind that observes it. This is the ghost in the machine, in the memorable words of the philosopher Gilbert Ryle. But as long as I think of myself as separate from my body, then obviously, claims that the

Norman Cousins.

mind can influence one's general health will be met with skepticism—even antagonism.

The notion that the mind can heal arouses much skepticism in the scientific community. "The dark side of assuming there is a connection between emotions and health is that people who fall ill may blame themselves and feel even guiltier if they get worse," notes Dr. Marcia Angell, an editor at the *New England Journal of Medicine*. "Our belief in disease as a direct reflection of mental state is largely folklore."

Yet the medical community readily acknowledges the positive effects of the sugar pill, or placebo—perhaps the most stunning example we have of the power of mind over health. The best demonstration of these effects came in 1964 when Dr. Robert Sternbach administered to a group of volunteer subjects a pill containing no active ingredients. (The pill was basically nothing more than a magnetic tracer that permitted the measurement of stomach activity.) The subjects were told that they were receiving a drug that would stimulate a strong churning sensation in their stomachs. On another occasion, the subjects were given the same pill but told instead that the pill would reduce their stomach activity and make them feel full and heavy. The third time he administered the pill to the subjects, they were told that the pill was a placebo and would serve as a control in the experiment. Though the same pill was administered on all three occasions, two thirds of Sternbach's subjects demonstrated changes in stomach activity consistent with the instructions they had received.

It is clear that all the pills Sternbach administered, not just the last one, were actually placebos. Whatever effect was produced owed nothing to their chemical composition—they were all inert. Instead, the effect came entirely from what the volunteers had been led to *believe* about the pills. What we are talking about here is commonly, and sometimes derisively, referred to as the placebo effect. This is a poorly understood process in which psychological factors such as belief and expectation trigger a healing response that can be as powerful as any conventional therapy for a wide range of medical and psychological problems.

On the average, about a third of patients given placebos will experience satisfactory relief from a wide variety of conditions. And these placebos may involve procedures as well as pills. In the 1950s surgeons enthusiastically touted an operation for angina, severe chest pains stemming from heart ailments. The operation involved tying off the mammary artery along the chest wall. They believed at the time that this created a redistribution of blood flow that improved circulation to the coronary arteries serving the heart, thus cutting down pain. Three quarters of all patients were said to benefit from this procedure. But a closer look revealed that even sham operations involving skin incisions alone produced a reported improvement in almost half the patients.

The placebo response obviously plays a major role in healing, though sometimes its effects are confusing. It's true, for instance, that it has made it difficult for researchers to gauge the effectiveness of new drugs. On the other hand, it has been quite useful in helping to explain the occasional success of quack remedies. In fact, it helps explain a wide range of otherwise mysterious phenomena. At one end of the spectrum is voodoo death, in which a person's heart may go into an irreversible arrhythmia (abnormal rhythm of the heartbeat) at the sight of a harmless object he or she has been led to believe can kill. At the other end of the spectrum are the many instances of recovery that defy medical explanation. Since 1954, for instance, thirteen cures at Lourdes have been declared "scientifically inexplicable" by the International Medical Committee of Lourdes.

That placebos work is no longer in doubt. How they work is another question entirely. But perhaps the most important determinant in their success is the setting in which placebos are administered, according to Dr. Jon Levine, a neurobiologist at the University of California, San Francisco. "The wearing of a white coat by the doctor, along with a stethoscope and other medical accoutrements, will help provide an image to the patient which suggests that the interactions should produce a therapeutic effect," says Levine.

If the conditions of placebo administration are changed—if, for instance, a drug is computer dispensed at a time unknown to the patient and doctor—the placebo response largely disappears. "That's because there's no cue for the patient," says Levine, "no white coat, no nurse, no indication at any point that the patient should improve."

The physical characteristics of the placebo itself have an effect on how the patient will respond. Red or pink stimulants seem to work better than blue ones. Multicolored tablets, particularly with a good deal of orange or red in them, appear to be more effective than small white tablets. In some patients, pills don't work at all; these people respond only to injections. And when placebos fail, success can often be achieved by supplying the patient with a "new and improved" version: another placebo.

The placebo response is not magic, nor is it mere "suggestion," Levine cautions. If the opiate-antagonizing drug naloxone is administered, the pain relief effect of the placebo is canceled out. This suggests that placebos help patients turn on their own pain relief mechanism. "We believe," says Levine, "the patients turn on an endogenous [internal] pain control circuit that is in their brain, and that this circuit uses substances called endorphins, which are morphine-like substances made by the brain, to produce pain relief. By psychologically intervening, we are able to get the patient to turn on this system, and to decrease the level of pain."

Physicians who can successfully elicit a placebo response tend to be optimistic and hopeful. In the face of uncertainty they emphasize affirmative emotions while encouraging confidence and expectations for recovery. Such physicians encourage their patients to develop a positive sense of themselves and their body, as well as to cultivate a trust in the body and its capacity for recovery.

This kind of an attitude does not come easily to physicians trained in traditional medical schools, where the emphasis is on caution and never promising more than one can deliver, lest false expectations be aroused. These physicians tend to view the patients as passive participants in the treatment process. It is the doctor who brings about a cure or improvement. On the other hand, physicians capable of eliciting a placebo response see patients as active participants in their own care. In this case, the patients, in cooperation with the physician, help to effect their own improvement. The distinction, although subtle, is important. In a phrase, the physician stimulates the patient's "will to live."

"It is doubtful whether the placebo, or any drug for that matter, would get very far without a patient's robust will to live," writes Norman Cousins in *The Mysterious Placebo: How Mind Helps Medicine Work*. "For the will to live is a window on the future. It opens the individual to such help as the outside world has to offer, and it connects that help to the body's own capability to fight disease. It enables the human body to make the most of itself. The placebo has a role to play in transforming the will to live from a poetical conception to a physical reality and governing force."

My own experience as a physician tells me that Cousins is correct. Many times throughout my career I've witnessed patients recover, or at least improve temporarily, by sheer willpower, pure determination that "this thing isn't going to get me." At such times I have often felt that my own role as the physician, ostensibly the most important one, was actually subsidiary to other processes I couldn't precisely define. In saying this I recognize that such an opinion, though interesting in its own right, sheds little light on our understanding.

No doubt, however, the plasticity of the brain and its component neurons forms the basis for the healing effects wrought by positive, hopeful states of mind, as well as for adverse effects wrought by despair and discouragement.

Any given neuron has the potential to switch from one neurotransmitter to another and thereby alter the message it sends and the regions of the brain it influences. It is likely that the subtle shifts of mind required for healing—particularly hope and confidence—involve alterations in neuron-to-transmitter relationships on the molecular level, alterations, in other words, of the brain's chemical structure. It should actually come as no surprise that the brain would be anything but dramatically responsive to our attitudes, emotions, thoughts, hopes, and other states of mind.

"Over the years," notes Norman Cousins, "medical science has identified the primary systems of the body—circulatory system, digestive system, endocrine system, autonomic nervous system, parasympathetic nervous system, and the immune system. But two other systems that are central to the proper functioning of a human being need to be emphasized: the healing system and the belief system. The two work together. The healing system is the way the body mobilizes all its resources to combat disease. The belief system is often the activator of the healing."

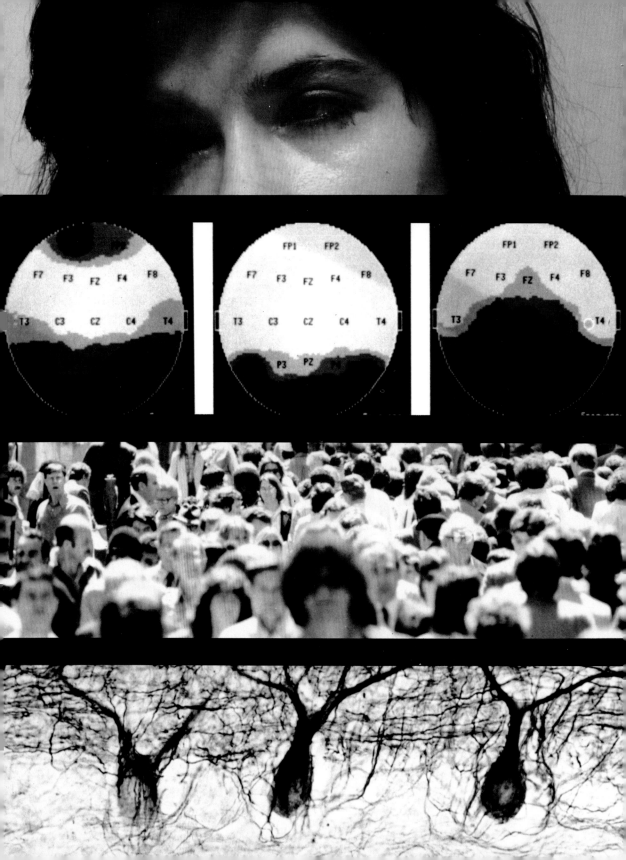

6.
DEPRESSION

Everyone of us goes through changes in mood. We are sometimes exhilarated and optimistic, at other times "in the dumps," "feeling low," unhappy. These moods are often a direct response to something that has happened to us—a pleasurable event or a sense that things are going our way, or a rebuff, a disappointment, a letdown. But a particular event isn't necessary to generate mood. Environment alone can affect how we feel; a succession of gray days in winter makes many people gloomy or irritable, and the balmy promise of April puts a spring in our steps and turns us cheerful and eager.

There are also many times when we can't pin down an explicit reason for why we feel as we do. For most of us, however, whether or not we know the reason, our moods do not dominate our lives. Even when we're "not in the mood" because we're feeling morose or sad, we force ourselves to do those things that need to be done. We are able to do this because over the years we have learned to control our moods instead of allowing them to control us.

But not everyone is capable of this. Some people are so dominated by their moods that these moods are in charge of their lives. When they're on a "high," they believe, and *act,* as if anything is possible. All constraints vanish. They may spend money they don't have, go virtually without sleep, work with such wild intensity that they often do a day's work within hours. The term for this behavior is "manic." When they're "down," in contrast, they can barely force themselves out of bed, often lose interest in food, isolate themselves from others, cannot summon up the will or energy to carry out even the most routine of activities, and are pervaded by a sense of hopelessness. If depression is sufficiently severe, individuals in its grip may even kill themselves.

Hippocrates, "the Father of Medicine"
(460?–377 B.C.).

When we talk about behavior like this, we are not referring to those ordinary variations in mood, ranging from happiness to unhappiness, that characterize most people. Rather, we are describing a specific kind of illness called *mood* or *affective disorders* ("affect" is a scientific term for an emotional state). As we will see, these disorders may express themselves differently, may have different causes and triggering mechanisms, and may be treated differently. But regardless of these differences, we are talking about a group of *diseases* when we describe clinical depression—the term for a major depressive episode. It affects the body as well as the mind, and is the most prevalent of mental illnesses.

Depression has been recognized and described throughout recorded history. Priests in Egypt three thousand years ago treated it. They operated within a theological rather than a medical framework, but their observations were acute and they noted two characteristic aspects of the disorder: depression is often (though not always) associated with the experience of loss, and it is often repetitive. In the Old Testament King Saul is described as suffering from recurrent depressive episodes. This pattern of depression alternating with periods of normal mood holds true for most depressive illnesses. However prolonged the attack of depression may be, almost no one is depressed all the time. Depressive episodes come and go.

Not until around the fourth century B.C. was depression first thought of as a medical problem, rather than an affliction of the gods not amenable to rational inquiry or the healing efforts of physicians. It was the Greek "Father of Medicine," Hippocrates, who first attributed mood change to natural rather than divine causes. He placed the site of mental functions and malfunctions in the brain and speculated that in mental illness, the brain suffered from an imbalance of the "four humors"—fluids—that he believed circulated throughout the body. He introduced the terms "mania" and "melancholia." His descriptions of patients exhibiting these behaviors, which he saw as the extremes of a continuum, with melancholia, or depression, at one end and mania at the other, remain as valid today as when he first articulated them.

Today we speak of chemical imbalances of neurotransmitters in the brain, rather than imbalances of humors. But the underlying concepts are remarkably similar: mood disorders result from or are associated in some way with disturbances within the brain, as well as with environmental influences.

Aretaeus, a Greek physician of the second century A.D., discarded the ancient theory of humors, and was the first to make a distinction between exogenous (externally caused)

depressions, in which the condition is triggered by an actual event, such as the loss of someone close, and endogenous (caused from within) depressions, in which there is no precipitating event. Both forms often exhibit the same symptoms, though treatment may vary. Aretaeus was also the first to note that mania and depression frequently occur in the same individual.

In the Middle Ages there was a resurgence of the supernatural theory of mental illness. The ancient gods had long been forgotten, but witches and the malevolent influence of the stars took their place, and evil spirits were thought to have seized the afflicted person. Beginning with the Renaissance, however, the emphasis shifted permanently toward natural causes for mood disorders. Though this certainly did not end popular belief in witchcraft or possession by evil spirits as the explanation for mental illness—beliefs that civil authorities continued to exploit for their own ends—by the middle of the sixteenth century thoughtful observers had come to agree that the brain was in some way implicated in depression and mania.

There was little change in the actual treatment of mental illness despite this insight, but it did stimulate an important change in the quality of care. Greater humaneness began to replace brutality. One of the most moving scenes ever captured on canvas is that of Philippe Pinel, the founder of modern psychiatry, removing the chains from the patients at Salpêtrière, the fearsome asylum in Paris, in 1795. Pinel's action was as revolutionary as any of the other upheavals in that time of revolutions.

Philippe Pinel removing the chains from patients in the Salpêtrière, 1795. Painting by Robert Fleury.

Vincent van Gogh, Late Self-Portrait,
1889–1890 (?).

The care of the mentally ill has varied in quality since then, ranging from the humane to the abysmal, and until this century asylums continued to be the chief repository for these patients. But it is accurate to say that Pinel's removal of the chains ushered in a new era in which mental disorders, including severe depression, were recognized as *illnesses,* and those who suffered from them as human beings in distress, not subhuman creatures in the grip of some demonic force.

Today we categorize the major mood disturbances as *unipolar disorder,* in which depression is followed by a return to normal mood; and *bipolar disorder,* in which depression often alternates with episodes of intensely heightened mood, or mania. (Other names for bipolar disorder are manic depression and the outmoded term manic–depressive psychosis.) One percent of the population suffers from bipolar disorder and at least 5 percent from unipolar disorder; yet because depression often goes unrecognized, and less than 6 percent of its victims ever seek or receive treatment for their illness, the incidence is very probably higher than these figures suggest.

Clinical depression is much more severe and prolonged than a simple case of the "blues." Depressed patients report they are incapable of experiencing pleasure, even when they recognize that the events or circumstances around them are inherently pleasurable. They cannot summon up interest in the people, things, or events around them. Their energy level is low. Ordinary tasks become overwhelming. Their horizons are narrowed, the future as dark as the present. They may also evidence other signs and symptoms, such as agitation, weight loss or gain, sleep disturbances (insomnia or hypersomnia, in which they sleep more than usual), a decline in self-esteem, guilt feelings, and difficulties in concentration, calculation, reasoning, and decision making. But the overriding characteristic of the illness is the appalling sadness and hopelessness that pervade the sufferer's life, envelop him or her without surcease.

"This new attack came upon me in the fields when I was in the midst of painting," wrote Vincent van Gogh to his brother from an asylum in the south of France a century ago. "I finished in spite of it. I am terribly distressed that the attacks have come back. It is abominable. To learn to suffer without complaint, to look on pain without repugnance. It is exactly in that that you run the risk of vertigo. Nevertheless, you catch a glimpse of a vague likelihood that on the other side of life we shall see reason for the existence of pain. Seen from here, it fills the horizon and takes on the proportion of a hopeless deluge." The deluge swamped him within a year.

Recovery from depression is slow. It can be spontaneous; but when it is enhanced by a combination of drug treatment and psychotherapy, it is likely to come more quickly. When the person suffers from bipolar disorder, however, the end of the depression is often not the end of the illness. Within a period ranging from a few weeks to a few days—and sometimes literally within hours—mania may ensue. The mood shifts dramatically into a blaze of heightened self-esteem, elation, expansiveness, euphoria. Suddenly no task is too difficult, no challenge too daunting. Manics think and speak rapidly, have difficulty sitting still, require little sleep, express themselves not only with great confidence and assurance but often with contempt for what they perceive as the limitations of others. They have boundless energy, taking up one project after another but often completing none of them. It is difficult for these individuals to hold to one idea at a time, and they are utterly certain of the rightness and importance of those ideas, greeting opposition with argumentation, more talk, disdainful dismissal, and—if pushed far enough—assault. Not surprisingly, this constellation of personality traits brings them into conflict with their family, their neighbors, and often with the law.

They sign contracts for things they can't afford to buy, drive recklessly, impulsively start up sexual liaisons, call up friends and acquaintances in the middle of the night to harangue them on topics of interest to no one but themselves. They may even begin to hallucinate, demonstrating behavior that by any definition can be termed psychotic. Here is a description of the illness written by a person suffering from manic depression:

"There is a particular kind of pain, elation, loneliness, and terror involved in this kind of madness. When you're high it's tremendous. The ideas and feelings are fast and frequent, like shooting stars, and you follow them until you find better and brighter ones. Shyness goes, the right words and gestures are suddenly there, the power to seduce and captivate others a felt certainty. There are interests found in uninteresting people. Sensuality is pervasive and the desire to seduce and be seduced is irresistible. Feelings of ease, intensity, power, well-being, financial omnipotence, and euphoria now pervade one's marrow. But somewhere [along the line] this changes. The fast ideas are far too fast, and there are far too many; overwhelming confusion replaces clarity. Memory goes. Humor and absorption on friends' faces are replaced by fear and concern. Everything previously moving with the grain is now against it—you are irritable, angry, frightened, uncontrollable, and enmeshed totally in the blackest caves of the mind. You never knew those caves were there. It will never end. Madness carves its own reality. It goes on and on and finally there are only others' recollections of your behavior—your bizarre, frenetic, aimless behaviors—for mania has at least some grace in partially obliterating memories. What then, after the medications, psychiatrists, despair, depression, and overdose? All those incredible feelings to sort through. Who is being too polite to say what? Who knows what? What did I do? Why? And most hauntingly, when will it happen again? Then, too, there are the annoyances: medicine to take, resent, forget, take, resent, forget, but always to take. Credit cards revoked, bounced checks to cover, explanations due at work, apologies to make, friendships gone or drained, a ruined marriage. And always: when will it happen again? Which of my feelings are real? Which of the me's is *me*? The wild, impulsive, chaotic, energetic, and crazy one? Or the shy, withdrawn, desperate, suicidal, doomed, and tired one?"

Testimony such as this underscores the anguish of mania, which, unlike the pain of depression, often goes unrealized by those who have not encountered it directly. This lack of awareness may be caused in part by the erroneous perception that mania is simply a continuous "high." It may also be linked to the belief that there is a close relationship between madness and creativity. It is an ancient belief. Pre-Grecian myths describe vivid Dionysian–Apollonian struggles between violence and creation, madness and reason. By the time of Plato and Socrates, priests and poets were believed to be capable of communicating directly with the gods through their daemons, or "geniuses." These daemons, who were guardian spirits and helpful agents of the gods, inspired the concept of "divine madness." Inspiration was believed to be directly related to extreme states of mind. Aristotle, for example, held that "all who have been famous for their genius, whether in the study of philosophy, in affairs of state, in political competition, or in the exercise of the arts, have been inclined to insanity."

Emil Kraepelin, the nineteenth-century psychiatrist who formulated the first scientific description of manic depression, concurred that on occasion the illness conferred positive benefits: "The volitional excitement which accompanies a disease may, under certain circumstances, set free powers which otherwise are constrained by all kinds of inhibition. Artistic activity may, by the untroubled surrender to momentary fancies or moods . . . experience a certain furtherance."

It is certainly true that during the milder stages of mania (*hypomania*), the expansiveness of thought and the heightened sense of well-being may lead to enhancement of the power to think and perform creatively and to associate ideas and concepts that are likely not to be linked during "ordinary" states of consciousness. Thoughts are speeded up, as we have noted, and associations facilitated, unique ideas generated, in response to the combination of elevated mood, expansive self-esteem, high energy, diminished need for sleep and rest, increased productivity, and, in many instances, a capacity to experience a heightened depth and breadth of emotions.

Psychologist Kay Redfield Jamison, Associate Professor of Psychiatry at the Johns Hopkins University School of Medicine, explored the relationship between manic depressive illness and creativity by studying successful artists and writers in Great Britain. She discovered during her research that mood, madness, and genius are often intertwined in ways that defy simple analysis. She found that fully 38 percent had been treated for mood disorders. One half of the poets in this group had been given drugs or been hospitalized for their illness. These figures are extraordinarily high.

Nonetheless, though many creative artists have certainly suffered from bipolar illness, the majority of creative people have not. Moreover, among those with the illness are many examples of lives as haunted and tragic as their works were brilliant; not only van Gogh, but the poets Robert Lowell,

Sylvia Plath, and John Berryman come to mind. Nor is the impulse to romanticize manic depression limited to lay people. "The psychiatric literature often suggests that mania is a condition to be envied rather than treated. The suggestion is clinical nonsense," says Dr. Robert Cancro, Chairman of the Department of Psychiatry, New York University Medical Center.

Nonetheless, it is important to remember that at least some forms of mental illness exist upon a continuum with normal behavior. An excess of good spirits may merge into hypomania and contribute to creativity. Further along the continuum, hypomania can give way to outright mania, with its attendant disorganization and uncontrollable actions, the need for medication, and perhaps even prolonged hospitalization. At the other extreme, somber reflectiveness may also contribute to the creativity of the artist or the writer. But increasing somberness may culminate in a depression marked by a complete cessation of all activity and perhaps even suicide. There is value in reminding ourselves that while depression, both unipolar and bipolar, is an illness, it is also an exaggerated form of the human condition—encompassing responses that all of us share, though in attenuated forms.

And as an illness, depression can have a disastrous outcome. It is linked inextricably with suicide. One person in six—more than 16 percent—of those with an affect disorder, if untreated, eventually commits suicide. Indeed, the overwhelming majority (60 to 80 percent) of all adolescents and adults who commit suicide suffer from a depressive illness. It is known that more than two thirds of moderately to severely depressed people have suicidal thoughts.

Breaking the suicide figures down by age reveals a striking disparity between age groups. Although those over sixty years of age comprise 20 percent of the population, they commit 40 percent of all suicides. After age seventy-five the suicide rate is three times the average for the population at large. Despite these troubling figures, however, suicide among the elderly has actually decreased slightly over the past thirty years. The real, and terrifying, increase is among the young.

The suicide rate for those between the ages of fifteen and twenty-four has gone up 150 percent in the last twenty years. This age group, which once accounted for 5 percent of all suicides, now makes up 20 percent of male and 14 percent of female suicides. Among adolescent males, suicide is now the second most common cause of death, exceeded only by accidents. Depression, like other psychiatric illnesses, can begin early in life, though it is only in recent years that the extent of its prevalence among the young has really

been recognized and investigations into youthful suicides begun.

The above figures are alarming enough, but there is reason to believe the actual situation may be even worse. In many parts of the United States death records are notoriously unreliable. In general, coroners are primarily concerned with ruling out homicide as the cause of death, and once that can be ascertained, they are often acquiescent to the pleas of relatives that a suicide not be labeled as such. Moreover, when deaths occur as a result of automobile crashes, overdoses of medication, or falls from heights, it is often impossible to know with certainty whether the victims intended self-destruction or died accidentally.

It has long been noted that suicide, like depression, tends to run in families. Ernest Hemingway killed himself with a shotgun; so did his father and so did his brother. But separating out a possible genetic trait from environmental, psychological, and biochemical factors in suicide is complex and uncertain. All three men in the Hemingway family suffered from depression and drank to excess. If there was a predisposition, was it to depression, to alcohol abuse, or to suicide itself? Given our current state of knowledge, all we are able to acknowledge at this time is the apparent existence of familial tendencies to self-destruction.

Ernest Hemingway (1889–1961), creative artist, depressive, and suicide. He epitomized many of the complexities often found in people suffering from depression.

In different eras, cultures, and religions, suicide has been considered everything from a mortal sin to an honorable method of dealing with ignominy, pain, incurable illness, or loss. Moral issues have always troubled lawyers, philosophers, and thoughtful lay people who grapple with unanswerable questions about suicide: Does a person have the right to take his or her own life? Are there circumstances that justify suicide, circumstances under which a reasonable person would freely choose this course? But the questions that confront psychiatrists, physicians, and the close family and friends of a severely depressed person are urgent and specific, not abstract: Is this individual suicidal? Does this possibility of suicide come out of a treatable or curable illness, such as depression? How can I prevent the actual act?

If we are to attempt to answer these questions, we need to look at why people kill themselves.

As we have noted, depressive disorders are found in the vast majority of those who commit suicide. Among the immediate precipitants of the act of suicide, data indicate, are physical illness (especially significant in elderly males), loss of a loved one, alcohol abuse (15 to 25 percent of suicides are alcoholics), and drug addiction (the rate of suicide among narcotic addicts is five times the average rate for the general population). Most significant of all triggering factors, however, is overwhelming hopelessness. This is why suicide is so common among the severely depressed, who must combat hopelessness on a daily basis. A high level of hopelessness is the strongest sign that a person intends to attempt suicide, and if unsuccessful, is likely to try again. While external circumstances, guilt, delusion, and the depth of the depression are also important, they have much less influence on the victim's decision than hopelessness.

(This use of the word "victim" in regard to suicide is intriguing. Under no other circumstances do we call someone a victim whose own actions cause him or her injury or death. But the term seems appropriate in suicide: one part of the self takes control and destroys the whole organism. Often the person is extremely ambivalent about killing himself. Only one out of four suicide notes is hostile. Indeed, half express some gratitude, affection, or other positive feelings. The remaining quarter are neutral: no rage, no hatred. Nonetheless, even in the absence of expressed hostility, suicide is the ultimate hostile act against the self.)

What generates a depression with hopelessness so deep, pervasive, and persistent that suicide can seem the only way out? Until comparatively recently, explanations focused on the interplay of social and psychological forces. Tragedy, the death of a spouse or child, severe and prolonged stress, and adverse life circumstances such as divorce and job loss,

The Scream, *lithograph by Edvard Münch.*

were thought to be likely causes. But data do not support these assumptions. Though factors like these are often present in the lives of the depressed, on average, more than 85 percent of people subjected to them do *not* develop a serious depression. Further, divorce, job loss, and many other major stresses are often the result rather than the cause of depression. When people are withdrawn, unfriendly, morose, and sometimes directly hostile, they become extremely difficult to live and work with and drive other people away. Later, when these individuals, now wholly alone, are identified as depressed, it is easy to jump to the conclusion that their depression is the outcome of the adversities to which they have been subjected, instead of the other way around.

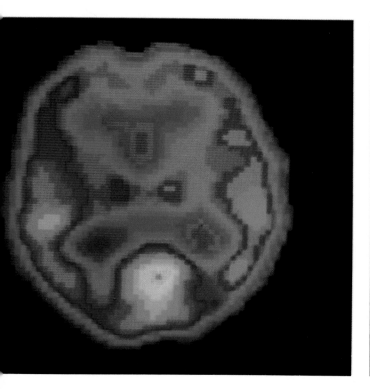 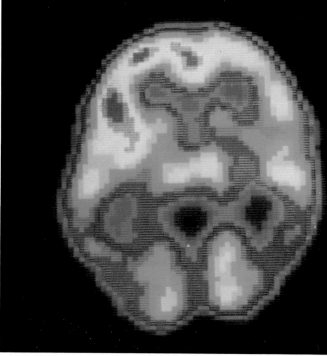

Other factors that have figured prominently in the construction of "explanations" for various mood disorders include gender, age, and social class. Unipolar disorder occurs more frequently in women (the lifetime risk for a major depressive episode is between 20 and 26 percent in women, 8 and 12 percent in men). The risk is highest among women who are younger, poorer, who have lost their mothers during childhood, and who lack supporting social ties. Bipolar disorder, in contrast, occurs as frequently in men as in women, and the correlation with socioeconomic class is reversed: better educated and more affluent individuals of both sexes are at greater risk.

These PET scans demonstrate a sharp contrast between a normal brain (left) and the brain of a bipolar depressive (right). The scan of the normal individual is characterized by bright red and yellow areas that indicate a high level of glucose utilization. Blue areas predominate in the depressed patient.

As in the analysis of social and psychological factors, however, when each of these variables is scrutinized, it proves to be insufficient explanation for depression. Depression may be more frequent in women who lost their mothers before age fifteen, for example, but the fact remains that two thirds of depressed women did not lose their mothers in that period.

Relating character traits such as introversion, shyness, "moodiness," or awkwardness and withdrawal in social situations to clinical depression is equally tenuous; again, the vast majority of those with these traits do not become depressed. Dr. Hagop Akiskal, Professor of Psychiatry at the University of Tennessee at Memphis, calls efforts to establish such links "a nightmare." For one thing, he notes, these efforts do not take the influence of the environment into account. In addition, even when personality traits seem independent of environmental influences, it is often difficult to ascertain whether these traits are the consequence or the cause of depression. All we know with certainty is that in at least 60 percent of depressive episodes, no precipitating psychosocial factor can be pinpointed.

Frustrated in their attempts to "explain" depression with any consistency on the basis of character traits, family background, or reactions to major stresses, investigators over the past two decades have turned to genetics. There is good reason to do this. It has been recognized for centuries that depression, and mood disorders in general, tend to run in families. But children also tend to imitate the behavior of those around them, so the increased incidence of a mood disorder within a family is not necessarily an indication of heritability. In the early twentieth century, for instance, pellagra, an illness marked by hallucinations, depression, and episodes of mania, appeared to run in families. Not surprisingly, many authorities considered it an inherited disease, as well as one with drastic consequences for the afflicted; fully 10 percent of the mentally ill confined to state asylums in the southern United States suffered from pellagra. But in 1915, Dr. Joseph Goldberger showed that the principal cause of pellagra is a deficiency of the B vitamin niacin. When niacin was added to a family's diet, the disorder was prevented. (Corn, which was a major component of the diet of poorer families in the south, is deficient in niacin.) Pellagra was a classic example of the complexities (and traps) inherent in the nature/nurture, genetics/environment dilemma. In this case environment—in the form of the family diet—proved unquestionably to be the culprit, rather than a genetic factor passed down from parent to child.

How then to clarify the roles of genetics and environment in what appear to be familial patterns of depression?

A FAMILY AFFLICTION

Genetic factors loom large in the family of Douglas Barton, who has suffered from depression since he was a child. His sons Clinton, age twelve, and Matthew, twenty-one, and his daughter Rebecca, nineteen, all exhibit symptoms of what Mrs. Barton calls "the family curse," and she thinks she sees early indications of the disorder in their youngest child, Joseph, who is eleven. "He has some of the signs that Douglas had when he was that age, when we check back in family history," she says.

Douglas Barton remembers being seven years old and going to his uncle's farm. "I should have been excited when I got there. And I wasn't. The animals were there; the barns and granaries were there. Just joyous things to do. There was no joy in it at all. It was absolutely bleak. I felt hopeless. I couldn't understand what was going on."

"What Doug is an exemplar of," says psychiatrist Paul Wender, who is treating him, "is someone who has had a depression ever since childhood. He suffered thirty-six years of pain. Sometimes it got better, sometimes it got worse; but it never went away. And it was the kind of pain that he was embarrassed to have because he, like many people, believed this to be a manifestation of some kind of personal weakness or spiritual difficulty, rather than a disease."

Because of the familial pattern of depression, at Wender's request Douglas Barton checked back into his family tree and found that his grandmother, born in 1873, had been institutionalized for depression and had died in a state hospital. The biological origins of Doug's depression were confirmed by his responsiveness to medication, the first treatment that has helped him in three and a half decades. "Two of my antidepressant pills a day make all the difference in my life as to whether I live in misery or I function," says Doug.

Dr. Wender has been able to help the Barton children as well. "I'm delighted Doug has responded the way he has," says Wender. "He has been able to discuss this illness with his kids. This articulate man has been so open about this that I believe the children's unhappiness is going to be mitigated somewhat by the fact that their father takes this as an unfortunate disease, not as a sign of psychological weakness."

Douglas Barton.

Drs. Seymour Kety, Paul H. Wender, and David Rosenthal, among others, addressed this by examining the incidence of depression among identical twins (possessing the same genes, from the fertilization of a single egg) as compared to fraternal twins (only half of whose genes are shared, because they are the products of two separate fertilizations). The researchers discovered that if one member of an identical twin pair suffers a depressive disorder, the average concordance rate—the likelihood that the other twin will also develop depression—is 50 percent. The rate for fraternal twins is only about 10 percent, no different than that for siblings.

This wide difference in concordance rate between identical and fraternal twins lends strong presumptive support to the role of heredity in depression, but it is essential to remember that most twins also share the same environment. They are raised in the same household with the same structure, routines, meals, and discipline, are often dressed in the same clothes, go to the same schools. There is a special impetus to treat identical twins as if they were identical in all respects because of their startling physical resemblance. To what extent does this environmental uniformity affect the high concordance rate of depression in identical twins? Would the rate be lower in identical twins who did not share the same environment?

Kety, Wender, and Rosenthal had explored the incidence of schizophrenia in twins in Denmark who had been separated at birth, reared in different families, and were now adults. They extended their research to study manic-depressive illness as well. They discovered that the concordance rate for depression among these separated identical twins was similar to the rate in such twins reared together by their biological parents. Heredity as a predisposing risk factor turned out to be strongly relevant for bipolar depression.

But there is an important caution to keep in mind. Although the concordance rate between twins in the Denmark study was sometimes as high as 75 percent, it never approached 100 percent. If genetic inheritance was the sole factor for the development of bipolar illness, then in all instances in which one member of the identical twin pair developed depression, the other twin should develop it too. Since this was not the case, it is clear that even in situations in which deterministic factors—in this case, genetic predisposition—loom large, there is still room for variations. Not every person with the genetic predisposition becomes depressed—or drinks excessively or commits suicide, two other conditions with heavy genetic "loading." There are genetic constraints on us all, but we are not automatons who are programmed to act out the scenarios written for us by our genes. No one can predict that an infant born today to a parent subject to manic-depressive illness will necessarily suffer from the disease. The most that scientists can do, bookmakerlike, is to tabulate odds.

By far the largest investigation of genetic factors in depressive illness is a study released in April 1987, that provides a major insight into the biological basis for depression. Over the past decade, twelve thousand Old Order Amish in Lancaster County, Pennsylvania, volunteered to cooperate in a groundbreaking study of human chromosomes under the direction of Dr. Janice A. Egeland, Professor of Psychiatry at the University of Miami School of

Medicine. The Amish had observed over the generations that mental illness was not evenly distributed throughout the entire community; as with certain other health problems such as diabetes and particular forms of cancer and heart disease, it appeared to run in families. "Sis im bloot," they said: it is in the blood.

Statistical analysis strongly suggested a hereditary pattern to the appearance of manic depression in these families over the generations. Then, using the most modern techniques of molecular biology, the researchers, affiliated with the University of Miami, Yale University, and the Massachusetts Institute of Technology, discovered a "strong predisposition" to manic-depressive illness in subjects who showed a genetic marker near the tip of the short arm of chromosome 11, one of the twenty-three pairs of human chromosomes. Though the incidence of the illness among the Amish is no greater than among the general population, those who demonstrate this genetic marker have a 60 to 80 percent chance of developing the disorder. One particularly tantalizing finding in the study is that this genetic marker for manic-depressive disorder is located near the gene that codes for the enzyme tyrosine hydroxylase, which is involved in a critical step in the synthesis of the neurotransmitter dopamine. Defects in dopamine metabolism have long been suspected as a possible biological cause of depression.

Within weeks after the Amish study documented the link between manic-depressive disorder and the indication of a defect in a gene on chromosome 11, Dr. Miron Baron, Professor of Psychiatry at Columbia University and Director of the Division of Psychogenetics at the New York State Psychiatric Institute, reported the results of a study of patients with manic depression at the Jerusalem Mental Health Center in Israel. Baron and his colleagues identified a genetic marker on the X chromosome (one of the sex chromosomes) in a group of subjects who, like the Amish, came from a highly homogeneous background. The fact that the X chromosome rather than chromosome 11 is suspect is not a concern; researchers have long theorized that there are multiple sources for manic depression. It is the pursuit of these possible sources that is the objective of the research. "Different biological defects may lead to the same clinical picture," Baron notes.

By using genetic markers like these to identify individuals at risk for manic depression before they become ill, psychiatrists in the near future may be able to spot the first signs of the disease and start early treatment. In the more distant future it may be possible to alter the course of the disorder—perhaps cure it or even prevent its expression—by altering the chromosomes with defective genes through some form of genetic intervention.

Studies of closed populations, as in the Amish and Jerusalem studies, are extremely valuable in tracking the etiology of an illness, and these findings provide exciting confirmation that at least some forms of manic depression are biological and heritable disorders; but many issues remain to be resolved. Because different genetic defects may be involved in the illness, much research remains to be done. So far, genetic studies among other homogeneous groups with a high incidence of manic depression, including isolated residents of Iceland and populations living in various solitary parts of North America, reveal no genetic markers for the illness. There may also be different subtypes of the illness, some with strong genetic loading that makes a defective gene a powerful influence in the emergence of the disease, others more dependent on life experiences and environmental factors. With manic depression, as often happens with an illness, a unitary definition that has served in the past may need to be reformulated over time to accommodate new knowledge discovered through modern neurobiological research.

But certainly the dimensions and the findings of the Amish study—for the first time in scientific history, a genetic mechanism was discovered for a mental illness—are a stimulus for a more complex approach to the origins and treatment of mental disorders. All known treatments for depression at this time deal with the symptoms of the disease, not the causes. Genetic investigations are targeted at possible causes. "This study ushers in a new era of psychiatric research, involving sophisticated molecular genetic techniques to reveal a physiologic basis for a mental illness," according to Dr. Daniel C. Regnier, Chief of Research at INSERM, in Paris.

Along with this new power to pinpoint the genetic bases for mental illness come new responsibilities. Chromosome analysis will almost certainly make possible prenatal confirmation that a fetus carries a genetic marker for manic depression. Is a 60 to 80 percent chance of developing manic depression a reasonable cause for aborting that fetus in the hope that prenatal tests of the next pregnancy will show no sign of the marker?

That issue aside, certainly much good can come from knowing ahead of time that a child *might* be predisposed to depression. Allowances can be made, environmental stresses perhaps reduced, early detection and treatment initiated. But there is a darker side to this knowledge too: the self-fulfilling prophecy.

What should adoptive parents know, for instance, about the genetic background of their adopted child? If they are told that one of the parents had died a suicide after a life marked by cycles of manic depression, would they wish to adopt that child? And whether their child was adopted or not, what effect would the knowledge of a genetic marker for the illness have on parents the first time that child came home from school crying in reaction to criticism from his favorite teacher? Would they overreact and see this normal response to a mild rejection as a sign of "pathologic" behavior? In other words, can they inadvertently induce in a child the very condition that by their efforts they are trying to prevent? Difficult questions like these extend beyond genetic and medical issues.

Depression is a prime example of an illness marked by helplessness and hopelessness in the face of forces that the patient envisions as inexorable and beyond his control. Imagine the effect of learning that genetic studies show you have a 60 to 80 percent chance of developing a major depression in the course of your life. Might this knowledge alone initiate a depression? It is certainly likely to deepen the feeling that your fate is not in your hands.

We will encounter this conflict between freedom and coercion at other points in our search for mind. We human beings need to believe that we are free despite increasing scientific evidence that our freedom operates within the bounds of biologically determined constraints. Depression is a disease of the mind, not only the brain. It involves our sense of purpose, destiny, autonomy, dignity—considerations that extend well beyond biology to fundamental issues of who we are, why we are here, and where we are going. Every technological advance that occurs brings with it challenges to our assumptions about ourselves.

Efforts to treat depression go far back in history and literature. The first recorded use of a drug to ease depression is found in *The Odyssey,* where Homer describes Helen of Troy giving nepenthe (an opium derivative) to Telemachus to relieve his grief. "Presently she cast a drug into the wine . . . to bring forgetfulness of every sorrow." At about the same period contemporary accounts describe a radical nondrug treatment; temple priests on an Aegean island threw depressed patients into the sea from a very high cliff. Other priests waited in boats in the water below to rescue them. The accounts say that many of the subjects of this unorthodox procedure recovered, cured by the shock of the harrowing experience.

In the second century A.D. a specific treatment for mania was suggested by the Greek physician Seranus Ephesios: "Natural waters such as alkaline springs." Over the centuries that followed, melancholy patients often "took the waters" at fashionable mineral spas throughout the world. We know now why this treatment often worked; the waters in these springs frequently contained lithium, the same chemical substance that is given today in the form of lithium salts to patients suffering from manic-depressive illness to bring them out of or avert an acute episode.

But except for this unidentified use of lithium, nothing new in the way of biological treatments for depression appeared for hundreds of years. The impetus for modern drug treatment of depression did not come until 1928, when psychiatrist J. Lange published this observation: "Opium appears to have a specific effect on melancholy, admittedly only a symptomatic one, and this is particularly striking because opium itself causes some effects that resemble the symptoms of melancholy."

Lange's statement led to a testable theory—namely, if one drug, opium, was able to alleviate the symptoms of depression, it should be possible eventually to find better and more effective drugs with similar effects.

In the early 1950s it became very clear that certain medications strongly affected mood. One was reserpine, derived from rauwolfia, the root of a plant used in India for centuries as a sedative, and now discovered to lower blood pressure in persons with hypertension. But about 15 percent of patients treated with reserpine for high blood pressure became depressed, showing the same symptoms of lethargy and detachment from their surroundings that characterize serious depressive episodes. Another drug, isoniazid, developed a few years later to treat tuberculosis, proved to have the side effect of heightening mood and increasing the sense of well-being.

Investigating the possible biochemical aspects of depression, researchers discovered that both these drugs affected the supply of the neurotransmitters serotonin and norepinephrine in the brain. Reserpine stimulated *monoamine oxidase* (MAO), a brain and liver enzyme, to break down these substances chemically when they were about to be released from the neurons where they were stored, resulting in a deficiency of the two neurotransmitters. Isoniazid had the reverse effect, inhibiting monoamine oxidase production and thereby increasing the supply.

Given these observations, it seemed plausible to hypothesize that depression results from a deficiency of norepinephrine and serotonin, and the hypothesis was tested by giving isoniazid to nontubercular patients suffering from depression. Their depression lifted dramatically over the weeks that followed.

Research based on this theory led to the development of antidepressant drugs specifically targeted at restoring the neurotransmitters involved in depression to normal levels. The development process began in 1952 with the first psychopharmacologic agent to be useful in treating schizophrenia, chlorpromazine. It was hoped that it might also alleviate depression; but when this did not happen, Dr. Roland Kuhn, a Swiss psychiatrist, who was seeking a workable antidepressant drug, theorized that another drug chemically similar to chlorpromazine might be more effective.

In early 1956 Kuhn administered such a drug, then known simply as G22355, to three patients suffering from severe depression. They showed improvement within a month. In September 1957 he reported on this new and successful treatment for depression before an audience of barely a dozen people attending the Second International Congress of Psychiatry in Zurich. "Our paper was received with a great deal of skepticism," Kuhn recalls. "This was not surprising in view of the almost completely negative history of the drug treatment of depression up to that time."

But the skepticism gave way to acceptance when the effectiveness of compound G22355, later known as imipramine, was reconfirmed. Imipramine belongs to one of the two classes of drugs that were developed in the late 1950s for the treatment of depression. These drugs modify the chemistry of the brain by altering the interactions between neurons mediated by neurotransmitters. Different antidepressants affect different neurotransmitters and thus alleviate depression in different ways.

Imipramine belongs to the *tricyclic* class of antidepressants, which acts on the catecholamines, a major group of neurotransmitters comprised of dopamine, norepinephrine, and epinephrine. Ordinarily a neurotransmitter is released from a neuron, travels across the synaptic cleft, attaches to a specialized receptor on the cell membrane of a neighboring neuron, and then is rereleased and taken up once again by other neurons. Imipramine and related tricyclic drugs block this reuptake mechanism and thus allow more of the neurotransmitter to remain available in the synaptic cleft for a longer time, thereby reversing the deficiency.

The second major class of antidepressants, the *monoamine oxidase inhibitors,* or MAOIs, works slightly differently in achieving the same result. These drugs block monoamine oxidase's chemical breakdown of neurotransmitters within the synaptic cleft.

During the 1960s neuroscientists believed that a satisfactory chemical theory of depression could be based on catecholamine levels within the brain. According to this overly simplistic theory, depression was caused by a deficiency of catecholamines, particularly norepinephrine, at functionally important brain synapses. Mania, in contrast, was believed to result from an excess of catecholamines.

This theory has been discarded because additional research has revealed that other neurotransmitters with chemical structures different from the catecholamines—serotonin and acetylcholine, to mention only two—may also be in-

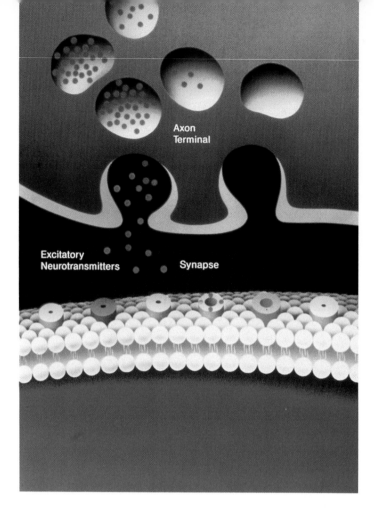

Axon Terminal

Excitatory Neurotransmitters

Synapse

This computer graphic shows the mechanism of action of antidepressant drugs. They increase the amount of neurotransmitter available at the synapse by reducing reuptake, so that it remains available longer in the synaptic cleft, or by inhibiting MAO (enzyme) breakdown of the neurotransmitter.

volved in the development of depressive illnesses. Moreover, as indicated in Chapter 5, depression is not limited to disturbances in neurotransmitter balance and brain function alone. Mood disorders also involve the endocrine and immune systems, which affect every organ system within the body. When people are depressed, as we have noted, they suffer from more than the "blues"; they undergo changes in appetite, sleep, activity, and energy. They appear to be more susceptible to infection and other illnesses, perhaps including cancer, strongly indicating that the immune system is affected.

Research in these areas is being pursued, but at the present time studies of the human brain continue to offer the best "window" for observing the biology of depressive illnesses. One particularly valuable approach involves monitoring levels not only of neurotransmitters but also of their breakdown products—metabolites—after these neurotransmitters are metabolized. For example, the major metabolites of catecholamine neurotransmitters appear in the spinal fluid. One of the major metabolites of brain norepinephrine is also found in the urine. By monitoring the levels of these and other chemical substances in the spinal fluid, urine, and bloodstream, neuroscientists have discovered that depressions that often appear similar to an observer actually possess very different chemical signatures.

Consider two patients who come to a physician complaining of sleep difficulties, depressed appetite, and feelings of hopelessness and despair. Despite the similarities in what they experience and report, tests reveal that one patient's spinal fluid contains a lower than normal level of a serotonin metabolite, while the second patient's spinal fluid contains a low level of a norepinephrine metabolite. Each patient is exhibiting a biologically distinguishable form of depression that will require a different medication. The situation is similiar to what happens when two people come to a doctor for the treatment of heart disease. Each may have the same complaints—shortness of breath, easy fatigue, swelling of the legs—but despite the parallels in their symptoms, one proves to need only a diuretic to diminish fluid retention, and the other requires a stronger, more specific drug capable of acting directly on the heart.

For a while neuroscientists had another simplistic theory that separated depression into two categories, serotonin-associated depression and norepinephrine-associated depression. No one believes that now. There are too many interrelated variables. Many, many chemicals affect functioning in normal and depressed people in ways that scientists are only beginning to appreciate. There are reasons to believe depression can result from specific disturbances of the hypothalamus and its interconnections with the body's master gland, the pituitary, and its hormones. Many of the clinical signs of depression can be observed in other disturbances affecting the hypothalamus, including weight loss, poor appetite, insomnia, fatigue, and loss of sexual potency. Through its connections to the pituitary, the hypothalamus exerts a powerful influence on neuroendocrine function. Indeed, the neurotransmitter systems most strongly implicated in depression—serotonergic (serotonin-producing) neurons and noradrenergic (noradrenaline-producing) neurons—play important roles in neuroendocrine regulation. It is unlikely that a truly comprehensive understanding of depression can be arrived at until more is known about the different chemical pathways within the brain, how they affect each other, and how they interact with hormonal systems within the hypothalamic–pituitary–adrenal axis.

Until we understand more about these complex interrelationships, the most that can be achieved—and it is a significant step forward—is to formulate classifications of depression, based on specialized laboratory tests involving neurotransmitters and their metabolites along with hormones and other chemicals derived from the endocrine and immune systems. Such classifications are not simply an exercise in orderliness; they have significant consequences.

Consider one laboratory test and its practical implications:

In the mid-1970s Dr. Marie Asberg, a psychiatrist at the Karolinska Hospital and Institute in Stockholm, Sweden, began checking into the effects of antidepressant drugs. Why do some drugs work with certain patients and not with others? In order to find out, Asberg looked for chemical markers that might separate out subgroups of depressive patients. She noticed that the spinal fluid of about one third of the depressed patients at the Karolinska Hospital contained a low level of a chemical called 5-HIAA (5-hydroxyindoleacetic acid), a metabolite of the neurotransmitter serotonin, which is known to affect mood and emotion. She wondered if 5-HIAA might be a marker. If so, what is it a marker of? Asberg got her answer from an unexpected source.

In July of 1975 two patients committed suicide after a period of psychiatric hospitalization. Their spinal fluids while in the hospital had contained low levels of 5-HIAA. "All of these low-5-HIAA patients kill themselves," said a psychiatrist on hearing of one of the deaths.

"I thought, my God, what is she saying!" Asberg recalls.

Asberg reviewed case records and found more than twice as many patients with low 5-HIAA levels among those who had attempted or committed suicide than among those with normal levels. In addition, many of those with *very* low 5-HIAA levels chose violent methods: hanging, self-injection, drowning. The methods used by patients with moderately low levels of 5-HIAA were gentler and less effective: most often drug overdoses too small to be lethal.

In the years since her initial recognition of the possible significance of low levels of 5-HIAA, Asberg has analyzed the cerebrospinal fluid of over two hundred patients with depression and a history of at least one suicide attempt. She has found a low 5-HIAA level to be repeatedly associated with suicidal behavior, and especially with serious suicide attempts. "Among people who have attempted suicide and survived, you can expect two percent of them to be dead of suicide within one year," says Asberg. "But among people with low levels of 5-HIAA and a previous suicide attempt, the figure jumps to twenty percent."

Asberg believes that low levels of 5-HIAA may serve as a marker for vulnerability to depressive disorders and suicide. It can serve only as an indicator of heightened risk of suicide, however, not as a predictor. Low 5-HIAA concentrations also occur in mentally healthy people who have never been depressed or contemplated suicide. Asberg says, "A suicide attempt is unlikely to occur unless the individual finds himself in a situation which he conceives of as desperate or when he is without hope for the future."

According to Asberg, low levels of serotonin, of which 5-HIAA is a metabolite, might render an individual more

recognizing the signs of a clinical depression, refers him to a psychiatrist.

In response to the psychiatrist's inquiry, Steven admits to feelings he has never shared with anyone before this.

"I know I have everything that I ever wanted—a successful career, a reasonable amount of money, good health, a loving family—but I feel that it's all a sham. I feel empty inside. Nothing gives me pleasure or joy any more. Not sex, not vacations, not my work, not even my children. All I can see is the down side of everything. And I'm constantly exhausted, can't work up enthusiasm for anything, hate to face people. I don't want to answer the telephone when it rings. Even the briefest, most superficial conversation seems like a burden, a heavy rock that I have to carry around with me all the time. Sometimes I just wonder if it wouldn't be better for everybody if somehow or other all of this could end permanently."

Had Steven's depression been so severe and unremitting and his sense of hopelessness so deep that his psychiatrist feared suicide was a real possibility, he might well have been hospitalized and given electroconvulsive (electroshock) therapy to bring him out of the episode quickly. But his depression does not appear to be that acute, so he is likely to be given a tricyclic drug. If the medication works (in about 15 percent of cases, depressed patients do not respond to antidepressant medications or cannot take them because of serious side effects), Steven will notice over the next several weeks a gradual, almost imperceptible improvement in some of his symptoms. He will begin to sleep more soundly and awaken feeling refreshed. His appetite will improve, sex may be appealing again, his work situation seem less onerous.

It may take longer for Steven to experience a better self-image (less "hollow," less "empty") but in time this too will improve. In fact, if all goes well, within another month or two Steven may return to the way he felt before he became depressed. At this point both patient and psychiatrist must make several important decisions. Should the antidepressant be stopped? If not now, when? Equally important, what is Steven's understanding of what happened to him?

In general, most patients are maintained on antidepressants for several months or longer after their improvement. This not only prevents relapses but puts them in a better position to understand the nature of their illness and plan ways in which to prevent future depressions, if possible.

That understanding is likely to come not through drugs alone but through a combination of drugs and psychotherapy. Drugs are not the only way to treat depression, though there are some psychiatrists who rely on them exclusively, just as there are some who rely wholly on one of the "talking therapies" in treating mood disorders.

Until recently, psychotherapy often aroused fierce debates between psychiatrists trained in the biological sciences and those who became committed to psychiatry at a time when psychoanalysis and other psychodynamically oriented therapies dominated American psychiatry. To the biologically focused psychiatrist, the sheer profusion of different psychotherapeutic techniques—among them behavioral, cognitive, psychoanalytic, supportive family, group, and gestalt therapies—argued against the effectiveness of this method of treatment. On the other side of the aisle, psychotherapeutically oriented psychiatrists often saw their biologically oriented colleagues primarily as technicians, who too readily abandoned psychiatry's most important contribution: the psychiatrist's willingness to listen, understand, empathize, and respond with insight to what patients are experiencing.

Happily, the hostility between these two camps has abated somewhat over the past decade. By now it is obvious that medications alone cannot cure mental illness. All human beings need to talk, be listened to, be understood, and be consoled; and those with mood disorders need this with special urgency. Recognizing this, most psychiatrists now combine medication with some form of psychotherapy.

One promising psychotherapeutic approach for the treatment of depression is interpersonal psychotherapy (IPT), developed by the New Haven–Boston Collaborative Depression Project. This treatment approach emphasizes the importance of role conflict, grief, and faulty or deficient interpersonal relationships in the development of depression. The therapy stresses the here and now, rather than traumas or deprivations going back to infancy and childhood.

Another form of psychotherapy that appears to work well with depressed patients is cognitive behavioral therapy, developed by Dr. Aaron Beck, University Professor of Psychiatry at the University of Pennsylvania. Beck believes depressed people have learned inappropriate ways of interpreting their experiences. With training, these maladaptive tendencies can be reversed. His twelve- to twenty-week treatment technique is designed to correct three major thought distortions characteristic of depressives: seeing oneself as worthless and deficient; viewing the world as cruel, unyielding, and punishing; and viewing the future as hopeless. Cognitive therapy actively counters these views by pointing out to patients instances in which they employ one or more of these thought distortions. Recognition makes it possible to alter them.

"The *goal* of cognitive therapy is to relieve emotional distress and the other symptoms of depression," says Beck. "The *means* is by focusing on the patient's misinterpretations, self-defeating behavior, and dysfunctional attitudes. The therapist needs to be able to empathize with the patient's painful emotional experiences as well as to be able to identify . . . the linkage between negative thoughts and negative feelings."

A major controlled study comparing four treatments of depression—cognitive therapy, IPT, drug treatment with imipramine, and placebos—was begun in 1981 under the direction of Dr. Earleen Elkins of the National Institute of Alcohol Abuse and Alcoholism. Called The Treatment of Depression Collaborative Research Program, it has been conducted at George Washington University, the University of Pittsburgh, and the University of Oklahoma. Two hundred thirty-nine subjects have been studied, all outpatients suffering from unipolar disorder; their average age was thirty-five, and 70 percent of them were women. They were divided into four groups, receiving either cognitive therapy, IPT, imipramine, or a placebo. The psychotherapists participating in the study utilized training manuals provided by the program, and their therapy sessions were videotaped.

After an average of sixteen weeks, between 51 and 57 percent of the patients in the three treatment groups had returned to normal as gauged on a variety of widely used depression scales, in comparison to 29 percent of those in the placebo group. The speediest results came in patients given imipramine, but by the end of the trial period there was no significant difference in outcome for any of the three forms of treatment. Only the untreated patients—those given placebos—showed a lower recovery rate.

The findings of this research, which is ongoing and is by far the largest study of its kind, suggest that certain talking therapies relieve depression as effectively as does drug treatment with imipramine. They also suggest that it is futile to pursue the either/or issue of which treatment is "better" for depression—an antidepressant drug *or* a psychotherapeutic approach. Even when satisfactory drugs are selected, administered in the correct dosage (surprisingly often, physicians prescribe dosages that are too low to be effective), and are effective, most patients will benefit from concurrent psychotherapy.

Take our patient Steven Robinson as an example. His depression begins to improve while he takes an antidepressant, but his wife, Jane, overburdened by the expense, tension, worry, and need over the past several months to sacrifice her own interests to his, may turn some of her resentment onto him. His children, both teenagers, may resist his efforts to reassert his authority by imposing limits on their comings and goings. Steven's department chairman may have discovered during Steven's absence that he actually *enjoyed* teaching that introductory literature course and is wonder-

RAPID CYCLER

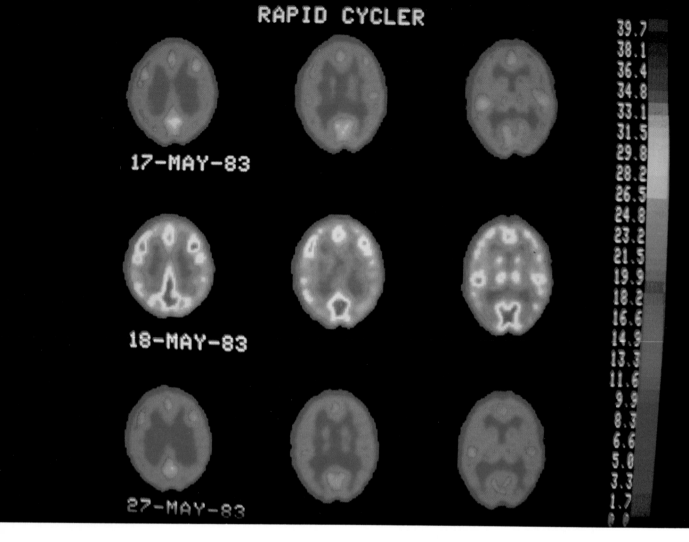

17-MAY-83

18-MAY-83

27-MAY-83

39.7
38.1
36.4
34.8
33.1
31.5
29.8
28.2
26.5
24.8
23.2
21.5
19.9
18.2
16.6
14.9
13.3
11.6
9.9
8.3
6.6
5.0
3.3
1.7

These PET scans, taken by Dr. John Mazziotta of UCLA, show the brain of a bipolar disorder patient who moves quickly from depression to mania and back to depression (a "rapid cycler").

Low levels of glucose utilization, demonstrating low brain activity, are indicated by the blue areas that predominate in the scans in the top and bottom rows. In the middle row, the manic cycle (which occurred one day after the top depressive cycle) is marked by vivid coloration indicating hyperactivity. This pattern can be contrasted with the PET scan of a normal brain seen on page 175.

ing aloud whether Steven is really ready to resume teaching the class. None of these problems, and the stress they induce, is going to be managed by medication alone, no matter how much better the medication makes Steven feel. He is going to have to express his appreciation for his wife's efforts; understand why his teenage children have become accustomed to setting their own hours and why they don't want these kinds of choices taken away from them; and know how to approach his departmental chairman firmly but tactfully.

If Steven is going to maintain his restored resilience and improved self-esteem and avoid another depression, he's going to have to use important aspects of mind: intelligence, insight, and observational and communicative skills. Like all of us, he seeks meaning and purpose, employs language and symbols, responds to comfort and caring, and needs to feel worthwhile. For people who are depressed or vulnerable to depression, the best way of fulfilling these needs, coping with stress, and recognizing patterns of thought and behavior that may have increased that vulnerability is by combining psychotherapy with medication.

Reliance on special tests to diagnose and treat mood disorders such as depression is likely to increase over the next decade. Researchers at UCLA have already discovered PET (positron emission tomography) scan abnormalities in depressed patients. The scans show a decreased rate of glucose metabolism, which returns to normal as the depression lifts. Metabolic images of the brain also allow neuroscientists to tell whether depression is localized to the left or right hemisphere. In preliminary studies, a more profound decrease in metabolism is found on the left side of the brain, in areas thought to be involved in language and analysis.

The illustration on the opposite page shows the PET scan of a bipolar depressive during the depressive phase (top and bottom rows) and during the manic phase (middle row). As the patient shifts into mania, there is a global increase in glucose utilization that shows up as a bright red, yellow, and orange glow throughout the brain. Although much of this work is preliminary and requires the study of additional patients, it is likely that PET scans will profoundly affect our understanding of the brain changes associated with mood disorders. "PET has the ability to demonstrate functional changes in cerebral biochemistry associated with behavioral disorders," according to Dr. John C. Mazziotta, an investigator at the UCLA School of Medicine.

Within the next decade the diagnosis and treatment of depression is likely to take the following form. Patients with depression, unless they have a personal physician, will first be evaluated at the intake unit of a health maintenance organization (HMO). Thanks to greater awareness of depression on the part of primary physicians, the diagnosis won't be missed as frequently as it is now (more than 60 percent of depressed patients aren't initially recognized as suffering from depression). A careful history by a psychiatrist will then pinpoint distinguishing features of the illness, allowing an informed decision on what treatment may be the preferred approach: psychotherapy or antidepressant drugs or electroconvulsive therapy, or some combination of these treatments. Computers will cross-correlate symptoms and recommend possible treatments based on this synthesis. "Patients with sleep disorders, weight loss, and phobias generally do best on an MAO inhibitor," the computer printout might read.

Analysis of blood, urine, skin cells, and spinal fluid will help identify biologically distinguishable depressions. Decreased levels of such chemicals as 5-HIAA will serve as warning signals that some patients may be suicidal or otherwise overly impulsive. Closer observation and perhaps some form of legally sanctioned restraints may then be imposed to prevent these patients from harming themselves.

PET scans and electrophysiological studies such as evoked

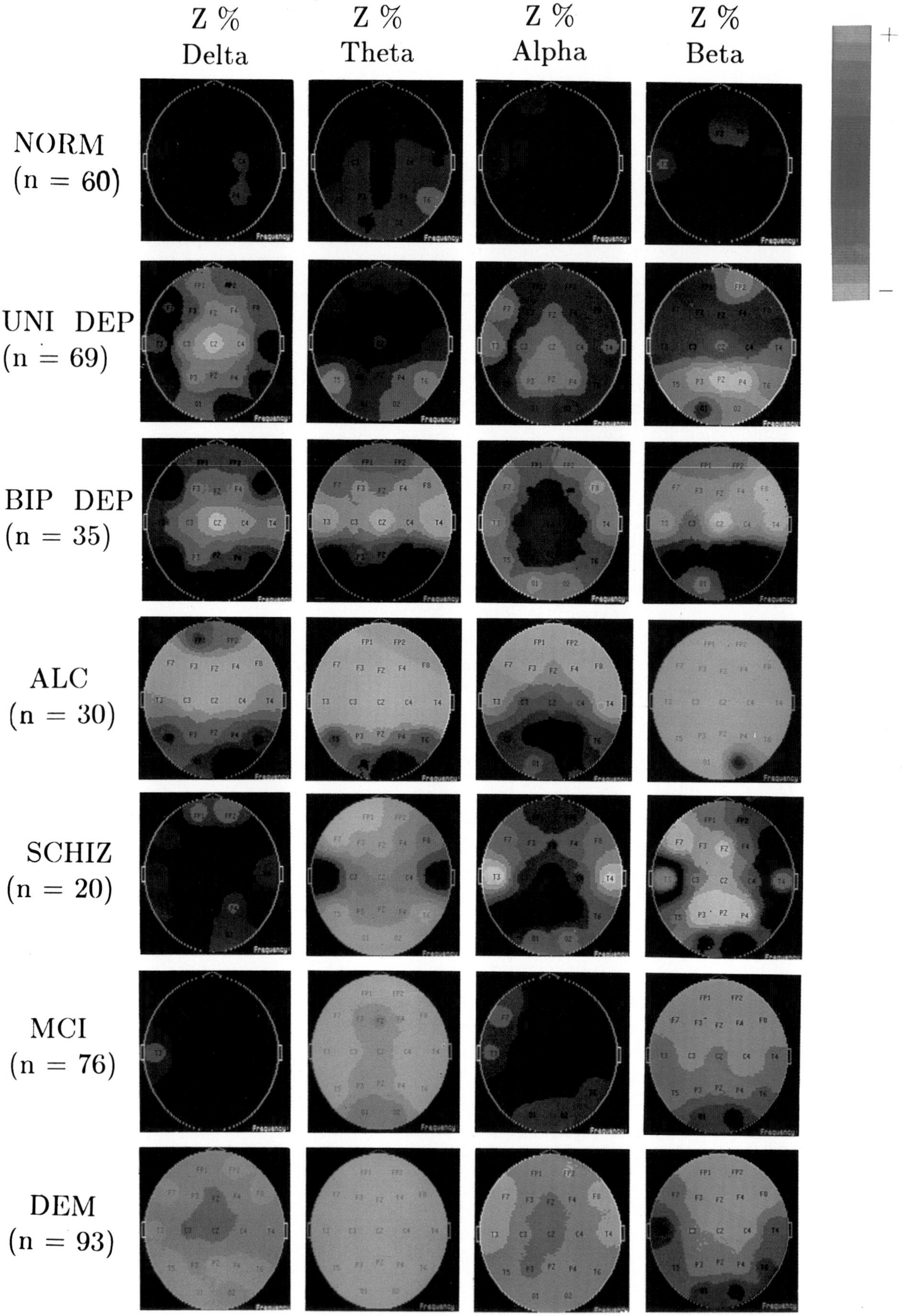
Z % Delta
Z % Theta
Z % Alpha
Z % Beta
+
−
NORM (n = 60)
UNI DEP (n = 69)
BIP DEP (n = 35)
ALC (n = 30)
SCHIZ (n = 20)
MCI (n = 76)
DEM (n = 93)

potential recordings or brain electrical activity maps will aid in both diagnosing depression and evaluating the success of treatment. Starting with a baseline recording such as PET scans, psychiatrists will be able to monitor changes in brain activity and correlate them with the patient's progress.

Finally, once patients have improved with the help of drug and psychotherapeutic treatment, medications such as lithium may be prescribed to maintain that improvement, especially in cases in which depressions are recurrent. (Findings suggest that lithium is useful in controlling the cyclicity of depression in bipolar disorder.) In addition, patients will be encouraged to look upon their depression not as a sign of personal failure but as a disease that is as biologically based as diabetes or high blood pressure. Those conditions aren't treated by moral exhortation but by medication, information, and placing responsibility on the patients for maintaining their health. Depressed patients should be informed in the same way about the nature of their illness, the importance of their medication, and the role they play in their emotional health.

As we have noted, today only a handful of those with diagnosable depressions receive *any* type of treatment, biological or otherwise. The reasons for the reluctance of people to seek help are varied: ignorance that depression is an illness, is treatable, and is not a reflection of personal failure; denial; fear of being stigmatized as "mentally ill"; hopelessness brought on by the depression itself; the unavailability of psychiatric services; poverty; and a stoic approach that says problems should be "toughed out," not brought to physicians in the effort to resolve them.

More than any other subject that we explore in our search for mind, depression illustrates the difficulties that can ensue when the "mental" is set off from the "physical," when mind is arbitrarily separated from brain. Depression is a uniquely human affliction. It never exists in a vacuum. It always affects a particular human being who occupies his or her special world and has a past and present that are like no one else's. It has different meanings and consequences for each sufferer. It is crucial that we recognize this, and accept the fact that depressions are diseases of the mind that affect the brain and body as well—diseases that could strike any of us at any point in our lives. They are diseases, as we have seen, involving genetic, biological, and environmental factors. The need to understand depressive illnesses in all their ramifications is not only urgent but a formidable challenge. When we understand depression, we will reach an important landmark in our search for mind.

(Opposite) A new neurological recording system, Neurometrics, outputting directly as a statistical analysis of electroencephalograms (EEGs). When taken of people without known neurologic or psychiatric disease, it can provide reliable patterns of brain electrical activity in individuals from six to ninety years of age. Healthy persons display only chance deviations beyond predicted ranges. Patients with neurologic impairments or psychiatric disorders show a high incidence of abnormal values, indicated here by variations in color coding. The more the color varies from that seen in the healthy population, the more likely it is that the brain of the individual in question is functioning abnormally.

7.
LANGUAGE

We take language for granted, yet it is one of the most complex things we do. Language allows us to convey our emotions, to share ideas, to create fresh forms of expression, and to communicate our most intimate thoughts. Without language the very notion of human civilization would be unthinkable. It is not only vivid confirmation of the mind within us; the need to communicate with other humans through language seems as fundamental as the existence of the mind itself.

All creatures are capable of some form of communication bound to basic drives linked to survival: hunger, danger, lust. Some animals have calls so distinct that we could almost label them "words." But can we say that such animals actually have language? And can we determine the point at which animal communication ends and human language begins?

Early researchers thought that one way to find out was to see if animals were capable of learning and responding to language-oriented material or processes in ways similar to humans. The best candidate for such experiments seemed to be the chimpanzee. In the evolutionary process, monkeys separated from humans about twenty-five million years ago, but chimps (which are apes) and humans parted company less than five million years ago. We not only share 99 percent of our genes with the chimpanzee, there are psychological commonalities as well. Unlike monkeys, chimps are always ready to return a curious gaze and seem pleased by the attention. Intelligent and sociable, they became the subjects of language research beginning in the 1950s. Two psychologists, Drs. Keith and Virginia Hayes, moved a baby chimpanzee they named Vickie into their home and tried to teach it to talk. The experiment was a failure for a fundamental reason that is now obvious: apes possess neither the vocal tract nor the agile tongue of humans. But though Vickie couldn't speak, she did manage to communicate her intentions by movements of her body and her hands.

Another husband and wife team of psychologists, Drs. Allen and Beatrix Gardner, of the University of Nevada in Reno, inferred on the basis of seeing a movie of Vickie that a chimp's capacity to gesture could be turned to good advantage. They put this theory to the test by teaching American Sign Language to a one-year-old chimp they called Washoe. Their objective was to learn as much as they could about the chimp's potential for communication. Washoe is still vigorous—and still signing—thirty years later, and continues to be the subject of research at the University of Washington. Since then, several other chimps have joined the roster of language research subjects, including Noam Chimpsky, or "Nim"—a spoof on the MIT psycholinguist, Dr. Noam Chomsky—taught by Dr. Herbert Terrace, of Columbia University, and Sarah, taught by Dr. David Premack, now at the University of Pennsylvania, who worked with her at the University of California, Santa Barbara. Although all these researchers were trying to find out whether chimps could learn a language and employ it in a manner similar to humans, Premack's interest extended beyond this.

"Our attempt to teach language to an ape was based on our interest in the human mind. In order to understand the mind of the human, it was essential, we thought, to compare it with other minds. But were there other minds that were comparable?"

To Premack there seemed two possible answers to this question. One rests on the theory that there is essentially only one kind of mind in the universe, so that the differences we observe from species to species result from elaborations on the fundamental plan common to all creatures. Just as a house and a castle share basic aspects—an enclosed structure constructed with windows, doors, walls, ceilings, and floors, and divided into rooms—but differ in dimensions, space, elaborateness, and multiplicity of functions, so it may be conceivable that the human mind is simply a more complex version of the mind that also exists in "lower" creatures. Language doesn't play a particularly important role in this theory: the house is fundamentally similiar except for the addition of a room called "language."

According to the second theory, language is unique, something so special that it completely transforms the house. In Premack's words, "The differences are no longer those between a house and a castle but between a house and an airplane. Thus, no proper comparisons could ever be made."

Premack's research over the past three and a half decades has been directed toward deciding which of these two alternatives is valid. Rather than employing a sign language,

Premack developed an artificial language of his own for testing the communicative abilities of chimpanzees. "I devised a very simple language for the chimp," he said, "which didn't require that it have the basic machinery of human language. It simply required that the animal be able to learn rules."

He uses a set of metal-backed plastic tokens of various colors, sizes, and shapes, each of which represents a word. The initial step is to train the chimp to develop an association between a chip and the object it represents—between, for example, the particular chip that by its shape, size, and color is intended to be the "word" for apple and an actual apple. "Essentially all chimp words are learned in this fashion," says Premack, "by directly associating the word with some object."

In an early experiment, Sarah learned after many trials to place the plastic chip for a fruit she liked on a magnetized slate, or "language board." Her trainer then rewarded her with the fruit. Next, she learned the "name" of the trainer, the donor of her fruit, as represented by a different chip. From then on, if she wanted the fruit, Sarah had to name both the donor and the fruit correctly. "Mary apple" had to be placed on the language board instead of simply the chip for "apple." Finally Sarah, the recipient of the fruit, was herself identified by a chip. This made possible the construction on the board of "Mary give apple Sarah."

Premack's system made it possible to probe Sarah's mind. He discovered that she could recognize similarities and differences. Two apples, for example, were set slightly apart on the work table and Sarah was handed an orange plastic token representing the word for "same." Next, a cup and a spoon were separated and Sarah was given a red token, the word for "different." Did she form the desired associations? Yes, as subsequent testing revealed. Sarah reliably selected the token for "same" when two similar objects were placed on the table and the token for "different" when the objects were dissimilar. After a while, according to Premack, "her performance was so close to perfect in all the tests that, in principle, it was possible to picture Sarah going about her cage picking up an infinite variety of pairs of objects and easily labeling them 'same' or 'different.'"

Subsequent fascinating research, more fully described in Premack's book, *The Mind of an Ape,* established that after training, Sarah was capable of matching a part object (half of an apple) with a partially filled glass cylinder. To carry out such a task, Premack believes, Sarah must be capable of forming a "representation" of objects. To pair a half-filled cylinder with a half apple, she must mentally reconstruct a filled cylinder and a whole apple, and then judge the half-

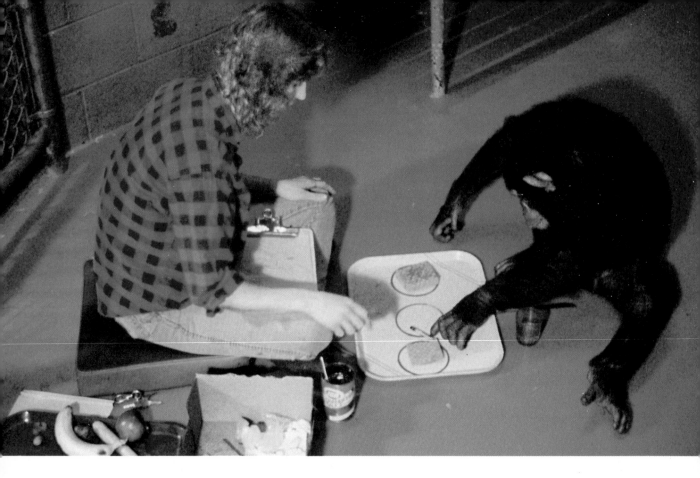

An experimenter, utilizing the technique developed by Dr. David Premack, tests a chimpanzee's ability to use language by employing plastic chips that represent specific words.

full and full cylinders to be equivalent to the half and whole apples. She must also be able to formulate the concept of quantity.

We know from the experiments of Jean Piaget that this kind of representation is impossible in children until about age six. Before then, even though the children have actually watched the identical quantity of liquid being poured into a tall, narrow glass and a short, wide one, they will insist that the tall glass contains more liquid. At that stage of their mind's development, they associate the amount of liquid with the level of water in the glass. Sarah, however, didn't make this error. When given her plastic words for "same" and "different" and asked to judge levels and amounts of liquid, she wasn't misled into equating a higher water level in a narrow container with "more." Instead, she chose the token for "same."

Premack investigated other aspects of the chimp mind as well. He tested Sarah's knowledge of causality by presenting her with a series of paired items, one of which had been altered. A whole apple, for instance, was paired with a cut apple, and Sarah was challenged to match the pairs with a tool that could bring about the alteration, in this case a knife. Since she hadn't actually seen the apple being cut, in order to do this successfully she would have to retain in her mind a representation of the action of cutting. In most instances, Sarah selected the appropriate tool. In fact, she performed just as well with objects that were novel to her as with familiar ones. Cause and effect relationships held no mystery for her.

To test whether Sarah could infer intention, Premack showed her a series of videotapes portraying a person caught in a dilemma. In one situation, a man is shown jumping up toward a bunch of bananas that is slightly beyond his reach. Sarah was then shown a series of pictures, only one of which contained a solution to the problem, a ladder. On this, as on most occasions, she chose the correct picture. She was able to recognize that a problem existed that required solving, to choose the solution, and to realize that the person on the tape had a purpose or an intention in mind. In short, Sarah was able to impute a mental state to a human being.

But fascinating as these experiments are in exploring the functioning of mind in chimpanzees, they don't really tell us whether the animals are capable of language as we know it. Despite the experiments with Sarah, Premack now thinks it unlikely. She may have been taught to comprehend and produce simple "sentences"—"Sarah cut apple," "Sarah wash apple," "Sarah take apple." "But we couldn't have gone to Sarah," says Premack, "and given those sentences to her and said, 'Tell us, what do these sentences have in common? Could you, for example, tell us what's the subject of these sentences?' There isn't the slightest suggestion that she had any such notion. The main deficiency in the chimpanzee is that there is no evidence it has any grammatical competence."

Grammatical competence means the ability to understand concepts like subject, noun phrase, and verb phrase, without which, as Premack says, "you cannot formulate the rules of human language." The young child's tendency to omit certain parts of a sentence is an illustration of this competence. On one occasion he'll say, "Daddy home," and on another occasion simply, "Home." "Children often omit the subject from their sentences," Premack notes. "It's impossible to do that unless you have a notion of sentences. In some sense the notion of sentences has to be in the head so that you can systematically omit the subject of that sentence. If you look at the sentences produced by chimpanzees, you never find that kind of thing. There is no suggestion that there is any omission of any grammatical category."

And without grammatical competence, there is no understanding of syntax, the relationship of words to one another in a sentence.

Syntax involves far more than simply word order. Obviously, "Sarah give Mary apple" differs from "Mary give

Sarah apple." But to fully understand a sentence, it's necessary to be able to put the same information in many different forms: "The book is sitting on the table." "On the table is the book." "The table has a book sitting on it."

"A sentence is not merely a thought expressed in words. It is a thought expressed in words arranged in a sequence chosen from infinitely many other possible sequences," according to Premack. "Provided you have genuine knowledge of a sentence, you can express the thought in a countless variety of ways."

According to Premack, chimps are capable of stringing together plastic "words" in the form of constructions: one-to-one correspondences between the words and the items in the world that the words refer to. But unlike sentences, constructions lack an internal organization. Implicit in the understanding and use of a sentence is the grasp of an internal structure that is considerably more sophisticated and advanced than a mere construction.

When a two-year-old child holds a toy car in his hand and says, "Daddy plays with big one, me play with little one," the child isn't only referring to the object in hand. He is taking into account an array of facts about the object, such as its size in comparison to the family car, who "plays" with which car, which car is smaller, who "owns" the two different cars. Sentences are creative and novel, whereas constructions are determined entirely by physical situations.

It's possible to test chimps for their understanding that a banana is "yellow," but only a human being could understand why an army deserter might be referred to as "yellow." The late philosopher Bertrand Russell captured the essence of the difference between a construction and a sentence when he was asked, "Will apes ever learn to speak?" "I'd be prepared to accept that an ape can speak," Russell answered, "when someone presents for my consideration a specimen that could fathom the meaning of a sentence such as 'My father was poor but honest.'"

It seems clear from all this that language does not in any way constitute the addition of another "room" to a basic floor plan of mind. Creatures who possess language can certainly build a representation of the world within their own mind and manipulate it. But human language is a quantum leap beyond mere representation. It makes possible a complete transformation of the human mind. It entails the capacity for abstract representation, as in your reading of the words in this sentence and applying the "abstract representations" the sentence contains to situations and questions you may have encountered in the past, and to your formulations of the future. It is this that differentiates us from the apes.

"While it's true the chimpanzee can do various things

with the pieces of plastic outside of its head, on the board," says Premack, "there's not the slightest suggestion the pieces of plastic taught the animal have in any way entered its head, and become a part of the system which is used for the representation of language. That contrasts powerfully with the human case, where we have very good reason to suppose that quite interesting things are going on inside the head with the use of language."

If language is built in to us as a species, where in the evolutionary record did this miracle first occur? Why did language evolve in man alone of all living creatures? Clues to the origins of modern language come to us from fossil records.

Dr. Philip Lieberman, of the Department of Linguistics at Brown University, has examined Neanderthal and hominoid skulls in his laboratory. "You can tell how a fossil could talk, even though you have only bones and not the soft tissues that go along with them, by using the method of comparative anatomy. You can locate living animals, like chimpanzees and human newborns, that have skeletal structures like the fossil's. On these living creatures, you can see directly how the soft tissues connect to the skeleton. Then you can reconstruct. It's really very similar to the way you tell how fast a dinosaur could run. Although there are no living dinosaurs around today, you've got lizards who have skeletons that look like dinosaurs', although they are much smaller. You then observe how the muscles attach to the bones on the living animal, then put together the fossil. Now once you have that, you can also tell a fair amount about the brain and how the brain could control the anatomy."

The power of language to affect history is exemplified by these two spellbinding orators and passionate enemies: Adolf Hitler and Winston Churchill.

Why do we assume Neanderthal man was capable of a language at all? Mostly on the basis of the culture in existence at that time. "The evidence of Neanderthal culture, which is apparent in their tools and their tool-making techniques, their rituals, and their social order—which involved care for the infirm—all point to the presence of language," says Lieberman.

But not human language as we know it. From his analysis and reconstruction of fossil remains, Lieberman does not believe Neanderthals could have had human speech. They had short necks, a very long tongue, larynxes placed very high, and relatively small, immobile throats, so they would have been unable to produce vowel sounds like *ee* or *oo* or *ah,* or consonants like *cuh* or *guh.* A round tongue, and the ability to seal off the nose and lower the larynx, are necessary for these sounds. He is convinced Neanderthals communicated vocally, but, he says, "it would have been at a slower rate, with more errors."

As the vocal tract evolved, so did the nature of language. The key developments were the gradual evolution of the round human tongue, the longer neck to accommodate it, and the lowering of the larynx, a process that can be seen starting in fossils about one hundred thousand years ago. There was also the assumption of a more upright posture, which made possible better and more stable head balance. All these changes indicated increased development of the brain, Lieberman says, "because the changed vocal tract would be useless for speech without the parts of the brain that run it." Speech is complicated. The precise coordination of tongue, lips, and larynx forms an elaborate, high-speed choreography. "The selective advantage for speech must have been one of the strongest things in human evolution," says Lieberman, "because the airway we have is really good for speech but it's good for practically nothing else. We've ended up with an airway that causes us to choke to death much more easily than any other animal."

He notes that the parts of the brain that developed in concord with changes in the vocal tract "are also involved in other aspects of human language, human thought, and human culture. So in a very meaningful way, I think the evolution of speech is the key to the evolution of modern human beings."

In Lieberman's opinion, language didn't evolve in a single path, with our present day language existing as a kind of "theological–linguistic great chain of language." Other forms of language probably existed in the past and, indeed, may still exist in other living animals today. This certainly doesn't imply, however, that our language is not better than, say, the communication system employed by the apes. More efficient and intelligible speech carries its own reward: clearer communication becomes possible; the amount of "noise" in the system decreases; subtleties of meaning can emerge.

Lieberman: "Modern speech is very efficient. We don't think about it because we do it all the time. So it's perfectly natural. But it turns out that it's almost ten times faster than any other sound, such as the sound that chimpanzees make. It's also phonetically distinct: about 30 to 50 percent better perceived than other sounds."

The ability to communicate at a rapid rate provides a selective advantage, Lieberman believes, for the development of human culture.

"To paraphrase Charles Darwin, human culture really is the infinitely complex relations of human beings to other human beings in all aspects of the material world. It's really impossible to conceive of human culture without language. Language enters into everything. You can't have human culture without human language. Further, language facilitates thought. I think it's impossible to conceive of human thought without human language. The two are integral elements tied together."

Words, phrases, sentences, all evoke images in our minds. They all contain meaning—the driving force in human language. Distinguishing various meanings, and the different sounds that *trigger* meaning, is so crucial to humans that infants seem programmed to respond to it.

Dr. Patricia Kuhl, Professor of Speech and Hearing Sciences at the University of Washington in Seattle, studies speech perception in early infancy. She operates on the hunch that humans, like bats, tree frogs, birds, and macaques, are biologically predisposed to respond to different but specific signals that are important to their survival.

"Like the bat and the bird, the human baby comes into the world well prepared to pick up signals that are critical to its survival," says Kuhl. "Evidence supporting this idea comes from studies demonstrating infants' early responsiveness to the human face and the human voice. Young infants prefer to look at faces rather than other complex visual stimuli."

Kuhl's research has focused on demonstrating the presence in infants of what linguists refer to as the "special mechanisms" arrangement. Briefly, this theory holds that the brain mechanisms underlying speech perception are "special": speech signals are processed differently than other auditory signals. In adults this seems obvious. All of us can recognize human speech when we hear it, even in instances when the language spoken is totally unfamiliar to us. We don't, in other words, confuse speech with other auditory signals. But can a baby perform the same feat? And if so, how early?

To find out, Kuhl and Professor Andrew Meltzoff, also at the University of Washington, designed an experiment aimed at determining whether six-month-olds could recognize the critical and often subtle cues that separate even the simplest units of language.

In the first part of the experiment, a six-month-old sat on her parent's lap while, to the baby's right, an assistant

In this experiment designed by Drs. Patricia Kuhl and Andrew Meltzoff, the six-month-old baby turns from a toy when she hears a change in a speech sound coming from the loudspeaker to the right, and is rewarded by the illuminated sight of a toy bear beating a drum.

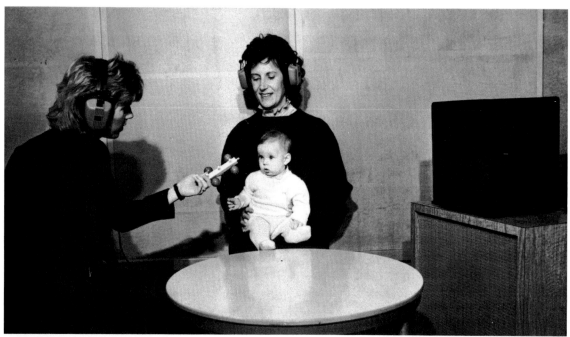

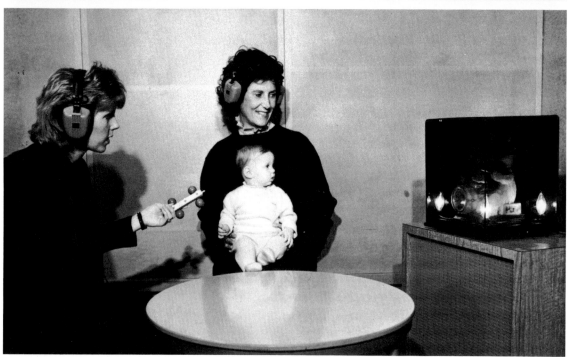

showed toys to attract and hold the baby's attention. At the same time, a loudspeaker located to the baby's left repeated a consonant or vowel sound. Periodically and unpredictably, that sound changed. Coincident with this change, a dark box on top of the loudspeaker lit up. Inside the lighted box was a toy bear that began pounding a drum. In order for the baby to see the bear, she first had to recognize that a change in vowel or consonant sound had occurred, and then turn her head quickly to the left. After the few moments it took to "get the hang" of the experiment, six month-olds had no problem in recognizing vowel and consonant changes. As soon as the changes occurred, they turned their heads quickly to the left in order to see the bear.

In the second part of the experiment, twelve different kinds of recorded voices were used instead of only one. Could the baby pay attention to the category differences— a change from an *aw* sound to an *ee* sound, for instance— and ignore all the *in*-category differences—the high squeaky voices of the children, the loud booming voices of the men, the softer, clearly articulated voices of the women in the recordings?

Kuhl found that six-month-olds had no problem recognizing vowel and consonant changes regardless of the pitch or volume of the voice.

"What we observed is that once babies are trained on a particular speaker's voice, this training generalizes to the voices of all kinds of different people. That is really remarkable: Babies are able to ignore all of the differences between male, female, and children's voices and pay attention to the category difference only: the change, say, from an *aw* sound to an *ee* sound."

With this performance, babies are far ahead of even the most sophisticated and advanced artificial intelligence devices. The design of human voice synthesizers has foundered on the requirement that the machine be able to recognize similiar sounds when spoken by many different people, some of whom may mumble or slur the words or speak too rapidly or too loudly.

Several things can be concluded from the six-month-old's successful speech performance. First, babies are able to recognize the similarities between speech produced by a man, by a woman, and by a child. Secondly, babies must somehow be able to recognize the similarities between their own "speech"—early babbling—and that of an adult. (This is no mean performance, because the vocal tract of a baby is very different from that of an adult. This is why the sounds produced by the infant are so distinctive. No actor, however skilled, can really "cry like a baby" or speak "babyese" because of these changes in the vocal tract after infancy and young childhood.) How do we know this? By inference. Infants, before they can speak, must first imitate. To do this, they have to be able to perceive similarities between their own speech and the speech of an adult.

Next, Kuhl and her associates turned their attention to another question: Can a six-month-old recognize that a speech sound is usually accompanied by certain lip and tongue positions? When the sound *ah* is pronounced, for instance, the mouth is opened wide and the tongue drops to the floor of the mouth. When the sound changes to *ee*, the lips are retracted and the tongue elevated slightly. Sounds, in short, correlate with lip and tongue movements that are visual rather than auditory.

Kuhl wondered whether babies at six months of age could recognize these auditory–visual correlates—whether, in other words, they could do what we all do in a crowded, noisy room: pay attention to the lips of the persons we're speaking with in order to "hear" what they're saying over the din that muffles or drowns out their voices.

To find out, Kuhl and Meltzoff designed an experiment in which babies were shown, side by side, two faces of the same woman pronouncing different vowel sounds. One of the faces silently made repeated lip and tongue movements of the vowel sound *ah,* and the other face produced movements of the vowel sound *ee.* Both faces moved in perfect synchrony. A loudspeaker located between the two faces pronounced only one of the two vowel sounds. Could the baby, given two visual choices but only one sound, match that sound to the appropriate face? Would it turn its gaze preferentially to the correct face in order to bring into synchrony what it saw and what it heard?

"We find that eighteen-week-olds who heard the sound *ah* looked back and forth at the two faces and then focused on the face pronouncing *ah*. And babies who heard *ee* focused on the face producing that sound," says Kuhl. "These skills are remarkable. They demonstrate that in infants, speech organization is quite complex. They are capable of appreciating cross-modal correlations: associating something heard with something seen."

But most remarkable of all, the infants who were listening to these sounds tended to try to produce the sounds themselves. They tried to "talk back" to the female speaker, taking turns with her voice. "This shows that the baby recognizes not only the auditory–visual correlates of speech but the auditory–motor ones as well," says Kuhl.

These findings suggest that the infant brain is "hard-wired" with the ability very early—certainly by six months—to sort and categorize the sounds of speech. Kuhl's discovery of this capacity helps resolve a longstanding debate: Is speech a special subsystem of the mind, or can it simply be explained by general auditory and cognitive abilities? It wasn't until Kuhl discovered that infants can link what is seen with what is heard that a resolution of this question became possible.

Kuhl: "The discovery of cross-modal perception abilities definitely swung the pendulum back again in the direction of thinking of infants as born specially prepared to perceive speech, the sound of human speech."

In a laboratory at the University of Edinburgh, a mother is sitting across from her baby, who smiles and waves at her from a little seat. He is two months old. Both are participating in an experiment in which mother and baby are encouraged to do the most natural thing in the world: spend time together, pay attention to each other, play with each other.

Through a one-way partition in a booth behind mother and infant, Professor Colwyn Trevarthen, a neuropsychologist, is watching them in order to detect the earliest beginnings of language. Over the past two decades, Trevarthen has concentrated his research on what actually occurs when a mother is simply asked to "chat with her baby." He discovered that infants show two different kinds of intention, two ways of spontaneously responding, depending on whether they are interacting with a small toy suspended in front of them or with the mother. The expressions of face, voice, and hands are the most revealing. Babies, it turns out, have considerable control over these movements when they are interacting with their mother. The movements are apparently purposeful and regular enough in form and perceptibly adapted to changes in the environment for "an observer, such as the mother, to have some grounds for imputing intentions to them."

How can an interaction between a speaking adult and a speechless baby tell us anything about the origins of language? In a typical exchange between the mother and her two-month-old, the infant may smile at the mother and then respond to gentle baby talk with cooing and a sudden movement of one hand. Trevarthen has found that these hand movements, particularly when involved in a gesture above the shoulder, are correlated with "prespeech" movements of lip and tongue.

When one watches one of these filmed encounters between a mother and her baby, it is virtually impossible not to be convinced that infants this age are capable of a vast array of emotions and feelings. Both mother and baby smile at each other. Mother says, "Come on, then." Baby coos. Mother further encourages the baby by making lip and tongue movements. Baby responds by smiling. Without being aware of it, mothers move into behavior that complements every action of their baby. Both enter into a kind of dance—

a controlled interplay of gestures and expressions—with movements that underlie true human conversation.

"The foundations of speech and conversational behavior are present from birth," says Trevarthen. "Many important features of the structure of the movements involved, and of the perceptual capacities that are necessary to perceive another person communicating, are active from birth. So you really are studying language, studying some of the forms of communication that will be incorporated into language, even though it hasn't been turned into speech yet."

Trevarthen's findings clear up two points. First, infants are capable of differentiating themselves from the world, and second, of distinguishing things from people. Further, infants' responses are specific and exquisitely sensitive to the ongoing "dialogue" with their mother.

"In many of our samples of spontaneous communication, the infant is clearly adjusting to what the mother does, not just detecting her face or her voice, but modifying responses to match the particular thing the mother has just done. The infant watches the mother with intense focalization of gaze and an attentive expression. The mother sees this and responds with speech, touching, and changed expression. The infant may then be excited to smile, gesture, or vocalize," says Trevarthen.

Discovery of this embryonic speech communication in babies fits in very well with the view that language is embedded in a context of nonverbal communication. As adults, we speak for the purpose of informing, instructing, and directing the actions or experiences of others. Trevarthen finds that very young infants make speechlike patterns of lip and hand movements intended to influence or impress another. Even though, literally, no "information" is being exchanged, the interaction is one of psychological communication, or "intersubjectivity," as Trevarthen terms it. This intersubjectivity is the first stage in the development of infant communication.

Trevarthen: "The baby is born into the world driven to communicate, at times playing the role of leader in its prelinguistic conversations with mother. The infant's development is, to a degree, actually spurred on by the emotional component, by the will to communicate. This interaction is as finely tuned as the speech system the infant will later master. At this stage, his response may take the form of a gesture or an intonation matching the mother's. But it is highly coordinated to the mother's voice, analogous to the call-and-response improvisation between jazz musicians. In the intervals between mother's cooing and short phrases, the baby contributes a carefully timed response which either mimics or cues the mother's next contribution in terms of pitch and intonation. The infant's proficiency in this early cooperative interaction implies that this kind of communication is hardwired in the species."

Communication of meaning by gestures, expression, voice, and, at a later point, formal language, is an inherently social process. Language, therefore, is linked with culture, socialization, the cooperative search for knowledge, indeed cooperative ventures of all kinds.

"If you look at language in its natural use, you find that it's used for cheating people, for persuading, for giving information in an honest way about a task that interests people," Trevarthen says. "But it's also used for creating affection, antagonizing people, and gaining power. It's also used for all kinds of play. In all these instances, humans are essentially sharing consciousness. Language is the principal medium of sharing the details of experience."

Although it is the "principal medium," language is not the only medium of communication. Nonverbal communication is often just as important. Smiles, tones of voice, angry glares, impatient gestures, rolling upward of the eyes, deep sighs, looks of befuddlement—no translator is required to interpret the meaning of these universal tokens of human exchange. Yet none of them employs spoken language.

Trevarthen says, "It's possible to communicate internal changes in the mind across a distance by means of seeing another's face, hearing his tone of voice, watching his hands. In the case of babies, the communication at a distance regulates the state of the baby's mind. It provides the

As in Dr. Colwyn Trevarthen's experiments, a father "chats" with his two-month-old baby, and the baby responds with intense attention, body movements, and mouth utterances—in effect, embryonic language communication.

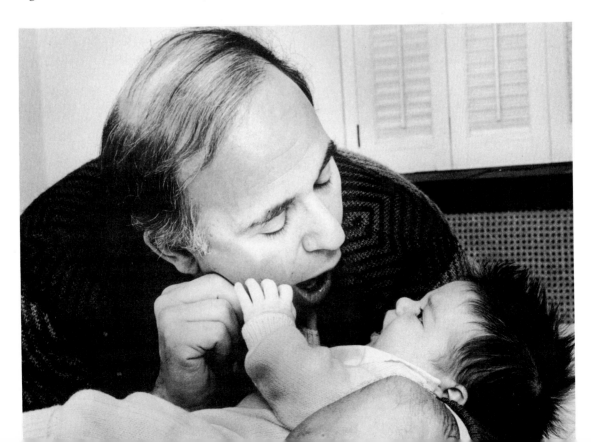

foundation for future transferring of information about interests and intention."

The beginning of this process can be traced to the infant brain. "Communication of meanings by vocal signs is an invention of the baby, something synthesized in the young brain," according to Trevarthen. "When this baby, too young to say a word, is able to understand the name of a familiar person or thing, he or she is already a part of the society's culture and language."

Trevarthen has coined the term *proto-communication* to describe the communication of very young infants and their mother. "To an astonishing extent, a six- or eight-week-old baby can perform its part in what seems very like conversational behavior. The timing, the use of voice intonation, the combination of gesture with facial expression, and the attempt to make utterances with the mouth—all of these are present in infants despite the fact that the word 'infant' comes from a Latin word *infans,* which means 'without speech.' But although the infant may lack speech, it still can take part in a conversational interaction. Besides, infants express themselves with vocalizations which resemble the core sounds of speech. They move their hands in ways which are systematic and expressive. Most important of all, it works! Mother responds to these infant communications."

Trevarthen's work with infants has convinced him that the communication of meaning and shared symbolic awareness is more basic than spoken language. Prior to language, humans must communicate needs, share emotions, convey internal states of mind. Language refines this process, "fine tunes" it in ways that are unavailable to a creature that lacks language. Further, the underpinnings of language—the need to communicate emotion and influence others to respond in certain ways—most probably involve the right hemisphere of the brain.

"If we take a more natural view of human communication, a deeper view, and try to think about why people communicate and what they get out of it and what their motives are, I think that we will find that a very important component of language may be carried out by the right hemisphere. I think that this deep psychology of language will contain many activities that are regulated from infancy onward more on the right half of the brain, more on the emotional side than on the interpersonal side. There are signs now that the expressive activities that go into language are distributed asymmetrically even in a newborn baby's brain."

Thanks to our brain, we enter the world equipped with the capacity to interact with other human beings who, as our caretakers and progenitors, know the world much better than we. From this dialogue, to which we contribute at first by gesture and cooing, and then by single words and finally sentences, emerges nothing less than the vast, culturally diverse world in which each of us finds himself.

Because of advances in neurology, language processing within the human brain is beginning to be understood. Observations of language-impaired individuals have made this possible.

In 1861, the secretary of the Anthropological Society of Paris, Paul Broca, a surgeon and neuroanatomist, described what he had found at autopsy in one of his patients.

For many years, Broca had attended a man who had suffered from a severe difficulty in speaking, or *aphasia*. He was known as Tan because that was the only word he could utter. In Tan's brain after his death, Broca discovered an isolated defect of the third frontal convolution of the left cerebrum. In subsequent autopsies, Broca turned up other instances of brain damage, always on the left side, that were coupled with loss or impairment of speech, or "aphemia," as Broca referred to it. Based on this discovery, Broca claimed that the left frontal convolution was the center for articulate language.

Thirteen years later, a German neurologist, Carl Wernicke, reported on another type of language disturbance associated with damage to a different area in the left hemisphere, the posterior portion of the superior temporal region. Further, Wernicke suggested two broad categories of aphasia. In the first, named after Broca, the sufferer understands what others are saying but cannot respond in a natural and spontaneous manner. The speech is telegraphic. "Buy newspaper, get job," the Broca's aphasic would say to a family member, instead of, "Go to the store and bring home a newspaper so we can look in the employment section for a suitable job for you."

In Wernicke's aphasia, comprehension of speech is severely impaired, and the patient talks on with great speed and fluency, but most of what is said doesn't make sense. "Oh sure, go ahead, any old thing you want," said one Wernicke's patient. "If I could I would. Oh, I'm taking the word the wrong way to say, all of the barbers here whenever they stop you it's going around and around, if you know what I mean."

Thus, by 1874 two different language disturbances were known to be associated with damage in two distinct areas in the left side of the brain. In the years since then, neurologists have discovered additional forms of aphasia associated with damage in distinct brain areas.

At the University of Iowa, Dr. Antonio Damasio, a behavioral neurologist, has been studying the ways in which the brain processes language. He looks at language capability in patients who have suffered strokes.

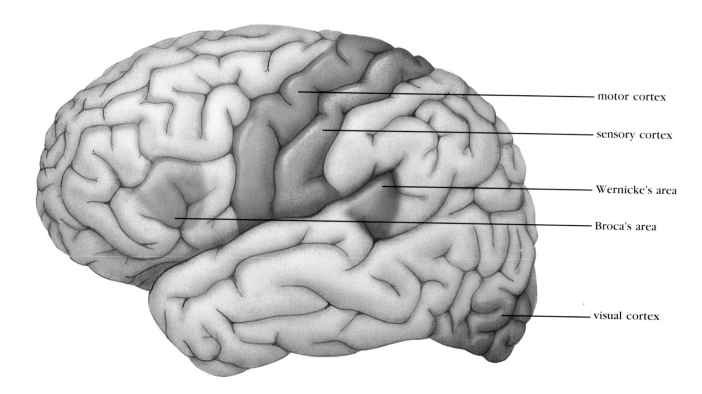

labels: motor cortex, sensory cortex, Wernicke's area, Broca's area, visual cortex

Functional anatomy of the motor and sensory areas of the brain (right lateral view), showing speech centers—Broca's area and Wernicke's area.

"The hallmark of aphasia is the use of words that are off target, words that are related but not quite correct," says Damasio. "For instance, 'president' may be rendered as 'pressman'—a combination of 'president' and 'man.' Aphasics also frequently have trouble with grammatical structure, particularly when the sentence contains a passive clause. 'The boy was pushed by the girl.' "

On superficial observation, patients recovering from aphasia may appear to have no difficulties in their use of language. But if they're tested with a sentence such as, "The bird that the cat watched was hungry," and then shown a picture of a cat watching a bird in a cage, they cannot answer the question, "Who is hungry?" They will invariably take their cue from the picture and make assumptions based on experience; and experience says that cats usually eat birds rather than the other way around.

"What these patients are unable to do," says Damasio, "is to sort out who does what to whom in the sentence. They'll be derailed by the sentence that contains the cat, and they will actually point to the cat in the picture. They do not relate the bird and the state of hunger. This is something that any of us would promptly recognize. We wouldn't be derailed by that sentence."

"Such a performance tells us a lot about the state of mind of these patients," according to Damasio. "They're confused by the sentence. Attempts at simple repetition also produce performance failures. 'The orchestra played and the audience applauded,' often cannot be repeated despite the fact that the patient knows perfectly well who played and who applauded."

One aphasic patient referring to her handicap told Damasio that the words "turned into mush." Although she could retrieve the meaning (who applauded?), the image of the words necessary for prompt repetition simply disappeared. Further, there was nothing that she could do to bring the words back.

Even with good recovery from aphasia, something is lost forever. This loss may be very subtle and be discovered only by sophisticated testing. Further, the recovery that takes place is largely a spontaneous process. It results from other areas in the same and opposite hemispheres taking over and compensating for the defect. Because it is capable of parallel processing, when a primary area is damaged, the brain falls back on auxiliary systems that enable it to perform the same function, although often less efficiently. Spontaneous speech, for example, may return almost to normal. But the recovered aphasic will still go into a tailspin when asked to process, "The girl that the boy asked to go to the dance said that she couldn't."

"Within the brain, you have very large networks that work together to perform certain functions. They all perform slightly different roles. There is no single area to which you could localize language, or to which you could localize such gross areas of language as, say, the lexicon or syntax," says Damasio. "It would be a grave mistake to think, for instance, that you have grammar in one part of the brain and words in another part of the brain, and that somehow the two working together will make sentences. That is simply not the way things work in the brain. Language is so central to the human mind that its key functions are not limited to any one brain area. Nor is the brain limited, of course, to any one language," says Damasio.

When Damasio's patients are given the sentence, "The bird the cat watched was hungry," and cannot say who was hungry, they are unable to grasp the meaning not because they have a problem with the words in the sentence, but because they have a problem with the syntax.

Consider a patient with a classical Broca's aphasia. This patient's verbal productions are sparse and telegraphic. "Butter . . . bread" may have to do for "Please pass the butter so that I may butter my bread." His comprehension is a bit better than this might suggest, but two-part commands may easily throw him: "Take your right hand and touch your left ear." Most apparent are difficulties in "who is doing what to whom" kinds of sentences.

"CREOLE" LANGUAGES

There are about five thousand languages in the world. To be in at the birth of one of them would be a marvelous opportunity to see the way in which language emerges naturally. This is just what Dr. Derek Bickerton, of the University of Hawaii, is doing. He studies languages called "creoles," which are created when established languages are useless.

Bickerton, a linguist, does not agree with Antonio Damasio's contention that mind can exist apart from language. "As far as I'm concerned," he says, "the relationship between language and mind is that language produces mind. Without language, I wouldn't say that it is impossible to have mental experiences, but I'd say that the mental experiences would not be very coherent."

To Bickerton, language is not so much a means of communication as it is a representational system. By means of language, we acquire symbols for everything in our experience. At the same time, we learn to manipulate these symbols to formulate things that don't yet exist but can be made to exist.

Bickerton has arrived at his theories about the relationship of language to mind by study-

ing native speakers of creole languages around the world, including the speakers of the creole languages of Surinam, a former Dutch colony in South America. We can see how a creole language develops by looking at what happened in colonial Surinam when people who had no common language were forced together.

Berry Vrede, who was born in Surinam and now teaches school in Amsterdam, Holland, is fluent in English and Dutch, as well as a Surinam creole. "They come from the western coast of Africa, my ancestors," says Vrede. "And when slaves were taken away from different areas of Africa, they spoke different languages. In Surinam, they were bought on the slave market by owners of the different plantations, who also spoke different languages at that time. People can't stop communicating with each other, and in that process, you develop a lot of languages."

Many slaves in Surinam fled from the cruelty and oppression of their lives to form their own communities. It was in these communities that they evolved pidgin speech, an improvised language that had a sparse vocabulary and no real grammar. Pidgin made communication pos-

In recent years, linguists have joined the teams studying language breakdown in stroke patients, a development that is providing new insights into the nature of language. Indeed, language is an area in which specialists of diverse persuasions can work together: biologists, psychologists, neurologists, and linguists. Linguists bring a more sophisticated conception of language to the task. They can employ tests that isolate grammatical knowledge from semantic knowledge (knowledge of meaning), and with these tests, they are then able to pinpoint the specific system at fault in aphasia.

"The leopard was killed by the lion. Who died?" is a favorite test sentence that most aphasics can't handle. The explanation for this failure? The patient is incapable of retrieving the syntactic structure of a sentence: who did what to whom. He understands that a leopard and a lion appear in the sentence and, perhaps, that one of them is killed. But he fails miserably on the task of which animal killed the other. What makes "The leopard was killed by

sible among people who had no common tongue. Thus, their children also lacked a true language. By spontaneously bringing grammar to their parents' pidgin, Bickerton believes that the children created a completely new language in one generation. This language is a creole.

Bickerton says, "The Surinam creoles are the most interesting of all creole languages, in that they were formed under severe deprivation. Surinam was a kind of natural testing ground for the linguistic capacity, providing a situation that doesn't normally exist in the course of human communities."

In computer terms, as Bickerton puts it, the hardware of a language is its syntax—the way in which words are put together so that the ideas expressed by the words are logical and follow in reasonable order—and the software is its vocabulary. Pidgin, lacking grammar and with a scanty vocabulary, has very little hardware *or* software. "The adults who make the pidgin are not able to provide it with any structure," says Bickerton. "They're past the critical age at which syntax develops. The children, however, are not. Syntax develops in them just as naturally as any other physical part of their bodies. It's natural, it's automatic, it's instinctive, and you can't stop them from doing it. I think the only explanation you can have for the way syntax works is that somehow, this is built in to the hard wiring of the neural circuits in the brain."

Creoles are found worldwide, wherever in the tropics there has been a plantation economy populated by people brought together from different parts of the world who lack a common language. Pidgin is the first stage in their efforts to communicate with one another. Creoles are an order of magnitude different. They are full languages, rich in syntax even if limited in vocabulary. Bickerton believes that the most probable scenario for the development of language involved the construction of a pidgin language in *Homo erectus,* perhaps a million or a million and a half years ago. Then followed, in our species, the gradual emergence of syntactical languages, beginning with creolelike languages and culminating in our own sophisticated languages. To this extent, language evolved as the brain evolved. Interestingly, the language of young children evolves too: pidginlike at first—"Bread ... knife ... me," says the toddler—and only later with the ability to speak with correct syntax: "Cut the bread with the knife and give me some, please."

the lion" and "The lion was killed by the leopard" different is, of course, syntax: the organization of the words in each of the sentences.

Does this mean that the patient is not capable on *some* level of recognizing syntax? In order to answer this question, neuropsychologist Myrna Schwartz, along with her colleague, Dr. Eleanor Saffran, and linguist Marcia Linebarger, developed a series of tests in which aphasic patients are probed for their ability to differentiate syntactically correct sentences—as "The little girl carries the kitten around"—from syntactically incorrect or nonsense sentences—"The kitten carries the little girl around." They have found that despite an aphasic patient's inability to produce sentences such as "The leopard was killed by the lion," and despite confusion when asked to assess these sentences when questioned (who killed whom?), the patients nonetheless can demonstrate an almost perfect recognition knowledge of syntax.

LANGUAGE PROCESSING
IN THE BRAIN

There are several means you can use to read the words on this page. If a word is unfamiliar, you may sound it out. Young children, like my three daughters in their classes at a Montessori school, often learn to read by moving their lips as they sound out the way a word would seem to be pronounced. This is sometimes serviceable, but it is still an unreliable guide to the way many English words are actually pronounced; no one could produce a word like *colonel* by sounding it out. Moreover, even successful sounding out is not necessarily a guide to meaning or correct pronunciation. Reading involves many components, among them the application of the rules of sound, the use of familiar word forms and of context to infer meaning, and the generation of sentences that incorporate the new word.

Our understanding of what occurs in reading has been somewhat aided by observations of people with brain injury because such cases suggest that the components of reading involve different areas of the brain. Thus, patients with damage to Broca's area in the left hemisphere have difficulty with producing and pronouncing words. Damage farther back in the same hemisphere affects comprehension and repetition, and tends to induce a flow of unusual words used out of context.

But observations such as these have limits. It is difficult to ascertain the precise extent of brain damage in living people; only autopsy can delineate it accurately. Most important, studies like these do not tell us how words are handled in the normal, healthy brain.

That has changed over the last decade, thanks to the work of Drs. M. E. Raichle, Michael Posner, and Steven Peterson, among others, at the Washington University Medical School in St. Louis. Using PET scanners, they have watched the living brain at work as it deals with the basic building blocks of language, words. The technique generates color-coded maps that display the areas of the brain involved when a person reads, listens, or speaks.

Very low, harmless doses of a short-lived radioactive isotope, oxygen 15, in water are injected into the volunteer subjects' arms. The areas of the brain that are activated when they use words absorb the radioactivity and are visible on the scanner. There are four stages to the experiment: a resting stage, in which the subject closes his or her eyes and does nothing, or else watches a blank screen; the appearance of single words on the screen; the subject reading the words aloud as they appear; and, finally, the subject producing a use for each word, in the form of another word, as it appears on the screen.

Each of these stages elicits images on the scanner. When the subjects simply look at the words on the screen, areas at the back of the brain that are processing the visual image of the words are highlighted. When they say the words aloud, areas of the brain that are concerned with motor activity of the vocal apparatus, the movements of the mouth and tongue and larynx, are also highlighted. And finally, when they are asked to produce other words, an entire array of regions is illuminated: the frontal areas in the left hemisphere crucial for language, areas devoted to motor control, and areas often activated during stress.

When Patty, a volunteer in one experiment, came to this last stage, Peterson said, "If you'll open your eyes now, you'll see that the words going by on the screen are all nouns. What we want you to do is to generate a verb that's appropriate to the noun, or a use for it. So if, say, *cake* came up, we'd like you to say 'eat,' or if *gun* came up, to say 'shoot,' or something like that."

Patty proved to be adept. The verbs came pouring out in reaction to the words that passed across the screen: "Bake. Fly. Twirl. Climb. Heat. Watch. Listen. Hit. Swim. Drink. Drive. Blow. Ride. Knit. Ring. Turn. Sit. Shoot. Sniff." And as they did, the images of all her brain areas involved in the different processes came vividly alive.

The pictures produced by the PET scanner at these different stages are placed in align-

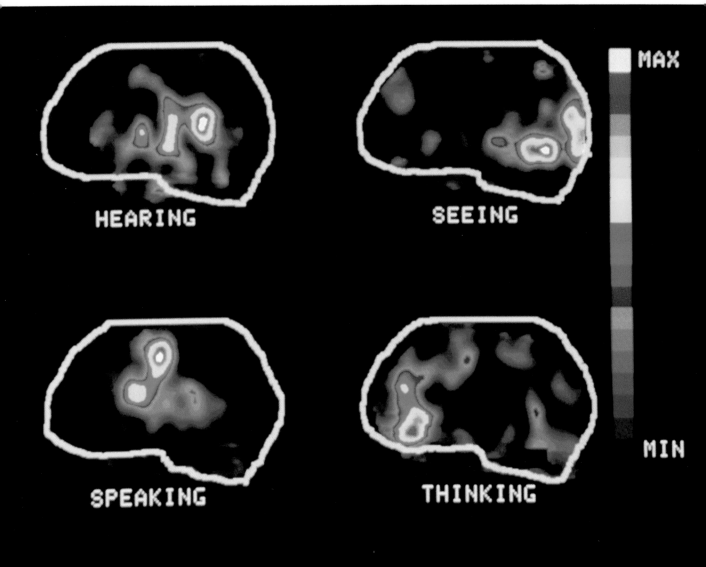

PET scan of the left hemisphere of the brain, contrasting the different areas used in aspects of language activity: hearing, seeing, speaking, and thinking.

ment, which allows the researchers to subtract the activity in one task from the others, or to average the activity in the same task when performed by different people. This technique of subtraction lets the investigators see exactly which areas of the brain are involved in a particular activity. As Raichle notes, "The brain is involved, in a very discrete way, with the processing of language."

PET scans in normal subjects promise to provide very important, fresh understanding of how different regions of the brain are involved when we read, when we listen, and even when we think. Mental activities can be objectively measured with this technique. When a person merely *thinks* about a word, or does something "in his head," there is visible activity in the premotor and supplementary motor areas. That familiar sentence we all remember from our elementary school classes is proving to be literally true. The brain is visibly active, very much at work, when we "do it in our head."

Schwartz: It's perfectly correct to say, "John looked over the new cars." Can we say, "John looked the new cars over?"

The patient points to a board on which is written the simple word *yes*.

Schwartz: Can we say, "He stood in line very patiently?"

Patient points again to *yes*.

Schwartz: How about, "He stood the line in very patiently?"

Patient points to a board on which is written *no*.

As the testing continues, it becomes obvious that the patient is capable of isolating grammatical English sentences from those that are not. Again and again, simple recognition of the correct response occurs despite the patient's inability to produce such a sentence or answer questions about it. "Our findings are incompatible with the view that the aphasic speaker has no access to information about what constitutes a well-formed sentence in his language," Schwartz, Saffran, and Linebarger have written.

Several practical as well as theoretical implications follow from this new research. "In the controversy over whether syntax is 'real,' we've learned to say that it must be real. A person does it effortlessly even when he or she has suffered massive brain damage," says Schwartz. What seems to be involved here is an *innate* ability to correctly process syntax. Even when language production and processing are disturbed, there remain certain unaltered predispositions toward the recognition of syntactically meaningful sentences.

Does this mean there is a "universal grammar"—a deep structural similarity underlying all the diverse languages of the world? Or is language processing in the human brain dependent upon culture?

To answer this question, Dr. William S.-Y. Wang, a linguist at the University of California, Berkeley, and Dr. Ovid Tzeng, a psychologist at the University of California, Riverside, traveled to Taiwan to study how the special characteristics of the Chinese language affect brain organization and the processing of language. Specifically, they were interested in learning whether the "Chinese brain" handles language in the same way as the brain of a Westerner.

Chinese differs from a Western language such as English or French in one eminently important way: words are constructed not only by means of vowel and consonant combinations, but also based on the distinctive tone of each syllable that is associated with a particular word. Wang explains it this way:

"There are numerous languages in the world, called tongue languages or tonal languages, that use the pitch of the voice as part of the intrinsic form of each word. For instance, the word *ma* can mean 'mother,' 'hemp,' 'horse,' or 'to scold,' based on the pitch at which the segments are pronounced. These differences are based on the frequency of the vibration of the vocal cords. In this respect, Chinese is quite different from the way the pitch of the voice is used in English in such words as *contract*, as a noun—a written agreement—and *contract*, as a verb—to contract an illness. Or consider constructions like *White House* versus *white house*. Notice that in these instances in English, we are talking about *grammatical* issues, whereas in a tonal language the pitch of the voice is part of the intrinsic form of each word."

Since the variations in pitch in the Chinese language sound almost like music to the Western ear, one might expect that Chinese would be processed in the right hemisphere, as music is. But in actuality, the Chinese language is processed the same way as English: in the left hemisphere of all right-handers and the great majority of left-handers. (See page 20.) Wang has confirmed this by his studies of the effects of brain damage on language in adult Chinese.

Wang: "Both the tones of spoken Chinese and the pictorial characters of the Chinese writing system are strongly lateralized to the left hemisphere. Patients with damage to the left hemisphere have great difficulty spontaneously producing Chinese characters in their writing. They have no difficulty in drawing fake characters; that is, the components are those of a Chinese word, but they don't really form a word. The 'word' *bick*, for instance, doesn't violate any of the rules of English grammar, but you can't find this configuration of letters in a dictionary. *Bick* triggers a vacuous spot in the sound system. The same thing can be said for Chinese. For instance, if something is drawn that looks like a Chinese character but isn't, left-hemisphere-damaged patients experience no difficulty in copying these fake characters. Their difficulty is with real Chinese characters.

"This indicates that the Chinese writing system, even though it is based on a different principle—each graph typically refers to both a meaning and a phonetic syllable—lateralizes to the left hemisphere by virtue of its being linguistic."

In all languages that have been examined to date, the human brain is organized to distinguish linguistic from nonlinguistic stimuli. This holds true even in languages that have strong pictorial and musical qualities. This brain organization suggests that there is a powerful connection not only between language and mind, but between language and the formation of mind.

Wang agrees. "Language is the best window through which we view mental life. But it's probably even more than that. It also plays a major role in shaping the mind. I think how we relate to others, how we see things, how we represent reality within ourselves, to ourselves, are all very critically influenced by the choices that our language makes available to us. 'Another language, another soul,' as language teachers sometimes like to repeat, is a somewhat romantic view, but I think there's a lot of truth to it."

Outside, as I write these words, snow is on the ground. To a city dweller like myself, the word *snow* refers to white precipitation that covers the roads and streets. When I use the word *snow,* I don't need to elaborate any further; other city dwellers like myself "know" exactly what I mean. But "what I mean" is very much related to that "reality within ourselves" that Wang notes above. I am a city dweller. Snow may delight my children but from my vantage point, I am likely to think of it in a unitary sense, as something that clogs the streets and makes me late to my office. If I were a dedicated skier, I would have more precise and varied terms for it: Is it powdery? Packed? Will it form a crust? Is it corn snow? And snow to an Eskimo is an order of magnitude different. In the Eskimo language there are nearly one hundred words for snow—*apikak,* first snow falling; *aniu,* snow spread out; *pukak,* snow for drinking water.

Language determines perception, which in turn helps to mold mind. Does language, therefore, also mold the environment or culture in which we find ourselves? Would an Eskimo's process of thinking be different from ours because his language stresses differing priorities? Does language so influence the thinking of those who speak it that it imposes a specific view of the world upon their minds?

In the 1930s, while studying the Hopi Indians in the American southwest, Dr. Benjamin Whorf, an anthropologist, decided that this was so. He claimed he had found a language that defined the world so differently from any other language that the Hopis, living in isolation and bound by traditions handed down over countless generations, had a unique world view. Their language, Whorf concluded, was "timeless," lacked any word for time, and the Hopis, therefore, were completely divorced from the phenomenon of time that the rest of us all know.

Dr. Ekkehart Malotki, of Northern Arizona University, a linguist and for the past fifteen years a student of Hopi language and culture, interviewed native Hopi speakers to explore the idea that the reason the Hopis have no perception of time is because they have no vocabulary for it. When one Hopi said that they "went to pray to the sun with cornmeal," for instance, Malotki caught a particular phrase and asked, "Does this mean the *time* when you do this?" "Yes," was the answer. "Barely sunrise." As Malotki points out, "They are living with time in every point of their lives. But not necessarily in the way *we* perceive time today.

Before the encounter with the white man, there had never been a need for naming hours or minutes or seconds. In Hopi society, time is probably experienced as a more organic or natural phenomenon." Its source is the Hopi environment, in which each season evolves gradually into the next, each day shades subtly into the night, each crop is planted in its time, the rhythm of life is shaped by the cycles of harvest. The Hopi language mirrors its world as surely as all other languages mirror theirs.

Malotki points to the importance of the planting and harvesting of corn in the Hopi culture. In their semi-arid environment, moisture plays a paramount role in whether or not the corn will come to harvest. Therefore, the Hopis developed a great interest in the phenomena of weather and weather ceremonialism: inducing the gods to produce the life-giving moisture in sufficient amounts.

The Hopis.

THE THREE S's

Despite its complexity and universality, language allows only three formats for communication: speech, sign language, and script. As you read these words—a printed version of a typewritten version of what was originally a handwritten manuscript—you may decide to read some of it aloud to a friend. Under appropriate conditions, your spoken language can be transformed into signs by someone familiar with American Sign Language. But in all these instances, there are common requirements. The brain of the language *user* must be capable of selecting, sequencing, and timing appropriate motor commands; and at the other end, the language *receiver* must be capable of understanding what has been written, spoken, or signed.

All three language formats—the three S's—are based on the transmission of signals through motor activities. In order to speak, the lips, tongue, jaws, and larynx cooperate to shape the vocal tract to make various sound patterns possible. In the case of sign language, hand shapes and movements are employed to create layered configurations. Handwriting or typing uses script to convey meaning to the reader. We see these language channels as separable, but this was not true centuries ago. Reading was done aloud, to listeners who could not usually read themselves; and those who knew how to read did not necessarily know how to write. So universal was reading aloud that reading and speaking were thought to be joined. St. Augustine, writing in the fifth century about St. Ambrose, commented in surprise, " . . . a remarkable thing . . . When he was reading, his eyes glided over the pages and his heart sensed out the sense, but his voice and tongue were at rest."

Eight centuries later, reading, writing, and speaking were still linked. Monks assigned to copy manuscripts identified the words by their sounds, mouthing the phrases as they bent over the manuscripts in their tiny cubicles, or carrels. Today, most of us as children repeat this process as our reading abilities mature. At first, we mouth the words, move our lips, or run our fingers over the lines on the page. The more sophisticated the reader, the fewer muscles are employed, culminating in silent reading in which only the muscles moving the eyes are engaged.

This separation of reading from spoken language enables us to read much faster than would be possible if we spoke the words aloud. Speed reading techniques are the culmination of this separation. But in every instance, no matter how rapidly we can speak, read, or sign, biological limitations exist. The motions of tongue, larynx, and jaw can be speeded up only to a certain point, beyond which gibberish takes over. Handwriting has similar limitations. If we write too fast, the time we have saved is paid for in the difficulty of deciphering our scrawl and the errors in interpreting it. There are similar constraints in typing and signing. At all times, we are forced to accede to limitations on how fast *and* effectively we can communicate.

"It was not the language that led the Hopis into developing agriculture revolving around corn. The momentum came from their interests and not from the language," according to Malotki. Language is not simply a reflection of "the reality that is out there." For language to mirror exactly what's confronting us, we would need millions of words more than the human brain could possibly store. People are not different because of their language; they are different because of their experience in this world and whatever becomes important to them. In that sense, we find a tremendous variety of cultures and languages, but deep down we're all the same and it couldn't be otherwise."

At the Bacavi school in Northern Arizona, Hopi Brian

Honyouti is attempting to sustain the Hopi language amid the wider culture in which the Hopis are now immersed. "We can base our knowledge on the things around us. Our language is the language of the plants and animals and the rocks and the winds and the birds. In order to know who we are and what's around us, we have to know that." To Honyouti, learning the Hopi language is "a very integral part of being Hopi. . . . It's an organic entity."

Benjamin Whorf was clearly wrong in saying that language determines our thinking. If Whorf was right, translations from one language to another would be impossible. Each culture would be hermetically sealed from every other and communication impossible. But we do communicate and learn from each other despite differences in our languages. This holds true even in languages in which speech plays no part. American Sign Language—ASL—which is wholly gestural, is an example.

Dr. Ursula Bellugi, Director of the Laboratory of Language and Cognitive Studies, of the Salk Institute in La Jolla, California, is an expert in the sign languages of the deaf. She studies ASL in search of insights into all language. "We are interested in sifting out the properties of language that are due to the mode in which language developed, and the properties that are more fundamental to the human mind—that is, intellect and cognitive processes." Language is so central to the human mind that it emerges in everyone equipped with normal mental abilities, even when hearing is absent from birth. ASL has developed an alternative to human speech, with, as Bellugi says, "the transmission system in the hands, rather than the vocal tract, and the perception in the eyes rather than the ear."

Bellugi reports, "We have found after a long series of studies that American Sign Language is structured at its core very much like spoken language. It has the same kind of organization into different levels. Signs are built up into more complex signs. This is like the morphology of spoken language. And signs are also organized into sentences, like syntax in spoken language."

But there are differences in this organization. English, for instance, relies heavily on word order for meaning and relationships—"The dog chased the cat," versus "The cat chased the dog." Other languages, such as Latin, use verb inflection or case markings. "In ASL the syntax, meaning, is set up in space and is spatially organized."

Signs are made up of several components. One aspect has to do with hand configuration; another has to do with location in space. For instance, the signs for *summer, ugly,* and *dry* differ only in the positions in which they are made with respect to the body.

Bellugi has studied an unusual population in a school in

Fremont, California, where most of the teachers and students come from deaf families. Signing is the first language they learn; no other language has influenced their development. The children's signing language is as vivid as would be the spoken language of a hearing child. A little girl, asked what firemen do, answers in ASL, "I know. They fight fires. They go in and break out all the windows, *bam, bam, bam, bam,* and they pull the people out." Her responsiveness and expressiveness and vocabulary are identical to that of all children her age everywhere. Only the language she uses is different.

Bellugi explores how this language of gestures enters the youngsters' minds, and whether the *form* of the language alters the way they learn to communicate. "We know by now, from experiments, that deaf people rehearse in signs, plan what they're going to do in signs, even dream in signs. We've seen little children signing to themselves. So to the extent that we hearing people think in words, it's perfectly clear that deaf people equivalently think in signs." It turns out that the learning process is no different than it is for hearing children. When they're first acquiring the language, Bellugi has discovered, the children make exactly the same kinds of errors as hearing children learning English. They proceed in just the same way as hearing children, with the errors disappearing as their minds mature.

But for Bellugi, "The most interesting aspect of sign language is the way in which the grammar is built up. For example, many verb signs are mutable with respect to space. The basic sign, *give,* a very simple form, can be changed to mean *give to you, give to me, give to him, give to each other, give to the two of them,* and so on. In addition, there are a wide variety of ways in which you can change the meaning of a sign to include how events occur over time. Examples are *give over and over again, give regularly,* and *give for a long time.* In each .of these examples, the basic sign form is the same and yet it's nested in spatial patterns."

Understanding a language expressed in spatial movement rather than sound is not something that comes easily to most of us. It takes considerable time and effort to learn ASL. But some appreciation of the subtleties conveyed by sign language can be gained by means of computer graphics.

Dr. Howard Poizner, of the same laboratory as Bellugi, has attached lights to the major joints of both arms of persons speaking in ASL. By videotaping their movements in a darkened room, Poizner has been able to capture sign forms as dynamic light displays—patterns of moving dots. With the aid of computer graphic analysis, Poizner found that it is possible to analyze the underlying structure of the linguistic movement system that forms the basis of ASL.

"By isolating the movement and studying it directly, we can peel off one of the many simultaneously occurring levels of structure in sign language, that of essential grammatical information," Poizner explains. "Whole-arm movements of signs in space are constructed from such building blocks as planes of motion, shape of motion, and rhythmic patterns of motion. This is the correlate, in a spoken language such as English, to establishing a temporal order of information by stringing signs together in a particular sequence."

ASL and English differ markedly when it comes to this temporal order. If a person speaks too rapidly or mixes in too many qualifiers, meaning becomes lost. This is because spoken language is based on the analysis of signs presented in a linear pattern. Not so in ASL, however.

"The trajectory shape in which the hand is traveling and the rhythmic properties of the movement are all elements which build up grammatical processes. These, in turn, are conveyed in space in a simultaneous way," says Poizner. "Grammar in ASL is conveyed not by hand or finger movement, but rather by arm movement through space. By placing the lights at the major joints of the arm, therefore, we

Research by Dr. Ursula Bellugi has discovered that deaf children's acquisition of American Sign Language entails the same learning process as language acquisition by hearing children.

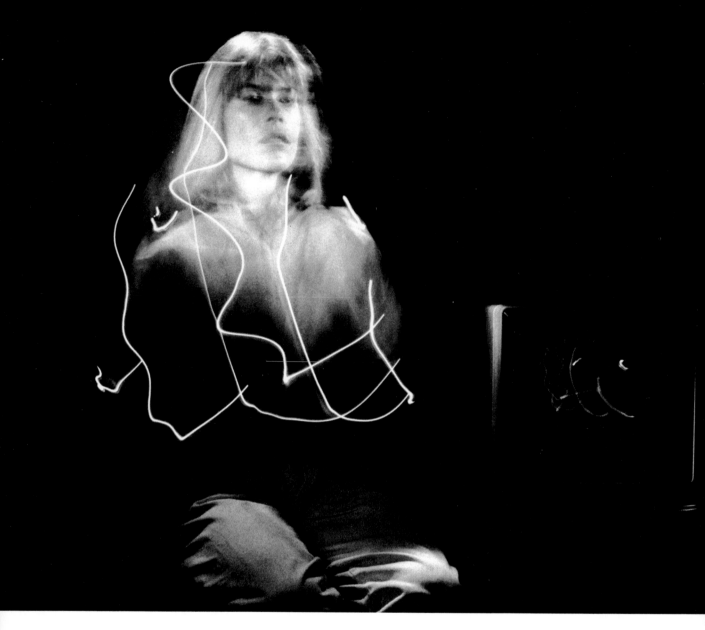

By placing small points of light at the arm joints of a person using American Sign Language, Dr. Howard Poizner demonstrates that these movements convey grammatical processes.

are able to capture that whole-arm movement through space, which by itself is enough to convey grammatical processes."

Poizner has carried out perception experiments employing only a few moving points of light. Despite the paucity of data, deaf persons familiar with ASL can read the grammatical inflections, thus demonstrating that meaning structures, conveyed through whole-arm movement patterns, can be isolated. To the person unfamiliar with ASL, on the other hand, these moving dots of light remain just that: pinpoints of light veering erratically and meaninglessly against a curtain of darkness.

The way in which the brain processes sign language has been studied by Dr. Helen Neville, Associate Professor of Neuropsychology at the University of California, San Diego, School of Medicine. "There's a great deal we don't know about the relationship between language and the mind," says Neville. "A good way of approaching this relationship involves studying those many, many deaf people who basically do not acquire any formal language at all. They haven't acquired American Sign Language since they weren't born to deaf parents. Nor have they acquired English. This means they can't be said to have a formal language. Despite this, many of these people function very well in the world. They have communicative skills despite the absence of a formal language."

Neville has been scrutinizing the cognitive faculties and operations of these individuals and their brain organization, as well as those of deaf persons who use ASL, utilizing evoked potential recordings of ongoing brain activity (see Chapter 4). There have been some surprising findings. In most hearing, right-handed adults, the left hemisphere of the brain plays a greater role than the right in the production and comprehension of speech. This is also true for the deaf; ASL is processed in the left hemisphere. But deaf and hearing people process *movement* differently in the brain.

Most neuroscientists believe that in most hearing right-handers, the right hemisphere is active in tasks such as detecting the direction of motion of a small white square on a computer screen. "But in this kind of situation, deaf subjects show a greater role for the *left* hemisphere," Neville reports. "We think this is because motion is critical to the perception of ASL. As a result, the detection of motion is moved into the neural systems of the left hemisphere, which are specialized to produce and comprehend language." In effect, motion is the fundamental mechanism for all communication in the deaf, serving the same purpose as sound in persons with normal hearing.

"It's as though there is an initial bias for the left hemisphere to mediate all formal language, English and ASL alike," Neville says. "But the perception of information which is critical to the language, such as the perception of motion, will be organized within the system that processes the motion."

Thus, the familiar sequence of genetic predisposition, redundancy of neurons, plasticity, and commitment that shapes the unfolding of other constituents of mind is applicable to language, too. These differences in hemisphere specialization between deaf and hearing persons illustrate the enormous adaptability of the brain. "When we do this kind of research, we learn about the plasticity of the human brain," Neville points out.

Sign languages are true languages, with all the formal complexity and expressive power of spoken languages. Separate and mutually unintelligible sign languages exist in the United States, Austria, Denmark, Finland, France, Germany, Norway, Portugal, Rumania, Sweden, Switzerland, the Soviet Union, the United Kingdom, and Yugoslavia. A person employing the sign language used in Norway would find the sign language of a Frenchman incomprehensible. Intriguingly, sign language exhibits an independence beyond what is usually encountered in a spoken language. The sign language used by a Londoner can't be understood by an American signer even though the spoken language in their two countries is the same.

The research of Bellugi, Poizner, and Neville provides a "window" on a basic process of mind: the human capacity for language is so profound that even in the absence of hearing from birth, a completely separate and autonomous language system develops.

Where do all these converging insights into the nature of language lead us? Certainly not to a logical, internally consistent theory that neatly ties up brain, language, and mind.

Bellugi: "The capacity for language is fundamental to the human mind, so fundamental that even in the absence of hearing and speech from birth, language emerges in its great richness and flowering and complex organization. Man perfects an alternative system to give explicit expression to ideas."

Lieberman: "The evolution of language is, in my view, an interactive process involving virtually all aspects of human and animal behavior and the biological mechanisms that underride these behaviors. The search for the 'uniqueness' of human language and the 'unique' mechanisms that may underlie it are, so far as I can see, a search for the Holy Grail. Language is probably not unique, nor is it an isolated biological component."

Premack: "The sentence is the most abstract representation of which humans are capable and, as such, is far beyond the capacity of the chimpanzee."

Damasio: "The language system is, in a way, a constant shadow of everything that is happening in terms of non-language in our minds. It acts as a go-between . . . a sort of public representation of what is going on in our minds prior to the use of any language."

Bickerton: "Without a language, it would not have been possible for mind to develop. Without a representational system such as language, there would be no mind."

Kuhl: "Language is one of the skills that separates humans from the rest of the animal kingdom. We've yet to see any sign that an animal, such as a chimpanzee, is capable of producing anything related to syntax. Language is really a separate system. It's also one of the most complex things that human beings are capable of."

Trevarthen: "Language doesn't only convey intentions

and information. It also regulates personal relationships, positions, roles, rank, and so forth. Language is something that has to be considered within the whole fabric of what humans are trying to do."

Wang: "Knowing more languages makes available to you more ways of looking at things, more ways of relating to things, to others. All these are, of course, aspects of how the mind is shaped."

Malotki: "In my view, language is a coping mechanism that helps us to classify, to categorize, what is out there. And we will categorize, of course, according to our specific interests, our specific concerns. People are not different because of their language; they are different because of their experience in this world and whatever became important to them. We've a tremendous variety of cultures, but deep down we're all the same. And it couldn't be otherwise."

At various points in our search for mind, we've heard that language made possible the development of mind; that language provides the basis for such cognitive processes as memory, perception, and reasoning; that only a creature endowed with intelligence, an aspect of mind, could evolve a language.

Perhaps our minds *are* in part molded by language; perhaps language merely *reflects* the workings of brain and mind. There are too many loose ends, too many intriguing observations, for us to be able to know. We are perhaps best satisfied by what psycholinguist Michael Studdert-Kennedy says: "The development of mind, thought, and language is simply a nexus in which it is impossible to separate one from the others."

8.
THINKING

At 2 P.M. on a clear May afternoon, the U.S.S. *Saipan* leaves the naval base in Norfolk, Virginia, headed for the Middle East. The helicopter carrier, over eight hundred feet long, is equipped with the ultimate in high-tech navigation. Thanks to radar, computers, scopes, charts, and the cooperative endeavors of its crew, the ship's course is plotted out in advance with such precision that, barring unforeseen circumstances, it will arrive at its destination exactly as calculated.

At 8 A.M., halfway around the world, a forty-foot outrigger canoe slips into the South Pacific from a launch point on a Micronesian island. Its crew consists of several oarsmen and, at the helm, a navigator who has no technology, just himself, to chart and maintain the vessel's course. But the outrigger, too, will reach its destination, a dot of an island set amid a vast expanse of water, as unerringly as the carrier.

Two seagoing craft, two contrasting ways of traversing the sea, two very different modes of thinking to get to those destinations. Though changes in course will be made if unforeseen conditions develop, most of the planning is done before the carrier leaves port. The outrigger's position is under constant revision at sea in order to keep the craft on course. Thinking here is continuous, a series of informed improvisations more like those of a jazz musician than the playing of a classical musician performing a set piece of music from a score.

There is another important difference between the two navigators. The navy man can describe fully *in words* the strategy that he's employing. He has an overall plan in his mind, based on information from compass readings, computer calculations, radar readings, and charts. He can give

Navy navigators aboard the U.S.S. Saipan are surrounded by intricate technological aids.

Micronesian islanders study rocks they have set on the ground in a "star compass," as a navigational aid for a prospective voyage.

you a report of the carrier's progress and, if you ask him, he can draw a line on a chart connecting his on-course position at the moment with his destination.

The Micronesian cannot spell out his plans or pinpoint his position in the way the navy man does, but he can point accurately toward his destination over the horizon, something the navigator on the carrier would find extremely hard to do. Over time, the islanders have developed a "star compass," a map that pinpoints the positions of hundreds

of stars. At sea, they utilize knowledge drawn from the environment and passed from generation to generation: the flight of birds, the formations of clouds, the location of the sun and stars, the direction in which the ocean waves flow.

Yet different though their approaches to navigation may be, every time he sails, each navigator must pass the strictest test of all—the test of either reaching land or floundering till he dies. The thinking process of both has crucial elements in common. Dr. Ed Hutchins, of the University of California, San Diego, explains it: "Navigation is a task that clearly involves many kinds of thinking. There has to be reasoning about where one wants to go, how to get there, where one is at the moment. Both navigators have to get information about the world and employ it to form a representation about the world. This representation, or mental model, is a means of thinking about how to organize observations in the world in order to get the job done. Although the mental models are far different for the navigator of a pocket carrier than for a canoe, in both cases mental models are employed in order to think."

To psychologist Philip Johnson-Laird, of the University of Cambridge, the notion of a mental model is very much akin in function to an architect's model. "It allows you to anticipate how something will occur. But, of course, the difference between the architect's model and a mental model is that the architect's model is a physical thing, out there in the real world, whereas a mental model is something that is constructed computationally by the brain."

Mental models are shaped by thinking. The art of navigating a ship is a demonstration of what we all do all our lives: construct models, solve problems, anticipate the future. These mental processes reach their culmination in the human brain.

"The brain exists in order to construct representations of the world, " says Dr. Johnson-Laird. "Very simple organisms have no brains, construct no representations of the world. And the reason we probably have such large brains is in part because we live in a very complicated world, a complicated *social* world. We're social animals. So the brain has to do a great deal of computation in order to solve the very intricate problems that social life poses for us."

On some occasions, our thinking is like that of the navigator of the carrier. We employ words, concepts, highly abstract representations of the world around us. At other times, in difficult, sensitive, or challenging situations, we think in the way the native navigator does, and intuit or "feel" our way. There are no fixed rules, no set approaches, that will invariably work at such times. But though we, like the native navigator, "play it by ear," interpreting the situation as he interprets the direction, shape, and feel of the ocean swells that rock his tiny craft, the mental models in both these kinds of thinking are similar, drawing on a store of accumulated knowledge and experience.

Thinking is easier to name than to define, but we can begin to explore what it is by noting elements we have highlighted in describing the process of navigation. Hutchins has pointed out some of these: reasoning about where one is at the moment and about one's objective and how to reach it, using information about the world, and forming representations or mental models that organize this information. We have used other terms that are intrinsic to thinking as well: developing concepts, solving problems, using words, abstracting, intuiting, anticipating the future. Nor are these all. As we shall see, learning, memory, creativity, communication, generalization, insight, logic, and rationality are all aspects of thinking. Many of these terms, too, can be difficult to explain, but we can advance our understanding of them by concentrating on how we think under different circumstances.

Consider the following biographical sketch: Jonathan dropped out of school in the mid-sixties, drifted into antiwar activities, experimented with drugs for a while, and eventually returned to take a degree from Berkeley in 1970. Today Jonathan lives in Greenwich Village. Question: Which is more likely, that Jonathan is a teacher at the New School, or that he is a teacher at the New School and an occasional user of cocaine?

Based on your knowledge of people, you might have answered that Jonathan is both a teacher at the New School and an occasional user of cocaine. But the *logically* more correct answer is that Jonathan is a teacher at the New School. According to probability, it's impossible for two categories (A and B: teacher and cocaine user) to be more probable than one category (A: teacher).

If you chose incorrectly, you were no doubt misled by the description provided, which says nothing very typical of teachers but quite a bit about people in their late thirties and early forties who are likely to dabble with drugs. Jonathan's background is more representative of an occasional drug user than it is of a teacher.

It is true that people with a background in statistics would not have been taken in by the description of Jonathan, but few of us have studied formal statistics. Besides, there is a huge literature that indicates probability exerts only a weak and inconstant influence on decision making. We usually base our decisions on our personal experiences, to the exclusion of how things stand in the larger world.

Now consider this question: Are there more words starting with the letter *r* or more words in which *r* is in the third letter position? When Drs. Daniel Kahneman, of the Uni-

THE CHESS PLAYERS OF
THE SOUTH BRONX

The entire chess club of the Roberto Clemente Junior High School in New York's South Bronx is playing against Bruce Pandolfini. Their opponent is a member of a group of chess masters who have begun a program in New York's inner-city schools in the belief that chess can improve the children's ability to concentrate and help them learn to think more carefully.

It does, and the children know it. Felix spells it out: "Chess is like life because if you make a mistake, you aren't going to be able to put it back." Jeannie is equally explicit. "It develops your thinking so that it's tuned to think of what might happen later, what might happen in the end," she says. "And when you do something you'll think of what'll happen." Jeannie would neither have realized this nor have been able to articulate it before the chess club came into being.

"Most of the kids from the inner city are used to doing things intuitively, impulsively," says Pandolfini. "Chess instills a feeling for very careful thinking and logical reasoning, which they're unused to at first. And when you bring both of these together, the intuitive and the analytic processes, you redress the balance and you get a full person."

Pandolfini is convinced that ghetto kids are uniquely qualified to become good chess players. "Chess is a game that is suited for fighters, for people who enjoy the struggle and can stay with it and don't quit. And that's what we're talking about when we're talking about inner-city kids."

The children's schoolwork also shows the effects of the chess club. "Chess does a lot for these kids," says Pandolfini. "It improves their concentration, their memory skills, and their discipline. But there's also a carry-over effect. The kids learn to make analogies, arrange ideas in logical sequences, spot patterns, visualize, and determine what's relevant. In a word, chess makes them *think*."

But even though chess requires talents that are essential to thinking, it is more than a logical exercise played out on a board arranged in sixty-four squares. At all times, the fledgling player, as well as the grand master, seeks *meaning*. For instance, it is difficult for chess players, both the very best and the worst, to memorize chess positions when the pieces are arranged haphazardly on the board. But when the pieces are arranged in sensible positions, the game takes on a life of its own, with each player participating to the extent of his or her knowledge and skill.

Although the program is still in its early stages, some gratifying results have already been achieved. The youngsters' self-esteem has improved and they are willing participants in the civilities that accompany the game. They respond to the behavior required of them. Bambi: "Little after little I talked less 'cause every time I talked, I lost. And finally I started beating some opponents. The only words I really say now are, 'Hello, my name is Bambi.' And I say, 'Check,' 'Checkmate,' and 'Thank you for the game.' That's the only words I really say. And 'When's lunch?' "

The members of the chess club are thriving.

The chess club of the Roberto Clemente Junior High School. Chess master Bruce Pandolfini often plays the entire club.

versity of California at Berkeley, and Amos Tversky, of Stanford University, asked this of test subjects, they discovered that "Most people judge words that begin with a given consonant to be more numerous than words in which the same consonant appears in the third position. They do so even for consonants such as *r* or *k* that are more frequent in the third position than in the first." How can we explain such results? What do they tell us about how we think?

For most of us, our ability to think of words beginning with the letter *r* far exceeds our ability to rattle off a list of words with *r* in the third position. Put differently, if our brain was "wired" to count letters and encode the count in memory, we could probably make the relevant calculation within our head and come up with the correct response: "More words with *r* in position three than in position one." But our brain isn't wired that way, so we're perpetually at risk whenever we rely simply on our inner "blueprint" of how things are in the world. Obviously, many of these difficulties can be avoided by asking the right questions and examining the data: actually locating the words with *r*'s on a page of a book and counting the placement of the *r*'s. But such examination is often impossible. More important, we usually don't feel the need for it because we're confident that our incorrect assumptions are correct.

Here is another example. Consider the difference between the cash price and the credit card price for gasoline at many gas stations. This difference can be formulated in two ways: a discount for buying with cash, or a surcharge for buying on credit. To most people, a credit surcharge is much less acceptable than a cash discount. "This is because we treat gains and losses in quite a different way," says Kahneman. "Accepting losses such as a surcharge on our gasoline somehow hurts a great deal more than giving up a cash discount. This difference in attitude indicates that the same objective or the same state of affairs is not necessarily recognized as the same."

None of these scenarios is the result of stupidity, flawed thinking, or malfunctioning within the mind. Rather, they illustrate how the mind actually works. Put in evolutionary terms, the mind has evolved to be effective in situations that are most likely to arise. Mechanisms have developed to respond to these situations. Logic is one of these mechanisms, but it's not the only one, nor, often, is it the most useful, adequate, or even the most important one. Most of the time, few of us operate according to strict principles of logic. Our minds are not logic machines, and for good reason.

In what way does logic help us choose a mate, vote for a politician, pick friends, keep ourselves from catching a cold, be the first in line to get tickets for a rock concert? In each of these instances logical inferences are only slightly helpful. Even the situation here that seems most susceptible to logic is constrained by conflicting demands: If I get there early enough, I'll be the first in line. But how early is "early enough"? Other considerations are often more important than logic. Most of us are prepared to spend only a certain amount of time waiting in line. "Overall, I have more important things to do no matter how much I want to hear the concert." Concepts such as "overall" and "more important things to do" are critical when it comes to understanding thinking. Rationality, which is closely correlated with logic but not identical to it, often helps us utilize these concepts. Thinking is formed on the basis of compromise. If we insisted on examining *all* possible alternatives that are open to us, we could never make any decisions. Most of us most of the time settle for "rough and ready" choices that enable us to move on. There are always limitations of time, resources, and mental energy that must be taken into account, as well as individual life experiences unique to each individual. Our decisions are always based on what seems best "under the circumstances." This doesn't imply that the mind is flawed. On the contrary. The point is simply that more important considerations influence the formation of thought than mere logic or even rationality.

Because our use of language often suggests that we tend to equate rationality and mind, it is important to emphasize this point. "He must have been out of his mind," we exclaim when we learn that our neighbor lost all his savings at a blackjack table in Atlantic City. "She has an incisive mind," the mathematics teacher comments about his most brilliant pupil. As we will see throughout this chapter, *nothing* about thinking lends itself to simplistic explanations or relationships.

Here are three questions: Who was the sixteenth president of the United States? How far is Los Angeles from San Francisco? Are the toes of a pigeon arranged differently from those of a parrot, and if so, what is the difference?

Each of these questions required you to think, but the thinking involved wasn't the same. If you're like most people, you answered the first question either by referring back to some inner listing of presidents until you reached Abraham Lincoln, or by having his name come immediately to mind, suggesting a listing that exists outside of your consciousness.

Your approach to the second question has a lot to do with where you live or how much you've traveled. If you live on the West Coast, you simply "know" that San Francisco can be reached by a fifty-minute flight from Los Angeles or a six-hour drive—about four hundred miles. If you live elsewhere, you have to draw on what you remember from reading or other sources to answer the question.

Assuming you're neither a zoologist nor an ornithologist, the answer to the third question also depends a good deal upon your experiences as well as your powers of observation. However, the question also involves a dramatically different kind of thinking. In order to come up with the answer (both birds have four toes but differently arranged: three forward and one backward in the pigeon; two forward and two backward in the parrot), you have to mentally visualize the foot of a pigeon and compare it to that of a parrot. If, like most people, you never look carefully at pigeons and parrots, you won't be able to answer the question. Your *image* of these two birds is insufficiently detailed.

On occasion, thinking consists of working with words and concepts: the sixteenth president. At other times it requires vivid images: parrots compared to pigeons. On still other occasions, thinking may use either of these approaches—you can deduce the distance between San Francisco and Los Angeles by reasoning, or you can dispense with words altogether and consult an "inner map" based on your travels. Often, thinking involves all these processes.

For a very long time, images were thought to be intrinsic to thinking—*the* form of internal representation. For Aristotle, "thought was impossible without an image." At the opposite extreme was the psychologist J. B. Watson, who in 1913 ushered in a half century of behavioral psychology based on a mistaken view that images don't exist:

"They remain unproven—mythological, a figment of the psychologist's terminology. If our everyday vocabulary and the whole of literature had not become so enmeshed in this terminology, we should hear nothing of imagery. What does a person mean when he closes his eyes or ears (figuratively speaking) and says, 'I see the house where I was born, the trundle bed in my mother's room where I used to sleep—I can even see my mother as she comes to tuck me in and I can hear her voice as she softly says good night'? Touching, of course, but sheer bunk. We are merely dramatizing."

Watson believed our mental activity consists of scenes that had been "put into words long, long ago and we constantly rehearse those scenes verbally whenever the occasion arises. . . . What we mean by being conscious of events which happened in our past is that we can carry on a conversation about them to ourselves (thought) or with someone else (talk)."

Today we know better than that, though there are indeed many occasions when our representations are far removed from anything that can be "pictured" within the mind. No image is adequate to convey the subtlety and range and richness of much of thinking. $E = mc^2$ cannot evoke an image that does justice to the intricacies underlying Einstein's famous theory. In such instances, language plays a part in the internal constructions of our minds. Certainly, many of our ideas seem to exist independent of any images. Imagine yourself *not* watching television. The idea makes perfect sense but it's impossible to form an image of yourself *not* doing something. Images are specific, and many of our ideas are too general and encompassing to be captured by a specific image. "No image could ever be adequate to the concept of the triangle in general," wrote philosopher Immanuel Kant. "It would never attain that universality of the concept which renders it valid for all triangles, whether right-angled, obtuse-angled, or acute-angled.... The schema of the triangle can exist nowhere but in thought."

Nonetheless, our thinking at times takes the form of images that can be manipulated like the objects they represent in the real world. The line from Shakespeare's sonnet, "Shall I compare thee to a summer's day?" not only is amenable to an image; we literally call the linguistic device here an image, in this instance a metaphor. Further, images, like beauty, reside in the mind as well as the eye of the beholder. My image of a summer's day will differ from yours, based on our individual life experiences.

In exploring the nature of thinking, it is useful to know when an image is the vehicle of thinking and when it is not. To investigate this question, psychologists Roger Shepard and Lynn Cooper measured the time that it takes for a person to mentally rotate a geometrical shape so as to bring it into alignment with a second geometrical shape. When we see the letter *E* turned on its side, for example, it requires a certain amount of time to mentally turn it to an upright *E*. In other tests, complicated geometrical figures were shown in pairs and the subject asked if the shapes were different or the same. Here, too, a mental rotation of the figures was required. Shepard and Cooper discovered that the more the figures had to be rotated relative to each other, the longer the reaction time was. This is very similar to what happens if the two figures are picked up and rotated manually. Indeed, most people performing the Shepard-Cooper experiments explain their performance in these terms: "I look at the figures and sort of turn them around inside my mind until they match." It's as if a crude mental photograph exists within the mind that can be turned around, inverted, inspected. We know this is not so. There aren't any photographs inside the brain, only neurotransmitters and neurons. But when we try to summon up the differences between the feet of a pigeon and a parrot, or when the subjects in the Shepard-Cooper experiments attempt to rotate a geometrical figure, all of us *seem* to see them within the "mind's eye."

Moreover, even with ideas that lend themselves to imaging, there are limits to the complexity of the images our minds can generate and maintain. Imagine a small arrow on a blank piece of paper. You are instructed to move the arrow in your "mind's eye" to the north, and then to the southwest and then the west and then the northeast, and so forth for ten moves. At this point, you are asked, "In what direction is the arrow pointing?" Most people do poorly at this test, because they are unable to sustain a steady and reliable image of a path that heads off consecutively in many different directions.

Neither images nor what Watson called "carrying on a conversation," however, are sufficient by far to explain the mind's operation in thinking. Here, for example, is an everyday situation: two people meet on a beach. Michelle recognizes that she's encountered Michael before, but can't come up with his name. But she does recall that he's a doctor, specializes in pediatrics, and lives in New York City.

Michael remembers Michelle's name but can't dredge up from his memory any biographical details about her. He recalls they met previously at a party given by a friend to celebrate the completion of his residency. Michael can bring vividly to mind what Michelle was wearing that night and how attractive he found her.

Ordinary experiences like this raise important questions about how thinking is organized. Why is it that Michelle can recognize Michael's face, remember significant facts about him, but can't come up with his name? In Michael's case, the organization would seem to be different: he can remember names but specific life details are only a blur. What kind of mental organization in Michael might account for these differences?

The most popular metaphor for the human mind is that of a huge and intricate filing system. When Michelle and Michael encounter each other, facial recognition sets off an elaborate search through "files" stored within billions of neurons. How are these files organized? Are there separate files for names and faces? If so, why does Michelle do so much better than Michael in accessing the facial files? Is information stored in chronological order? It would seem not, since recognition of someone met a year ago often comes more easily than someone encountered only last week. One possibility is that the filing system in some people's minds is more comprehensive and more efficiently organized than in others; but that raises the question of who or what does the organizing so that, in Michael's case, the sight of Michelle immediately brings her name "to mind."

Communication within this vast filing system proceeds outside of awareness, so neither Michael nor Michelle can explain why they remember what they do. Further, if it doesn't occur to Michelle spontaneously, there is nothing that she can do to retrieve Michael's name. The filing system metaphor breaks down at this point.

We know from surgical experiences that electrical stimulation delivered to the temporal area of the brain elicits images of events that occurred in the patient's past. This is confirmation that such memories are "stored," but in most instances they cannot be voluntarily recollected. Thus, all of us "know" more than we are aware that we know. Moreover, the access that we do have to the words and images within our mind varies according to time and circumstances. This suggests the existence of a mechanism, activated at some times and not at others, that translates messages back and forth between the language of the brain—let's call that language "neuronese"—and the English that I employ in conveying to you the contents of my own mind. The brain doesn't store words and images directly, but as electrochemical signals. My brain deals only with these signals. I understand only English, not neuronese. Who or what does the translating? Are these two realms of discourse unified?

In recent years a new discipline has arisen directed toward answering some of these questions. Cognitive science—a blend of psychology, philosophy, linguistics, neuroscience, and computer science—attempts to explain in scientific terms the workings of the human mind. Basic to cognitive science is the belief that the mind is a representational system.

When you read a moment ago about Michelle's and Michael's meeting on the beach, the word *beach* evoked a complex series of mental events corresponding to the inward representation of all the beaches you have ever encountered, directly or through hearsay or movies and books. Beaches are sandy, often hot, gleam in the sun, are dotted with umbrellas. They create a shoreline, merge with water, are linked with holidays. Sand, sun, water, and umbrellas were never mentioned, yet you thought of them immediately. Neither the five letters that comprise the word beach nor the word itself is actually a beach, but together they evoke in the mind associations having to do with beaches. This is a representational system.

How does the mind construct this representational system? What goes on in the brain so that the word beach evokes a host of associations? Certainly simple introspection doesn't offer an answer to this question. Although you are subjectively aware of each association when it arises, you haven't any idea why it has sprung to mind. Many of the mind's operations remain permanently inaccessible. Every one of us sometimes "knows" a certain word, yet can't get it out despite its being "on the tip of our tongue."

Even when we believe we know how we think, we may be wrong. An experiment conducted several years ago shed some light on the degree of access we have to the operations of our own mind.

Volunteers memorized lists containing randomly generated numbers between one and ten. The lists varied in length from one to six digits. In each trial, the list—for example, the numbers 4, 8, 6, 3—was displayed for just over one second. Two seconds later a test digit appeared, 6. The subjects were instructed to pull lever A if the test digit was on the memorized list, lever B if it was not. Each subject's reaction time—how long it took before the lever was pulled—was measured.

The results: the reaction time varied directly with the *length* of the memorized lists. It didn't matter whether the test digit appeared early or toward the end of the list (pull lever A), or even whether it didn't appear at all (pull lever B). The length of the list was the operative factor. This finding indicates that our minds perform an exhaustive sequential left-to-right search whenever we carry out a task such as this. Yet when most people are asked to specify what they have done in experiments like this, they say, "I see the numbers in my mind and move across from left to right until I get to the test digit, and then I stop and pull lever A. I certainly don't continue to scan along the list once I've encountered the test digit. The only time I scan the entire list is when the test digit comes at the end or when it's missing entirely."

It is clear from this number-scanning experiment that our intuitions are not reliable when it comes to discovering the mechanisms that underlie the mind's operation. Despite our best efforts, we can't simply peer into ourselves and observe how we think.

This disparity between the mind's operations and our access to those operations is an aspect of trying to discover how we think. Is the mind organized in a unitary fashion, such as seems to be implied when I speak of "making up my mind?" Or is the mind a committee, an association of members who carry out different operations but have only the loosest communication with each other? The experiment mentioned a moment ago suggests that some of the mind's activities are rather rigidly rule bound. Most of the time we don't bother to inquire what these rules are and how they are applied. Furthermore, when we do inquire by observing our own thinking, we're often wrong about what's going on. Yet most of us experience ourselves as reasonably unified. The interruptions in consciousness that accompany many of our mind's operations don't seem to bother us.

The fact that we can't explain (or are wrong about) the process of thinking does not make us feel in the least diminished.

The question of whether the mind is a unity or a diversity has practical implications when it comes to an important constituent of the mind, intelligence. If the mind is truly a unity, then intelligence can be considered as a single generalizable set of abilities: A person is or is not intelligent. But if the mind is organized into separate faculties that do different things with varying skills and abilities, then "intelligence" must always be qualified: What is being measured? How well does a person do in areas other than the traditional verbal and mathematical skills that are probed on IQ tests? Is it in fact likely that IQ tests don't really measure intelligence at all, but only a few aspects of it?

Psychologist Alfred Binet was the first person to try to quantify intelligence. In 1905, the French government asked him to devise an intelligence test that would identify students who were below average. Modified many times since that date, Binet's test remains central to the debate that asks the fundamental question: What *is* intelligence? Dr. Patricia Goldman-Rakic, of the Yale School of Medicine, says, "I like to think it is associated with a broad range of knowledge, not just one type of information, and that it is the ability to keep that broad range of knowledge in mind as one makes the appropriate choice and decides upon the appropriate action. How much information can be brought to bear on that decision is a reflection of the capacity for intelligence."

Intelligence tests were originally devised as instruments to predict academic achievement. That function is separate from the usefulness of the tests in ascertaining other aspects of thinking and mind, such as one's ability to function effectively and independently, or to utilize knowledge productively in the ways Goldman-Rakic describes.

Alfred Binet (1857–1911).

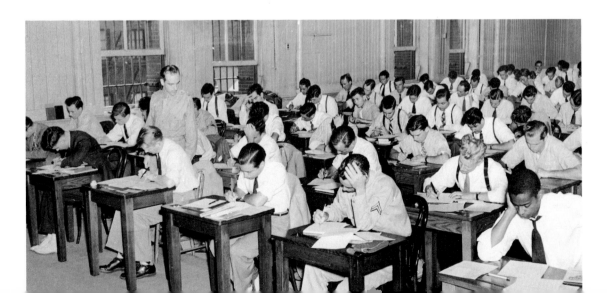

Mass I.Q. testing was used to screen army recruits in World War II.

Dr. Howard Gardner, of Harvard University, is convinced of the existence of at least seven different types of intelligence. The intelligence of the mathematician is different from that of the athlete or the musician or the poet. Moreover, each kind of intelligence is semiautonomous. If you have abilities in music but do poorly in athletics, what you possess is an enhanced musical intelligence. The absence (or, for that matter, the presence) of athletic gifts exists separately from your musical capability.

On occasion this heightened ability may coexist with profound deficiencies in other areas. Noel Patterson is an autistic young Englishman, filmed for the television series, *The Mind,* who rarely speaks sentences of more than two or three words, has only a limited ability to care for himself, and will probably remain in an institution for the rest of his life. Yet Noel possesses a rare "island of ability"—a phenomenal talent for music. He plays the piano and the guitar and can almost instantaneously memorize a piece after having heard it once and then play it back perfectly. But in contrast to musicians who are not autistic, Noel cannot think about what he's played or impose upon it his own feelings or personality. He can only play the music exactly as he heard it. A bandleader will often instruct his musicians in rehearsal to "play it with feeling." Noel can't play it with feeling. He can only play it with fact—the fact of what he hears. As Robert Reynolds, the principal of the residential community in which Noel lives with other profoundly autistic adults, notes, "Any further development depends on his having the ability to conceptualize, to think, to plan, to transfer his performing into new situations. And he's unable to do that because of the nature of autism." Noel has one talent that is off the charts, a gift that some might term "thinking" at a high level if only he had the capacity to think in an integrated fashion. Lacking that, he must be considered profoundly retarded.

Contrast Noel's isolated gift with the talent of concert violinist Nadja Salerno-Sonnenberg, who spends "months and months and months in analyzing a piece of music. This process is intense and never ends because you always feel differently about the musical piece. You reanalyze it and reanalyze it. Where's the theme? Where's the second theme? Where's the development? How does it fit? In effect, you're breaking the musical piece down to nothing and perfecting each of the little details. And then you put it back together like a model airplane. And then you've built your model airplane and it's ready to go. When you walk out on the stage, that's the finished product."

Noel's mind is unintegrated, with one extraordinary talent standing out like a beacon in a wasteland. Salerno-Sonnenberg's mind, in contrast, is concentrated and focused

Violinist Nadja Salerno-Sonneberg in performance.

as she attempts to reach what she calls the zone. Her thoughts and her emotions come together on stage. "Playing in the zone is a phrase that I use to describe a certain feeling on stage, a heightened feeling where everything is right," she says. "By that I mean everything comes together. Everything is one. Everybody agrees. Everybody sees what you're saying and everybody is enjoying it. Everybody is with you and you, yourself, are not battling yourself. All the technical work and what you want to say with the piece comes together. It's very, very rare but it's what I have worked for all my life. It's just right. It just makes everything right. Nothing can go wrong with this wonderful feeling."

As in the study of so many aspects of human beings, explorations of animal behavior may help us discern processes in ourselves. Philosophers and scientists alike have long been intrigued by the question of whether or not animals think. The Nobel Prize–winning neurophysiologist, Sir Charles Sherrington, believes that they share with us at least some aspects of thinking, among them feeling, the ability to feel emotion, and the expression of preferences. As the experiments and observations below make clear, many animals certainly carry out processes that require thinking. If so, how do they do it? Further, how does their thinking differ from ours?

Alex is an African Gray Parrot owned and trained by Dr. Irene Pepperberg, of Northwestern University. When asked, Alex can name more than eighty objects. He can recognize seven colors and five shapes. When shown a green square, for instance, and asked, "What color?" or "What shape?" he usually gives the correct answer. Such a performance is difficult to explain in terms of conditioned responses because Alex's answers vary according to the question asked. A blue square requires the answer "Blue" to the question "What color?" but "Four corners" to "What shape?" It's difficult to deny Pepperberg's claim that this African Gray Parrot has some understanding of at least two abstract categories, color and shape, and can distinguish examples of these categories (blue, square) in concrete objects (a blue square).

The most famous example of an animal capable of novel, even creative forms of thinking was Wolfgang Köhler's "insightful" chimpanzee. In his experiments with chimpanzees, Köhler hung a banana, out of reach, from the ceiling of a room that contained only a box and a chimpanzee. Despite the chimp's best efforts, he couldn't reach the banana by simply jumping up at it. After numerous unsuccessful trials, one chimp suddenly shoved the box toward the banana, climbed up on it, and retrieved the fruit. It was a novel approach to a hitherto insoluble problem.

Psychologists questioned the experiment because several of Köhler's chimps had been obtained from a circus and might have been accustomed to climbing on boxes. In response to this objection, Köhler's original experiment has been replicated with pigeons, who presumably have no experience with either boxes or bananas.

The pigeon is taught two separate tasks: to push a box along the ground (*not* to climb up on the box), and to peck a suspended banana by standing on a box placed directly underneath it. Later, in a different test situation, the pigeon is confined with a banana out of reach and a box located some distance to the side. What does this pigeon do? Here is a description, by Dr. Robert Epstein and his colleagues, of the experiments done when they were at Harvard University.

"At first, each pigeon appeared to be 'confused'; it stretched and turned beneath the banana, looked back and forth from banana to box, and so on. Then each subject began rather suddenly to push the box in what was clearly the direction of the banana. Each subject sighted the banana as it pushed and readjusted the box as necessary to move it toward the banana. Each subject stopped pushing in the appropriate place, climbed on the box, and pecked the banana."

A minimalist interpretation of such an experiment would read something like this: When the elements needed to solve a problem have all been rehearsed, pigeons, chimps, and a host of other animals ranging from voles to honey buzzards can carry out mental operations that are worthy of the term *thinking*. Given this, how far down the scale of living organisms can one go and still encounter behavior that involves some form, however primitive, of thinking and reasoning? Can a bee behave intelligently? Can a bee think?

In 1945, the Austrian zoologist Karl Von Frisch described the communication system of bees. When a foraging bee finds a new source of nectar or pollen, she returns to the hive and recruits helpers. By means of a ritualized "waggle dance," she informs the others of the distance, direction, and quality of the food. The helpers "memorize" the information, process it, and then, after compensating for winds and movements of the sun, fly out directly to a flower patch.

To an objective observer, the participants in this timeless drama seem to be conveying information and acting on it in an intelligent, even logical way. But closer analysis reveals that bees employ a series of navigational routines. The sun is used as a compass and compensation is made for its changing position as it moves from east to west. This trigonometric adjustment occurs *automatically* and relies on a memory of the sun's position relative to the bee's destination on a previous trip, along with an extrapolation of the sun's current rate of movement. When the sun is obscured, two other backup systems emerge: the bee responds to the pattern of polarized light generated in the sky by the gathering of sunlight, or it responds to landmarks that have been previously encountered. The "thinking" carried out by the bee is actually the result of an interplay of several subroutines based on stimulus recognition and simple processing over time. In a phrase, the bee seems to be behaving in a very machinelike manner.

But as one delves deeper into the bee communication system, unmistakable signs of what most of us would be willing to accept as thinking begin to emerge. In an experiment carried out by Von Frisch, bees were trained to forage for an artificial food source. Von Frisch then began moving the food source increasing distances away. Each time he moved the food source farther away, the bees had to travel longer distances. Eventually some of the bees began to anticipate Von Frisch's experimental design and flew straight to the anticipated source. It was as if they had formed a "cognitive map" of the terrain and calculated, on the basis of Von Frisch's previous maneuvers, where next he was likely to put the food source. Were the bees employing reasoning here? Is such an operation consistent with thinking?

Based on standard definitions, the answer would seem to be yes. L. V. Krushinsky, a Russian ethologist, defines reasoning as the "ability of an animal to grasp primitive relations linking objects and phenomena in its surroundings, and to demonstrate this understanding through adaptive behavior in new situations."

Using these criteria, the honey bees as a colony are engaged in an elementary form of reasoning. Yet no single honey bee processes by itself all of the necessary information for the location and retrieval of nectar. Thinking here is a *communal process* in which many, many bees working together are capable of thinking. We are dealing here with a collective intelligence that evades definition at the level of the individual organism.

"What is remarkable about this collective intelligence is that it arises from fundamentally decentralized information-processing," writes neurobiologist Thomas D. Seeley in his book, *Honeybee Ecology: A Study of Adaptation in Social Life.* "The colony's allocation of foragers seems to be guided by an 'invisible brain.' . . . A bee colony's cognition results from thousands of foragers collecting, processing, and sharing information about a tiny portion of the foraging operation."

A bee colony is a good metaphor for the mind. Operations such as thinking can be carried out when many of the components work together. Yet when the colony is broken down into its components, the individual bees, the thinking capacity is much reduced, although not eliminated entirely. Individual bees, as we have seen, are capable of anticipation and the formation of "cognitive maps."

A curious situation: mind exists at one level of complexity, the colony, but is much reduced in the individual bee. Mind here seems to be a social structure requiring the interaction of simpler components. Is the human mind constructed on the same principle?

Within the brain, vast numbers of cells interact by means of neuronal networks that form and dissolve throughout our lifetime. Every experience is embedded somewhere within these networks. But each cell retains its individuality. Moreover, there is no master cell (such as Descartes located in the pineal) that oversees and integrates and interprets experience. Somehow, these processes emerge from the action of many independent *parallel* activities.

The human mind—like the bee colony—is decentralized. As one of the consequences of this arrangement, any attempt on our part to delve within the landscape of our own mind ushers us into a house of mirrors. The behaviorists solve this dilemma by denying mind altogether; for them, all animals, including the human animal, "think" by associative learning or trial and error. But the discovery that animals can construct cognitive maps of the world in which they live changed all this.

Vervet monkeys use auditory signals to transmit complex and subtle messages. They emit distinct alarm calls in response to different predators (eagles, snakes, leopards). They also respond to taped predator calls from loudspeakers hidden in the bushes. If the alarm call warns of a leopard, the animal runs for the nearest tree. An eagle call stimulates intense scanning of the sky, and a snake call causes the vervet to stand on its hind legs and look down in the surrounding grass. There is more involved here than simple stimulus and response. The warning calls serve as symbolic "words" that represent complex features of the environment. The researchers who first described this phenomenon in vervets, Drs. Robert Seyfarth and Dorothy Cheney, of Stanford University, suggest that this display of intelligent behavior evolved in response to the need to establish and maintain a social system.

Thinking, like language, is a social phenomenon. None but the demented or the insane talk to themselves. Is it pure coincidence that the more intelligent and highly evolved an animal species is, the more social it is as well? As one progresses from unicellular to multicellular organisms, increasingly sophisticated capabilities are demanded in order to adapt to the environment. Little evidence of intelligence exists in a paramecium but quite a lot in a colony of primates. The most difficult, unpredictable, and volatile environment to adapt to is, of course, other creatures like oneself. Thinking, therefore, provides social benefit. Fighting and uncontrolled aggression can be reduced; elementary reasoning abilities can further group selection. Nonaggression and cooperative efforts benefit both the group and the individual. In fact, complex societies can exist only if the animals living in them are capable of anticipating and predicting the social consequences of their behavior, recognizing and acknowledging dominant members of the society, and gauging what the other members are likely to do under changing conditions. All these are processes that involve thinking.

Animals experience pain; they cry out if we hurt them or mishandle them in some way. Like ourselves, they prefer warmth, comfort, and a ready supply of food to hardship and starvation. These predilections are based on similarities between an animal brain and our own. But moving beyond similarities of this order to evidence of more sophisticated mental processes in other species, like thinking and conscious intention, is much more difficult.

Several years ago Dr. Emil Menzel, of the State University of New York at Stony Brook, carried out an experiment with captive chimpanzees. One of the chimps was shown the location of some hidden food in a large outdoor enclosure. Later the animal was released back into the enclosure with other chimps who had no idea that food was hidden there. Menzel observed that the knowledgeable chimp, in the presence of dominant, higher-ranking companions, wouldn't go anywhere near the food; it went in every direction but the correct one.

Dr. David Premack added a different twist to Menzel's experiment. He was curious whether his language-trained chimps (described in Chapter 7) would gesture toward a food source so that an experimenter could find the hidden food. They would. But if the experimenter ate the food himself instead of sharing it with the chimp he was working with, the chimp adopted a different strategy in subsequent tests, misdirecting the experimenter to an empty site.

Both these experiments are very difficult to explain unless one attributes thinking and conscious intention to the animal. The chimps clearly intended to hide the treasure from others—chimp or human—who would consume rather than share the bounty. Performances like this make it difficult not to conclude that animals, at least at the higher primate level, are capable of thinking about a problem, reaching a conclusion, forming an intention, and concealing that intention from others.

The role played by deception here is particularly intriguing. If the chimps had merely sought out the hidden food source, the most that we could postulate as an operative principle would be their ability to return to a "reward site"—the kind of stimulus/response exchange that behaviorists have advocated for more than half a century. But a very sophisticated level of thinking must be postulated for the food source to be concealed under appropriate conditions (the presence of a dominant monkey or a diabolical experimenter intent on eating the chimp's food): a memory of the location of the food, a sizing up of the relevant variables, an intention to hide the true facts, the capacity to carry out the act of deception successfully.

But it makes us uneasy to say this. Proving conscious intention in creatures other than ourselves is a hazardous enterprise. The experiments of Menzel and Premack, however remarkable, involve inferences only, because the chimp can't tell us of his intentions. Are we conferring intention on the basis of a circularity in our own reasoning: the chimp concealed the food cache because that's what it intended; we know that was its intention because that's what it did?

Experiments that explore the nature of mind in animals, including those that test their capacity to think, tell us much about the human mind as well—and as can be seen from the Menzel and Premack research, may leave us with other discomfiting questions. If animals are capable of intelligence and cunning sometimes equal to that of their human counterparts, are there reasons beyond human ego or vanity for our insistence that our minds truly differ from those of animals? There does seem to be one outstanding indisputable difference. We of all species are capable of self-awareness; we can step back from ourselves and our world, and reflect. We do not know at this point whether this reflective capacity is a consequence of language or some other higher cognitive ability; as we have seen in Chapter 7, even in human beings we postulate thinking and consciousness in others largely by analogies with ourselves.

A three-and-a-half-year-old boy was asked, "What do you do when you think?"

He considered the question a while before he answered. "If someone tells you something hard which you don't know, you have to think what it is. If you don't know what to say, you just stand quietly and don't say nothing and something comes into your brain."

That youngster isn't a cognitive psychologist, but his explanation of what goes on when we think isn't a bad first approximation of the process. Ultimately our brain does our thinking for us, but how?

Dr. Jerry Fodor, of the CUNY Graduate Center in New York, believes that the brain is vertically organized—that separate "modules" are specialized to deal with particular information, such as, for instance, the input of electromagnetic waves to the eyes that produces vision. Visual information is processed through a series of modules that initially do not communicate with other systems in the brain. In the visual system, at least, this theory is consistent with everyday experience. At a magic show we "know" that one thing is taking place before our eyes but we continue to "see" something quite different. It's as if two separate modules are operating independently, each exerting only the faintest influence on the other.

But when it comes to processes more advanced than simple perception, the modularity concept begins to break down. Aspects of thinking like self-awareness, memory, and logical inference communicate within the association areas of the brain. On one level, the brain is a localized organ, with "parts" concerned with vision, hearing, touch, and so on. But at the same time the brain resists our attempts to impose a geography upon it. As we saw in Chapter 2, if one part of the brain is damaged, resulting in loss of a specific function, another brain area may take over and make possible a complete or partial restoration of that function. The younger the patient, the more likely the loss of function can be compensated for in this way. But with increasing age, the brain loses this plasticity and deficits become permanent. That's why young people sometimes recover from strokes completely, whereas older people sustaining the same brain injury may never walk or speak normally again. One of the factors in this difference is that neither walking nor speaking are modular activities. Speaking is entwined with logic, abstraction, memory, and learning. Walking involves complicated alliances with the sensory and cerebellar systems. Both speaking and walking can go awry, therefore, depending upon where in the brain the damage occurs.

This situation is far different from the breakdown of a machine. If your car can't start on a cold morning, it makes little difference functionally whether the problem is a broken starter, wet spark plugs, or a short in the ignition system. Each of the "modules" can be checked by the mechanic and the necessary repairs or replacements made. But in the brain there are no modules to be replaced in order to restore normal functioning. A modular plan doesn't accommodate the complexity of the mind's operations, most especially thinking.

Modules within the brain have obvious appeal as an explanation for mind in a culture such as ours that is enamored with computers. But the concept of the brain as a thinking machine has a long history, as we have seen in Chapter 1. During the eighty years following Descartes's publication of *Traite de l'homme* in 1664, much was learned about the human brain. Crude but serviceable distinctions were made about the activities carried out by the cortex, the cerebellum, and the brain stem. Added to this, the comparative neuroanatomy of humans and several other animal species contributed to the gradual replacement of the unlocatable soul of Descartes by the brain itself, which came to be regarded as a "machine" producing thought.

In 1747, La Mettrie, a physician and philosopher, proclaimed the death of the soul in a provocative book, *L'Homme machine.* All forms of conscious life—sensation, passion, memory, thinking, will—are dependent upon the "organic machine," the human brain. La Mettrie spoke of a "thinking and feeling" machine into which ideas entered as coded symbols and were stored, compared, combined, and modified by emotions and instinctual forces. But La Mettrie's machine was a far more sophisticated device than anything Descartes had ever conceived.

"The human body is a machine that winds its own springs—the living image of perpetual motion. . . . Man is an assemblage of springs that are activated principally by one another, without it being possible to say at what precise point of this human circle nature has begun."

As an example of this new machine, La Mettrie could point to an automated "duck" built by Vaucanson to simulate biologic processes. The mechanical animal could paddle itself about and "digest" food within a mechanical "stomach." This equating of a machine with a living organism was extended to the brain. "We conclude that the brain somehow digests sense impressions, that it affects organically the secretion of thought," wrote one commentator in the late eighteenth century. As ridiculous as this statement seems today, it set the tone for interpreting the relationship of the brain to mind thereafter. The brain was a "machine," the mind merely one of its by-products. Further, the rules that governed the brain must, according to the brain machine model, be identical to those governing mechanical systems.

Today, the computer revolution has made the old brain-as-a-machine argument seem persuasive as well as appealing. Remembering, learning, reasoning, judging, foreseeing, and problem solving are all activities traditionally associated with mind that can now be carried out, in certain respects, by machines. Information-fed computers can play chess, forecast the weather, compose music, translate from one language to another, diagnose and suggest treatment for illnesses. In some quarters, computer science and cybernetics have brought the man/machine theory to a position of dogma. "The mind is the brain and the brain will one day be simulated by a computer"—this in a nutshell is the machine doctrine in its current formulation.

Much of this enthusiasm is based on the capacity of computers to outperform the human brain in many respects. The most obvious example is the inexpensive hand-held calculator, which can out-tally even the swiftest of human mental calculators. How much is $17 \times 18 \times 26 \times .07 \times 83$? The device can spit out the answer as fast as a finger can punch in the numbers. The brain performs less impressively, because of synaptic delays and the time that it takes for a nerve impulse to pass along the axon—the most that is possible is fifty serial steps in a quarter-second. Whatever the differences between brain and machine, it is clear that computers, with their remarkable and burgeoning capacities, have much to tell us about the human brain.

In 1936 Alan Turing, a British mathematician and intelligence agent, conceived a theoretical machine capable of carrying out any mathematical operation. A Turing machine is simply a scanner that can read a tape of instructions printed in binary code: 0's and 1's, not all that different from an on–off function or a yes–no response, or even the dots and dashes of Morse code. Turing proved mathematically that a Turing machine could, at least theoretically, carry out any logical task provided the tape was properly coded. This theory provided the framework for the modern computer.

Turing also proposed the famous Turing test for artificial intelligence. If a human observer cannot distinguish between the performance of a programmed machine and a human being, then the machine has passed the Turing test. A contemporary version of the test might involve a chess-playing computer that could fool its human competitor into believing that he was competing with another human instead of a computer in the next room.

Based on Turing's ideas, Dr. John von Neumann devised and built the first modern computer in the 1940s. Almost immediately, certain similarities between computers and the human brain became obvious. As artificial intelligence experts Warren McCullough and Walter Pitts pointed out, a nerve cell and its connection to other nerve cells—the basic neural network—could be expressed mathematically as a system of on–off signals. A nerve cell either fired or it didn't, so they claimed its activity could be represented as a binary system.

These ideas spurred research in two directions. First, scientists asked whether the brain could be understood as an extremely complex computer. Second, they wondered whether computer programs could be designed that simulate the brain.

The argument for the human brain as a computer typically takes the following form. All experience and thought are made possible by the human brain; all decision functions in the brain are reducible to a binary yes–no process; the brain is nothing more than an elaborate computer with its synaptic junctions performing on–off functions. Ergo, experience involves nothing more than symbolic coding, wherein thinking at every level can be expressed in various binary codes: yes, a nerve fiber will fire; no, the organism will not go for ice cream. The objective of computer science is to learn how the brain's symbols represent the external world and how the brain's circuitry regulates "input" and "output."

According to the brain-as-a-computer model, the external world impinges on our sense organs, which convert these signals into a "code." The brain then processes these codes electrochemically and translates the processed neurophysiological information into consciousness.

This model fits very nicely with what we know about computers. Letters and numbers are typed out on a computer keyboard and then converted to electrical pulses—a coded form of the information contained in these letters and numbers—in the computer's hardware. These electrical signals are processed within the computer's circuits. Finally, through a set of preprogrammed commands or rules (algorithms), the processed electrical signals are reported out in the form of intelligible and useful words and numbers.

Given these similarities in the translation of raw data into codes in both brain and machine, is there validity to the claim that the brain is really nothing more than a complicated biological computer? That thinking in the brain isn't really that much different from thinking in a machine?

Although not complete or even unassailable, the following inventory notes distinctions between brains and machines.

Each brain cell or neuron is alive and altered by its experiences and its environment. In their interactions with one another, neurons form and dissolve and reform chemical and electrical patterns that correspond to changes in the internal and external environment. As you read these words, neuronal networks are forming and interacting with other networks drawn from a memory store. With time, these patterns may disappear because of disuse (you may fail to keep alive your interest in the mind by reading additional books). In a computer, in contrast, the chips aren't alive, don't spontaneously organize and reorganize themselves, don't demonstrate *on their own* modifications in their functioning.

In general, most computers are designed to deal with information serially, that is, one bit at a time. Brains, in contrast, operate via subsystems that function in tandem, what in computerese is called parallel processing. While reading this book you can drink your tea without spilling it, listen for the doorbell announcing the arrival of a friend who is expected any moment, monitor the weather report on the radio that is playing softly in the background. This is parallel processing, and our brains thrive on it. Parallel input and output present little difficulty for brains, but only the most recent and sophisticated computers are capable of significant parallel processing. Most important, even those that are endowed with this capability deal with information only according to specific programs. Brains are not so restrained. Impulsiveness is characteristic of brains. You may suddenly decide, for instance, that you will stop reading and finish this chapter in the evening so that you can play a round of golf this afternoon.

Despite McCullough and Pitts's hypothesis, neurons don't operate according to a binary code of on–off. Whether or not a particular brain cell fires depends to a large extent upon the influence of the many other cells that make contact with it. Subtract several hundred inhibitory influences from the neuron and it may fire. The same result can be produced by adding several hundred excitatory influences. What one nerve cell "tells" the next depends upon the "conversation" going on between networks of hundreds and sometimes thousands of cells at varying distances from one another in the brain. Neuroscientist Donald Hebb termed these networks cell assemblies:

"Any two cells or systems of cells which are repeatedly active at the same time will tend to become 'associated,' so that activity in one facilitates activity in the other," Hebb wrote in 1949, in perhaps the most influential book on the brain written in this century, *The Organization of Behavior*.

THINKING MADE VISIBLE

To think—any kind of thought—is to activate an entire network of nerve cells in the brain. The brain is dynamic, always active, always changing. Dr. Alan Gevins, of EEG Systems Laboratory in San Francisco, studies the brain while it is working and is able to produce spectacular images of the process of thinking.

Gevins describes what goes on when a test subject makes a simple finger movement. "We measure just those signals in the brain that are related to a four-second finger pressure task. This is a tough problem, like finding a needle in a haystack, so in order to help us, we use lots of computer analysis. That way, we can enhance or bring out those signals in the brain that are related to the finger pressure task, while making all the other signals of the brain basically disappear."

The subjects wear a hat full of electrodes. Their task is to press a button, either lightly or with more force, when numbers are shown on the screen before them. The entire task requires about four discrete thoughts. Signs of each thought can be measured through the electrodes and converted into a visual image. Gevins likens these images to the shadows cast on the walls of Plato's cave: "the shadows of the actors who were dancing. Well, these are the shadows of thoughts. They're not the thoughts themselves, but you may say they're the low-resolution images of the traces made by thoughts cast off that we're able to record."

Each image involves patterns of neuroelectric activity that demonstrate that the brain is changing even as our thoughts are changing. When a subject prepares to respond with a finger movement, for instance, the left prefrontal cortex may send signals back to alert areas involved in vision, touch, and fine motor control. These are physical signs of simple versions of the mental models we form when we navigate, play chess, solve problems.

"Perception isn't a passive process," Gevins notes, "where stimuli come from the environment and impinge on our sensory organs. Perception is a very active, probing process. I have an idea in my mind. I probe the environment. I move my eyes around. I tune my hearing. I look for information. I compare that information with the model in my mind. And then I might take some action."

Our mental models change from moment to moment, depending on our expectations and experience. If a person wakes up in a strange city and thinks for a moment that he's at home in his own bed, he has to revise that mental model. "In such an experience," says Gevins, "I have to instantly re-form my mental model

Nothing resembling this exists within computers, which is one of the reasons why a six-month-old child can recognize her mother while a computer capable of specific facial recognition is only the stuff of science fiction. To phrase it slightly differently, our brain, over our lifetime, works as a self-assembling structure whose functional capacities are *distributed*. That means, in practical terms, that when one part breaks down, another part can often be recruited to take its place.

"I can't remember the name of the store where I bought this coat but I can tell you exactly how to get there from here," we may say to a friend when we can't come up with a name. "Graceful degradation" is the intriguing term for this loss of clarity and precision. We exhibit it—or rather our brains do—but computers don't. A computer either comes up with the specific information requested or it doesn't.

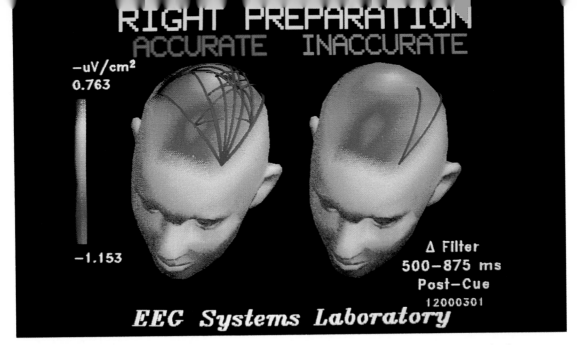

Dr. Alan Gevins of EEG Systems Laboratory in San Francisco uses an advanced EEG imaging system to display thought process pathways. Here, different pathways were activated when the subject was alerted beforehand to respond to a number shown on a video screen, and when the subject had no advance preparation. In addition to the sharp difference in pathways, the response was accurate with preparation, and inaccurate without it, suggesting that even brief advance warning can help avert errors.

to take into account that I'm in a strange room in a strange hotel in a strange city. In order to do this, functional neuronal networks will have to be reconfigured. We interpret the world through our mental models. In a sense we create reality in our brains and our minds. To a large extent, we see what we expect to see. We hear what we expect to hear. There is an interaction, a negotiation, between our expectations and what's really going on out there." And he emphasizes, "If we have any hope at all of getting some insights into human behavior, human thought, the human mind, we've got to see the whole system functioning, and in near real time. It's not going to do us any good to see one or two neurons firing; it's the integration of all these pieces that produces our behavior, our thoughts."

This is because brains but not computers are good at employing alternative neuronal networks to signify the same thing. Cell assemblies make this possible.

If a sufficient number of cell assemblies are coupled together, generalizations become possible that are beyond all but the most advanced computers. For instance, we recognize a Chippendale chair, a pew, a tree stump, and an empty orange crate as things to sit on. This recognition is based on many cell assemblies overlapping to form a meta-assembly that is responsible for the abstract concept, "something to sit on." These cell assemblies are also responsible for humor, insight, inspiration, and creativity. The brain can cross-reference ideas and concepts that at first seem to have nothing in common. "Brainstorming" is an apt term for the process of getting together with others and letting the "creative juices" flow without inhibitory restraints. What happens from the brain point of view is that cell assemblies in one person's brain and those in another's are establishing new and different approaches to problems. Such communal exercises raise an interesting question: if my ideas, the product of my brain, represent one brain–mind, how do we describe many people working together to produce ideas that no one of them could have come up with individually? Is this Mind, or is it mind with subscripts to distinguish one from another: $mind_1$, $mind_2$ and so on? The latter isn't satisfactory either, since more is involved in the outcome than the sum of the individual contributions of each brain. Finally, truly creative ideas often appear spontaneously, as if—in a telling phrase—they have a "mind of their own."

Why should the parallels between computer performance and human cognition be so surprising? After all, it is human cognition that programs the computer and creates the "symbols" that are entered into it. At all times the computer hardware generates nothing more than electrical pulses. We are the ones who program the computer in such a way that the pulses will illuminate the screen with "Flight 603 has been canceled." The computer knows no more about flights or delays than a tape recorder knows how to differentiate a Brahms concerto from a Bach fugue. Symbols within a computer are not the same as symbols within the brain. We design computer circuits and program computers in such a way that a given series of pulses *stands for* "Flight 603." But it makes no sense to say that the brain engages in similar translations. To search for symbols within either the brain or a computer is a hopeless enterprise. There are no symbols within the brain, only statements that we can make about the brain. Nor are there symbols within a computer; only pulses and pauses that we ourselves have arranged in a way that conforms to the symbols of our language and our thinking.

Jonathan Swift's "thinking machine" in Gulliver's Travels. *Swift suggested acerbically that books on all manner of subjects could be written simply by turning the appropriate handles.*

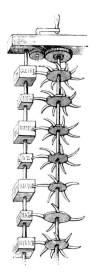

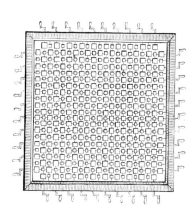

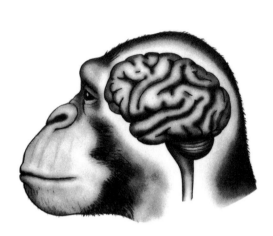

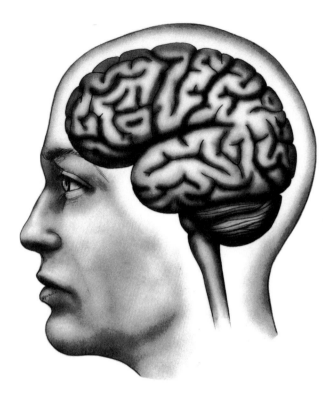

Dr. Daniel Weinberger, of the National Institute of Mental Health, says that "In some ways, it is almost easier to characterize frontal lobe function by saying what it doesn't do. It's not the part of the brain that allows us to see; it's not the part of the brain that allows us to hear; it's not the part that allows us to touch something and recognize what it is that we've just touched. It's not really by itself the part of the brain that remembers. It doesn't seem to be involved in any particularly discrete perceptual, sensory, or motor function. But in spite of this, it seems to have a very critical role in how we use the kinds of information that other parts of our brain are dedicated to determining."

Patricia Goldman-Rakic, who is an authority on the prefrontal cortex, notes, "If thinking is the process of using information to make decisions, then the frontal lobe is crucial for thinking. Without the frontal lobes, we're at the mercy of our environment. We respond to events without reflection. We are unable to plan for our future. And it is this capacity to plan for the future that distinguishes us from all other species."

Damage to the motor–premotor component of the frontal lobes can produce the typical symptoms of a stroke: weakness, alteration in muscle tone, and aphasia (speech loss or impairment). Damage further forward, in the prefrontal cortex, leads to disturbances of a far different sort. Neuroscientists have cataloged a remarkable variety of changes in thinking and behavior brought about by injury to the

Because chimpanzees are the animals closest genetically and in intelligence to human beings, they are often the subject of experiments exploring the nature of mind. However, though these investigations show that chimps are able to perform often startling mental activities, they lack the capacity for the highest cognitive functions of the human mind. As can be seen here, frontal lobe development in the human brain has evolved far beyond that in the chimpanzee.

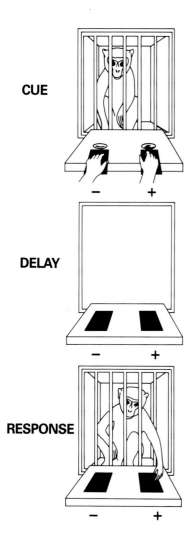

CUE

DELAY

RESPONSE

Dr. Patricia Goldman-Rakic of Yale used two types of monkeys to study comparative brain development and thinking processes. In this experiment (top), *the monkey sees the experimenter bait one food well (cue) before both wells are covered. Then a screen is dropped that blocks the monkey's view for several seconds. When it is raised* (bottom), *the rhesus monkey, which has greater frontal lobe development, remembers where the food is hidden. The galago monkey, with less frontal lobe development, does not remember on its first try.*

prefrontal regions. Here is a description by Dr. M. Marsel Mesulam, a neurologist with the Division of Neuroscience and Behavioral Neurology at the Harvard Medical School:

"Some of these patients become puerile, profane, slovenly, facetious, irresponsible, grandiose, and irascible; others lose spontaneity, curiosity, initiative, and develop an apathetic blunting of feeling, drive, mentation, and behavior; others show an erosion of foresight, judgment, and insight, lose the ability to delay gratification and often the capacity for remorse; still others show an impairment of abstract reasoning, creativity, problem solving, and mental flexibility, jump to premature conclusions, and become excessively concrete or stimulus bound."

These alterations are sufficiently out of the ordinary to attract the attention of even the casual observer. But there are other disturbances of a subtler sort in frontal lobe damage that tell us a great deal about thinking and the brain.

Mesulam: "The orderly planning and sequencing of complex behaviors, the ability to attend to several components simultaneously, and then flexibly alter the focus of concentration, the capacity for grasping the context and gist of a complex situation, resistance to distraction and interference, the ability to follow multistep instructions, the inhibition of immediate but inappropriate response tendencies, and the ability to sustain behavioral output . . . may each become markedly disrupted."

What all this tells us, in sum, is that frontal lobe damage interferes with those aspects of our thinking that distinguish us from the rest of the animal kingdom: reasoning, abstract thinking, the organization of behavior over time and space, the attainment of future goals, initiative, creativity, feelings of personal autonomy and identity, and the ethical and moral components of behavior. Not every patient with frontal lobe damage demonstrates all these disturbances, of course. Sometimes only a few alterations in thinking may be detectable. Nonetheless, it is clear that in order to function as thinking human beings, we must rely on the integrity of our frontal lobes.

Take, for instance, our sense of personal autonomy. At any given moment, our behavior, including this sense, is influenced by the outer environment and our inner psychological state. Indeed, these two influences coexist in a dynamic balance that is constantly shifting and thereby affecting our behavior. How might damage to our frontal lobes affect our sense of autonomy?

For the past several years, at the Hôpital de la Salpêtrière in Paris, Dr. François Lhermitte has been carrying out a series of experiments involving everyday situations with subjects who suffered damage to their frontal lobes second-

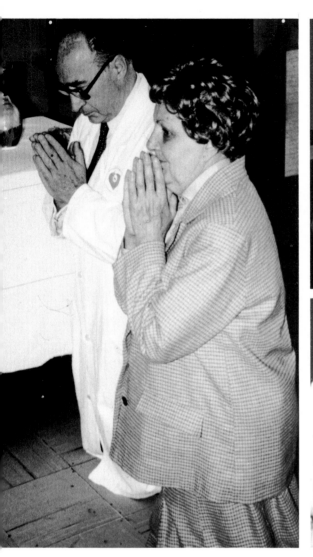

ary to tumors, strokes, or trauma. None of the patients, however, was other than normal in terms of intelligence. Nonetheless, these frontally damaged patients exhibited a peculiar and irrepressible urge to imitate Lhermitte.

In a typical experiment, Lhermitte would sit across from his patient and start to comb his hair. The patient would remove another comb and imitate this behavior. In one instance Lhermitte arose from his chair and knelt down and began to pray. The patient immediately arose, knelt down, and bowed her head in silent prayer. In each instance the patient behaved as if he or she was totally dependent on the environment and could not express or assert any degree of autonomy.

"The sight of a movement is perceived in the patient's mind as an order to imitate that movement; the sight of an object implies the order to use it," says Lhermitte.

Subjects without damage to their frontal lobes in similar situations did not imitate, nor did they think that they were

Frontal lobe damage in these patients of Dr. François Lhermitte causes them to imitate his behavior without any sense of why they do this.

being requested to do so. Lhermitte's actions had no effect on their behavior.

Most interesting of all, imitative behavior in the frontally damaged patients was an integrative part of their consciousness; they were aware of what they were doing and not responding reflexively. When asked, "Why did you do what I just did?" the patients would respond that since Lhermitte had made the gesture, they felt they had to imitate him. Even when Lhermitte specifically told them *not* to imitate his gestures, most patients imitated him anyway. "On being reminded afterwards that they had been told not to imitate the gestures, their answer was that obviously, since the gestures had been made, they must be imitated," says Lhermitte.

Lhermitte attributes his patients' compulsion to imitate to the loss of inhibitory influences from the frontal lobes. Without this inhibition, activities in other brain areas, principally the parietal lobes, are enhanced. The patient is thus compelled to respond to events in the outer world: "Frontal lobe damage results in liberation of parietal lobe activity, leaving the patient subject to all external stimuli," says Lhermitte.

In an effort to probe the depth of the patients' dependence on their environment, Lhermitte next studied how they would respond in natural settings, such as a garden or an apartment. Here is his description of the response of a fifty-one-year-old engineer.

"A buffet had been laid out in a lecture room where there were about twenty people. When the patient came in, he clearly indicated his delight by word and gesture. He helped himself to the food and drinks. He behaved like a guest, not even thinking of offering anything to me or to anybody else. . . . In front of the audience I presented him with the insignia of 'Officer of the Order of Medical Merit.' I embraced him in the traditional manner and then made a short speech. After bowing his head to acknowledge the applause, he said he would like to make a speech. He thanked the gathering and said how happy and proud he was."

Another patient, a woman, followed Lhermitte when he arose from his chair, walked out to his car, and drove to a garden. Later, as he walked along a line of flower beds, she did the same. When he leaned over as if to pick flowers, the patient gathered a bouquet herself.

"We walked into a square and posed like tourists for a photographer," Lhermitte said. "We then returned to my office. Not a word was spoken during this outing. When asked about it a few days later, she recalled the outing clearly and considered it quite normal. I pretended to be surprised because I had not asked her to do anything. She did not understand why I was surprised."

Each of these strange responses was characterized by the patients' nearly total dependency on the social and physical environment. Missing from their explanations for their behavior was the sense of autonomy that normally accompanies the exercise of free choice. Instead, they exhibited what Lhermitte has termed an environmental dependency syndrome (EDS).

"For the patient afflicted with EDS, the social and physical environments issue the orders to use them, even though the patient himself or herself has neither the idea nor the intention to do so," according to Lhermitte.

The psychological functions of attention, motivation, and emotion, like autonomy, also are affected by frontal lobe damage. The overall result is a lessening of the individual's free will.

Because traditionally we have been taught to think of ourselves as acting freely most of the time, the extensive consequences of frontal lobe damage are profoundly disturbing. Our thinking and behavior involve a delicate balance between two opposing factors. As a result of parietal influences, we are directed outward to the world about us. Frontal influences, on the other hand, turn us inward toward those intrapsychic processes necessary for insight, abstraction, planning, and a sense of personal autonomy. A disturbance in either the frontal or the parietal region throws off this delicate balance. Most troubling of all, these disturbances can be so subtle as to escape detection. Sizeable frontal lobe lesions may remain "silent" for years. Standard intelligence tests and other measures of thinking are of no use. Afflicted people may seem unchanged except to those who know them well. Only by being aware of their prior personality and comparing it with present thinking and behavior can we detect the alterations induced by frontal damage to the most subtle aspects of thinking: judgment, an innate feeling for what's appropriate, and the ability to take the "long view" and look beyond one's immediate circumstances.

Reasoning and communication underlie all human thought. The experience of Joseph Kovach, who was a fifteen-year-old Hungarian schoolboy when he was imprisoned in a Soviet gulag, is a powerful example of this. For four years, he lived in an isolated, frightening environment, each day an eternity. "When I look at the months, the years, they were empty," Kovach remembers. "There's nothing in terms of thinking, of planning, of remembering the past or planning for the future. It felt almost as though I was hibernating."

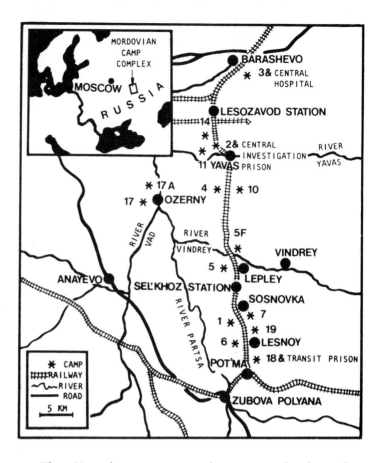

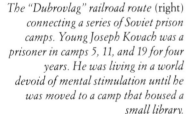

The "Dubrovlag" railroad route (right) *connecting a series of Soviet prison camps. Young Joseph Kovach was a prisoner in camps 5, 11, and 19 for four years. He was living in a world devoid of mental stimulation until he was moved to a camp that housed a small library.*

Ten years after his release from the gulag, Kovach is shown (above) *as a graduate student at the University of Chicago.*

Then Kovach was transported to a camp that housed a small library. "It was an altogether new world for me. I suddenly discovered an escape out of the starkness of the prison world into the beautiful world of words and poetry. But it was more than that. It marked the opening up of a whole new sense of thinking and of intellectual activity. From then on, I had an immense preoccupation and interest in anything relating to ideas, to language, to anything I could learn about. Although I had no way of doing anything about my physical condition, I was free. I had access to the inner workings of my own mind, my thinking, and my ideas. I was completely free to think whatever I wanted and to combine my ideas in whatever way I wanted. And that gave me freedom."

Thanks to our mind, we can change our perceptions of ourselves and our world. Joseph Kovach, free, built a life of the mind and the spirit, and today is Dr. Joseph Kovach of the Menninger Foundation. We can create science, music, and art. We can read one another's feelings, put ourselves in somebody else's shoes, formulate our ideas, or respond to the genius of a violinist like Nadja Salerno-Sonnenberg. Her gifts express themselves in the delicate balance between pure thought and experienced emotion that lies at the basis of her music. "One thing that goes to the heart of human beings is the importance of an emotional life. We take great pleasure in having our emotions moved either by the real world or by imaginary events," says Philip Johnson-Laird. "It's a great mystery why we take such pleasure in having our emotions moved in this way. But it certainly seems a central part of human mental life."

"Ultimately," says Kovach, "it is our mental apparatus, our capacity to think, our capacity to deal with ideas, our capacity to find unities, coherences in variations—that's what makes us free and that's what makes us human. We have a way of creating worlds for ourselves, in our heads, and sharing those worlds."

9.
THE VIOLENT MIND

One night in August 1985, Colin Kemp, a thirty-three-year-old salesman in Caterham, England, went to sleep as usual. About two hours later he encountered two Japanese soldiers in his bedroom. They began to chase him. One soldier had a knife, another a gun. Although Kemp ran very quickly, he wasn't fast enough to lose his pursuers, who eventually cornered him. Convinced he was about to die, Kemp wrestled with the soldier carrying the knife. The other soldier then approached him with a gun and aimed it at Kemp's head. Kemp tripped him to the ground, put his hands around his neck, and squeezed as hard as he could. Despite these efforts the soldier slipped away, aimed the gun at Kemp, and fired. As smoke poured from the gun, Kemp awoke in a panic, drenched in sweat. In terror, he turned to his wife, who was lying in the bed beside him. She was dead. Kemp had strangled her, and not the Japanese soldier.

At the trial nine months later, Kemp claimed that he had been asleep when he killed his wife. He pleaded not guilty to the charge of murder and stated that he had intended to kill the Japanese soldier, not his wife. Psychiatrists testifying on his behalf told the jury that Kemp had suffered a *night terror:* a sudden arousal from sleep, accompanied by intense fear coupled with appropriate physical alterations such as accelerated heart rate, rapid breathing, profuse perspiration, loud piercing screams, and, most important to Kemp's case, physical movement.

On two previous occasions prior to the fatal event, Kemp had experienced night terrors. Both times he was being pursued in his sleep. In one instance he had punched at his wife, who awakened to ask what was happening. The second time he kicked her in the back.

Strangling someone to death is a more elaborate and sustained activity than pushing or kicking someone. Is it possible that an act such as Kemp's—strangling a person to death—could really happen during sleep? It is known that night terrors often merge into sleepwalking episodes, during which complex acts may be carried out. Sleepwalkers have been known to get dressed, talk on at length, get into their automobiles, and drive short distances. So why should it not be possible when asleep to strangle one's mate?

Kemp was acquitted. His action was considered the result of an *automatism,* defined in both law and medicine as a state in which a person, "though capable of action, is not conscious of what he is doing."

Claims that a person has acted as a result of automatism fly in the face of several of our most cherished beliefs. Most of us would agree that for the most part, people are responsible for their actions. Indeed, the concept of responsibility is fundamental to our way of life.

We give and take responsibility for ourselves, just as we attach praise or blame to other people's actions, according to whether or not, in our judgment, they have acted responsibly. We also define criminal behavior in terms of responsibility, but we add to this an important additional factor: criminals are responsible for their actions based on our best judgment of their *intentions.*

For instance, if I walk out of a restaurant with somebody else's overcoat, it matters a good deal whether I took it by mistake or intended to steal it. If I strike someone on the head with a baseball bat, it's important to know whether the injury was inflicted accidentally during the warm-up part of a game or whether I intentionally tracked my victim down and bludgeoned him with the bat in order to "pay him back" for some real or imagined injury.

The criminal law is a formal recognition and codification of the paramount importance of responsibility and intention. When a person is accused of a crime, the prosecution has to prove that the individual both carried out the alleged illegal action and *intended* to do so. In Colin Kemp's case, there was no doubt that he had actually killed his wife. But the jury held that he did not consciously intend to do this and therefore was not responsible for his actions.

"It's a tradition of Anglo-American law that nobody can be convicted of a criminal offense unless he has had deliberate intent to commit the crime. In the law we refer to this as *mens rea:* a Latin term which literally means 'a guilty mind' but which generally has been meant to stand for a specific 'intent,'" says Potter Stewart, retired Justice of the U.S. Supreme Court.

In our search for mind, intention and responsibility are important factors. We human beings, alone among animals, are capable of standing back from ourselves, weighing the consequences of one action over another, and then choosing what we will do. It is an awesome capacity. But does each of us have this capacity to the same degree? Most of us believe that we do, excepting only very young children, the profoundly retarded, and those in the extremes of insanity. In this chapter we will explore that assumption and the consequence that flows from it: that those who of their own free will misuse their responsibility to live according to the dictates of the law, and willfully decide to injure or kill another human being, should be punished for their offense. While such determinations are not new, the approach that we will take is very recent. Rather than concentrating on theories of criminology, we will be taking our direction in regard to intention and responsibility from the neuroscientist.

Under ordinary circumstances, intention involves the activation of certain parts of the brain and the inhibition of other parts. Suppose my next door neighbor has called me on the telephone to complain about the barking of my dog. As I listen to him, several possible scenarios flash across my consciousness: keeping the dog indoors except for periodic walks; having a measured and dispassionate discussion with my neighbor about whether or not the barking is excessive; retorting angrily that the barking is none of my neighbor's business; and finally, going over to my neighbor to argue the matter "head to head." Notice that each of these scenarios involves an increasing loss of impulse control: discussion is replaced by verbal abuse, which in turn gives way to confrontation and the likelihood of physical combat. Fortunately, few of us give in so easily to angry feelings; we inhibit our aggressive impulses. But those who do lack this power of inhibition make up a large proportion of the individuals who come before the courts accused of acts of violence. Traditionally such cases were considered simply as examples of "a hot temper," but as they have learned more about the brain, neuroscientists have discovered physical mechanisms that can result in aggression.

As long ago as 1892, Dr. F. L. Goltz demonstrated that removal of the forebrain of a dog changes a gentle animal into one that explodes into rage and launches a vicious attack on minimal provocation. But it was not until 1937 that Dr. James Papez identified the limbic system in the brain as the area from which emotions emanate (See page 18.). Further, the violence that erupts from limbic system discharges often does so despite the absence of any intent on the part of the perpetrator. Consider this response of a young woman, who, as her doctor described her, "was a very mild-mannered person and very sweet and who was always concerned that she would say the right thing and not hurt anybody." As part of medical treatment, an electrode was inserted in this woman's amygdala, an area at the tip of the temporal lobe and a component of the limbic system. As the current was slowly increased the woman became "hostile" and spoke in an angry tone. She said, "If you think you're going to keep me here, you had better get a lot more men." She stood up and attempted to strike the examiner, who, not surprisingly, quickly reduced the electric current. At once she reverted back to her pleasant and cooperative self. "The woman's anger could be turned on and off with one flick of a toggle switch," recalls Professor Kenneth Moyer, a psychologist at Carnegie-Mellon University.

But an electrode inserted into a person's brain is hardly a "normal" situation. What about episodes of violent behavior not provoked by such intrusions? Is there any evidence that such discharges of electricity in the brain can occur in the natural state?

For many years neuroscientists wondered what would be observed if someone were to electrically monitor the brain of a violent person during an actual attack. Dr. Vernon H. Mark, a neurosurgeon now at Harvard Medical School, once had the opportunity to investigate this question. Mark's special interest in the violent mind has occupied him throughout a long and successful neurosurgical career. The most memorable of the many patients who have come under his care was Julie.

"One day a physician in another city called me about his 21-year-old daughter. He told me she was suffering from epilepsy and sudden, unpredictable outbursts of violence," Mark recalls.

Before the age of two Julie had suffered a severe inflammation of the brain in the wake of a mumps infection. As a result, she began at about age ten to have epileptic seizures consisting of brief lapses of consciousness, staring, lip smacking, and chewing. Often after such a seizure, Julie, overcome by panic, would run away as fast as she could. Between seizures she flared into sudden outbursts of anger and temper tantrums, followed by remorse for what she had said and done. On four occasions she was sufficiently depressed to attempt suicide. But the most troubling aspect of Julie's behavior stemmed from a series of impulsive assaults directed against other people.

"By far the most serious attack occurred when Julie was eighteen. She was at a movie with her father when she felt a wave of terror pass over her body, 'a knot of fear in the pit of my stomach,' as she termed it. She went to the ladies' room and stared at herself in the mirror while clutching a dinner knife which she always carried to defend herself during those occasions when, after an attack of running away, she would 'come to' in an unsavory part of the city."

While Julie stood before the mirror, another woman came into the room and accidentally bumped against her. Julie reacted with an outburst of violence: she plunged the knife into the woman's chest. "There was a blood-curdling scream from the restroom. Julie's father rushed in and administered first aid to the stabbing victim and saved her life," says Mark. Sometime later, Julie was transferred to his care for investigation.

There is agreement among neuroscientists that the sites within the brain that are most important in triggering violence are the frontal and prefrontal areas, and the amygdala, the hippocampus, and the hypothalamus, which are part of the limbic system.

Through several small burr holes in Julie's skull, Mark inserted electrodes into the hippocampus and amygdala on both the right and left sides of the brain. Abnormal electrical discharges were detected from these sites. Mark then added telemetry: a recording technique whereby Julie could be monitored as she moved about rather than remaining confined to a chair or a bed in the recording laboratory.

"By using telemetry, we were able to stimulate Julie's brain with electrical impulses. On most electrodes we got nothing . . . no seizures, no attack behavior. But there was one specific pair of electrodes in the amygdala that brought on a dramatic change in her behavior. On the first occasion when we stimulated these electrodes, Julie became unresponsive and stopped answering questions. She began to stare and then took on a facial grimace characteristic of a primitive rage response. All the while seizure activity continued in the amygdala and hippocampus." Then, suddenly, Julie launched an explosive attack, smashing her fists against the wall. When that seizure was at an end, Julie's EEG showed the typical slowing that occurs in the postseizure period.

In order to confirm that Julie's violent episode was directly related to the electrical impulses, Mark repeated the stimulation a second time without her knowledge. "She was playing a guitar and was quite unaware that any stimulation was going to take place. There was a neuropsychiatrist in the room watching her play the guitar. Within five seconds of stimulation, Julie stopped playing and stared blankly ahead. She didn't answer any of the questions that the neuropsychiatrist was now asking her. A cascade of abnormal, spikelike epileptic brain waves from her amygdala was then recorded. This was followed by a sudden and powerful swing of her guitar. She smashed the guitar against the wall, narrowly missing the doctor's head. Obviously, that was the last time we have ever stimulated that particular electrode.

At that point we certainly had significant evidence that there is indeed a focal point that caused seizures, followed by attack behavior."

Based on the demonstration of epileptic activity emanating from the right amygdala, Mark "destroyed the abnormal tissue by using radio frequency current and raising the temperature by heat coagulation in a sequential fashion over a period of many months."

Five or six years after the surgery, Julie's aggression attacks had ceased, and she returned to her music once again. Today, fifteen years later, she shows no evidence of difficulty controlling her anger. I asked Mark whether he thought Julie was responsible for her behavior during one of those attacks.

"I think that someone like Julie has very little control over her activities," he said. "She had attack behavior that was related to a brain abnormality. She had very little ability to control this by free will."

When it comes to understanding violence, Mark is convinced that one must concentrate on both the environment and the brain. Alcohol and drugs can bring about a temporary situation very similar to what was happening within Julie's brain. "During a time when an individual is poisoned with alcohol or cocaine, he or she may be just as incapacitated as a person affected with a brain tumor or brain infection," Mark notes. "The only difference is the time sequence: when the drug or alcohol disappears from the system, the 'brain lesion' disappears with it."

Violence is very rare in epilepsy, but when it occurs, it provides a clear example of how a brain abnormality can lead to behavior over which the afflicted person has little control. Under such circumstances, the mind is incapable of controlling the impulse to strike out. Should Julie be held responsible for attacking the woman in the movie theater? Based on experiences with patients like Julie, neuroscientists have come to appreciate the difficulty in attributing "responsibility" to someone suffering from a brain lesion.

It is humbling and frightening to consider that our rationality is dependent on the normal functioning of tissue within our skulls. As we probe into the mysteries of the violent mind, we will encounter our Januslike nature; thanks to our brain, our lot is cast both with angels and demons. We have the capacity, if everything is operating correctly within our brain, of composing a bill of rights or the Constitution. But in the presence of a barely measurable electrical impulse within the limbic system, our much vaunted rationality can be replaced by savage attacks and seemingly inexplicable violence. What's more, the violent mind is violent only sporadically and explosively. Only when Julie received electrical stimulation to her amygdala did she smash

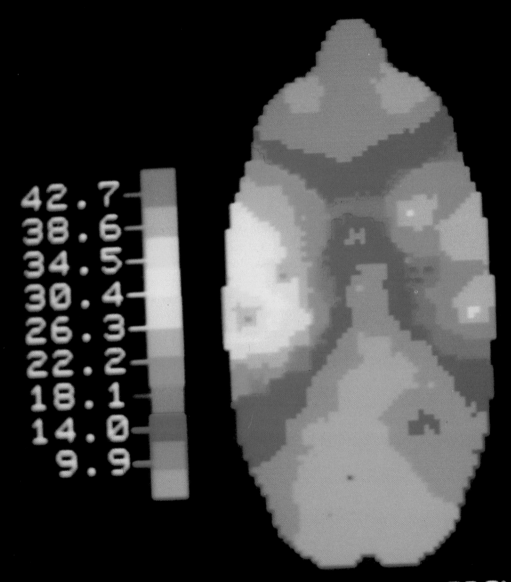

42.7
38.6
34.5
30.4
26.3
22.2
18.1
14.0
9.9

TEMPORAL LOBE EPILEPSY

the guitar against the wall. Moments later she was contrite and puzzled. "What happened?" she asked. "Why did I do that?"

But Julie was lucky; in her case brain scientists were able to demonstrate in a conclusive manner that something was amiss within her brain and that she could not possibly form the necessary intent to be fully responsible for her actions.

Our new insights into the role of the brain and aggression have highlighted the need for some way of predicting ahead of time those individuals who, as a result of brain injury and other contributing factors, are at an increased risk of committing an act of violence in the future.

Dr. Dorothy Otnow Lewis, Professor of Psychiatry at the New York University School of Medicine, believes that she has discovered a predictive profile of child delinquents who are at great risk for later acts of aggression, particularly murder. A study by Lewis of delinquent boys who later became murderers showed patterns of aggressive and sometimes violent behavior in childhood, as well as other factors in common: close relatives with psychotic illnesses, severe parental abuse, major neurologic impairments, and a history of head injury.

The last two characteristics warrant special note. Many children are exposed to violence at home, suffer physical abuse, even have one or both parents with a history of psychosis, a possible genetic factor. But as a rule, these children are not going to commit murder unless childhood head injury and significant neurological impairments are also present.

As we will see in the course of this chapter, brain damage, the major cause of such impairments, is very common in persons who have been examined by a neurologist because of their violent behavior or acts. The damage is confirmed by abnormal EEG readings and PET scans. But as the profile developed by Lewis suggests, a complex interplay of biological *and* social factors often underlies such behavior; it's very difficult to pinpoint a single cause for violence.

Given this, and clear evidence that control, responsibility, and intention can be altered by abnormal electrical discharges within the brain initiated either by epilepsy or by electrical stimulation of the limbic structures carried out as a medical or laboratory procedure, what can we infer about the origins of violence?

"The formulation which best fits these facts is that the capacity for aggression is present in all of us but most people learn to control it, and that this control can be reduced by biological factors," says Dr. Frank A. Elliott, Professor Emeritus of Neurology at the University of Pennsylvania School of Medicine. Elliott, who has spent a lifetime studying violent people, is convinced that genetic inheritance is one of the biological factors influencing the capacity for aggression. This capacity is mediated by a system of neurons and neurotransmitters extending from the prefrontal cortex down to the lower brain stem. "Most of this equipment is situated in the deep central portions of the brain which we have inherited, almost unchanged, from our reptilian and early mammalian ancestors," says Elliott. Experiments have made it clear that electrical stimulation of key sites along this pathway within the limbic system can provoke angry aggressive behavior or childhood predatory attacks.

Implicit in Elliott's formulation is a fundamental principle of brain activity: the preeminent role played by *inhibition*. Most of us think of the brain as an excitatory organ, in which one neuron excites another. In fact, inhibition rather than excitation is the hallmark of the healthy brain. If all the neurons in the brain were excitatory, we wouldn't be able to do something as simple as reaching out for a glass of water. Movement is sculpted within the brain by an interaction involving stimulation of certain neurons, that activate specific muscles that enable us to reach for the glass, and the inhibition of others, muscle groups not specifically involved in the act of reaching. Inhibition also plays a pivotal role in our emotional responses.

Think back to the last time you encountered a noisy or an aggressive drunk. Alcohol dampens the influences of inhibitory systems so that aggressive impulses that would ordinarily be held in check emerge uncensored and uncontrolled.

Drugs, particularly barbiturates, also increase aggression. Marijuana seems to reduce it. But when marijuana is laced with PCP (phencyclidine)—a concoction known on the street as Love Boat—an explosive and deadly violence is frequently unleashed.

Radioactive labeling of PCP reveals that it exerts its influence within the limbic system, effectively shutting off the emotional parts of the brain from the influence of the overarching cortex. Insight, judgment, and reasoning are impaired. Responsibility and intention melt away, leaving the individual at the mercy of his now unleashed aggressive impulses. Episodes of sudden unprovoked violence secondary to PCP have become common in many of our major cities. A patient under my care several years ago who had no history of violence bludgeoned his wife to death with a shovel several hours after smoking Love Boat. He had a sudden "insight" that his wife was a devil and had to be destroyed.

But bizarrely violent episodes can occur in the absence

of chemicals. In the later part of the nineteenth century, psychiatrists first described recurring attacks of sudden uncontrollable rage. A century later a group of psychiatrists at Harvard described 130 self-referred patients who sought help for their explosive outbursts. These attacks of *episodic dyscontrol,* as the syndrome is now called, are unlike ordinary anger or outbursts of temper in response to frustration. Rather, the attacks come on suddenly, often without any provocation. "There is a dramatic change of personality, voice, and manner," says Frank Elliott. "The violence often has a primitive quality—gouging, kicking, clawing, biting, spitting—and the attacks are carried out so quickly and with such power that the victim is hard put to escape." In his practice Elliott has encountered a sixteen-year-old boy who tore the door off of a refrigerator, and a woman weighing only 105 pounds who hurled a large upholstered armchair over the dining room table.

A striking aspect of such individuals is their mental condition between attacks. A study of 286 patients followed over eleven years showed that two thirds were psychiatrically normal. Many of them were married, parents, holders of steady jobs—indistinguishable from their neighbors and co-workers. Moreover, they did not live under deprived social or economic conditions. They were private patients drawn from the middle and upper social classes. Ninety-five percent were white, and most were young. Men outnumbered women three to one.

Despite their apparent normality, however, neurological examinations, supplemented by EEG and CAT scans, turned up neurological deficits in 94 percent of the group. Of the remaining 6 percent, most came from families, in some instances extending back two or three generations, in which one or more members exhibited explosive behavior.

In 102 of the cases the episodic dyscontrol syndrome occurred for the first time following a specific brain injury such as head trauma, encephalitis (inflammation of the brain), stroke, or brain tumor. In the other 184 cases the violent outbursts had been present since childhood, starting out as temper tantrums. As children, many of them had exhibited developmental defects and had a history of injury or oxygen deprivation at birth.

Now picture in your mind a person, ordinarily under good control and not different in any easily distinguishable way from normal, who suffers from episodic dyscontrol and breaks out into an uncontrollable act of violence that terminates in a death. Is that person guilty of murder? Would he conform to the legal requirement that he fully *intended* to commit the act of murder?

His lawyer might well suggest that he was temporarily insane at the time of the murder but was insane no longer, and was now perfectly capable of assisting in his own defense. If you were a juror, what would you make of these claims?

It should be clear by now that responsibility and intention, aspects of mind that do not seem too difficult to grasp in the abstract, may prove to be extremely difficult to pin down in specific instances. In response to this difficulty, a basic principle of law has emerged over the centuries: a person should not be convicted for an offense if he is mentally disturbed.

The first legal pronouncement on insanity in English law dates from the Wild Beast Test of 1723: "It is not every kind of frantic humor, or something unaccountable in a man's behavior, that points him out to be such a man as is exempted from punishment; it must be a man that is totally deprived of his understanding and memory, and doth not know what he is doing, no more than an infant, than a brute or wild beast; such a one is never the object of punishment."

Obviously, a person would have to be totally mad to pass this test, which ignores the plight of those with less flagrant forms of insanity. But the Wild Beast Test did accomplish one purpose: the insanity plea, if successful, led to acquittal and freedom. Then, three quarters of a century later, that changed.

In May 1800, James Hadfield, an English soldier who six years earlier had sustained a serious head wound in a battle against the French, fired a pistol at the king as he entered the royal box at the theater in Drury Lane. The ball narrowly missed the king and Hadfield was charged with treason. At the trial the accused's insanity was obvious to all. But it was also unacceptable to all parties that Hadfield should go free. Parliament therefore hastily passed "an Act for the safe custody of insane persons charged with offenses." The act introduced into English law the so-called Special Verdict of not guilty by reason of insanity, which leads not to release but to indefinite confinement in a mental hospital.

A half-century later, in 1843, the definition of insanity was broadened as a result of the trial of Daniel McNaughton.

Convinced that the Tory party was singling him out for persecution, McNaughton attempted to shoot the Tory prime minister, Robert Peel, and by mistake shot and killed Peel's secretary, Edward Drummond. At the trial, McNaughton was found not guilty by reason of insanity. The "McNaughton rule" set out by the House of Lords for judges to apply at insanity trials required that to bring an insanity verdict, "it must be clearly proved that at the time of committing the act, the party accused was laboring under such defective reason from disease of the mind as not to know the nature and quality of the act he was doing, or if he did know it, that he did not know that he was doing wrong."

A great public outrage followed McNaughton's acquittal. *The London Times* captured the spirit of the public protests:

Ye people of England! Exult and be glad
For ye're now at the will of the merciless mad.
Why say ye that but three authorities reign
Crown, Commons and Lords?—You omit the insane.
They're a privileged class whom no statute controls
And their murderous charter exists in their souls.
Do they wish to spill blood they have only to play
A few pranks—get asylums a month and a day.
Then Heigh! To escape from the mad doctor's keys
And to pistol or stab whomsoever they please.

Public outrage at psychiatric courtroom testimony continues today. The acquittal of John Hinckley by reason of insanity unleashed a similar barrage of public protest. "Psychiatrists are often hired to put an acre of embroidery around a pinhead of 'fact' so that they bandy about diagnostic categories that are as evanescent as snowflakes," wrote columnist George Will in response to the Hinckley verdict.

Two weeks after the Hinckley trial, a survey of public opinion showed that 40 percent of the public, if they had been jurors in the Hinckley trial, would have had no confidence in the psychiatrist's testimony, while another 20 percent would have had only slight confidence. Put at its plainest, most of us believe that a person is responsible for his actions except under the most extraordinary circum-

John Hinckley's acquittal on grounds of insanity for his attempted assassination of President Reagan generated widespread anger.

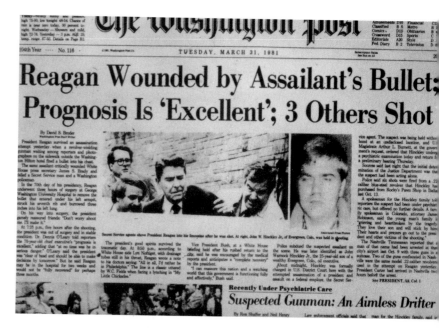

stances. Psychiatrists are in a position to define these circumstances. But they do so in the face of a challenge:

> Tell me, ye judges of our moral sins,
> where madness ends, and sanity begins?

This query is from a ninety-nine-verse poem, "Monomania," published in 1843 in angry response to the McNaughton verdict.

Attempts to answer this question have resulted in several modifications of the McNaughton rule. One modification says that the accused cannot be held responsible if his act is "the product of mental disease or mental defect," but these terms are too broad; there are minor as well as major mental disorders, and psychiatrists often disagree about the relationship between a person's behavior and the mental illness he may be suffering from.

The American Law Institute's Model Penal Code makes another modification and refers to "a mental disease or defect which results in a lack of substantial capacity to appreciate the criminality of one's conduct or to conform one's conduct to the requirement of law." But how can one be certain about an individual's ability to conform to what is acceptable behavior? How does one distinguish between an impulse that is irresistible and one that is merely not resisted?

The complexities of defining insanity are compounded by new insights into the workings of the human brain. We know now that the brain can malfunction—sometimes only temporarily—because of conditions over which a person has no control, and that this malfunction can impair the person's capacity to know what he is doing and to remember afterward what he has done. How is responsibility to be determined in situations such as this? How is sanity to be gauged?

Consider the case of William Quick. On December 27, 1971, Quick, a nurse at Farleigh Mental Hospital, Flax Bourton, Somerset, England, accidentally overdosed himself with insulin. A diabetic since he was seven, Quick regularly self-administered insulin. On at least a dozen other occasions the amount he gave himself had been excessive, plunging him into states of unconsciousness and semiconsciousness that required medical treatment. On three or four of these occasions, according to Quick's doctor, his patient had behaved violently in response to the lowered blood sugar brought on by the excess dose of insulin.

After taking his insulin dose on that December day, Quick ate almost no breakfast and skipped lunch altogether. In the afternoon he drank an unknown quantity of whiskey and a quarter bottle of rum.

At 4 P.M. a nurse summoned to the patients' lounge

observed Quick assaulting one of the patients. Quick was "glassy-eyed" and made no reply when asked what was happening. Moments later he collapsed into a coma.

Quick was charged with assault. Medical testimony in Quick's behalf included this statement: "If a patient is going unconscious with a falling blood sugar, for a while he would be more than aggressive, for a while he may start being physically violent, and then he will be in a semi-comatose state. Then he may have a fit, then he may stay deeply unconscious for quite a while. It would sound from the evidence . . . that this man developed an increasing effect of a falling blood sugar from sometime in the afternoon until when he collapsed after the episode of attack. At least the events fit with that."

Did Quick suffer, at least temporarily, from a disease of the mind? Certainly precedence in English law tends to support this contention. A judge commenting on an earlier defense based on an epileptic automatism had said, "It seems to me that any mental disorder which has manifested itself in violence and is prone to recur is a disease of the mind."

But if any violence-producing mental disorder is a "disease of the mind," would it then be correct to say Quick was insane at the time of his offense? If so, he might be consigned to psychiatric care. But obviously no mental hospital in the world would admit a diabetic merely because of a low blood sugar. "Common sense is affronted by the prospect of a diabetic being sent to such a hospital when in most cases the disordered mental condition can be rectified quickly by pushing a lump of sugar or teaspoonful of glucose into the patient's mouth," said Lord Justice Lawton, who presided over the case.

What then should be done with William Quick? Did his medical condition so impair his mind that he wasn't acting freely when he assaulted the patient? With that question the interests of medicine and the law diverge.

"It does not matter for the purpose of law whether the defective reasoning was due to a degeneration of the brain or some other form of mental derangement. That may be a matter of importance medically, but it is of no importance to the law, which merely has to consider the state of mind in which the accused is, not how he got there," wrote one attorney, commenting on the case in the *All England Law Reports*.

But limiting considerations to the determination of a defendant's "state of mind" and "not how he got there" can lead to some bizarre consequences, in which "insanity" can be distorted beyond recognition. Imagine a football player, for instance, who sustains a concussion after a particularly hard tackle but nonetheless gets up and continues the game in a state of automatism. If while in that state—which he cannot recall afterwards—he assaults an official, it hardly makes sense to excuse the player from the consequences of his action on the basis that he is "not guilty by reason of insanity." Impaired, yes, but certainly not insane.

"There is no question that the legal profession has not caught up with the medical profession as far as the mind is concerned," says the Honorable Robert A. Barton, Justice of the Superior Court of Massachusetts. "Unfortunately, the law cannot fit into cubbyholes and categories all gradations that the medical profession may use as far as mental disease or defects or limited responsibilities are concerned."

For example, the law distinguishes between diminished capacity that is voluntarily or involuntarily entered into. If I drink down a bottle of bourbon and some time later lose control and assault someone, I cannot excuse my action on the basis that my ability to control my temper was impaired by the alcohol. That's because when I took that first drink, I knew what I was doing, and should have foreseen the general consequences (confusion, irritability, loss of impulse control) that finishing off the whole bottle would probably bring about. My diminished capacity was *voluntarily* entered into; at least that's how my behavior would be looked upon by the courts.

But in Quick's case he didn't deliberately overdose himself with the insulin. What's more, the disturbance in his state of mind was caused by an external factor, the insulin, not by disease. To complicate matters further, there was the alcohol. Was his confused mental condition the result of an overdose of insulin (diminished capacity of involuntary origin) or too much alcohol (a voluntary incapacity, at least in the early stages)? If the insulin dose was to blame, to what extent had Quick brought about his own condition by not following his doctor's orders about eating regular meals? Finally, it seems likely that in the earliest stages of his impaired state, Quick should have suspected something was amiss and tried the simple antidote of a lump of sugar, as he had been instructed to do under such circumstances.

Quick pleaded not guilty to the assault on the grounds of automatism. The judge ruled that the defense that had been raised was insanity, not automatism. In response Quick changed his plea to guilty. He was convicted. On appeal the conviction was overturned on the grounds that the verdict was "unsatisfactory." Quick was not responsible for his behavior, which occurred during an automatism, but he was also not insane within any reasonable and acceptable use of the term—a reference to McNaughton and the modifications of the Rule that had passed into law thereafter. He suffered, in other words, from a temporary, perhaps episodic, condition and not a permanent defect of the mind.

The Quick case and others like it broke new ground. A person suffering from an episodic illness, with psychological complications arising during an episode of the illness, may be no more responsible for his behavior than a defendant who is declared "insane" by traditional standards. What is still required, according to some psychiatrists and attorneys, are refinements of the insanity defense that liberalize the doctrine of diminished responsibility. One such defense, already upheld in English courts, is that of premenstrual syndrome (PMS).

Sandie, an eighteen-year-old student, suffers from premenstrual syndrome. During eight days out of each month, the paramenstruum that begins several days before the onset of her period and reaches peak intensity either during the final four days or during the first four days of actual menstruation, Sandie often acts erratically. On various occasions she has swallowed weed killer, run away from home, shaved her head and eyebrows, cut her face. She once set fire to her house, and while serving a prison sentence for arson attempted to strangle herself, cut her wrists, and set the prison on fire. All these episodes occurred during the paramenstruum. Prolonged treatment with progesterone, a female sex hormone, terminated her bizarre behavior. She was freed on probation and displayed no further symptoms. She is now married and employed in a full-time managerial position.

Suppose, however, that just prior to one of her menstrual periods Sandie had injured or even killed someone. Should her hormonal imbalance be considered a mitigating factor in determining Sandie's guilt or innocence? Dr. Katharina Dalton, of the Premenstrual Syndrome Clinic at University College Hospital, London, believes that premenstrual syndrome may be responsible for many violent acts carried out by women. She has found that among female patients admitted to psychiatric hospitals, 46 percent are admitted during their paramenstruum. Women suffering from premenstrual tension constitute 53 percent of attempted suicides. Among 156 new inmates to a prison, 49 percent had been sentenced for crimes committed during their eight-day paramenstruum. "Premenstrual syndrome was present in an incapacitating severity in 27 percent of the prisoners overall and in 67 percent of those who had committed their crimes during the paramenstruum," according to Dr. Dalton. She would favor incorporating a "hormonal influence" defense into accepted definitions of insanity.

Under the defense of premenstrual syndrome, a woman defendant to a violent crime could claim that she was not responsible for her actions, that at the time she suffered from a variant of temporary insanity. "It is not a great step to include hormonal aberration within the scope of the insanity defense, assuming that such aberration resulted in

the individual being unable to appreciate the wrongfulness of her acts or to conform her conduct to avoid that wrong,'' says Dr. Dalton.

But there are difficulties with the premenstrual syndrome defense. According to the best available estimates, between 20 and 27 percent of women suffer from premenstrual syndrome severe enough to demand medical attention or to result in loss of time at work. Only a small minority of these women are violent. But depression, lethargy, and irritability do occur in the majority. Given the proper trigger—frustration, humiliation, perhaps even physical abuse—that irritability has been known to erupt into murderous violence. Where does one draw the line? Should every woman who commits a violent act during the eight-day paramenstruum be considered to have acted in a state of temporary insanity? According to Dalton's statistics, this would constitute about 50 percent of women accused of a crime. Or should the defense of premenstrual syndrome apply only to some women? If so, which women? What criteria will be applied to distinguish ''irritability'' from ''temporary insanity,'' and who will be applying this standard?

Neither the McNaughton Rule nor changes in the laws and statutes pertaining to the insanity defense that have evolved since McNaughton provide consistent answers to these questions and many others.

Neither women like Sandie who suffer from premen-

Sandie, whose many acts of violence were linked to severe PMS, has not shown these behaviors since she was given hormone treatment for the condition.

strual syndrome nor diabetics such as William Quick would be considered insane by the McNaughton Rule, which requires demonstration of a "defect of reason, from disease of the mind." Under this rule insanity is a cognitive, not a behavioral disorder. "Was the defendant able to appreciate the significance of her act?" takes precedence over "Was she able to control her conduct?"

But under a provision in the American Law Institute's Model Penal Code known as the "substantial capacity" rule, both Sandie and William Quick could be found not guilty by reason of insanity. The provision states, "A person is not responsible for criminal conduct if, at the time of such conduct, as a result of mental disease or defect he lacks substantial capacity either to appreciate the criminality (wrongfulness) of his conduct or to conform his conduct to the requirements of the law." (Katharina Dalton would modify the rule to read "as a result of mental *or hormonal* defect or disease . . .")

Under the Durham formula or "Product" rule ("an accused is not criminally responsible if his unlawful act was the *product* of mental disease or mental defect"), both Sandie and William Quick could also be considered not fully responsible and therefore not fully accountable for their violent acts.

But what does it say about our understanding of the violent mind when a person accused of violence is fully responsible under one standard and insane under another? What is needed are fresh ways of looking at what goes wrong in the mind of a violent offender. Further refinements in psychological or legal approaches are unlikely to provide this. There are indications, however, that in some instances the brain sciences may help provide new insights into the violent mind. As an example of this new perspective, consider the mystery surrounding David Garabedian, who is now serving time for first-degree murder.

On March 29, 1983, David Garabedian, a young man employed by the Old Fox Lawn Care Company in Massachusetts, arrived at the home of Eileen Muldoon. After knocking at the front door and receiving no response, he inspected her front lawn, worked out some calculations, and came up with an estimate of the costs of spraying the lawn with insecticides. At about that time, according to Garabedian, he experienced the urge to urinate. He walked around to the back of the yard and urinated near the side of the house. Suddenly Mrs. Muldoon appeared. "She was very angry at me . . . began yelling . . . I became confused."

Garabedian apologized but Mrs. Muldoon turned around, angry and unwilling to listen to further explanations. "At that point I just tapped her on the shoulder to say, 'I'm sorry.' She just turned around and gouged me in the face.

That's when I grabbed her by the neck and I just remember squeezing and then both of us falling off the ledge. At that point a drawstring fell out of my jacket. I just picked it up and put it around her neck and I just started squeezing."

If events had stopped at this point, the mystery surrounding David Garabedian's behavior that fateful day would be far less problematic.

"He went to a nearby wall built from large boulders and picked up boulders which probably weighed fifty or sixty pounds and repeatedly threw these large boulders at Mrs. Muldoon's head and face, disfiguring her greatly," stated the psychiatrist who examined Garabedian prior to the trial.

"At that point I was very confused and didn't know what to do," Garabedian recalls. "I didn't know how I could tell my father about this awful thing." He drove back to the chemical plant, but told no one of the killing or even of his visit to the Muldoon house. He then drove home and sat down with his father, still unable to tell him what happened. Then he went to bed, and at one A.M. policemen burst into his room, guns drawn, and took him into custody.

Prior to the attack on Mrs. Muldoon, David Garabedian had given no indication of violence. He was described as shy, mild-mannered, passive, even docile. But about a month prior to the murder he had undergone a striking personality change.

"David was unusually fatigued, withdrawn, irritable, jittery, and hypersensitive to noise. On one occasion he quite uncharacteristically argued with and struck his younger sister. He drank unusually large amounts of orange juice or water. He had repeated episodes of abdominal pain and diarrhea. His father noted that his son was salivating excessively at night and complaining of headaches during the day. On one occasion after mixing chemicals at work, the headache became so bad that David had to leave work early. Nausea, loss of appetite, and five- to ten-pound weight loss ensued during the first three weeks of March. He complained that his skin itched and that he was urinating more frequently and with a great sense of urgency. In addition, he felt light-headed, tense, nervous, and impatient." This is the report of Dr. Peter S. Spencer, a toxicologist and Professor of Neuroscience at the Albert Einstein College of Medicine in New York, who evaluated David Garabedian and formulated an explanation for the murder:

"David Garabedian was involuntarily intoxicated with a chemical present in the lawn products that he was exposed to on a daily basis both while mixing and spraying these agents."

The chemical referred to by Spencer is chlorpyrifos (Dursban). It interferes with the neural transmission within the brain. The interference occurs because the chemical inactivates a normal protein, cholinesterase, located at the ends of many nerve fibers. Under ordinary conditions cholinesterase terminates the action of the neurotransmitter acetylcholine. But in the presence of an anticholinesterase inhibitor, acetylcholine remains within the synaptic cleft.

Excessive exposure to anticholinesterase chemicals produces a spectrum of ill effects that reflect the degree to which acetylcholine activity in the brain is disturbed. With the most powerful anticholinesterase agents, total paralysis ensues. Less potent agents are routinely utilized in pesticides.

Depending on the amount of exposure, the potency of the anticholinesterase drug or chemical, and the brain area involved, a host of different impairments can result, among them loss of appetite, abdominal cramps, diarrhea, urinary frequency, increased sweating and salivation, and easy fa-

Computer graphic model of acetylcholine, the neurotransmitter whose excessive retention in the synaptic cleft is thought to have triggered David Garabedian's violent behavior.

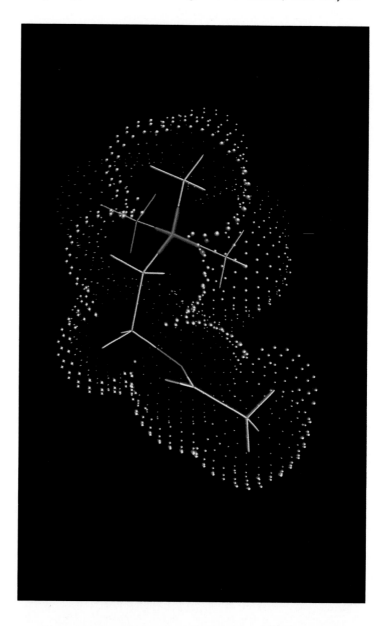

tigue. David Garabedian reported all of these symptoms. In addition, there are symptoms of a more subjective variety: anxiety, jitteriness, restlessness, emotional instability, combative behavior, and light-headedness. The affected person may also complain of headaches, difficulty in concentrating, slowness of recall, and mental confusion.

At the trial, Spencer testified that "it seems likely that David Garabedian's behavioral changes, caused by involuntary exposure to chlorpyrifos, played a role of indeterminable magnitude in the action that resulted in the death of Mrs. Muldoon."

The psychiatrist who examined David put it in even stronger terms. "In my view, David did not have the capacity to control his behavior because his brain was poisoned."

The claim that a chemical had induced a state of insanity had never been made in the United States prior to the Garabedian case. But the defense was unsuccessful: the jury decided that Garabedian was guilty of first-degree murder. Among the factors that influenced the jurors were the following:

Other workers had been exposed to anticholinesterase chemicals, often in higher doses, and they hadn't murdered anyone.

Only moments before the murder David Garabedian had surveyed the lawn and had calmly, coolly, and accurately carried out computations and calculations, and had come up with a cost estimate. In other words, he had acted most reasonably.

At no time in David Garabedian's life had he given any indication of mental illness. "He is a person who had no previous background of mental illness or mental disease. That's a problem. In most of your successful insanity cases there is always a background or prior history of mental illness which we didn't have here," says David's attorney, Robert M. Mardirosian, who had has more than twenty-five years' experience as both a former prosecutor and a public defender.

At the moment, David Garabedian is serving a life sentence. But in contrast to most prisoners in his situation, he still has hope that he will receive a new trial. He bases this on a bizarre series of incidents involving a professor of medicine, his companion, and a mild-mannered cat that suddenly turned killer.

Professor Claude Lechenne: "I had a large dog who was heavily infected with fleas. When nothing else worked, I started using a very potent insecticide. Since I also had a cat, I sprayed the chemical on him as well. Within days the cat, who was usually very gentle, began chasing mice and birds. He would drag them into the house, free them, and then run after them and kill them. Soon almost every room of my house was filled with rows of animals. The cat was continuing to go outside and bring in more animals, which he then killed."

Angry at this behavior, Dr. Lechenne pushed his cat out of the house and told his companion: "That cat is becoming a murderer." At that moment, he learned an important fact about his own behavior, a fact that might some day gain a new trial for David Garabedian.

"She told me that my mood was extremely changeable and that I was constantly picking a fight with her over trivial matters. When she said that, I realized that something was terribly wrong—wrong with me, the cat, even the dog. All three of us were sleepy all the time. Then there was the increased aggression by me and the cat. When I checked into the composition of the insecticide I found that it contained an anticholinesterase inhibitor."

When Lechenne stopped using the insecticide, his symptoms and the cat's promptly disappeared. The involuntary intoxication was over. But David Garabedian wasn't so lucky, according to psychiatrist David Bear, who believes that "David should not be in jail because he did not have the capacity to control his behavior . . . his brain was poisoned."

Within the insecticide that David Garabedian mixed and sprayed on the lawns of his town was the anticholinesterase chemical. "Let's imagine what might have been happening inside David's brain that day," Bear suggests. "The nerve cells in the hypothalamus are firing their usual signals at a low rate. When Mrs. Muldoon walks up and the encounter takes place, a tremendous emotional reaction follows. Nerve cells in the hypothalamus that had been resting, idling, firing very slowly, suddenly began firing extremely rapidly."

With that increase in firing, the amount of acetylcholine at the synapse increases. But since the enzyme that ordinarily inactivates acetylcholine is inhibited by the insecticide chemical, the acetylcholine continues to build up.

"Suddenly, the circuit does something it's never done before. There's a feeling which we can only describe as overwhelming rage, a feeling David Garabedian probably never experienced in his whole life. The environment may have combined with the chemical poisoning to produce a terrible event that neither alone could have produced. I don't think David Garabedian had the structures, whether we say nerve cells or psychological preparation, to handle that burst of temper. A chemical from outside his brain led to this anger. The brain was fooled by a substance from outside that mimicked the action of its normal signals. This was not rage directed at the environment but a mistake in the brain based on chemical poisoning."

Garabedian's lawyer, Robert Mardirosian, is now seeking a new trial for his client, based on Bear's theory. Both men believe that Garabedian did not have the capacity to commit a crime. "If the case were tried again today, it is quite possible that a different result would be reached because we now know what these chemicals are doing. Professor Lechenne is an example of such a case. I think there are others out there and I intend to find them."

Bear compares the Garabedian tragedy to the *Challenger* disaster. "Just as it wouldn't make sense to direct our anger at the pilot of the *Challenger* when the problem was in fact a defective O-ring, it would be a mistake to direct anger at David. If the real villain in this piece is the insecticide, then there may be no human villain. I think we run the risk of mistaking the cause of this tragedy and not correcting that cause."

While the explanation suggested by David Bear is entirely possible, there is no way of proving it. One expert on poisons has suggested that David be deliberately exposed to the chemical—challenged—so as to reproduce the physical signs of intoxication that he experienced on that March day in 1983. But such an experiment is risky: long-term brain damage even from a single exposure cannot be absolutely ruled out. In any event, it is likely that both the chemical poison and the psychological stress would be required in order to reproduce the rageful violence that occurred on that fateful day. Most damaging to David Garabedian's case is the speculative nature of the pesticide theory. "Anything can have an impact on your behavior," says Dr. John Clark, Associate Professor of Toxicology at the University of Massachusetts at Amherst. "There is absolutely no proof for or against this theory. He could have gone out and had five chocolate bars and that could do it."

At issue here are two conflicting standards, science and the law. Typically, scientists examine their "data," formulate a theory, test that theory, and, if necessary, give some "benefit of the doubt" in the individual case; not every experiment need turn out as expected so long as the overwhelming majority are supportive of the theory. But with the law, theory and speculation, no matter how interesting conceptually, are insufficient. David Garabedian confessed to killing Mrs. Muldoon. The "facts" were beyond dispute. At issue is the explanation for David's behavior. Put at its simplest, the jury did not believe that David Garabedian suffered from a brain-related defect that impaired his ability to conform his behavior to the law.

Sudden repeated explosive outbursts of rage correspond to just about everybody's notion of some forms of mental illness. If, in addition, violent paroxysms are based on an epileptic discharge or brain abnormality that comes out only during sleep, there is even more reason to assume that the perpetrator of violence isn't responsible for his or her actions. But what about situations in which the violence is an outgrowth of years of maladjustment and creeping psychosis that in its earlier stages could be seen simply as aberrant behavior?

On October 30, 1985, Sylvia Seegrist, aged twenty-six, put on camouflage pants, combat boots, a wool cap, and a shirt with the word *Jihad* printed on the back. She then proceeded to the Springfield Mall near Philadelphia, Pennsylvania, and opened fire with a semiautomatic rifle. Three persons were killed and seven seriously wounded.

Four years earlier, Sylvia had stabbed a young woman psychologist. Over the following three years she was hospitalized five times, on three occasions because of violent attacks against her mother. Several months before the mall shooting, Sylvia took to wearing army fatigues in combination with a shirt that had printed on the front, "Kill 'em all." Only three days prior to the shooting, she was observed behaving strangely at a shooting gallery. The police responded to a complaint, but nothing was done.

Ruth Seegrist, Sylvia's mother, recalls the events that occurred in the early weeks of that ominous October. "By the third week in October she was completely out of touch with reality—continuously agitated, vitriolic, restless, unable to concentrate or even comprehend questions directed at her. 'You!' she would screech, pointing an accusing finger at me, eyes ablaze with scorching anger, 'you gave me birth . . . you will be lucky if some day you don't die by my hand.' I was terrified. I did not doubt that she was capable of killing me."

During Sylvia Seegrist's trial medical records were introduced into evidence indicating that since 1981 she had stated on numerous occasions to different psychiatrists and psychologists, "I feel like getting a gun and killing a lot of people." She had also contacted crisis centers on several occasions and made similar statements.

The jury found Sylvia Seegrist mentally ill and guilty of three counts of first-degree murder and seven counts of attempted murder. The verdict meant that Sylvia's life sentence would be served either in an institution for the insane or in prison, depending on her mental condition.

What went wrong in the Sylvia Seegrist case? Why did no one listen to this agitated, distraught, and extremely ill young woman? "Why did her screams for help fall on deaf ears? Why did ours?" asks Ruth Seegrist. "Sylvia was in and out of psychosis for months and completely out of touch with reality for two or three weeks before the tragedy. Yet legally, there were no grounds on which she could be involuntarily committed."

Several months after Sylvia's transfer to a mental hospital, Ruth Seegrist appeared before a legislative hearing on proposed changes in the mental health system. She banged her fists on the table in frustration and anger. "I resent the fact that patients like Sylvia with extensive and well-documented histories of violence cannot be involuntarily committed when they are psychotic but before they are a clear and immediate danger. . . . Sylvia is as much a victim as the people she victimized."

Prior to the 1970s, it is likely that something would have been done about Sylvia Seegrist. Most probably she would have been involuntarily committed and retained in a mental hospital. This could have happened during any one of her five involuntary admissions. But starting in the 1970s, prolonged involuntary commitment of a psychotic, potentially dangerous person became increasingly difficult. In reaction to alleged cruelties and inequities in the management of mental patients, the courts and legislatures began making it harder and harder to lock up mentally ill people against their will. Today, patients' right to remain free often prevails over their need for psychiatric help. The right even prevails over their physical safety and, as in the Sylvia Seegrist case, the safety of other people. As a result many more psychotic people roam the streets now than at any time in our history. "Ma'am, the streets of Philadelphia are full of psychotics," Ruth Seegrist was told on one occasion, when she contacted a mental health office to ask for help in involuntarily hospitalizing her daughter.

A delicate balance exists between the rights of individuals to be protected against undue restrictions on their freedom and the rights of the rest of society to be protected against those few mentally ill patients given to violence. In previous periods the balance was overweighted on the side of societal protection. "I'm not sure whether it is not more necessary to hang an insane person than a sane person," said a nineteenth-century judge when passing the death sentence on a "mad man." Has the balance swung too far the other way today? Are we now overconcerned with the rights of the mentally ill to the exclusion of public safety? Ruth Seegrist thinks so:

"Just as it was cruel and unjust to indiscriminately lock up the mentally ill years ago, so it is unjust and socially irresponsible to allow the severely ill with established records of violent behavior to fend for themselves. . . . In doing this you have not given the severely ill 'civil liberty.' You have merely given them the right to be slaves to their own devastating and debilitating brain disease."

Within a week of reading those words by Ruth Seegrist, I encountered in my office a Vietnam veteran dressed in battle fatigues. He spoke of not wishing to live, nightmares, "tremendous anger." Then he told me that while working for a bail bondsman he had killed a man. "He threatened me . . . said he would get me. I took off the handcuffs and told him to 'get moving.' When he started to run I shot him."

"Why are you coming to me?" I asked.

"I have the impulse to take my gun down to the Vietnam Memorial and shoot everybody in sight. I really believe I'm going to do that some day."

He brushed off my suggestion of hospitalization and left the office. I put in an immediate call to the man's psychiatrist and suggested that the police be contacted. He disagreed. "I don't think he'll actually do it," he said over the phone. As a compromise we agreed to have the man evaluated by a third psychiatrist. He too doubted that the man would actually carry out his threat, although he felt "uncomfortable about that opinion since I know the guy has a houseful of guns."

In this instance, three psychiatrists with equivalent training, skills, and conscientiousness genuinely differ about whether or not a mentally ill person represents a threat to society. One psychiatrist recommends that the police be notified. The two others suggest that the man be "watched a little longer." Who is right?

Ruth Seegrist: "If the person is spiraling down into psychosis, then he or she should be picked up by the police and taken to a hospital . . . there are other Sylvias . . . walking time bombs, just as uncooperative and difficult as she was."

But the problem is that no one can be certain that something like the Springfield Mall tragedy will happen until *after* it occurs. The words of the Vietnam veteran mentioned a moment ago will seem prophetic if he ever does carry out his threat. "Why didn't the doctors do something?" is certain to be asked. But indeed, what are we to do? People can't be placed in mental institutions because of their thoughts or, with a few exceptions (a threat of presidential assassination, for example), for their words.

No one disagrees that a mentally ill person bent upon violence should be forcibly restrained and hospitalized. The disagreement involves: Who is going to make this decision? On what will it be based? How long will the person be confined? Psychiatrists are often not very helpful in answering these kinds of questions. For one thing, reformulations of what is and is not a mental illness occur every few years. For another, predictions of dangerousness are often made that are not borne out. On other occasions, as in the case of Sylvia Seegrist, dangerousness is ignored.

Psychiatrists are especially ineffectual when it comes to evaluating delusional beliefs. Sylvia Seegrist spent many months prior to the Springfield Mall incident studying the Middle East, Islam, and communism. "Unsolicited, she recited facts and opinions on these subjects to anyone within earshot, with passionate, bitter rhetoric, convinced that the Arabs, like the Soviets, were misunderstood and that they were provoked and angered by nuclear buildup and unfair treatment," her mother recalls. "She emphasized her points with physical gestures, whipping a double fist above her head or bunting a swift karate kick through the air." Obviously at a certain point Sylvia Seegrist's belief that she could affect Middle East policies should have been taken seriously. But when?

Here are two accounts of Sylvia.

"Sylvia Seegrist was a twenty-five-year-old schizophrenic woman who was well during the first fifteen years of her life. Over the next ten years she started using drugs, became sexually promiscuous, and grew erratic in her school performance. She assaulted her parents on several occasions, made verbal threats to students and, at a later point, other mental patients. At age twenty she stabbed a female psychologist. Between twenty-three and twenty-five years of age Sylvia became increasingly involved in Middle East affairs. She dressed in army fatigues, and Arab style headwrap, dark sunglasses, and a shirt with 'Kill em all' emblazoned on the front."

And the second account: "Sylvia Seegrist at age fifteen began a deterioration of her mental and psychological functioning that her psychiatrists described as schizophrenia. Although the causes are not presently known, schizophrenia is thought to be a brain disease that affects thinking, emotional behavior, and impulse control. The affected individual may be intermittently violent, delusional, may hear voices, may believe he or she has a special mission from God. Schizophrenics may also harbor deep-seated resentment and anger that, undeterred, can lead to violence directed at random. On October 30, 1985, Sylvia Seegrist's feelings that 'I wanted to get a gun and kill a lot of people' could no longer be controlled."

Both these accounts are accurate. But your reaction to each is likely to differ. The first emphasizes Sylvia's conduct and how she failed to conform to widely held societal standards. "Drug use," "sexual promiscuity," "violence against other people" are terms that operate as buzz words that prejudice us against the accused. Most of us, with varying degrees of effort, manage to control our tempers and curb our sexual passions. We don't use drugs and feel that at least initially other people can refrain from using them too if they want to.

The second account largely skirts the specifics of Sylvia Seegrist's behavior in the form of a more scientific concept

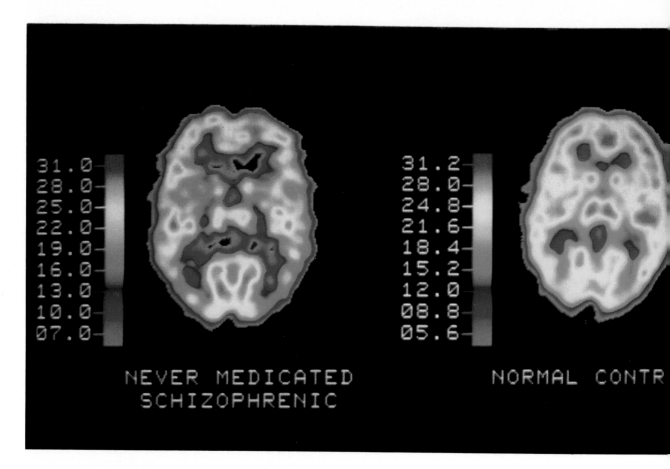

31.0
28.0
25.0
22.0
19.0
16.0
13.0
10.0
07.0

31.2
28.0
24.8
21.6
18.4
15.2
12.0
08.8
05.6

NEVER MEDICATED
SCHIZOPHRENIC

NORMAL CONTR

PET scan of a schizophrenic brain (left) *and a normal brain* (right). *The disease is sometimes marked by decreased brain activity as evidenced by diminished glucose metabolism.*

of the disease from which Sylvia suffers. Her behavior conforms to this description, or at least is compatible with it. "Sylvia is suffering from a disease and therefore is not responsible for what she did," seems a reasonable verdict when the facts of the case are so arranged.

Difficulties arise, however, if the psychiatrist is questioned too closely on the nature of the brain disease from which Sylvia Seegrist allegedly suffers. At the moment no one knows the exact cause of schizophrenia. Certainly a brain disease seems the best bet when it comes to causation. But in the Middle Ages demonic possession seemed the best bet. In the 1960s faulty parenting seemed the best bet. The courts and juries don't want "best bet" answers, but black and white answers. ("Does the defendant suffer from a brain disease? What is that disease? How does that disease affect the defendant's ability to control violent impulses?") Psychiatrists and neuroscientists want to talk in terms of possible and probable causes, thresholds for aggression, and so on.

"You can't really translate psychiatry into law and preserve science," says Dr. Loren H. Roth, Director of the Law and Psychiatry Program at the Western Psychiatric Institute and Clinic at the University of Pittsburgh.

Is it possible that the purposes and interests of psychiatry render it incompatible with the interests and purposes of the court? George J. Alexander, former Dean of the Santa Clara Law School, believes that psychiatrists should be kept out of courtrooms:

"Law does not make any sense at all unless it is premised on free will. What sense does it make to sentence somebody for a criminal act that he committed because of, for example, birth trauma? We would not have a criminal justice system except for the fact that through it all we believe, or at least we do not have an alternative to believing, that people are responsible for what they do. It may not be a good position, but it is all we have.

"Psychiatrists and psychologists necessarily are in the business of being nonjudgmental—of looking at factors in people's lives and looking at the deterministic influences and understanding why people do things in light of what has happened to them. They cannot make psychiatry work with free will and lawyers cannot make law work with determinism. It is about time we stopped trying to bring the two together."

Psychiatric influence in the criminal justice system begins even earlier than the courtroom. At all stages of the justice system, psychiatrists play a crucial role in evaluating the violent mind. For instance, consider this scenario that occurs daily on the streets of our major cities:

A police officer is called to an apartment building where a man has been observed acting in a violent manner. He is shouting and screaming, striking out at any person who approaches. He speaks of "killing all of you," and at one point threatens to reenter his apartment to "get a gun and waste everybody in the building."

Upon arrival the police officer subdues the violent man. At this point the officer is faced with a decision: Should he take the man to the station house or bring him to a hospital for psychiatric evaluation? Let's say that the officer takes the violent person to an emergency room for psychiatric evaluation. At that point the authority shifts from the policeman to the psychiatrist, who is authorized—indeed, required by law—to determine whether the person is dangerous to himself or others. Two decisions must be made: a treatment decision and a dangerousness decision. But each of these decisions is being made by the wrong person. The police officer is the one who decides whether the violent person should see a doctor and the doctor decides whether the person is dangerous enough to lock up. Further, many psychiatrists are fundamentally opposed to such things as the death penalty, and are in the position, unique to their profession in our society, of conscientiously employing their professional qualifications to further their own social and political opinions.

"Only with psychiatry and psychology do we bring experts to court who fundamentally disagree with the whole notion of criminal responsibility or human responsibility. In that sense we have a system that cannot be fixed up by minor adjustments," says George J. Alexander. "We probably should start over, dealing with responsibility without the help of psychiatrists and without the notion of insanity."

A suggested solution to this dilemma involves limiting the testimony of psychiatrists. This is based on the belief that no one can be *certain* that a particular mental state caused the person to become violent. Free will is a moral and legal issue that cannot be defined or converted into medical terms. "The more sophisticated psychiatric knowledge becomes, the less psychiatrists are able to say (and the less they should be allowed to say) that certain impairments *cause* certain criminal acts," according to Leonard Rubenstein, Legal Director of the Mental Health Law Project.

As things now stand, psychiatric testimony exerts a near-overpowering influence on the minds of the jurors. If psychiatric experts say that the mental illness was responsible for an act of violence, the jury is likely to defer to their judgment. Psychiatric testimony in such instances becomes the sole basis for the determination of guilt or innocence. The psychiatrist has replaced the jury as the determiner of responsibility.

If psychiatric testimony was limited, psychiatrists would be prohibited from speculating on the relationship of a defendant's mental illness to the violent crime he committed.

"It may be that psychiatry . . . cannot provide sufficient data relative to a determination of criminal responsibility no matter what the rules of evidence are," suggests the Honorable David Bazelon, a retired Judge of the United States Court of Appeals, and a specialist in mental illness and the law.

Under such a prohibition in the Hinckley case, for instance, psychiatrists for both defense and prosecution would have been free to describe John Hinckley's background, his fantasies, his dreams, his behavior on the day of the shooting, and even his mental state at the time he pulled the trigger. At that point each psychiatrist would step down from the witness stand and allow the jury to determine whether or not any or all of these factors caused John Hinckley to shoot President Reagan.

This approach would solve many of the problems concerning psychiatric testimony, but I think it would also undermine the purpose of the insanity plea: to absolve from criminal responsibility for their actions those persons who are incapable of exercising free and knowing choice of conduct. Often this capacity is affected in ways that only a trained psychiatrist or psychologist is able to appreciate. Further, strict emphasis on logic—the hallmark of the legal system—can create ludicrous and pathetic miscarriages of justice.

An eighteen-year-old man living in England in the last century told his friends that he was going to kill someone in order to be hanged. One day he "felt an impulse to kill someone," sharpened his knife, and proceeded to maim and murder a young child. At trial his counsel argued that his client's vehement desire to be hanged was the strongest proof of insanity. The prosecution, on the other hand, urged that the fact of the defendant's having done murder in order to be hanged showed clearly that he knew quite well the consequences of his act and he was therefore criminally responsible. The defendant was found guilty. At the sentencing the judge said: "This morbid desire to part with your own life can hardly be called a delusion; and, indeed, the consciousness on your part that you could effect your purpose by designedly depriving another of his life, shows that you were perfectly able to understand the nature and consequences of the act which you were committing, and that you knew it was a crime [for] which by law the penalty was capital. This was, in truth, a further, and may I say, a deeper aggravation of the crime!" When the death sentence had been passed, the prisoner, totally unconcerned as he had been throughout the trial, replied with a smile, "Thank you, my lord," and stepped down from the dock.

This is an obviously extreme example, culled from an age when psychiatrists hadn't the opportunity to advise about the ways in which mental illness can impair an individual's responsibility. Thanks to psychiatric testimony bolstered by experience and a well-documented psychiatric literature, we now know that people can intend an act without being able to control their behavior or without appreciating that it is wrong. People who hear the voice of God telling them to kill their next door neighbor, "a follower of Satan," fully *intend* to kill that person. Yet who would hold such people wholly responsible for their action? The mind is not a logic machine. Insisting that responsibility be judged strictly on the basis of a person's intention can lead to modern day equivalents of what happened to the young man who, killing in order to be hanged, was granted his wish by a psychologically unsophisticated court.

The fundamental goal of the insanity defense is to determine whether or not a person's mental condition—call it what you will—has become so impaired that he can be truly said to have lost his "free will," either in the sense that he committed a violent act while not knowing what he did, or that he knew what he was doing but remained incapable of stopping himself from doing it. Most mentally ill people know right from wrong and are able to control their actions. The law and the insanity defense, therefore, must emphasize *how* a particular mental impairment does or does not influence a specific violent act.

As an illustration, join me in the examination of another example of the violent mind.

At age thirty, Joseph B. Centifanti was a successful lawyer. Ambitious, hardworking, and indefatigable, Centifanti was the prototypical overachiever who could work three or four days at a stretch without any need for sleep or rest. At times his mind "raced," but he could usually get things under control with a few drinks of alcohol or by smoking a "joint." But in the summer of 1975, Centifanti's world began to come apart. First there was the breakup of his marriage. His wife moved out of the house in June and planned divorce proceedings and to obtain custody of their two children.

Second, and perhaps related to his marital problems, Centifanti was having increasing difficulty keeping his racing thoughts under control. Alcohol or marijuana no longer helped. He found himself unable to maintain his concentration. He began ruminating about his wife, the upcoming divorce, and the custody battle. But most distressing of all, he discovered that his wife now had a man friend, eight years her junior. On the night of August 15, 1975, Centifanti decided to take action.

Armed with a .38 caliber revolver, Centifanti waited in Philadelphia's 30th Street station. He knew that his wife and her friend had traveled to Swarthmore earlier in the evening and would be returning on one of the late-arriving trains. When he spotted the couple sitting at a window, he boarded the train. Here is Centifanti's recollection in 1987 of the events that took place on that train.

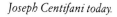
Joseph Centifani today.

"My plan was to terrify both of them, particularly her boyfriend . . . to show them both that I meant business." But Centifanti was also hearing a voice. "The voice said shoot her now even though I had no conscious plan to do that. It was as if someone took me over . . . something outside was telling me to do this."

According to the testimony of witnesses, Centifanti approached the couple from behind and fired three shots into his wife's back and one shot into her cheek. He then ordered her companion, "Get off the train now or I'll kill you." The man jumped at Centifanti's orders and tumbled out of the train and across the roadbed unharmed. Centifanti has no recollection of this. "I came to . . . I had already shot her . . . I had no recollection and the voice at that moment was telling me, 'You don't want to kill her.' " After forcing the engineer to jump from the train and terrorizing several of the passengers, Centifanti leaped from the train himself. "I could hear another message that said 'run.' I felt very agitated and wanted to find somewhere that was quiet."

Centifanti's "quiet" refuge was in the attic of his church, where he remained hidden over the next two months. On Sunday mornings he looked down through the grating and watched the congregation saying prayers on his behalf. One Sunday he even stared down at his wife, recently released from the hospital, while she sat in a pew beside a policeman assigned to guard her against a renewed assault.

On October 24, 1975, Joseph Centifanti surrendered and committed himself to the Norristown State Hospital. The psychiatrist who examined him recalls: "He was talking fast, had a flight of ideas, couldn't stay on one thing and couldn't focus. He was moving and walking all the time . . . couldn't sit still. He was hearing voices and receiving messages at various times . . . visionary kinds of things."

The diagnosis was manic–depressive illness. The psychiatrist, Dr. Robert Sadoff, contended that during the manic phase, Joseph Centifanti lost control and shot his wife. "His state of mind when he first came here was psychotic, out of touch with reality . . . he was so hypermanic that he was just rambling a mile a minute. This driving force of the manic phase of the illness pushed him beyond his ability to control the anger," says Sadoff.

On July 22, 1976, Joseph Centifanti was given a two-and-a-half-year sentence and ordered to continue his commitment at the state hospital. While there he was treated with lithium and regular psychotherapy sessions. At the conclusion of his sentence he was released. He has never again been violent, no longer hears voices, and has returned to living a normal life. He can now handle frustration, such

SERIAL MURDERS

In exploring the violent mind, we encounter individuals about whose sanity there may be some legitimate argument. But in the recent past a terrible form of violence has emerged that lies outside the bounds of simple sanity versus insanity. Some people believe that terms such as *evil* and *demonic* may be more appropriate designations. This is the serial killer.

Before me are reports on Donald Harvey, a thirty-five-year-old nurse's aide. They called him "the angel of death" because he was so often nearby when patients under his care died at Drake Memorial Hospital in Cincinnati. A man of gentle ways, a quiet smile, and an unusually conscientious interest in his patients, Harvey pleaded guilty in August 1987 to twenty-four murders of patients under his care. He told his lawyer that he had killed twenty-eight other persons but could not recall their names.

In appearance, Harvey is a slightly built white man with dark wavy hair and intense eyes that, under the proper circumstances, could help create an impression of deep sympathy, interest, or compassion. Overall, he fits the FBI description culled from experience with thirty-six serial killers: a white male in his twenties or thirties who is reasonably attractive and commands average or above-average intelligence.

The families of Harvey's victims recall him as a pleasant staff member who stood out because his personality was especially appealing. After he had completed a shift and was free to go home, he often remained in the hospital to comfort anxious or grieving family members.

All of the relatives interviewed agreed that he seemed a charming and compassionate man. Yet he was a killer. As if driven by some kind of inner demon, Donald Harvey injected cyanide or created air bubbles in intravenous tubes. On other occasions, he employed cleaning fluid or petroleum-based compounds as the lethal agent, and finally, in the murder that led to his arrest, he administered arsenic to a man brought to the hospital after a fall from a motorcycle.

After he was exposed, the relatives of the victims wanted to know why it took so long to discover that Donald Harvey was murdering patients. "Because they are charming and pleasant, serial killers like Donald Harvey are extremely difficult to detect," notes Dr. Emmanuel Tanay, a Detroit psychiatrist with extensive experience in the evaluation of serial killers.

Donald Harvey used his charm to disarm patients and their families, as well as his professional colleagues. He premeditated the murders, carried them out calmly and coolly, and skillfully covered his tracks so that no one would suspect that the deaths were other than natural. At no time did he evidence delusions, hallucinations, or other signs of mental illness. He never experienced a driving impulse to kill, but rather spoke of relief to the patients, whom he said he killed "out of mercy." Like Ted Bundy, the serial killer of college women, or John Gacy, convicted of killing thirty-three boys and young men, Donald Harvey selected a specific target population.

---

as the decision last year by the Disciplinary Board in Superior Court of Pennsylvania not to reinstate him to the practice of law in the Commonwealth of Pennsylvania.

"When the bar told me I could not practice I was upset. But I've learned control over my feelings and reactions. Thanks to lithium I don't feel as if I'm being internally driven. I've never again had another episode where I was out of control."

Today Joseph Centifanti is no longer violent. He has reentered society and, according to his psychiatrist, presents an extremely small risk of ever acting violently again.

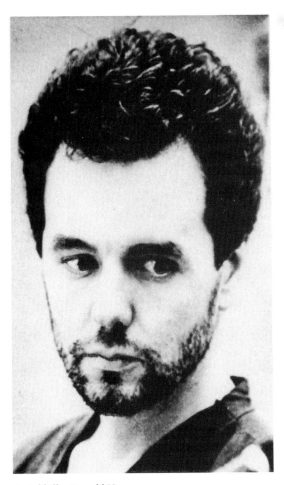

Serial killer Donald Harvey.

Otherwise, there is not the slightest clue that his behavior was ritualized, impulsive, or "driven" in any way.

Is Donald Harvey insane? Was he insane at the times of the murders? At the moment, serial killers such as Donald Harvey do not fit any of the definitions of insanity employed anywhere in the world. It certainly strains credulity to believe that Harvey, Bundy, and Gacy should be considered "sane." But is it possible that our conviction that they are insane—according to some as-yet-to-be defined criterion—is nothing more than a comforting form of circular reasoning: no sane person could commit such acts, these men committed them, therefore they are insane? Could this be a way of avoiding value judgments about good and evil? In short, is the defense of insanity in such instances anything more than an excuse for our unwillingness to confront the full gamut of human freedom? Donald Harvey's behavior seems less a form of insanity than it does an appalling distortion of ordinary human feelings best left to the explanations of theologians and moralists. After all, if we are free to do good, then it seems reasonable to suppose that we are also free to perform acts of extreme wickedness. If the human mind can evolve in the direction of a Mother Teresa, why can it not take a counterturn and produce a Donald Harvey?

Is it reasonable to suppose that future research on the human brain will produce some explanation for what went wrong in the mind of Donald Harvey? It seems unlikely. I think this asks more of neuroscience than we can reasonably expect.

But Sylvia Seegrist remains confined. She may spend the rest of her life under these conditions. Two forms of psychosis, two conditions of the violent mind—one, Joseph Centifanti, with a mental illness that isn't likely to recur under medication; the other, Sylvia Seegrist, a chronic, most probably untreatable psychotic. Obviously, the same approach cannot be applied to these two individuals, though both have acted violently. As we have seen in Chapter 6, manic depression can usually be controlled in a manner very similar to the control of diabetes: the patients aren't cured but if they take their medicine, they have a good chance of leading a normal life. Unfortunately, neuroscientists don't know enough about schizophrenia to cure it or even control it in a predictable and satisfactory way. Until we can understand what goes wrong in the brain of a violent person—whether that person is schizophrenic, manic depressive, or "normal"—it is unlikely that we will be able to come to grips with the complex medical, social, and ethical problems surrounding the violent mind.

Violence that is secondary to mental illness may involve hallucinations, delusions, and a host of other behavioral disturbances. But violence can also be cold, casual, callous, and deliberate. Neuropsychiatrist Frank Elliot describes the violent psychopath:

"They are not insane, and delusions or other signs of irrational thinking are usually absent. They are egocentric and lack the capacity to feel empathy and love. They have little or no conscience or sense of guilt, tend to project blame when they get into trouble. They are unreliable, untruthful, and insincere, but they are often convincing because they believe their own lies. There is a vast gulf between what they say and what they do. They are impulsive, the whim of the moment being paramount. They are given to periodic and often senseless antisocial behavior which may be either aggressive or passive and parasitic."

In the nineteenth century, a profile like this would have been considered from a moral viewpoint. Indeed, Benjamin Rush, the "Father of American Psychiatry," wrote, "There is probably an original defect of organization in those parts of the body which are occupied by the moral faculties of the mind." Today we no longer think of the mind as divisible into faculties. But we do know that psychopathic behavior is intimately linked with the brain and its disorders. It can result from brain diseases like encephalitis (inflammation of the brain), and can produce a profound behavioral distortion. Head injury that causes brain lesions can also transform reasonable and self-contained individuals into violent, destructive aggressors. "They can become destructive, quarrelsome, and cruel," says Frank Elliott. "They are egocentric and often exhibit total disregard for the welfare of others and a notable loss of affection for the family. They lie and steal, seemingly with total disregard for the consequences. In some there is also evidence of intellectual impairment, but it is the changes in personality and their liability to explosive rage in response to minimal provocation that are disruptive."

But not all cases of psychopathy or even the great majority of them are associated with head injury. In most instances, evidence of brain injury is not found. Here is a nineteenth-century description of a psychopath by the great English psychiatrist Henry Maudsley:

"There is a disorder of mind in which without illusion, delusion or hallucination, the symptoms are mainly exhibited in a perversion of those mental faculties which are usually called the active and moral powers—the feelings, affections, propensities, temper, habits and conduct. The affective life of the individual is profoundly deranged and his derangement shows itself in what he feels, desires and does. He has no capacity of true moral feelings; all his impulses and desires to which he yields without check are egotistic; his conduct appears to be governed by immoral motives which are cherished and obeyed without any evident desire to resist them. There is an amazing immoral insensibility. The intelligence is often acute enough, being not affected otherwise than being tainted by the morbid feelings under the impulse of which the persons think and act; indeed, they often display an extraordinary ingenuity in explaining, excusing or justifying their behavior. All their intellectual faculties are applied to the justification and gratification of their selfish desires."

Maudsley is describing persons suffering from what in the nineteenth century was labelled "moral insanity." In the twentieth century the term is "psychopathic personality disorder." But whatever such individuals are called, they present a profound challenge to our understanding. Here are people in whom the components of mind that make human beings moral beings, civilized beings—conscience, a moral sense, recognition of right and wrong, constraints that stop us from injuring others—literally appear to be lacking. What could be the cause of this troubling and troublesome disorder? Though our reactions of horror and fear when we encounter individuals with psychopathic personality disorder are justified, we have been wrong in assuming that the condition exists independent of biology. Neuroscience is confirming that Maudsley was correct when he also con-

Notorious psychopath Charles Manson, convicted mass murderer. "He used to say he was a man of a thousand faces," a witness testified at the Sharon Tate murder trial.

tended a century ago that, "Assuredly, moral insanity is a disorder of mind produced by disorder of brain."

Findings over the past few decades suggest that there are patterns common to many habitually violent individuals, including frequent low blood sugar levels and abnormal EEG readings. For instance, Dr. Richard Howard at Queens University in Belfast studied EEG patterns of men committed to Broadmore, a high-security facility that houses convicted murderers and mentally abnormal offenders who have committed acts of extreme violence. Howard finds evidence of low cortical arousal. "That means the general tone of the cortex is depressed, as if they were in a generally sleepy state." Associated with the state of low cortical arousal are "anomalous brain wave patterns in about fifty to sixty percent of the subjects." Howard believes these findings are related to trauma incurred during the perinatal period (pregnancy and birth). Such trauma can include a variety of damaging agents and events. In the womb, the mother's poor nutrition, alcoholism, or tobacco use can lead to abnormalities in fetal brain development, as discussed in Chapter 2. Problems can also occur during birth. If a baby suffers oxygen deprivation during a difficult or complicated delivery, it can cause subtle brain damage marked by low cortical tone, impulsiveness, and difficulty in controlling violent and aggressive feelings.

But how does a person, as a result of brain damage at birth, go from a state of low cortical arousal to violence? If anything, low cortical arousal would seem more likely to produce a placid or phlegmatic disposition. Dr. Jan Volavka, Professor of Psychiatry at the New York University School of Medicine, suggests a hypothesis. Socially appropriate behavior may be learned through the reduction of anxiety that comes when one decides *not* to engage in antisocial behavior. Volavka cites an example of a six-year-old boy who feels the urge to hit his little sister. When he considers the punishment that is likely to result from this action, his anxiety increases. He then decides against hitting her and the anxiety subsides. According to Volavka, anxiety reduction is a very powerful reinforcement, leading to civilized, restrained behavior. "What may be happening in the psychopath is that he is so relaxed and his autonomic nervous system so sluggish that the reduction of anxiety is very small."

Psychologist Robert Hare of the University of British Columbia believes that the brain of a psychopath is organized differently. For one thing, he's found that psychopaths usually don't process words on the left side of the brain as the rest of us do. Their language processing seems equally balanced between the right and left brain. Further, psychopaths respond differently to the connotative aspects of words.

For example, if the words *warm, loving,* and *cold* are presented and the psychopath is asked to select the two words that go together, he's likely to select *warm* and *cold* rather than *warm* and *loving,* which share connotative similarity.

"The psychopath doesn't make any distinction between neutral and affective words," says Hare. "This is important when it comes to conscience, which is partly internalized language. If a person says 'I shouldn't do something,' then that person will actually feel that he shouldn't do it. But a psychopath can say the same thing, 'I shouldn't do this,' but he doesn't *feel* that he shouldn't do this. The emotional or affective component of conscience is absent in the psychopath."

How common are the brain abnormalities found by Howard and others? Most impulsive or aggressive people do not commit murder. Moreover, research done in hospitals for the criminally insane may have little to do with violent behavior occurring in the outside world. Nonetheless, it is important to continue to clarify biological contributions to violence. We need, for example, to learn whether brain damage at birth is sufficient to produce a violent individual or whether it takes coexisting poverty, uncaring parents, and early exposure to violence for the damage to manifest itself in actual violence. If biological factors are found to be the most significant contributor to the violent mind, then the insanity defense—now a patchwork of conflicting and chaotic theories—may need to be based on

Dr. Robert Hare testing a psychopath who had committed multiple violent crimes. Hare's research is focused on the nature of the psychopathic personality.

evidence that supports or discredits neurologic–biochemical dysfunctions. Under such circumstances, "guilty but insane" would be determined on a neurologic rather than a psychological basis.

As things now stand, the violent mind is studied by psychiatrists with backgrounds in psychodynamics, the interplay of psychological and social factors in the production of mental illness. These studies do not utilize tests such as CAT and PET scans or EEGs that might reveal evidence of brain abnormality. Some people will argue that such tests are irrelevant; even if an abnormality is found, that doesn't release the individual from responsibility for his act of violence. But such a sentiment, I believe, leaves us with no other recourse than to abolish the insanity defense altogether, at least in its present form. Despite the most thorough evaluation, the inner world of another person's mind cannot be divined beyond a certain point. There is always room for doubt, reason for suggesting that the law will never be able to know with absolute certainty whether or not a person intended the violent act for which he is charged. What is the wisest course to follow under such circumstances? Henry Maudsley captured the essence of this dilemma, and its solution, in his essay, "Responsibility in Mental Disease":

"If the law cannot adjust the measure of punishment to the actual degree of responsibility . . . that is no reason why we should shut our eyes to the facts; it is still our duty to place them on record, in the confident assurance that a time will come when men will be able to deal more wisely with them."

AFTERWORD

We have now reached the end of our search for mind in these pages. Along the way, we have glimpsed our mind's earliest origins, at the union of sperm and egg carrying our parents' genetic heritage. We have learned that brain and mind are intertwined, that without the brain the mind could not exist, and that the mind evolves in tandem with the brain. Whenever the brain is maldeveloped or afflicted with organic disease, such as Alzheimer's, the mind fails. When the healthy mind is stimulated, the brain flourishes. Without the mind there would be no Chartres, no Declaration of Independence, no Beethoven quartets. With mind, it can sometimes seem that all things are possible.

But in relating mind to brain, we are left with as many questions about mind as we have answers. Each new understanding or insight into the brain, or new discovery about the relationship of mind and brain, can render our prior knowledge obsolete. Still, these findings can be liberating. By understanding the brain, and learning more about the way the mind functions, we may be able to assume more control over aspects of our behavior that have left us baffled or powerless.

Mind puts meaning and purpose into our lives. Mind is conscious awareness and unconscious processes operating together to provide each of us with a world view. No guarantees of quality come with this gift of mind. Mind has produced a saintly Mother Teresa and an Albert Einstein, and it has also spawned the demonic behaviors of serial killers. Still, another special gift of mind is hope. As we ask ourselves those questions unique to the human species— Why are we here? What is the purpose of our lives?—we forge new directions for ourselves and our fellows. The search continues.

GLOSSARY

adrenal glands A pair of glands, situated above the kidneys, that secretes a variety of hormones that have a wide range of effects on the body. Among them are hormones involved in metabolic functions.

amino acids Organic compounds that bond together into a sequence to form proteins, essential to growth and proper metabolism. Several amino acids are either precursors of neurotransmitters or function as neurotransmitters themselves.

amygdala An almond-shaped structure in the brain that plays a role in the emotions, particularly aggression. It also serves memory function.

antibody A protein produced by white blood cells to neutralize any foreign substance posing a threat to the body.

antigen Any substance that the body regards as foreign and that stimulates the production of an antibody.

autoimmunity A disorder of the body's defense mechanism in which its own tissues are treated as foreign invaders.

autonomic nervous system The self-regulating, or autonomous, portion of the nervous system supplying stimulation to the muscles and glands that control such functions as digestion, respiration, and circulation. It is divided into the parasympathetic nervous system, which maintains bodily functions, and the sympathetic nervous system, which serves arousal functions.

axon The long, threadlike projection of a neuron that carries the nerve impulse *away* from the body of the cell either to an adjacent neuron or to an effector such as a muscle.

basal ganglia Three small masses of nerve tissue located at the base of the brain involved in the subconscious regulation of movement.

blood–brain barrier A network of membranes controlling the passage of substances from the blood to the brain; permits passage of solutions but excludes particles and large molecules.

brain stem The central core of the brain that links the spinal cord with the cerebral hemispheres. It is comprised of structures that control and integrate reflex activities such as respiration.

CAT (or CT) scan A computer-processed, three-dimensional image derived from multiple low-dosage x-rays. The process, *c*omputerized *t*omography (or *c*omputerized *a*xial *t*omography), is particularly useful in brain imaging as it can distinguish between even slight variations in tissue density.

catecholamines A group of compounds with a specific biochemical structure that serve as neurotransmitters and hormones, all of which play significant roles in the functioning of the nervous system.

cerebellum The large, dorsally projecting part of the brain involved in muscle coordination and the maintenance of body equilibrium.

cerebral cortex The outer "bark" or "rind" of the brain, which is responsible for the control and integration of movement and the senses, as well as memory, language, and thought. The term "motor cortex" specifically refers to those areas of the cortex responsible for motion.

cerebrum The largest and uppermost part of the brain. It consists of the two cerebral hemispheres and connecting structures. It is considered the seat of conscious mental processes.

cholinergic system A neuron or neural pathway either involved in the release of, or stimulated by, the neurotransmitter acetylcholine.

cognition A process that refers to a broad range of mental "behaviors," including awareness, thinking, reasoning, and judgment.

conditioned response Any response learned through the repeated presentation of an initially neutral stimulus. For example, a dog hears a bell (neutral stimulus) each time before being given food. Eventually, salivation (the conditioned response) is elicited by the sound of the bell alone. This process is called conditioning.

convolutions The irregular folds on the surface of the brain. They increase the area of the cerebral cortex within the skull.

corticosteroids Hormones produced by the adrenal glands to regulate the use of carbohydrates, fats, and proteins and to maintain the salt and water balance in the body.

cross-modal transfer Information drawn from an experience in one of the five senses and associated with the features of an experience in another of the senses, as, for instance, when a discontinuous sound (hearing) is associated with a discontinuous line (sight).

dendrite A slender branching projection that conducts impulses from other nerve cells *toward* the cell body of the neuron.

differentiation A process in which a group of initially similar cells in the embryo generates a number of different kinds of cells, all specialized to perform particular functions in the various developing organs and tissues.

EEG An electroencephalogram, a graph of the electrical activity of the brain as detected by electrodes pasted on the scalp.

endocrine A gland, or system of glands, that secretes hormones directly into the bloodstream for use at distant sites throughout the body.

enzyme A protein, produced by a cell, that acts as a catalyst in biochemical reactions.

evoked potential The brain's reaction to a stimulus, measured by noting changes in the brain's electrical activity, as recorded by electrodes pasted on the scalp.

fibrillary tangles Thin black fibers present in the brain cells of those who have died of Alzheimer's disease.

frontal lobes The front portions of the cerebral hemispheres, thought to be the plan-making apparatus of the brain.

genes The units of heredity that determine the individual characteristics of an organism. Each gene is composed of genetic material known as DNA (deoxyribonucleic acid). Genes are linked together into long threadlike structures called chromosomes, which are found in the nuclei of all living cells. The term "expression of a gene" refers to the degree to which a genetic trait is observable in the organism; it can be mediated by environmental factors.

genetic marker Any specific gene that permits easy recognition of a genetic trait.

glucocorticoids Hormones produced by the adrenal glands and involved in the metabolism of proteins, carbohydrates, and fats, particularly when the body is subjected to stress. It is a type of corticosteroid.

habituation A waning or reduced response to a repeated or continuous stimulus. Similar to adaptation and desensitization.

hippocampus A long, sea horse–shaped brain structure involved in emotion, motivation, learning, and memory.

hormone A substance manufactured by cells and secreted into the bloodstream to regulate the growth or function of a specific organ or tissue in another part of the body.

hypothalamus A peanut-sized structure near the base of the brain that regulates a variety of functions essential to survival, including temperature and heart rate, as well as thirst, hunger, sex drive, and sleep.

immune system The body's defense system against disease. Any foreign or potentially dangerous substance (antigen) stimulates the production of specific proteins (antibodies) by the body's white blood cells (lymphocytes) to fight off the invasion.

inhibition Restriction or obstruction. The brain works not just by facilitation, or the transmission of impulses, but by inhibition, or the blocking out of impulses. Raising your forearm requires contracting your biceps muscle and *not* contracting your triceps muscle.

limbic system A complex, linked set of structures (including the hippocampus, amygdala, and hypothalamus) in the forebrain thought to be responsible for the emotions.

locus ceruleus A structure in the brain stem that controls arousal as well as the cycles of sleep.

lymphocyte A type of white blood cell that manufactures dozens of natural chemicals (antibodies) essential in the body's defense against disease. It is a constituent of the immune system.

medulla oblongata The lower portion of the brain stem that regulates such vital involuntary processes as respiration and circulation.

monoamine oxidase inhibitors (MAOIs) A major class of antidepressant drugs that operates by blocking the chemical breakdown of neurotransmitters in the synapse.

neurotransmitters The vehicles of communication between nerve cells; essentially chemicals that mediate the transmission of a nerve impulse across the gap between adjacent neurons. (For specific neurotransmitters see Chapter 2).

neurotrophic factors Substances within the brain that in and of themselves help keep brain cells alive. They are also known as trophic factors. The most important of these is a protein known as nerve growth factor (NGF).

nucleus accumbens A small, hook-shaped structure in the brain, apparently a pleasure center. It is linked to a craving for cocaine and identified as the reward site for amphetamines.

nucleus basalis of Meynert A small group of nerve cells in the forebrain with connections to many areas of the cerebral cortex. It is thought to play an important role in learning and memory.

parasympathetic nervous system A part of the autonomic nervous system. It is responsible for salivary gland secretions, decreasing the heart rate, promoting digestion, and dilating blood vessels. The sympathetic nervous system has the opposite effects.

parietal lobe The middle portion of each cerebral hemisphere responsible for motor and other bodily sensations.

peptides Organic compounds (amino acids) linked together. Long chains with more than fifty bonds are called proteins.

peripheral nerves The sensory and motor neurons connecting the surface of the body with the central nervous system.

PET scan A computer-enhanced image of the brain produced when special radioactive isotopes are injected into the bloodstream. *Positron emission tomography*, or PET, reveals the metabolic processes and shifts in blood flow that accompany various types of mental activity.

pineal gland A tiny, mysterious gland in the center of the brain. It was believed by Descartes to be the master gland controlling interactions between mind and body. It probably plays a role in sexual maturation and sleep.

pituitary A pea-sized gland that secretes hormones regulating the growth and activity of several other hormone-secreting glands. It is attached to, and probably controlled by, the hypothalamus.

pons A broad mass of transverse nerve fibers on the front side of the brain stem. It relays impulses between different parts of the brain.

receptor A cell, or specific site on the membrane of a cell, that is sensitive to a particular neurotransmitter or hormone.

reinforcement Anything, from food to electric shock, that strengthens the bond between a stimulus and a response.

reticular formation A complex network of nerve fibers occupying the central core of the brain stem that functions in wakefulness and alertness. It is also known as the reticular activating system.

senile plaques Degenerated networks of nerve cell terminals found in the brains of those who have died of Alzheimer's disease.

substantia gelatinosa The first two layers of dense nerve fibers at the tip of the spinal cord, which serve to integrate information being transmitted from the periphery, such as the sense organs, to the central nervous system.

synapse The junction between two adjacent nerve cells (i.e., between the axon ending of one and a dendrite beginning of the next). At the synapse, the cleft or gap between the two cells is minuscule (twenty to thirty nanometers). Nerve impulses breach this gap with the aid of neurotransmitters. Most neurons have more than one synapse.

temporal lobe A portion of the brain, located just above the ears, engaged in processing auditory information. It is also important in emotions, the sense of identity, and personal integration.

thalamus A complex, two-lobed structure located at the top of the brain stem. It serves to relay sensory information to the cerebral cortex and translate impulses into conscious sensations.

thymus A gland located behind the sternum (breastbone) that produces hormones that play a role in the development and regulation of the immune system.

tricyclics A major class of antidepressant drugs, the most common of which is imipramine, used in the treatment of certain mood disorders.

twins Two babies born from a single pregnancy. Identical (or monozygotic) twins develop from a single fertilized egg and give rise to separate individuals who are genetically identical. Fraternal (or dizygotic) twins result from a single pregnancy in which two eggs have been fertilized; these individuals are no more similar than brothers and sisters from single births.

FURTHER READINGS

Adelman, George. *Encyclopedia of Neuroscience.* 2 vols. Cambridge, Mass.: Birkhauser Boston, 1987.

Atkinson, Rita L., Smith, E. E., and Hilgard, E. R. *Introduction to Psychology.* 9th ed. New York: Harcourt Brace Jovanovich, 1987.

Beck, Aaron T. *Cognitive Therapy and Emotional Disorders.* New York: International Universities Press, 1976.

Blakemore, Colin, and Greenfield, Susan, eds. *Mindwaves: Thoughts on Intelligence, Identity and Consciousness.* Oxford: Basil Blackwell, 1987.

Chomsky, Noam. *Syntactic Structures.* The Hague: Mouton, 1957.

Descartes, René. *Discourse on Method, and Other Writings.* 1637. Reprint. New York: Penguin, 1968.

Dilman, Ilham. *Freud and the Mind.* Oxford: Basil Blackwell, 1984.

Erikson, Erik H. *The Life Cycle Completed: A Review.* New York: Norton, 1985.

Erikson, Erik H., et al. *Vital Involvement in Old Age in Our Time.* New York: Norton, 1986.

Flanagan, Owen J., Jr. *The Science of the Mind.* Cambridge, Mass.: MIT Press, Bradford Books, 1984.

Gazzaniga, Michael S. *The Social Brain.* New York: Basic Books, 1985.

Goodall, Jane. *The Chimpanzees of Gombe.* (Illus.) Cambridge, Mass.: Harvard University Press, 1986.

Gregory, R. L., ed. *The Oxford Companion to the Mind.* Oxford: Oxford University Press, 1987.

Hebb, D. O. *Inheritance and Environment: The Organization of Behavior.* New York: John Wiley and Sons, 1961.

Heilman, Kenneth M., and Satz, Paul, eds. *Neuropsychology of Human Emotion.* New York: Guilford Press, 1983.

Jacobson, Marcus. *Developmental Neurobiology.* 2nd ed. New York: Plenum Press, 1978.

Kandel, E. R., and Schwartz, J. H., eds. *Principles of Neural Science.* 2nd ed. New York: Elsevier, North-Holland, 1985.

LeDoux, Joseph E., and Hirst, William, eds. *Mind and Brain: Dialogues Between Cognitive Psychology and Neuroscience.* Cambridge: Cambridge University Press, 1986.

Minsky, Marvin. *The Society of Mind.* New York: Simon & Schuster, Touchstone Books, 1988.

Oakley, David A., ed. *Brain and Mind.* New York: Methuen, 1985.

Popper, K. R., and Eccles, John C. *The Self and Its Brain.* (Illus.) rev. ed. New York: Springer, 1977.

Restak, Richard. *The Brain.* New York: Bantam Books, 1984.

Restak, Richard. *The Infant Mind.* New York: Doubleday, 1986.

Shepherd, Gordon M. *Neurobiology.* 2nd ed. Oxford: Oxford University Press, 1987.

Squire, Larry R. *Memory and the Brain.* Oxford: Oxford University Press, 1987.

INDEX

Terry, Robert, 70, 79
Thalamus
definition, 18, 320
opiate receptors and, 129–32
pain signal and, 141–42
Thought process, xv, 233–73
animal experiments, 246–53
behaviorists' view of, 250
brain association, 9
chess in, 237
in elderly, 79–80
electrode studies, 258–59
frontal lobes role in, 266–71
images in, 240–42
and interpretation, 261
language and, 204–205, 222–25, 226, 271–73
logic and reasoning, 63, 236–39, 304–305
meaning in, 261–64
mental model, 233–36
mind development and, 58–63
organization of, 242–45
prefrontal regions and, 267–68
reasoning and communication, 271–73
as social phenomenon, 251
see also Intelligence; Intent; Learning; Reasoning and logic
Thymus, 146, 148, 320
Tissue transplants. See Brain grafts; Fetal tissue transplants
Tobacco. See Nicotine
Toda, Nurumi, 44
Tonal language, 220–21
Tongue, 204
Toronto, University of, 31
Traite de l'homme (Descartes), 10, 254
Transplants. See Brain grafts, Fetal tissue transplants
Trevarthen, Colwyn, 209–13, 231
Tricyclic antidepressants, 183, 187, 189, 320

Trophic factors. See Neurotrophic factors
Tulving, Endel, 31
Turing, Alan, 255
Tversky, Amos, 238
Twins, defined, 320
Twin studies
aging process, 92
alcohol abuse, 120–21
depressive disorders, 177–78
EP wave forms, 122–23
"Two brains." See Cerebral hemispheres
Tyrosine hydroxylase, 179
Tzeng, Ovid, 220

Unconscious, 15–16, 27, 31
Unipolar/bipolar disorders, 168–72

Valenstein, Elliot, 110
Valliant, George, 152
Van der Loos, Hendrik, 52
van Gogh, Vincent, 169
Vaucanson, 254
Ventral tegmental area, 115
Ventricular system, 36
Vietnam War, 119–20, 126
Violence, xvi, 275–309
amygdala and, 278, 279, 282, 290, 317
biological factors, 313–14
chemically produced, 294–97
child delinquents, 282
deliberate, psychopath's, 310–14
electrical brain impulses and, 278–80, 282
episodic dyscontrol syndrome, 284–85
intent and responsibility, 275–78, 280–82, 304–305
legal vs. psychiatric approach, 302–14
limbic system and, 277, 279, 280–83
maladjustment/psychosis and, 298–302
origins of, 282–83

premenstrual syndrome and, 290–92
serial killing, 308–309
Virus, Alzheimer's disease and, 83
Vision
brain grafts and, 88
fetal, 46–48
head injuries and, 21
newborn recognition, 51–52
occipital lobe and, 18–20
Vocabulary, 63
Volavka, Jan, 312
Von Frisch, Karl, 249
von Neumann, John, 256
Voodoo deaths, 161
Vrede, Berry, 216

Waldman, David A., 100
Wall, Patrick, 142–43
Wang, William S.-Y., 220–22, 231
Watson, J.B., 14, 240, 242
"Waxy flexibility," 107
Weinberger, Daniel, 267
Weizenbaum, Joseph, 262
Wells, Charles, 101
Wender, Paul H., 177, 178
Werker, Janet, 54
Wernicke, Carl, 213
Wernicke's aphasia, 213
Whorf, Benjamin, 222, 225
Wild Beast Test of 1723, 285
Will, 10
Williamson, Joy, 47
Willis, Sherry, 95
Wisdom, 75, 97–100
Wise, Roy A., 115
Withdrawal, addiction, 106, 113–27, 133–34
World War I, 21
Writing, 224

Youth, suicide among, 172–73